THE MYTH OF THE ADDICTED ARMY

THE

OF THE   ADDICTED ARMY

VIETNAM AND THE MODERN

WAR ON DRUGS

JEREMY KUZMAROV

UNIVERSITY OF MASSACHUSETTS PRESS Amherst and Boston

Copyright © 2009 by University of Massachusetts Press
All rights reserved
Printed in the United States of America

LC 2009022363
ISBN 978-1-55849-705-4 (paper); 704-7 (library cloth)

Designed by Richard Hendel
Set in Scala by The Westchester Book Group. Inc.
Printed and bound by The Maple-Vail Book Manufacturing
Group

Library of Congress Cataloging-in-Publication Data
Kuzmarov, Jeremy, 1979—
   The myth of the addicted army : Vietnam and the modern
war on drugs / Jeremy Kuzmarov.
      p. cm. — (Culture, politics, and the Cold War)
   Includes bibliographical references and index.
   ISBN 978-1-55849-705-4 (pbk. : alk. paper) —
ISBN 978-1-55849-704-7 (library cloth : alk. paper)
   1. Soldiers—Drug use—United States—History—20th
century.   2. Soldiers—Drug use—Vietnam—History—
20th century.   3. Drug control—United States—History—
20th century.   4. Drug abuse—United States—Prevention—
History—20th century.   5. Vietnam War, 1961–1975—Social
aspects.   I. Title.
   HV5825.K89   2009
   959.704'38—dc22   2009022363

British Library Cataloguing in Publication data are available.

To my beautiful wife, Ngosa,
and to my parents,
Donna and Irwin Kuzmarov

CONTENTS

ACKNOWLEDGMENTS

A work of this nature would not have been possible without the assistance of many people. First, I thank Brandeis University and the Crown family for funding my studies. I also thank the librarians at the Brandeis and Bucknell University libraries for responding to numerous interlibrary loan requests efficiently and the archivists at the research centers I visited across the country, including the National Archives in College Park, Maryland, for their outstanding professionalism and assistance. I am indebted to Ms. Sam Brawand of Bucknell for her help beyond measure in preparing the manuscript. Patricia Sterling and Mary Bellino improved it through their wonderful copyediting.

I thank especially all of the Vietnam veterans I interviewed in the greater Boston area and at the Texas Tech University Vietnam Center 2007 spring conference for taking the time to share their recollections with me, and for their candor. The same goes for the former drug "czar" Jerome Jaffe, as well as Roger Roffman, Clinton Sanders, and Peter Dale Scott.

David C. Engerman also deserves special gratitude. An outstanding mentor to me in many different ways, he helped to guide this book from the beginning. The same can be said for Michael Willrich, who provided careful and detailed feedback on early drafts.

My special thanks also to Clark Dougan, senior editor at University of Massachusetts Press, who took great care in reading drafts of the manuscript and helped me to expand on my original ideas. Jack Tobin, professor of English, Korean War veteran, and longtime antiwar activist, also helped me improve my writing and highlighted the importance of digging beneath the surface for hidden truths. Chris Appy provided indispensable advice, as did Jacqueline Jones of Brandeis and John Shrecker, from whom I learned a great deal about Southeast Asian history.

I am grateful to the two peer reviewers, Jerry Lembcke and William O. Walker III, whose detailed commentaries and expertise on the topic helped me improve the presentation and substance of the book; their own scholarship has also greatly influenced my analysis.

Additional thanks go to colleagues in the history department at Bucknell who have listened and responded to my ideas, including Leslie Patrick, Julian Bourg, and Richard Waller, as well as to my students and to teachers who stimulated my interest in history, including Kimberley

Ducey of McGill; her course on crime and punishment helped to shape my views on the War on Drugs.

I must also thank friends who housed me on research trips and those who made my time writing the book enjoyable.

Finally, my wife, Ngosa, and family deserve the last word. Their consistent support in good times and bad has sustained me through the years.

ABBREVIATIONS USED IN THE TEXT

ACLU	American Civil Liberties Union
ARVN	Army of the Republic of South Vietnam
BNDD	Bureau of Narcotics and Dangerous Drugs
BPP	Black Panther Party
CAT	Civil Air Transport
CCAS	Committee of Concerned Asian Scholars
CCP	Chinese Communist Party
CID	Criminal Investigation Division, U.S. Army
DARE	Drug Abuse Research and Education
DEA	Drug Enforcement Administration
DEROS	Date of Expected Return from Overseas
DOD	Department of Defense
FARC	Fuerzas Armada Revolucionario de Colombia
FBN	Federal Bureau of Narcotics, U.S. Treasury Department
GMD	Guomindang of China (anti-Communist troops)
GVN	Government of South Vietnam
INTERPOL	International Criminal Police Organization
JNID	Joint Narcotics Investigation Division
LSD	lysergic acid diethylamide
MACV	Military Assistance Command Vietnam
MRTA	Tupac Amaru Revolutionary Movement (Peru)
NIDA	National Institute on Drug Abuse
NLF	National Liberation Front
NORML	National Organization for the Reform of Marijuana Laws
NVA	North Vietnamese Army
ODALE	Office of Drug Abuse Law Enforcement
ODAP	Office for Drug Abuse Prevention
OJ OR O.J.	opium joint
ONNI	Office of National Narcotic Intelligence
OPS	Office of Public Safety
OSS	Office of Strategic Services
PRI	Partido Revolucionario Institucional (Mexico)
PRIDE	Parents Resource Institute for Drug Education
PTSD	post-traumatic stress disorder
R&R	Rest and Recuperation Leave

RLG	Royal Lao Government
SAODAP	Special Action Office on Drug Abuse Prevention
SWAT	Special Weapons and Tactics
THC	tetrahydracanibinol
UHV	Upper Huallaga Valley, Peru
UMOPAR	Rural Mobile Police Patrol Units
USAID	United States Agency of International Development
VVAW	Vietnam Veterans Against the War
WHO	World Health Organization

THE MYTH OF THE ADDICTED ARMY

INTRODUCTION

THE POLITICS OF SCAPEGOATING

Like the Germans after World War I who claimed that their troops were stabbed in the back by pacifists and other "unpatriotic elements" at home, we claim that our troops are being stabbed in the back by heroin and the pushers responsible for supplying it to them. As we de-escalate against the "Vietcong," we will escalate against heroin. No doubt we shall find it easier to control Americans who shoot heroin than Vietnamese who shoot Americans. —Thomas Szasz

It was not until this scourge of drugs started affecting our boys in Vietnam that the Congress and other public officials and the press started to be interested in it. —Morgan Murphy (D-Ill.)

By indiscriminately categorizing all users of opium and heroin as addicts and by suggesting that their involvement is more serious than street addiction because of the high purity of the drugs in Vietnam, the press has fanned a new wave of scapegoating and regressive legislation. The irony is that this climate has been fanned by both political persuasions—by the left to heighten antiwar sentiment and by the right in concern for the morale and strength of the armed forces. —Paul Starr, sociologist

On June 17, 1971, President Richard M. Nixon ushered in a new carceral age in American history by officially declaring a "War on Drugs."[1] In recent months, there had been growing public concern over revelations of rampant heroin addiction among American troops in Vietnam, compounding existing fears about the spread of middle-class drug use. The media were particularly sensationalistic in warning that addicted GIs from Vietnam would return home to exacerbate urban unrest and crime—and further tear at the nation's social fabric.[2] Seizing on the public mood, Nixon took the opportunity to rail against his political opponents for inculcating a "culture of permissiveness" that had ostensibly helped to foment drug-induced rioting and demonstrations by "criminal misfits" and had now crept into the most venerable of social institutions. He vowed to fight these new developments with every resource that he could muster, telling Congress, "Not very long ago, it was possible for Americans to persuade themselves, with some justification, that narcotic addiction was a class problem. But now the problem is universal. It has assumed the dimensions of a national emergency and I intend to take every step necessary to deal with it." Nixon added that he was particularly "disheartened by the use of drugs among American servicemen in Vietnam" who had brought shame on a proud citizen-soldier tradition and outwardly threatened vital national interests. He warned that addicted veterans might return to the United States and "slip into the twilight world of crime, bad drugs and all too often premature death."[3]

The timing of the speech was opportune for Nixon. Four days earlier the *New York Times* had begun printing excerpts from the Pentagon Papers—a top-secret blueprint of internal government war planning leaked by former CIA operative Daniel Ellsberg, which exposed the calculated imperial rationale shaping American intervention in Vietnam and the deceptiveness of successive administrations in repeatedly lying to the public.[4] Popular support for the war had generally reached a low ebb by this point—falling below 25 percent—with some of the most protracted opposition coming from within the ranks of servicemen. In recent years, a growing number of GIs had engaged in acts of insubordination and resistance to military authority, while returning vets had swelled the ranks of the peace movement in the United States.[5] In late April 1971, antiwar veterans—described by the *Washington Evening Star* as "hippies with combat infantry badges and Purple Hearts"—gathered for a special ceremony during which they denounced U.S. aggression and war crimes and hurled their medals at the Pentagon, vowing that the only way they would fight again would be to "take these steps."[6] Testifying before the Senate Foreign Relations Committee, Vietnam Veterans against the War (VVAW) spokesman John F. Kerry subsequently excoriated the Nixon administration for betraying the troops and urged immediate withdrawal so that no one else had to "die for the biggest nothing in history" and a "mistake."[7]

On June 18, 1971, amid all these developments, Nixon received a flurry of positive letters from constituents praising his commitment to solving the drug "crisis," which many considered to be among the "gravest social problems" of their time.[8] He had found the perfect political remedy, it appears, to deflect public attention from the horrors of the war in Vietnam and popular opposition to it—while pursuing the elusive and ultimate illusory goal of "peace with honor."[9] Nixon's speech further exemplified his manipulation of public fears over drugs as a mechanism for attacking

Great Society liberalism and the counterculture, which he disingenuously grouped together. Fueling a politics of polarization that would endure for over three decades, he blamed both for inducing moral decay in American society and eroding the nation's power.[10]

Throughout the previous years, Nixon had displayed a "visceral opposition" to the 1960s social movements, which he depicted as being Communist inspired and an affront to traditional American principles of hard work, self-reliance, patriotism, and thrift. During the 1968 election campaign, he characterized drugs as "the modern curse of American youth," akin to "the plagues and epidemics of former years" and threatening to "decimate a generation of Americans."[11] In June 1969, after winning the presidency, he made a special plea before Congress to expand federal funding for antidrug programs, and in September he initiated a sustained interdiction drive on the Mexican border called Operation Intercept. Nixon's initial focus was mainly on marijuana and psychedelic drugs such as LSD, which, he said, served as "the eucharist of a generation" and symbol of youthful rebellion. Divergent from the political New Left, which aimed to create a "participatory democracy," the hippies experimented in new lifestyles and philosophies that challenged the dominant technocratic and consumerist culture of the 1950s. They defied the prevailing assumption that material prosperity was to be the supreme goal in life—and were hence the target of a sustained political backlash by those committed not only to traditional moral values but to a preservation of the status quo.[12]

By 1970, Nixon had discovered a larger bogeyman in heroin, which appeared to represent an even more insidious threat to American life. Nixon portrayed the spread of heroin, historically a drug of the inner city, as a consequence of overly indulgent liberal social policies, whose focus on confronting the root causes of social deprivation and poverty absolved the individual from responsibility for his actions. As part of his new law-and-order program, which replaced Johnson's vision of the Great Society and mandated a harsher punitive approach to crime, Nixon called for more concerted government assault against the "tide of drug abuse." He declared, "It is no exaggeration to say that heroin addiction—if not checked by decisive action now—could cripple a whole generation or more of Americans in the critical years ahead. If we do not destroy the heroin menace, then it will surely and eventually destroy us and our great nation's future."[13]

Nixon's increasing resolve on the issue over the next year was due in part to his ability to exploit public concern about the extension of the so-called drug "epidemic" into Vietnam. In May 1971, two congressmen, Morgan F. Murphy (D-Ill.) and Robert H. Steele (R-Conn.), released a report—which Steele later admitted had been exaggerated—claiming that 10–15 percent of American GIs were addicted to high-purity heroin. They blamed the availability of the drug on the corruption of U.S. governmental allies and CIA covert operations in Laos and the Golden Triangle region (which also encompassed northern Thailand and Burma).[14] In response to dwindling public support for the war, Nixon stepped up his rhetoric and doubled the budget for rehabilitation and enforcement programs as part of the newly declared War on Drugs. He further initiated mandatory urinalysis testing in the military and a sustained interdiction campaign in Southeast Asia involving crop substitution, aerial defoliation, and the pressuring of governmental allies to crack down on drug-related corruption. In Laos the Nixon administration went so far as to contemplate bombing heroin refineries and set fire to a manufacturing lab once run by CIA asset Ouane Rattikone. In South Vietnam, meanwhile, the United States conducted intensive training of counternarcotics operatives and employed Special Forces units to gather intelligence and destroy locally grown marijuana. All these measures aimed to root out the source of supply reaching American troops, clean up the image of American allies, and bolster public confidence in the "Army in Anguish," as the *Washington Post* characterized it, thus allowing Nixon to perpetuate the war and restore the nation's international prestige. They represented a watershed in the evolution of federal drug and crime control policy, which had previously been more limited in scope and concentrated at the local and state levels.[15]

The so-called drug crisis in Vietnam—and its profound sociopolitical significance—has generally been ignored in historical debates about the origins and evolution of the modern War on Drugs. It was critical, however, in shaping the vigorous character of Nixon's policy and its international focus. The issue of drugs in Vietnam first grabbed the public's attention in January 1968 with the publication of a controversial article in the *Washingtonian* magazine, "The Importance of Being Stoned in Vietnam," by the son of the famous novelist John Steinbeck. Having served as a roving correspondent for the *Pacific Stars and Stripes*, John Steinbeck IV wrote that marijuana of a potent quality was naturally grown in Vietnam, was sold by farmers at a fraction of its cost in the United States, and could be obtained "more easily than a package of Lucky Strike cigarettes." He estimated that up to 75 percent of soldiers in Vietnam got high regularly. "The average soldier sees that for all intents and purposes, the entire country is stoned," Steinbeck observed. "To enforce a prohibition against smoking the plant [in Vietnam] would be like trying to prohibit the inhalation of smog in Los Angeles."[16]

Steinbeck had volunteered for service in Vietnam in 1966 because, as he wrote in his autobiographical book *In Touch*, he "wanted to know what was going on there, rather than hear the name mentioned a thousand times a day by people who never breathed Vietnam's air." By the end of his tour of duty, he was wearing peace beads, discovering Buddhism, and publicly expressing his disdain for the American intervention. Upon returning home to California, Steinbeck was arrested on charges of marijuana possession. He lashed out by writing the *Washingtonian* piece, which was designed to highlight the hypocrisy of governmental policies and its maltreatment of veterans. As he told his famous father, who sympathized with his antipathy toward the war and pro-marijuana stance, "My purpose in writing the piece was to dramatize the vast numbers of Americans who were smoking marijuana in Vietnam. If they were smoking it as respected and lauded soldiers over there how could it be they were criminals in America? I wanted to paint this ridiculous contradiction."[17]

By his own admission, Steinbeck overdramatized the nature of drug abuse in Vietnam for political purposes. Lee Dembart, a reporter with the Queens College student newspaper who wrote of his observations during approximately the same period, estimated that the actual rate of marijuana use in the American military was 20 percent. Studying the issue most systematically, military psychiatrists found that between 30 and 35 percent of American GIs likely got high during their tour—largely on an experimental basis, to escape the harsh realities of war and in some cases as an act of defiance.[18] Despite its exaggeration, Steinbeck's article had an effect far beyond his original expectation. It gave rise to what I term the "myth of the addicted army," which alleged that drug use was so widespread in Vietnam that it contributed to a breakdown in the military's fighting capacities. Adopting hyperbolic references to "epidemics" and "plagues," proponents of this myth equated all drug use with abuse and downplayed the differences among drugs—depicting marijuana, for example, to be equally as powerful and addictive as heroin. Neglecting the social context in which GIs got stoned, including the link to antiwar protest and the confinement of drug use mainly to the rear, they blamed drugs for a host of military problems—including lack of discipline, sabotage, combat refusals, and civilian atrocities—which could more reasonably have been attributed to the prolongation of a war that had lost any sense of purpose. By the time the myth of the addicted army reached its zenith in mid-1971 with the proliferation of reports over the spread of heroin, it had already had a pronounced public impact. It helped divert public attention from the policies that had produced and perpetuated the war in Vietnam, intensified public fears of the growth of the 1960s drug culture, and thus created an opportune political climate for an expansion of the federal drug war.

In his sweeping cultural history *Gunfighter Nation*, Richard Slotkin defines myth as a series of icons and clichés, drawn from a society's history, which develop over time, usually help to shape public memory of historical events, and provide a framework for a shared public belief system and ideology. The focal point of Slotkin's study is the frontier myth linking the spread of liberal democracy to the conquest of the Indians on the western plains and the "taming of the frontier."[19] The myth of the addicted army is consistent with Slotkin's paradigm in that it helped to skew public memory of the Vietnam War by advancing the impression that pure and innocent American youth had been corrupted by illegal drugs— and not by flawed policies, institutional failings, or cultural chauvinism, as most historians would conclude.[20] The myth also helped to solidify a widely held belief in the malevolence of drug use of any kind, while providing an excuse for American conduct which helped minimize in the public's eye the atrocities committed against the Indo-Chinese people. This view accorded well with a deep-rooted perception of national exceptionalism and greatness, which manifested itself, as Noam Chomsky and H. Bruce Franklin have best documented, in quagmire analogies put forward by even liberal "doves." These "doves" could not admit that the United States had acted coercively in South Vietnam, stressing instead the nation's honorable intentions.[21]

In preventing the kind of sustained national soul-searching and rethinking of values that might have emerged from an honest accounting of the war, the myth of the addicted army served an ideological function similar to that of three additional cultural myths related to the American experience in Vietnam. One is the Prisoner-of-War Myth, which the Nixon administration initially used to justify a prolongation of the war and later provided a rationale for condemning the peace settlement that ended it. Equally prominent in American popular discourse is the Stab-in-the-Back Myth, which bears resemblance to the German Dolchstoss legend after World War I. It blames weak-willed politicians, treasonous antiwar protestors, and dissenting journalists for failing to provide the necessary moral support to the troops in Vietnam and constraining American military power, hence breeding defeat. Intricately connected to this view is the Spat-upon-Veteran Myth, which indicts the antiwar movement for allegedly maltreating American GIs on their return home, even though hard evidence of such maltreatment is hard to come by.[22]

These myths have been promoted most vigorously by conservatives and neoconservatives eager to justify the revival of an aggressive foreign policy and to denigrate the Vietnam-era antiwar movement. Each took root because of an unwillingness on the part of many Americans to bear collective responsibility for the country's actions in Vietnam. Because the culture at large could not accept defeat at the hands of "an inferior people," or "raggedy-ass fourth rate power," as Lyndon B. Johnson characterized the Vietnamese, it searched for alternative explanations that became institutionalized over time. Together, these myths helped preserve the nation's vision of righteousness and the dominant internationalist creed, which asserted that America had both the duty and the right to export liberal-capitalist ideals in the developing world.[23] They helped refocus public hostility, moreover, on a series of scapegoats, including ineffectual bureaucrats, antiwar activists, and liberal journalists, along with the "pernicious evil" of drug abuse, which emerged as a symbol of the war's "tragedy" and whose eradication was deemed necessary to restore America's international credibility and prestige.

Though manipulated by political elites, the myth of the addicted army was not advanced solely from the top down. The mass media were particularly influential, in part because explosive drug stories helped to sell papers (or draw in viewers for television). Many journalists referred directly to Steinbeck's inflated estimates, which they accepted uncritically, and pointed to the ravaging effects of drug use in combat, even though such use was actually rare. Their narcophobic discourse, encompassing lurid metaphors and orientalist stereotypes depicting drugs as a foreign corrupting agent, was reminiscent of the worst antidrug propaganda campaigns of the past.[24] In one typical piece the *New York Times* warned about GIs while going into battle stoned on high-potency Vietnamese marijuana and opiates, experiencing hallucinatory visions, and firing at their own men. Other articles blamed drugs for provoking the internal collapse of the armed forces and the spread of uncontrollable crime and urban decay in the United States. In May 1971, *Newsweek* columnist Stewart Alsop went so far as to claim that the "drug epidemic" was worse than the My Lai massacre, in which U.S. soldiers rounded up and killed an estimated 504 Vietnamese civilians.[25]

A chief proponent of the myth of the addicted army, Senator Thomas J. Dodd (D-Conn.) had previously tried to blame drugs for My Lai. While chairing a series of subcommittee hearings on juvenile delinquency—which served in the words of one critic as a "platform for law and order hawks to tutor the public about the evils of narcotics"—he procured testimony from two soldiers claiming that they had smoked marijuana the night before perpetrating the killings.[26] Though military psychiatrists dismissed any causal connection, Dodd was adamant in depicting the massacre as a product of military indiscipline provoked by the 1960s drug culture: "School children are popping pills like peanuts and as my hearings have shown, tens of thousands of troops have gone into battle high on marijuana, opium or other drugs, with horrifying results. There is a drug culture in this nation that existing laws have failed to reduce." Dodd's focus on drugs provided him with a politically convenient explanation for the army's breakdown. It enabled him to boost his political profile as a champion of the antidrug cause, while evading responsibility for the grim realities of a war that he supported as a prominent member of the Senate Foreign Relations Committee.[27]

The scapegoating of drugs reached new peaks with Nixon, in part because it helped him to deflect criticism for his failure to engender "peace with honor" in Vietnam, as he had promised in his campaign rhetoric. As Larry Berman chronicles in his aptly titled *No Peace, No Honor*, Nixon achieved just the opposite. Delegating to national security Adviser Henry Kissinger, who shared an elitist disdain for "public input" and the "democratic process," according to staff assistant Roger Morris, Nixon subverted the Paris peace accords, eventually accepting terms in 1973 similar to those proposed nearly five years earlier.[28] He concurrently widened the war into Cambodia and Laos, where residents were subjected to brutal scorched-earth campaigns by American-backed forces and to withering bombing attacks that yielded "methodical devastation."[29] As in South Vietnam, "carpet bombing" by U.S. warplanes leveled dozens of villages, wounded and killed tens of thousands, and forced countless others to live in underground caves, while also radicalizing the political opposition.[30] Nixon's extension of the war resulted not only in the death of untold numbers of Southeast Asians and further destruction of the societal fabric but also in the loss of approximately 20,000 more U.S. troops without yielding any measurable difference in the outcome. By 1971, despite the enormously high human costs of a failed war policy, Nixon had somehow succeeded in making the alleged "drug crisis" an issue of comparable if not greater national concern than the war itself, as revealed through public opinion polls.[31] Through careful media manipulation and rhetorical flourish, he helped to arouse what sociologists refer to as a "moral panic," characterized by an exaggerated public fear that illicit substances, including marijuana, threatened vital security interests and the nation's social vitality.[32]

Ironically, given the political ramifications, the antiwar movement and political left played a crucial though largely unrecognized role in enhancing the "drug panic." They were often as vocal as conservatives in broadcasting the ravaging effects of drug abuse in Vietnam, in large part because they blamed the government for addicting its own troops. During the mid-1960s, rumors first emerged that the CIA was providing logistical support for drug traffickers in Southeast Asia who served as allies in the fight against Communism. Radical academics, student activists, and Democrats seeking the withdrawal of American troops seized upon this information—which proved to be largely true—and linked it to the burgeoning addiction crisis in Vietnam, whose scope they exaggerated for political effect. In 1971 the left-wing *Ramparts* magazine editorialized: "The U.S. went on a holy war to stamp out Communism and to protect its Asian markets and its conscripted sons have come home with a blood-stained needle as their only lasting souvenir. It is a fitting trade-off—one that characterizes the moral quality of the U.S. involvement, which has radiated a nimbus of genocide and corruption. . . . This ugly war keeps coming back to haunt us, each manifestation more terrifying than the last."[33]

Seeing the international drug trade as a form of economic imperialism, the antiwar left helped to cement the public impression that drugs were a lasting legacy of America's disastrous intervention in Vietnam and menace to the social order. They further contributed to a transformation of the image of Vietnam veterans from agents of imperialism—as many came to see themselves—and dissenters to pathological victims of an unpopular war, upon whom public fears became transfixed.[34] In his 1973 book *Vietnam Veterans: Neither Victims nor Executioners*, Yale psychiatrist Robert Jay Lifton observed:

> The particular taint of Vietnam finds appropriate, if tragic, [public] symbolism in the heroin epidemic. . . . The men who encounter evil in war take on its particular taint or sickness in the form of heroin. The

society that sent them becomes terrified of them, the fear of contagion remains acute, as do images of infected men returning to spread their "plague" through the mother country. Now the addicts instead of the war itself and the way we are fighting it become the locus of evil. The problem, when finally acknowledged, becomes drug addiction, and that we are told is what must be overcome.[35]

Benefiting from the displacement of public scrutiny away from his foreign policy, Nixon was able to present himself as a national savior, bent on eradicating the drug peril from American life. His rhetoric and policies appealed in particular to nationalist sentiment and to the so-called silent majority seeking a return to the social stability of the pre-Vietnam era. In spite of abundant contradictions—including Nixon's continued support for known drug traffickers out of geopolitical expediencies—they helped to consolidate the growing grassroots appeal of the conservative right, which was successful in cultivating a populist image as an embattled champion of working-class aspirations. It did so in part by playing off media stereotypes of the student, black power, and antiwar movements and blaming deep-rooted social problems on a series of artificial catalysts, most notably drugs.[36]

The image of the addicted army lingered in the consciousness of the American public beyond the Nixon era largely as a result of popular cultural media. Through the late 1970s and 1980s, Hollywood and network television reinforced the notion that drug abuse had provoked the nation's military collapse and at the same time linked drugs to the spiritually corrupting effects of the war. Building on earlier media stereotypes, they stigmatized veterans as depraved junkies, obscuring the fact that many had joined forces with civilian activists to form the "most significant working-class antiwar movement in American history." They further turned the story of America's massively destructive war effort in Southeast Asia into one of U.S. victimization through drugs.[37] This in the end bore powerful political consequences, drawing attention away from all the carnage and the popular mobilization against it, and allowing for a revival of the war's justifying ideologies. It further helped to inculcate popular support for the War on Drugs as a policy designed to strengthen the country and avert future military disasters.

During the 1980s, Ronald Reagan, who referred to Vietnam as a "noble cause," capitalized on this popular rewriting of history. He made drug control a vital aspect of his mandate to restore American national prestige and overcome the so-called Vietnam syndrome, which was defined by conservatives as the "sickly prohibition against the use of force in international affairs," engendered in part by the antiwar movement. Abandoning the treatment paradigm established by Nixon, Reagan launched a major antidrug campaign in the military to bolster public confidence in the "Big Green Machine" and prevent future "quagmires" of the Vietnam variety. As part of an interventionist foreign policy, including the waging of proxy wars across Central America and the invasion of the small Caribbean island of Grenada, Reagan further expanded the international drug war with an emphasis on aerial interdiction and spraying. He simultaneously initiated a domestic enforcement blitz, resulting in record arrest and seizure rates, as well as an unprecedented prison boom.[38]

Motivated by powerful nationalistic convictions, Reagan's drug war typified the workings of the post–World War II national security state, in which public policy often served the interests of American global supremacy. It also reflected deeply rooted fears of external encroachment, epitomized by the typecasting of drugs as a "foreign" menace.[39] Throughout the 1980s, government officials frequently claimed that Latin American "narco-guerrillas" were exporting drugs as a means of ravaging the nation. Rooted more in fiction than fact, this claim harked back to similar government charges during the Vietnam era, when fears of imperial decline had first manifested themselves.[40] In both cases, drugs were portrayed as a primary cause of America's weakening global status and symbol of its loss in social vitality, they thus needed to be eradicated at whatever the social cost. Apart from pockets of dissent in the medical establishment, academia, and some remnants of the 1960s left, few Americans challenged this consensus or questioned the underlying assumptions shaping the growth of the "new prohibition," as one analyst characterized it.[41]

Scores of books have recently been written on the War on Drugs, most of which are highly critical. Many are ironically housed in Drug Enforcement Administration (DEA) library in Washington, D.C., whose patrons have remained stubbornly committed to the punitive enforcement paradigm despite its documented failure at both a practical and a humanitarian level.[42] While spending billions of dollars over decades, the rate of supply and demand for marijuana, heroin, cocaine, and new synthetic drugs (such as crystal methamphetamines and ecstasy) continue to increase. Imprisonment rates meanwhile have skyrocketed, particularly among African Americans and other minority groups in the poor urban communities most directly targeted by heightened policing efforts.[43] In order to enforce punitive laws, federal and state and local governments have diverted badly needed funding from schools, medical care, and other vital social services, thus perpetuating the conditions in which the drug trade flourishes and poverty remains entrenched.[44]

As devastating an effect as the War on Drugs has had domestically, the disastrous international ramifications have been even more marked. In both Latin America and Southeast Asia, U.S. drug-control policies have contributed to political destabilization, escalating cycles of violence and burgeoning anti-American sentiment. They have further yielded protracted health and environmental damage through crop defoliation, as well as the loss of innocent life, and provided billions of dollars in technical and military aid to repressive regimes implicated in systematic human rights abuses.[45] In November, 2004 a civic-advocacy group, the Washington Office on Latin America, published a damning report that concluded:

> In one nation after another, U.S. drug control policies are undermining human rights and democracy by bringing back into domestic law enforcement the region's militaries, which have not been held accountable for widespread abuses and authoritarian dictatorships, and are causing enormous damage to some of the most vulnerable people in the hemisphere, including impoverished farmers ratcheted down into deeper poverty with the destruction of their most important crops. After 25 years and more than 25 billion dollars, we are no closer to winning the war, which is ultimately about reducing drug abuse. There has been no significant reduction of illicit drugs flowing out of the Andes or other countries.[46]

These findings should come as no surprise to readers versed in the scholarly literature of the War on Drugs, which has consistently exposed the failure of narcotics control programs.[47] Writing from a predominantly liberal disposition, many critics contend that the drug war originally emerged as a product of the conservative backlash against the hippie counterculture and the social upheavals of the 1960s.[48] Others insist that conservatives manipulated public opinion on the drug issue through inflated statistics in order to push forward a social agenda focused on "law and order" at the expense of social welfare programs.[49] Such arguments help explain how the War on Drugs served specific political ends, contributing to what deputy drug czar John Walters (1989–1993) characterized as a "conservative cultural revolution."[50] The problem with the emphasis on the role of the conservative movement is that it ignores the bipartisan character of the modern War on Drugs. Previous scholarship also neglects the broader global context and impact of the crisis in Vietnam in exacerbating popular anxieties over drugs, which were linked to deep-seated fears of national decline. International developments, I argue, should be viewed as among the pivotal factors shaping the growth of the modern drug war, whose history shows how federal policy has been transformed by overseas military intervention and empire, with far-reaching effect.[51]

The Nation implicitly recognized this when it editorialized in 1974 that "the causus belli that triggered the War on Drugs was surely Vietnam." Robert DuPont, director of the National Institute on Drug Abuse (NIDA), wrote four years later that "the critical triggering event for the federal government's involvement [in drug abuse] was the national agony over the American involvement in the Vietnam War."[52] Yet scholars writing on the topic, including some of the best historians of the Vietnam War, have ignored this interconnection. Often subscribing to the sensational media imagery of the early 1970s, they tend to exaggerate the scope of the so-called drug crisis and ignore its broader social implications.[53]

My study seeks to set the record straight. It examines the growth of powerful mythologies surrounding drug use in Vietnam and their crucial significance in shaping the expansion, institutionalization, and internationalization of the War on Drugs. It further emphasizes the interplay between foreign and domestic policies and identifies the drug war as among the key legacies of the war on the America side, reflecting an insular cultural mentality and the erasure from public discourse of the Vietnamese vantage point.

To be sure, Nixon did not initiate the War on Drugs. He was a direct heir of Harry J. Anslinger, head of the Federal Bureau of Narcotics (FBN) from 1930 to 1962, who publicly exaggerated the ravages of drug abuse in order to bolster the profile of his agency and push forward the 1937 Marijuana Tax Act and the harsh punitive laws of the 1950s.[54] Anslinger had made the FBN important to the waging of the Second World War in getting drug supplies to be considered as strategic materials that should be kept out of Axis hands and did all he could to insinuate drug control into the making of national security policy.[55] It was those endeavors that Nixon and his successors built upon as a crucial basis for their broader strategic designs, aimed at restoring American global credibility and power and at countering the social transformations of the 1960s.

Through an analysis of military records, psychiatric reports, and GI testimonials, the first chapter of this book provides an overview of drug use patterns in Vietnam and examines the social circumstance in which GIs used drugs. The second chapter shows how politicians and the mass media exaggerated the scope of addiction within the U.S. military and helped fuel public fears of an impending domestic catastrophe, while diverting attention from the ongoing catastrophe afflicting the people of Indochina. The third chapter looks at the role of military psychiatrists in advancing an alternative portrayal of the alleged crisis, one that was far more sensitive to the soldiers' perspective and, in the end, far more accurate. The fourth chapter explores ways in which the Democratic Party and the antiwar movement promoted the myth of the addicted army for their own political purposes, enhancing the specter of "moral panic" that unwittingly played into conservative hands. The fifth and sixth chapters focus on Nixon's skillful manipulation of the drug crisis to his political benefit and the expansion of control measures both domestically and in the international realm, with profound consequence. The seventh chapter details the influence of popular culture media in propagating the myth of the addicted army during the 1970s and 1980s and in falsifying public understanding of the war, in part by recasting the image of American GIs. The final chapter points to the legacy of Vietnam in shaping the evolution of the modern War on Drugs through the 1980s—and beyond.

The enduring quality of the myth of the addicted army in many respects demonstrates America's long-standing inability to come to terms with the moral consequences of the Vietnam War. By reimagining their soldiers as victims and the U.S. military defeat as a "tragedy," Americans were able to deflect responsibility for the massive destruction and loss of life inflicted on the people of Southeast Asia and thus to avoid serious reconsideration of the ideological principles that rationalized the American intervention. The silencing and demonizing of dissenting voices, including antiwar GIs typecast as psychopathic junkies, aided in this process. Today, few recognize how the addiction "crisis" in Vietnam—and its political manipulations—both helped to distort public memory of the war and created the sensational climate surrounding drugs that has endured for over three decades. Understanding how the myth of the addicted army came into being and shaped the War on Drugs and how it came to play an increasingly important role in American culture during the late twentieth century is the subject of this book.

"THE PRESS HAS DONE A TREMENDOUS DISSERVICE"

HISTORICAL PERSPECTIVE

The clatter of machine guns was like a Stravinsky percussion interlude from Le Sacre du Printemps. There isn't a psychedelic discotheque that can match the beauty of flares and bombs at night. —John Steinbeck IV, 1968

The nature of the problem is not such that military readiness is considered to be endangered. —Admiral William P. Mack, Deputy Assistant Secretary of Defense, 1970

In December 1970, comedian Bob Hope generated a wave of laughter from a crowd of American troops telling jokes about marijuana and the use of drugs in Vietnam. Sent to boost morale as part of the United Service Organization (USO), Hope proclaimed, "Is it true the officers are getting flight pay? I saw a Sergeant before the show standing on a corner with a lampshade on his head waiting to be turned on. . . . At one barracks, everyone was watching 12 o'clock high. And they didn't even have a TV set." He added, "I hear you guys are interested in gardening security. Our officer said a lot of you guys are growing your own grass." Hope drew the greatest cheers when he declared, "Instead of taking away marijuana from the soldiers—we ought to be giving it to the negotiators in Paris."[1]

Although worthy of some good laughs, Hope's remarks—and the reaction that they elicited—held deep social significance. They promoted recognition that drug use had different connotations for soldiers than for senior commanding officers or contemporaries back home. In calling for American leaders to smoke marijuana before going to the negotiating table, Hope further tapped into a growing antiestablishment ethos and mistrust of government pervading the military, which helped to account in part for the relatively high drug usage rates. Only from the perspective of individual soldiers can one assess the genuine scope of drug abuse in Vietnam and disprove claims that the crisis was all-encompassing. Why did some soldiers turn to drugs and in what circumstances? These questions are perhaps most important with regard to the impact of drugs on the military's fighting performance—which was far less destructive than has been conventionally understood. Though not intended as social satire, Hope's comedic insights were, in hindsight, quite sharp in pointing not only to the paradox of governmental prohibition policies but also to the scandalous public emphasis on drugs. What Hope missed, however, was how deeply significant drug use was to the social setting of the Vietnam War—and to the injustice of American foreign policy more broadly, which he uncritically supported.[2]

"Distorted Impression That Average Soldier Uses Drugs . . . "

Illegal drugs were readily available in Vietnam from the invasion of American combat troops in the early 1960s. Among them was a headache remedy known as Binoctal, which soldiers took alongside alcohol for a "quick high."[3] Throughout most of the war the military actually distributed amphetamines or "pep pills" to soldiers serving on long-range reconnaissance missions to prevent them from falling asleep or to help them lose weight.[4] Many soldiers claimed that the pills increased their irritability—including one who admitted to killing over 100 civilians in the Ia Drang Valley while coming off a high—though others recorded a more favorable effect.[5] The most widely used intoxicant in Vietnam was marijuana of a high potency which grew wild in the countryside.[6] GIs developed such nicknames as "Pleiku Pink," "Bleu de Hue," and "Cambodian Red," based on the province or locality in which it was grown. They got stoned overwhelmingly (upward of 90 percent) as a group activity, rather than in isolation. The Vietnamese themselves rarely smoked marijuana, preferring the chewing of betel nuts or the smoking of opium. Capitalizing on rising market demand, however, many farmers sold marijuana through local retailing merchants, often disguised as packs of Parker Lane and Kent cigarettes. These could be purchased for 400 Vietnamese piasters or $1.50—an unheard of price by American standards.[7] "Marijuana in Vietnam is cheap, easy to find—and potent," remarked one medical psychiatrist, as quoted in *U.S. News & World Report*. "The drug is everywhere. All a person has to do to get the drug in any village hamlet or town is say the word Khan Sa."[8]

In 1967, as a result of a growing wave of media attention, the Department of Defense (DOD) formed a special task force on narcotics and commissioned psychiatrist Roger A. Roffman to conduct a study at the Long Binh jail, where drugs were prevalent despite tightening security. He found that 63 percent of prisoners tried marijuana. In a follow-up survey, Roffman and Ely Sapol determined that 28.9 percent of GIs stationed in the Southern Corps experimented with marijuana at least once during their tour of duty in South Vietnam—comparable to user rates in the United States for men between the ages of eighteen and twenty-one (28 percent of those surveyed had tried the drug back home.)[9] They later testified before Congress as to how they had taken pains to ensure strict confidentiality with their subjects, who might have been otherwise reluctant to admit participating in an illegal activity. Both were deeply dismayed by the media's coverage, which inflated their data and issued "bombastic statements that 60, 70, 80 or even 90 percent of American troops" were addicts. "It is a distorted impression," Sapol remarked, "that the average soldier uses drugs."[10]

From 1968 through the early 1970s, the Pentagon funded a new array of studies which corroborated Sapol's analysis. They determined on average that approximately 35 percent of GIs tried marijuana, with rates increasing over time because of declining morale and cultural shifts. Soldiers who had experimented with drugs in the United States were far more likely to utilize drugs in Vietnam. Dr. Morris "Duke" Stanton, who worked with GIs near the demilitarized zone, documented a huge increase in the percentage of pre-service drug use through the middle and late 1960s. In 1967 a mere 9 percent of the enlistees he sampled had tried marijuana prior to joining the military; none had tried heroin or morphine; and only 12 percent said that they had tried drugs in Vietnam. In spring 1970, by contrast, 46 percent stated that they had smoked marijuana prior to their enlistment, and 6 percent had tried heroin or morphine.[11] Military totals thus do not appear to have been out of line with broader societal trends.

In 1971, at the peak of the media "scare," the U.S. Army Research Office conducted a comprehensive survey of 36,000 GIs—including navy and air force personnel, who were excluded from most previous samples—which found that 29.9 percent had tried marijuana; 17.9 percent, stimulants such as "speed" and other barbiturates; and 11.7 percent, narcotic drugs. Of senior noncommissioned officers, only 3 percent admitted to using drugs in Vietnam, with 1 percent reporting habitual marijuana use. In all the surveys conducted, significantly, only a small percentage of respondents recorded "heavy" or "daily" drug use.[12] One survey characteristically determined that nearly 50 percent of those who smoked marijuana in Vietnam did so fewer than ten times. Another concluded that less than 10 percent of soldiers used drugs more than two or three times, while less than 3 percent smoked not more than 200 times, or on a semi-daily basis.[13] Major Edmund Casper, a psychiatrist based in Chu Lai, reported, "Many individuals found that marijuana was either unrewarding or unpleasant, and indicate no desire to repeat the experience. Chronic abuse was in the minority." Dr. Richard Wilbur, Assistant Secretary of Defense (Health and Environment), further commented, "There is no question that much of the usage in Vietnam is of a much more casual type than what we are accustomed to seeing here in this country." Typical, it appears, was the experience of Jerry Lembcke, who, while serving as a chaplain's assistant in 1968 and 1969 at Qui Truong, tried drugs once but never contemplated regular use. "I never thought marijuana was such a problem and I would have known about it because of my job," he said. "Some guys smoked it casually, but it wasn't so out in the open and didn't affect the military in any way. Like many others, I personally didn't enjoy my one experience [with marijuana] and never tried it again."[14]

The pivotal distinction between use and abuse is relevant in weighing the impact of the so-called heroin crisis in Vietnam. Throughout much of the 1960s, the use of heroin and raw opium was rare. According to a military report, in fifty-two raids of known opium dens conducted by the Vietnamese police throughout the decade, only twelve Americans were arrested. One GI commented that during his first tour in 1967, "heroin simply wasn't on the scene at the time—neither for that matter was marijuana." By November 1970, however, the opening of transportation routes from the Golden Triangle through Cambodia, plummeting morale rates, and a crackdown on marijuana by the DOD had facilitated the spread of a highly purified form of heroin that was smoked. Known as "scag," it first began appearing in police reports in 1969 after being widely introduced in Vietnam by Thai soldiers trained by American Special Forces and the CIA.[15] Various studies estimated that 7 to 35 percent of lower-grade enlisted "grunts," a majority of them draftees, experimented with scag, which was openly sold in Vietnamese marketplaces for a fraction of what it cost in the United States. The highest proportion found "strung out" was 20 percent in some units. Many soldiers were apparently fooled into thinking that scag was harmless because of the method of ingestion.

Some also thought that they were using cocaine because the name for both drugs in Vietnamese is the same.[16] Military autopsy reports show that from April 1970 to January 1973, drugs factored into the death of 112 GIs, including at least 56 from heroin overdose and 14 from barbiturates. Hospital admission rates for drug abuse also doubled in these years. According to medical transcripts at Walter Reed Army Medical Center, 70 percent of patients were white and, compared with racial minorities growing up in tough inner-city communities, naive about the potential hazard of hard drug use.[17]

In June 1971 the DOD instituted a mandatory urinalysis test for departing soldiers. Under the direction of Dr. Jerome H. Jaffe, 3.6 percent were found to have heroin in their urine, and 5.5 percent were thought to have previously used the drug. Only 1 percent of 13,190 U.S. Air Force personnel tested positive, and 0.3 percent of the 5,754 from the U.S. Navy, Coast Guard, and Marine Corps By May 1972 the average for the entire armed forces was reduced to 1.5 percent, though this figure remains the source of controversy because of laboratory inconsistencies.[18] Several GIs insisted that they tested positive without ever having used heroin; others claimed to have passed the test while stoned or to have cheated in different ways, including ingesting mass amounts of alcohol to dilute their sample. According to journalist Richard Ashley, a "black market for clean urine" even developed among soldiers who desperately wanted to avoid prolonging their tour of duty in Vietnam, which was the punishment for a dirty sample.[19]

Despite the inaccuracies, which even Jaffe admitted to (telling reporters somewhat sarcastically that servicemen had tried to substitute everything from "beer to their grandmother's urine"), the low figures confirmed that public fears of an "epidemic" were overblown. They also indicated that in spite of the high purity of the heroin—which experts estimated to be 96 percent—the majority of GIs who smoked "scag" were neither incapacitated nor addicted and could stop smoking at any time in order to avoid detection. In a recent interview, Dr. Jaffe commented, "The test was a way for us to determine how extensive the scope of addiction was, which we did not really know going in. [It] proved the rates were lower than reported in the media and that soldiers who used heroin once or twice, contrary to myths about being enslaved, could stop at will. The deterrent quality of the test was further successful in limiting use."[20]

Dr. Jaffe still feels that the number of addicts in Vietnam was actually lower than the data presented because many casual users were "caught in the net"—particularly after a system of random testing was developed. Many clinical specialists responsible for administering the rehabilitation process agree.[21] On the whole, as both understood, the percentage of American soldiers who could be characterized as drug addicts during the war was a minority—even during the peak of the heroin influx in the early 1970s. Although a relatively high number of Americans experimented with drugs, many fewer used them on a regular basis, especially during the decisive phases of fighting. In short, at no point was the military incapacitated by drugs, despite media and governmental proclamations to the contrary.

"Problem Best Described as Minor"
The Impact of Drugs on Military Combat

Evidence that the crisis in Vietnam was publicly overblown comes from top-ranked generals who had the most reason to fear the spread of a drug "epidemic." Born of a generation that came of age drinking whiskey, rum, and other hard alcohol, most believed that drug use was a sign of "individual character weakness" and that GIs who partook were unfit for duty and should be thrown out of the service.[22] Lewis Walt, assistant commandant of the Marine Corps from 1968 to 1971, referred to drugs in Vietnam as "a contagious disease nearly as deadly as the bubonic plague. . . . The only explanation is that our enemy wants to hook as many GIs as possible." In spite of such views, unit commanders unanimously concluded in October 1968 that neither marijuana nor any hard drug had to that point "degraded the military's combat effectiveness."[23]

The headquarters of General William C. Westmoreland had previously issued a private report, based on interviews with high-ranking officers, which stated, "All agree there has been no discernible impact on morale, health, welfare efficiency or combat effectiveness that can be attributed to drugs. The total scope of the problem is best described as minor." The report continued, "The impact regarding public image is much greater and more serious. This is reflected in the current rash of press reports alluding to the widespread use of marijuana by our troops in Vietnam, which is not borne out by statistics or the best judgment of our senior commanders." Although it is true, as antiwar critics charged, that Westmoreland and his staff were dishonest in trying to minimize the scope of addiction, having mounted a public campaign to denounce sensational press reports as "Communist propaganda to discredit the troops," these comments vividly demonstrate that internal military estimates were *less* alarming than those of the media and public at large. They also show that the military's primary concern over drugs during the decisive phases of the war was more in the realm of public relations than in duty performance.[24]

Tellingly, in a 1976 article summarizing the findings of military psychiatrists, Morris Stanton concluded that there was "no hard evidence" that military capability was "seriously affected by drugs." One key reason, he explained, was that marijuana was not habit-forming, and a majority of GIs who got high did so almost exclusively while on rest and recuperation leave (R&R), on rear support bases, or during lulls in combat. One quantitative study found that less than 10 percent of men admitted to the use of marijuana on duty at some time; others placed the total between 6 and 12 percent. Within the air force, the peak figure was only 2.6 percent.[25] Having interviewed over 500 military personnel, psychiatrist W. B. Postel found that "the usual habit was to smoke the drug after a battle to calm down. Only one person indicated that he smoked while fighting." Frank Bartimo, assistant general counsel for the DOD, similarly concluded, "We have very little, about no, drug abuse among troops going into the field. Guys who use it say they never do it when they're going into combat." A Senate subcommittee staff report added that "the incidents where marijuana is used in combat situations are rare and isolated. . . . There is no evidence that any mission or operation has been jeopardized."[26]

Michael Herr reports in *Dispatches* that troops at Khe Sanh refrained from smoking marijuana even when it was accessible because they didn't want to be stoned during any ground attacks. Major General Raymond Davis proclaimed that there was no drug problem "out in the hinterlands because of self-policing by the troops themselves. Their life depended on a clear head." Marvin Matthiak, an infantryman stationed with the Alpha First Battalion Cavalry Division from 1969 to 1971, added, "The press has done a tremendous disservice to this country in portraying grunts as being out there doing drugs. We didn't have a drug problem, and as far as I know and as far as everyone else I ever talk to about it, there was essentially no drug use whatsoever in the bush. Everybody knew what the dangers were and nobody was stupid enough to incapacitate themselves."[27]

Many GIs relate that they took drugs predominantly as a tranquilizer to calm their nerves after heavy fighting. "When a lot of shit came down you would straighten up, but after it was over, you'd really get off," said one soldier. "We only used [drugs] after we got back from a mission, particularly if it was a hard one. Sometimes we'd just sit under a tree, smoke dope and cry. It was a good way to unwind; a wonderful anesthetic and escape." Marc Levy, a medic with the First Cavalry Division, recounted the story of a wounded GI who demanded a toke from a joint before being medevaced to a nearby hospital: "He was lying on a stretcher with shrapnel wounds on his leg, and just blurted out—give me a fucking joint. Now that's medical marijuana in action!" Levy said. "You have to realize that when we were out in the jungle the tension would build up like a coil over several days. Combat was the equivalent of sex in that it released all the emotional drain and produced an incredible rush of energy. You needed something to come down after that—and drugs like marijuana provided the perfect tranquilizing effect." These comments are consistent with the findings of military psychiatrists that most soldiers who used drugs did so for a distinctive social purpose and that drugs often provided a powerful antidote to the hazards and stress of combat. They helped GIs to cope with their anxieties—away from the theater of battle and usually without damaging their physical capabilities.[28]

"Drugs Got Me through the Day"
The Psychological Importance of Drug Use

The important psychological function of drug use in Vietnam was enhanced by the distinct social character of a war fought on behalf of a corrupt client regime against a popularly backed revolutionary movement—a point that was obscured in many media portrayals. Stripped of their youthful naiveté and idealism early in their tour of duty, most soldiers encountered bitter hostility throughout the Vietnamese countryside and were perceived as unwelcome foreign intruders, much like the French foreign legionnaires. They faced grave difficulty adjusting to the treacherous jungle terrain, in which the National Liberation Front (NLF), the Southern-based resistance movement, commanded deep support, and were constantly in fear of guerrilla attack.[29] Fighting at what one analyst termed the "butt end of a bad war," 43 percent of soldiers who used drugs, according to a study by sociologist John Helmer, cited "escape" as the key reason, and 37 percent cited "to forget the killing and relieve the pressure." In a personal memoir, *The Drug Hazed War in Southeast Asia*, Sergeant Jay Dee Ruybal, who served with the Fourth Battalion, Sixtieth Artillery from October 1967 to June 1969, commented, "For many of us, drugs were a form of self-medication. I daydreamed under their influence. They offered a temporary release from the constant fear and physical suffering." Bill Karabaic, a drug counselor with the 101st Airborne Division, similarly explained, "Vietnam is a bad place to be. Most people want to get through it as quickly and as painlessly as possible and drugs can help." Writing in *The Nation,* Private David Kashimba put the rationale in slightly different terms: "The Vietnam War has no purpose and that is the originator of the [heroin] problem. . . . [It helps men] to escape minds that have been shattered by killing for the sake of their superiors' thirst for blood."[30]

In "The Importance of Being Stoned in Vietnam," John Steinbeck IV related how drugs helped desensitize him to the violence and brutality of the war: "Because of what marijuana does to the brain's interpretation of light and what we call beauty—a wonderful change in war starts to occur. Instead of the grim order of terror, explosions modulate musically—death takes on a new approachable symbolism that is not so horrible." Though Steinbeck was prone to exaggeration, his description was genuine and applicable to many of his contemporaries, who, in the words of historian Gabriel Kolko, took drugs as an "anodyne for the minutes and days of terror and boredom." Dr. Peter Bourne, chief of the neuropsychiatry section of the U.S. Army Medical Research Team, who also participated in combat operations, explained, "The use of drugs in the combat zone has a particular appeal because the psychological anesthesia provides a ready antidote to environmental stress. Soldiers know how near they have come to dying and about the possibility of death in the future and feel no compunction about immersing themselves in immediate gratification."[31]

Dr. Bourne was among those who believed that the psychic benefits of drugs may have aided in the military preparedness of some soldiers. He wrote in a 1972 article that the use of marijuana "had various redeeming qualities. . . . One veteran told me, 'we never smoked grass in combat but I do not think I could have made it without cracking if I had not used it in between patrols.' The relaxing effects of marijuana are beyond dispute." Dr. Morris Stanton further concluded that in spite of all the negative publicity, "instances have been reported of 'good performers.' . . . Marihuana and some other illicit drugs may *help* certain individuals function on the job by assisting them in maintaining an adequate psychological adjustment while under the stresses of a combat environment and separation from home." Corroborating these sentiments, a GI named Bill testified before Congress that "if you are afraid of dying, I don't care what you do, it [marijuana] relaxes your nerves, and you don't have the feeling of what we call breaking up and just running. There have been quite a few people who have died in Vietnam by being scared and running off in the wrong direction."[32]

Contrary to public impressions, military reports frequently downplayed the detrimental effects of drugs—even in the case of soldiers who used them regularly. Commanding officers were sometimes, in the words of one army newspaper, "flabbergasted" to find that some of their best men were regularly getting high on scag. One colonel, who served as a military judge in a vast array of narcotics cases, estimated that to his surprise, 80 percent of the men appearing before him because of heroin use had top efficiency ratings from their superiors. A subsequent survey found that the performance of 75 percent of soldiers who used drugs was rated as "good" or "outstanding." General Michael S. Davison commented, "Heroin is the most insidious thing. A guy could be on it with a light to moderate addiction and you'd never tell, because he could still fly an airplane and do a complicated task." Colonel Douglas Lindsey added with regard to marijuana, "Many pot smokers are among the most intelligent members of the regiment and soldiers who smoke pot are more likely to be found among the better soldiers in the unit."[33]

Though dishonorably discharged after being caught possessing marijuana, Corporal Michael A. Posey was a Purple Heart winner who was looked upon as a leader of his unit. His lieutenant testified before a court of military appeals: "I could always count on [Corporal Posey]. He held high proficiency and conduct marks reserved for exceptional individuals. I was impressed with his attitude and capabilities."[34] Despite being arrested for possessing thirty vials of heroin, Private Gregory Franks received similar high praise from his superior officers, one of whom wrote in his criminal investigation file, "Franks is a quiet natured hard worker who [though suspected of using and trafficking heroin] is a highly valued member of his unit."[35] Thirty-five years after his service ended, William Leary, an aircraft technician stationed outside of Saigon from late 1969 through mid-1971, still takes pride in the fact that he never once faced reprimand from his superiors, despite using opium on a semiregular basis. "Apart from a few gung-ho idiots [like the type who bragged about pinning a 'Vietcong' to a tree with bullets], most of us hated the place. Drugs helped to get through the day. I can show you all my reports—I got the highest possible marks, and had comments praising my dedication."[36]

As in civilian life, many drug users became skilled at moderating their level of intake so as to avoid detection and ensure fitness for duty and work. Asked by an interviewer if using heroin or marijuana didn't make him drowsy or hung over, one GI commented, "No, man, you don't get into it that far. You take just enough to get up there and alert, but not too stoned." Several soldiers performed what the military considered to be gallant actions while high on either marijuana or heroin and received awards for meritorious achievement. Peter Lemon, a Congressional Medal of Honor winner told newspaper reporters that he was "high on marijuana" the night he fought off two waves of NLF soldiers and won America's highest military honor. Lemon later stated: "It was the only time I ever went into combat stoned. All the guys were heads [those who regularly smoked pot]. We'd sit around smoking grass and getting stoned and talking about when we'd get home."[37]

In a 1988 *Playboy* interview, Hollywood film director Oliver Stone attested that he got high prior to winning a Bronze Star for combat gallantry following the 1968 Tet offensive. Stone, who served with the Twenty-fifth Infantry Division near the Cambodian border and later undertook long-range reconnaissance patrol behind enemy lines with the First Cavalry Division, won the honor his pinpoint precision in striking an enemy enclave with a grenade during a sustained firefight; the act saved his platoon from being wiped out. Stone commented, "My baseball arm came through, I got the grenade in the hole my first time. If I'd missed, the fucking thing would have rolled into my own men." He added, "I smoked dope in combat and had been stoned that morning. It was no big deal. Drugs in Vietnam kept me sane, particularly after I had already been wounded twice."[38]

There is, to be sure, much new scientific data confirming that the use of even so-called soft or milder intoxicants such as marijuana inhibits cognitive reaction time, short-term motivation, and cardiovascular strength, while producing an overall "mental clouding" that limits intellectual rigor. These effects are magnified for heroin, which results in increased irritability and is potentially lethal when taken in immoderation.[39] Many officers worried that even casual marijuana use, which was most notorious in the Fourth Infantry Division, made their troops less alert and that soldiers in the rear could make fatal mistakes while stoned. A DOD survey reported that only 14 percent of *non*–drug users felt that they could "count on" people who used marijuana while on duty to "perform their jobs effectively" by contrast, 62 percent of drug users themselves believed that marijuana smokers could be counted on. Lieutenant Colonel Anthony Herbert related in his book *Soldier* an incident in which a unit was ambushed at night and did not fight back because many of the members were high. Some GIs reported experiences with high-potency drugs in

Vietnam during which they blacked out or drifted into unconsciousness. Others experienced hallucinatory visions that contributed in isolated cases to dereliction of duty. Marc Levy related, "Vietnam is the worst place to have a bad trip. I smoked a marijuana joint laced with opium, what they called an OJ (opium joint), while at Long Binh and I freaked out. I crawled into a bunker and thought I was getting shot at. I was scared and filled with anxiety in Vietnam as it is, and the marijuana brought me over the edge. I thought I was going to die while on the stuff, and was scared senseless."[40]

Clearly, in this state, Levy was a major combat liability. His comments, however, need to be taken with a grain of salt. As he himself recognized, the delusions that he experienced were a product as much of the war environment as of the actual physical properties of marijuana—which, according to one leading scientific expert, normally produce "mere mild euphoria and giggles without unpleasant after-effects." Emotionally shattered by the brutality that he had witnessed and terrified virtually every waking hour of the day of being killed, Levy was susceptible to being put over the edge by the slightest of inducements, including pot. In this respect, he was far from alone. On the whole, though drug use may have brought to the surface deep-rooted social anxieties—as in Levy's case—or in other instances hindered the stamina, judgment, and preparedness of soldiers, it did not cause paranoid or irrational behavior that was otherwise inexplicable. To the contrary, in a large number of cases, as psychiatrists such as Dr. Stanton and Dr. Bourne best articulated, drugs helped mitigate the harshness of war, serving as a psychological outlet for GIs living in nightmarish conditions.[41]

"A Beer Was Cheaper to Get Than a Soda"
The Alcoholic Army in Vietnam

It puts the scope of the drug problem in perspective to recognize that alcohol abuse in Vietnam was far more pervasive. The DOD concluded that 88 percent of soldiers reported drinking alcohol during their tour of duty, often in "prodigious amounts." Another study found that 73 percent of junior enlisted men fit the definition of being either "problem drinkers" or "heavy or binge" drinkers. The rate for senior enlisted men was little better at 63 percent, and even the rate for officers exceeded 30 percent.[42] In a secret memo addressed to all military chiefs of staff, General Westmoreland admitted that alcohol abuse was a "serious problem." A 1970 Criminal Investigation Division (CID) staff report analogously concluded, "The emphasis placed in recent months on drug abuse in the services has all but obscured the plodding efforts to overcome an older, more nagging problem: alcoholism. Career considerations still prevent many from even acknowledging their disease and this holds for Senior NCOs as well as officers."[43] Gonzalo Baltazar, a private serving in the 2/17 Cavalry, 101st Airborne Division, commented in a recent interview, "Everybody in Vietnam drank like fish, and every chance you got you drank yourself silly. Us infantry guys, we were a bunch of alcoholics."[44]

As in World War II, the high rate of abuse was partially shaped by the senior command, which adopted a tolerant attitude toward and in some cases virtually encouraged drinking. Before 1972, when it declared alcoholism to be a "disease," the DOD had no official policy outlawing drinking and left major decisions about the need for treatment or punishment to local platoon leaders, who were often themselves prone to abuse.[45] In 1966 the army opened an amusement center at An Khe with forty-eight bars in order to "boost morale." Many officers made sure that free beer was available at base camp and at times ordered it to be dropped via helicopter in combat areas. Age regulations were abolished, and in December 1970, Army Chief of Staff Westmoreland approved drinking in the barracks. Some commanders even utilized alcohol as a reward for proficiency in enemy kills. Private David Tuck of the Twenty-fifth Infantry Division testified before the 1967 Bertrand Russell War Crimes Tribunal, headed by the ninety-four-year-old British philosopher, about a passing fad in his unit, where, "the person who had the most ears was considered the number one 'Vietcong' killer. When we'd get back to base camp, they would get all the free beer and whiskey they could drink."[46]

Dr. Roger Roffman, who worked at psychiatric treatment facilities in Long Binh and Saigon from 1967 to 1969, commented, "Legality made drinking a far more legitimate form of social release than drugs in Vietnam. Within the stressful setting of war, young men of that age naturally look to alter their state of consciousness. Because the military sanctioned alcohol, it is not surprising that drinking, often to extremes, was commonplace." Roffman added, "Not only was alcohol more prevalent than drugs in Vietnam . . . [but] alcohol-related problems were also far worse."[47] Backing up this point, the CID files are replete with cases of soldiers instigating fights while drunk. Intoxicated pilots had a ritual of racing their motorbikes at dizzying speeds around the Bien Hoa airbase, causing various disturbances and accidents. Assistant Secretary of Defense Richard Wilbur, spoke before a congressional subcommittee about a hazing practice in which airborne officers drank alcohol out of the nose cap of an airplane propeller until they became unconscious. "Unfortunately," stated Dr. Wilbur, "some of the social aspects of the military have tended to emphasize alcohol. The need for getting drunk when one is promoted or gets a medal or a change of assignment has an adverse effect on military preparedness."[48]

Many soldiers publicly stated that they feared going into combat with soldiers who had been drinking the night before because of the effects of being hung over, which was not the case with drugs. One air force officer proclaimed, "When I get up in the wee hours to fly a mission, I need the [person] I'm with to be fresh. He's more likely to be so if he smoked grass the night before than if he got juiced [drunk]." Another added, "Alcohol makes people really weird, I mean you can't depend on them to do anything, they're virtually incapacitated. Marijuana is not quite as bad." Jay Pierson, of the Eighth Wing Tech Division based out of Ubon Thailand, spoke in a recent interview about a pilot who drank so much that he "[almost] literally turned into a grape," jeopardizing the safety of his crew before he was sent to detoxification. Marc Levy detailed the case of a doctor who, under the influence following a particularly brutal firefight, was unable to treat wounded GIs near the Cambodian border. "The guy was completely drunk, risking lives," Levy recalled. "While there were rumors about soldiers fucking up because of drugs, the only cases I knew of were with alcohol; guys drunk or hung-over who couldn't do their jobs or [who] made mistakes like stepping on a land mine, which cost lives. Drinking was simply part of the culture in Vietnam and it was everywhere. A beer was cheaper to get than a soda."[49]

According to various firsthand accounts, drinking was far more pervasive than drugs in the Army of the Republic of South Vietnam (ARVN), even before combat.[50] Alcohol was also more likely than drugs to provoke cases of psychiatric breakdown. In 1966, in his capacity as chief of the neuropsychiatry section of the U.S. Army Medical Research Team, Dr. Peter Bourne treated forty-six cases of character and behavioral disorder among ARVN soldiers, of whom thirty were alcoholics. According to Bourne, alcohol was a key factor in a huge number of cases of mental collapse throughout the war on both sides, whereas marijuana and other drugs created "almost no psychiatric problems." In a 1970 article, psychiatrist Edward Huffman reported that 18.5 percent of the patients he treated for combat fatigue and stress in Nha Trang and Saigon suffered from "severe alcoholic dependency," compared with less than 2 percent who engaged in "unquestionable drug abuse." And Dr. Edward Colbach commented, "I heard many horror stories about marijuana, but in a full year serving a psychiatric facility of 45,000 troops, I came across no case of drug related mental breakdown. In my recollection, alcohol caused most of the trouble of a sensational variety."[51]

In "GIs against Themselves—Factors Resulting in Explosive Violence in Vietnam," Drs. Vincent Becchinelli and Douglas Bey cited the case of a drunken U.S. soldier who shot his sergeant four times in the head, killing him instantly. They concluded that alcohol enhanced deep-rooted frustrations with the war and the "loss of ideological purpose," causing a breakdown in military discipline.[52] Dr. John K. Imahara, a psychiatrist stationed at Long Binh, testified before Congress similarly that alcohol intoxication was more common than drugs in cases of intra-unit violence. He related how a soldier who had been drinking for "several hours" bayoneted and killed a fellow GI in a fit of rage.[53] James Pederson, an officer at the Long Binh prison, recounted another case where in which a highly decorated air force pilot fired his rifle indiscriminately at the end of an airfield while inebriated, killing five Vietnamese maintenance technicians. In March 1971, Sergeant First Class Prentice B. Smith was convicted of unpremeditated murder after he fired several rounds from his M-16 into a crowd of officers while drunk, killing one and wounding five others. A psychiatric report concluded that he had suffered from "paranoid thinking" and "auditory hallucinations" induced by alcohol.[54]

These cases exemplify the pernicious consequence of alcohol abuse during the war, which helped to exacerbate internal dissension and violence and tarnished America's reputation more directly than drugs. Yet for deep-rooted cultural and political reasons, politicians and the media overlooked the alcohol "epidemic," instead painting a one-dimensional portrait of a drug-addicted army. This in the end helped to inculcate support for expanded drug-control measures, while ensuring that alcohol continued to be both socially and legally acceptable—despite the fact that it remains the most destructive of social intoxicants and, according to a 1994 Department of Justice report, frequently causes acts of "aggression and violence."[55]

"Soldiers in Revolt"
Drugs as Symbol of Military Resistance
More than alcohol, drugs served as a fundamental symptom—not cause—of the internecine conflict that plagued the armed forces, especially

after the 1968 Tet offensive. During the course of the war the military's composition changed from ideologically motivated volunteers to dispirited conscripts bent on challenging authority and resisting U.S. policy. In a rare bout of grounded reporting, the *Washington Post* captured this shift in its eight-part series "Army in Anguish," editorializing, "With their long hair, black power wristbands and peace medallions, the rumpled, half-bearded GIs lining up at Long Binh for their pre-departure heroin-detected tests bear little resemblance to the tough professionals who led the way into Vietnam eleven years ago." In the interim years, seditious activity had increased exponentially as a result of the antiauthoritarian influence of the counterculture and growing perception that the war was unwinnable and unjust (or a "criminal waste," as one GI put it). In 1969, Country Joe and the Fish's antiwar "I Feel like I'm Fixin to Die Rag" was the most popular song in-country. According to the best estimates, 37 percent of soldiers were involved in some kind of resistance to the military or dissent.[56] Many wore peace beads, grew their hair long, and developed subversive underground newspapers that published radical critiques of U.S. policy.[57] Court-martial rates skyrocketed, as did conscientious objection, combat refusal, and desertion. Several major prison riots and mutinies also materialized, though these were given little attention in the mainstream press.[58]

By 1971, Colonel Robert Heinl reported in the *Armed Forces Journal* that the military had disintegrated to a "state approaching collapse," with "individual units drug ridden and dispirited when not near-mutinous," avoiding or having refused combat and "murdering their officers and non-commissioned officer" through "fragging" (detonating a grenade in their barracks). The army eventually admitted to some 700 such incidents.[59] Following a fruitless offensive on the Dong Ap Bia Hill in the A Shau Valley, a group of veterans placed a $10,000 bounty on the head of Lieutenant Colonel Weldon Honeycutt, who had ordered the attack. Many underground newspapers at the same time featured a "Lifer [career officer] of the Month" to be targeted for assassination. This testified to the profound contempt held by many GIs for their senior commanding officers, which was due primarily to a sense of betrayal surrounding their justifications for the war and their willingness to sacrifice human lives for what their men perceived as trivial military gain.[60] The contempt was not drug induced.

Bearing the imprint of the 1960s counterculture, which pervaded the armed forces, many soldiers indeed did turn to drugs as an emblem of their collective defiance. Sociologist Paul Starr wrote that by the late 1960s, "acid rock, drugs and peace emblems were as common in I-Corps as they were in California." On July 4, 1971, over one thousand GIs at Chu Lai held an antiwar rally which, according to one participant, evolved into "the largest pot party in the history of the Army." Leslie Whitfied, who served with the Third Battalion, Tenth Infantry, commented, "The heads [short for potheads] were critical of the war, looked down on lifers, condemned the military and wore peace symbols and beads with their uniforms." As Dave Cline, who served in the Ninth Infantry's Delta Company near Cu Chi, added in a recent interview: "After six months, I came to the conclusion that we were the aggressors. I started to see the injustice of it all. Truck drivers would just run people down on the road and laugh about it. We'd be riding in helicopters and people would be working in rice fields and the door gunners would just kill them right on the spot and laugh. Something just started to go awry inside of me. This isn't right. This isn't mom and apple pie. So I was involved with smoking marijuana. At the time this was the symbol of the anti-war movement in the service."[61]

One interesting facet of the rebellious connotation of drug use in Vietnam was that it was not always ideological. Captain Larry H. Ingraham found that most "heads" who smoked scag in Vietnam embraced a conservative critique of the war. "In hostile zones, they expressed frustration at not being able to identify and engage the enemy and having to fight for limited objectives," he wrote, in an article appearing in *Psychiatry*. "They would call for greater escalation, so that 'we can get in, do the job right, and get out.' They were not pacifists and had no reserve about killing 'gooks.'" Jerry Lembcke added in a recent interview, "Drug use was definitely tied to a culture of resistance in Vietnam, but I don't know how much [of it] was antiwar. Most guys hated the Army and all the rules. They were naive, though, politically. They rebelled against the military, first and foremost, and not necessarily against the war."[62]

Because of the prevailing racial divide engulfing the military, African American GIs were most prone to use drugs as an expression of social dissent. Influenced by the Black Power movement, many formed revolutionary organizations—such as one titled De Mau Mau after the Kenyan anticolonial fighters—and instigated a series of racial riots, some at the Long Binh stockade, where they faced constant degradation and harassment by white guards.[63] The media, including *Playboy* magazine, later tried to associate their actions with the intake of marijuana, though these claims were repudiated by a long military inquiry on the matter.[64] Many African Americans had come to identify by this time with the Vietnamese revolutionary struggle for political autonomy and independence, which they likened to their own. They overwhelmingly viewed American policy as being "racist and imperialistic in design."[65] One black marine commented, "The black guys [in our unit] would say that as far as they were concerned, Ho Chi Minh was a soul brother. Along with a few college drop-outs, they formed a kind of coalition. They would listen to music all the time, get stoned and refuse to carry out assigned orders." Although some black radicals also frowned on drug use, which they felt diverted activist energies, these comments exemplify its importance as a symbol of nonconformity and resistance to military authority, which was most marked during the latter stages of the war.[66] They also highlight the growing antiestablishment sentiments of GIs, which lay at the root of the crisis in military discipline and insubordination—a crisis for which drugs received the blame in the media but which itself created the drug problem.

"Nobody Mentioned Drugs"
Spurious Link to GI Aggression and War Crimes

Among the most damning and baseless of indictments—which some historians have apparently accepted—politicians and the mass media charged that drugs were behind the high level of civilian atrocities and war crimes committed by American soldiers in Vietnam.[67] In a 1970 congressional subcommittee hearing, Senator Thomas J. Dodd (D-Conn.) declared that the My Lai massacre—where U.S. troops shot up a village of over 500 innocent civilians—was provoked by marijuana. He cited the testimony of a lieutenant named Charles West, who told Congress that five members of his unit had gotten high as late as eleven o'clock the night before perpetrating the killings. Dodd commented, "The marijuana user feels that he's being persecuted and given the proper conditions he can retaliate in a furious and vengeful manner. The implications of this occurrence such as the My Lai incident are obvious."[68] Military psychiatrists objected to Dodd's reasoning and his insinuation that marijuana could cause unprovoked violence. The army's CID concluded through lengthy interrogation of nearly seventy witnesses that the shootings were "in no way" influenced by marijuana. Ronald Ridenhour, a helicopter door gunner who witnessed and later helped to expose the atrocity, told the media that Senator Dodd had "stacked the evidence."

Noting that men in his unit rarely smoked marijuana prior to going out on missions, he commented, "Nobody mentioned drugs at My Lai after it happened, and they would have looked for any excuse. Many, many Americans are looking for any reason other than a command decision."[69]

As Ridenhour recognized, My Lai was neither unique to the war nor the consequence of undisciplined soldiers high on marijuana. It was rather the logical extension of American counterinsurgency doctrine and its assortment of violent relocation and search-and-destroy programs.[70] Because the NLF was inseparable from the Vietnamese population from which it drew its base, hundreds of thousands of civilians ultimately lost their lives at the hands of what Noam Chomsky aptly termed "Westmoreland's automated killing machine."[71] The army's own criminal files reveal a grisly record of U.S. atrocities, including a case where American troops shot up a village of over 100 Montagnards and cases where soldiers tried to smuggle mutilated corpses and heads out of Vietnam—with the support of their senior commanding officers![72] Certainly none of these incidents were attributable to drugs. In a recent interview, Michael Berhardt, a member of Lieutenant William Calley's platoon, which was responsible for My Lai, tellingly commented: "Something like My Lai happened many times. It was just a matter of scale. The whole war effort was built on three pillars—the free-fire zone, meaning shoot anything that moves, the search-and-destroy mission, which is just another way to shoot anything that moves, and the body count, which is a tool for measuring the success or failure of what you're doing. When you've got those three things, it doesn't take a genius to figure out how it's going to end up."[73] Colonel Oran Henderson, the highest-ranking officer to face court-martial charges for the My Lai massacre, added, "Every unit of brigade size has its My Lai hidden some place, though every unit doesn't have a Ridenhour [to expose its actions]."[74] These comments ultimately stand out in any effort to understand the context surrounding incidents like My Lai: they had nothing to do with marijuana or any other artificial intoxicant, as Senator Dodd and others had claimed, but were institutionalized within the fabric of the war.

"Fears Not Well Founded"
The Myth of the "Nam Junkie" Returned Home

Proponents of the myth of the addicted army were perhaps most disingenuous in spreading popular fears surrounding the extension of the drug crisis to the United States. In 1973, psychiatrist Lee N. Robins of

Washington University conducted a series of interviews with veterans who had tested positive for heroin in Vietnam and concluded that less than 10 percent used any drugs at all once back in the United States—an extraordinarily high remission rate, which she attributed to shifting social circumstances and their removal from the death-tainted environment of Vietnam (and not the success of army rehabilitation programs, as its architects tried to claim). Only 1.3 percent of those sampled were drug dependent, and less than 1 percent addicted to opiates. A follow-up determined that up to a third later relapsed, though their drugs of choice were amphetamines, barbiturates, or in most cases alcohol.[75] The Vietnam Era Research Project subsequently released a report, which found that drug use was actually "more common among non-veterans than Vietnam era veterans," and that GIs were "not inclined to heavy or problematic use" once back in the United States.[76] Egil Krogh, a key architect of the modern drug war, recently commented, "Public concerns surrounding the threat of drug addiction [emanating out of Vietnam] were fortunately not well founded."[77]

Contrary to later Hollywood depictions, DEA and army CID files and the public testimony of former narcotics agents downplay the degree to which smuggling networks out of Southeast Asia affected supply rates in the United States, particularly those run by active-duty or discharged soldiers, which were limited in scope. Of the Americans who were arrested for involvement in the region's black market economy, a majority were private citizens. The one exception was the shipping of heroin by three veterans, who were arrested in January 1972, via the U Tapao airbase in Bangkok using forged military documentation.[78] The heroin available in America was of much lower purity than that of Southeast Asia, further contradicting these claims. Drug use, on the whole, was *less* prevalent in American society than was portrayed in the media. In 1975, Dr. Lloyd Johnston, a sociologist at the University of Michigan, conducted a statistical survey which concluded that less than 1 percent of all school-aged youth had tried heroin during the previous two years. Gallup Polls documented that less than 12 percent of Americans had so much as tried smoking marijuana, though the rate for youths was around 40 percent.[79]

Governmental and epidemiological studies did record an upsurge in heroin use, particularly in major urban centers such as New York, though the peak figures remain in dispute: a range of 69,000 to 500,000—up from an estimated 25,000 to 50,000 during the mid-1960s. Rather than being fueled by addicted soldiers, the increase was the result of shifting cultural values, population growth among baby boomers reaching the age when delinquency rates are highest, and a decline of the nation's inner cities due to sociopolitical ferment and neglect. As political scientist Edward Jay Epstein argues, the alleged increase was also a product of more sophisticated drug reporting technologies drawn from local police reports, which did not employ uniform standards, and were "unreliable," as Bureau of Narcotics and Dangerous Drugs (BNDD) statistician Joseph Greenwood admitted. Even if one accepts the high-end total, which was likely inflated, the proportion of heroin consumers was only a tiny fraction of the population (estimated at less than 2 percent), with most use being of the casual variety, and often the result of despairing social conditions rarely acknowledged by the authorities. The situation never lived up to media cries of an "epidemic"—a value-laden term supportive of the disease model of addiction, which critics have derided for ignoring the psychosocial and environmental roots of drug abuse and the agency of users, for treating it as a medical condition, and for exaggerating the enslaving effects of heroin and other drugs.[80]

Though receiving far less attention, the rate of alcohol abuse meanwhile was estimated to be ten times more than that of drugs and caused far more substantial damage to the nation's social fabric. Alcoholism was linked more directly by sociologists to the spread of violent crime, in addition to a host of social problems such as domestic violence, highway accidents, and juvenile delinquency, as well as to tens of thousands of deaths per year from cirrhosis and poisoning. The rate of criminal conduct by veterans and nonveterans was generally overblown in the press. While the Federal Bureau of Investigation's crime index increased substantially through the early 1970s, sociologists have shown this to be an artificial indicator, connected as much as anything else to improvements in crime-recording technology, shifting demographics, and overpolicing in poor, minority communities. Ensconced in a culture of fear, the public was being misled on many different fronts.[81]

There is no secret to the fact that soldiers in Vietnam, just like soldiers from time immemorial, got high, often to blunt the pernicious social effects of war. Contrary to popular myth, however, drug use in Vietnam was far from omnipresent. It was confined largely to the rear and bore little effect in shaping combat breakdown or the military's collapse, which was based on political contingencies and the insolubility of trying to fight a popularly rooted guerrilla movement on its own terrain. Most soldiers who used drugs did so casually, off duty, and were not incapacitated; for some undoubtedly, drugs even had a positive therapeutic effect. Despite commanding a virtual media monopoly, drugs were *less* prevalent than alcohol and *less* socially destructive. To the degree that it did exist, the so-called drug problem was a product of social rebellion, personal despondency, and the crisis in morale that plagued U.S. troops during the latter stages of the war. Through exaggerated rhetoric and sensationalist metaphors, politicians and the mass media ultimately helped to obscure these basic facts and to color the public's view of the situation, with profound long-term results.

CREATING THE MYTH
OF THE "NAM JUNKIE"
MASS MEDIA AND THE
RISE OF A DRUG SCARE

Illegal drug abuse by military personnel in Vietnam was a "cause célèbre" surrounded by considerable rhetoric, conjecture and emotion from people of different political and philosophical persuasions. — Morris "Duke" Stanton, military psychiatrist, 1976

The screaming headlines said it all. In February 1969 the *Washington Post* published articles titled "Turn On, Tune In and Fire Away" and "GIs Deep into Drugs." The *U.S. News & World Report* subsequently declared, "Marijuana— The Other Enemy in Vietnam"; and *Newsweek,* "A New GI for Pot and Peace."[1] All these stories gave the impression that the military had been subsumed by a torrent of addiction and that soldiers were subverting American war aims by going into battle stoned. Written at a time of escalating atrocities and the expansion of the war into Cambodia and Laos, they helped to divert attention from the suffering of millions of Indo-Chinese, while generating what one analyst termed a "Pharmacological Gulf of Tonkin"—blowing the scope of the illusory drug crisis far out of proportion.[2] In the original Gulf of Tonkin incident, policymakers fabricated the idea that an American naval armada suffered an unprovoked attack by the North Vietnamese to justify the initiation of a sustained aerial bombardment campaign and declaration of war. Now, new myths were being created to justify the escalation of the War on Drugs. Drawing on the sensational testimony of several congressional subcommittee hearings, the mass media played an integral role in promoting a climate of fear surrounding drugs, in part by spuriously linking them to the nation's military breakdown. Fixated on the pathologies of American veterans to the neglect of deeper social variables, they attributed to them potent pharmacological properties disproportionate to their actual effect. They also raised alarm about the return of addicted soldiers to civilian life. This in the end helped to refocus public debate away from the consequences of the war itself and to harden social attitudes toward drugs, binding them in the public consciousness to the tragedy of Vietnam.

"You Could See Punctures Up and Down Their Arms"
Drugs and an Army in Anguish

The myth of the addicted army was born in the mid-1960s when the media began to report rumors of rampant drug abuse in Vietnam.[3] By mid-1968, following the publication of Steinbeck's "The Importance of Being Stoned in Vietnam," marijuana had become what psychiatrist Roger A. Roffman termed a "hot potato" in the press, in his view as a result of a "history of misinformation and hyperbole" surrounding the drug in the United States and the "reefer madness" campaigns of Harry J. Anslinger. During his tenure as head of the Federal Bureau of Narcotics (FBN) from 1930 to 1962, Anslinger was highly influential in promoting the belief that marijuana precipitated acute mental breakdown, paranoia, and aggression.[4] In order to boost funding for his agency, he frequently broadcast stories of individuals committing terrible crimes and even murder under the influence of drugs. A favorite story involved a twenty-one-year-old Floridian of Mexican descent named Victor Lacata, who allegedly hacked up his whole family with an axe while high on marijuana.[5] In a 1970 *Playboy* interview, Anslinger derided proponents of the 1960s counterculture for promoting "Hitler-type lies" surrounding marijuana, which he believed was capable of destroying American society from within. "History is strewn with the bones of nations that tolerated moral laxity and hedonism," he observed. "Legalizing pot will make highways worse than a second Vietnam."[6] During the Korean War, Anslinger had exaggerated the scope of military addiction and suggested that "Red China" was covertly supplying American troops with opium as an act of sabotage, a charge reported uncritically as fact by the mainstream press.[7] In a 1953 book titled *The Traffic in Narcotics*, he wrote, "The Communists know that a trained soldier becomes a liability and security risk from the moment he first takes a shot of heroin. They have planned well."[8] These comments epitomized Anslinger's characterization of drug use as a moral evil linked to enemy subversion. The portrayal of the situation in Vietnam by media pundits and government officials was, in hindsight, little different.

During the late 1960s and early 1970s the media became flooded with sensational stories linking drugs to the breakdown of the American military mission. Typical was a January 1971 *Newsweek* article, "The Troubled U.S. Army in Vietnam," which proclaimed the drug situation to be a nightmare. "Even some of the medics are on heroin, using needles from our own stores," the authors wrote, amid lurid photos of soldiers getting high. "You could see the punctures right up and down their arms."[9] The *Washington Post* had previously described wild drug parties at the army's R&R center at Vung Tau, nicknamed "Tijuana East" after the Mexican border town and narcotic capital. Journalist Nicholas Von Hoffman quoted a young private who stated, "A large majority of my buddies smoke. Man, the first thing we do in our outfit when we got a dead 'gook' [slur for Vietnamese] is search him for his dope stash. Then we look for his money and then we take his weapons." Von Hoffman editorialized, "Vietnam veterans now speak of whole units 'turned on' in combat and military policemen and junior officers looking the other way instead of cracking down. . . . This is a sorry state of affairs."[10]

In August 1970 the *New York Times* profiled a marine sergeant, Robert Parkinson, who claimed that members of his platoon had tried to "frag" [murder] him by rolling a grenade in his bunk after he objected to their use of marijuana. Although surviving the attack, Parkinson was severely wounded and left with a shattered kneecap and serious liver and intestinal damage. He commented, "Marijuana was everywhere you looked in Vietnam. Men smoked pot to the extent that they couldn't do their jobs and were useless."[11] In highlighting Parkinson's story without qualification, the *New York Times* insinuated that fragging incidents were ubiquitous and that the deep internal divisions plaguing the armed forces could be centrally linked to drugs—rather than to more deeply rooted factors such as loss of ideological purpose and GI enmity for commanders willing to sacrifice their men's lives for trivial military gain. In this respect, the piece was characteristic in both distorting the scope of the alleged drug crisis and obscuring the deeper political context in which the war was being fought.

Displacing the reality of burned villages, napalmed children, defoliated landscape, teeming urban slums, and tortured Vietnamese prisoners, many other articles similarly misled readers, raising public fears that U.S. fighting capabilities were being eroded by drugs. Implicit was the assumption that this was tragic because of a nationalist identification with the American side.[12] In the aptly titled "Vietnam: How Do You Turn Off the Turned On Troops?" the *New York Times* depicted GIs preoccupied with planning pot parties and too "strung out" to mount any effective military campaigns. Another *Times* piece profiled a soldier who, driving a tank while high on marijuana, nearly ran over his patrol. "You smoke it, you get wrecked and you don't know what you're doing," he said. Yet another piece spoke of soldiers reenlisting in the military to "get cheap marijuana and heroin"; the author quoted a senior addiction counselor, who spoke about a twenty-three-year-old marine discharged for drug possession. "This is one of the most pathetic cases I have ever encountered," he said. "He told me that he joined the Marines to get heroin in Vietnam. Not to steal it, but to buy it."[13]

In September 1970, CBS News broadcast a tale of American soldiers getting high by inhaling opium-laced marijuana from the barrel of their guns. A congressional inquiry later determined that the event had been staged by the soldiers as an antiwar ploy and to shed light on the decline in troop morale. The reporter made no mention of that fact, however, and thus helped to inflame public fears of a full-fledged epidemic. He editorialized, "Drugs are as plentiful as C-Rations, here. One pipeful, which the soldiers call a bowl, can easily take care of five or six men."[14]

Many journalists speculated that the drugs were imported by Communist agents in North Vietnam and China and peddled by guerrilla insurgents as a covert act of sabotage.[15] The basis for these claims lay in the hysterical assertions of military leaders such as William C. Westmoreland, Victor "Brute" Kulak, and CIA operative Edward Lansdale about an international Communist conspiracy, assertions designed for propaganda purposes and to discredit the opposing forces.[16] The State Department, FBN, and Military Assistance Command Vietnam (MACV) privately concluded through consultation with local intelligence that the NLF rarely handled any drugs except for a few "isolated and limited cases," that North Vietnam and China did not "figure prominently in international narcotics trafficking due to strong anti-narcotics legislation," and that they "produced only as much opium as was needed for internal medical needs." In 1971, it was reported by federal narcotics agents that there had not been a single seizure from China since the 1949 revolution. The officials further conceded the corruption of American regional proxies in Laos, Thailand, and South Vietnam.[17] The *New York Times* nevertheless was typical in asserting, without providing any evidence, that the NLF was peddling "brain dulling marijuana" to American GIs to help finance their "terrorist" operations (a term never applied to the United States, in spite of its responsibility for at least 80 percent of civilian atrocities, according to the most conservative estimates). In a November 1967 story, interviewing John Steinbeck IV, NBC News correspondent John Chancellor declared that the high prevalence of marijuana in the U.S. military demonstrated the wiliness of America's enemy. In introducing the piece, anchorman Walter Cronkite proclaimed, "The Communists are battling American troops not only with firepower but with drugs."[18]

Fitting with this theme, in October 1970 the *Washington Post* cited a close adviser to Egyptian president Gamal Abdel Nasser, who claimed that Chinese Communist Party (CCP) official Zhou Enlai had told Nasser in 1965 that he had planted opium in Vietnam in the hope of demoralizing American troops. Zhou allegedly told Nasser, "Do you remember how the West imposed opium on us? They fought us with opium, and we are going to fight them with their own weapons." The *Washington Post* later published an article headed, "China Drug Plot Seen to Incapacitate GIs," which quoted Jon Steinberg, a journalist for *Pacific Stars and Stripes*, who stated, "This looks to me like a Communist plot to incapacitate our troops in Vietnam by feeding them hard drugs at an absurdly low cost."[19] These comments conveyed the deep cultural conviction that drugs were a foreign menace capable of destroying America's fighting resolve. They also revealed the prevalence of a stark Cold War mind-set among journalists, who, easily susceptible to government manipulation, helped to construct the popular image of a monolithic Communist enemy willing to resort to any form of treachery and evil—including drug trafficking—to ensure global supremacy.[20] Cast aside were the factors shaping the strength of revolutionary movements, including the appeal to nationalist sentiment in Vietnam and the dedication to land reform and literacy campaigns, which had long won over most of the rural populace, as internal military intelligence reports conceded.[21]

Though reliable on other issues and a maverick investigative reporter, Jack Anderson of the *Washington Post* was at the vanguard among journalists in promoting the myth of the addicted army. Anderson claimed that Vietnamese guerrillas literally "sniffed at the perimeter of American outposts" for the smell of marijuana and planned their attacks accordingly. In his semiweekly column *Washington Merry-Go-Round* he frequently recounted horror stories of GIs crossing enemy lines under the influence of drugs and shooting fellow American soldiers. One particularly inflammatory piece reported that a group of Americans became so "stoned on super-strength Vietnamese marijuana" that they fired on their own helicopters—which supposedly struck back, killing them and a bunkerful of GIs, whose remains were allegedly found strewn with marijuana and cigarette butts.

In another column, Anderson wrote about a "drugged out" soldier who jumped out of a helicopter at 1,500 feet above the ground because he thought that he could fly. He further claimed that "drug craving GIs" at the American naval base in Okinawa were selling classified information to North Vietnamese agents, including data containing the precise timing of scheduled bombing raids over the Ho Chi Minh trail on the Laotian border. In return for sexual favors, marijuana, and heroin, according to Anderson, GIs traded these secrets to local prostitutes serving as liaisons with the North Vietnamese Army (NVA). There is no corroborating evidence to indicate that any of these charges were true. After the article was published, the military actually investigated the allegations regarding the compromising of classified information and found them to be unfounded.[22]

Reliant mainly on unverifiable sources and second hand rumor, Anderson's writings helped foster the belief that drug abuse was a threat to vital American security interests. They further exaggerated the physiological properties of drugs by linking them to paranoia, aggression, enslavement, and treachery, thus contributing to the revival of what one noted drug specialist termed a "dope fiend mythology."[23] Anderson's use of the drug issue to criticize governmental mismanagement of the war added to his penchant for embellishment, though in these respects he was far from unique. In April 1971 the *Washington Post* columnist Marquis Childs termed the drug situation in Vietnam "the most disastrous consequence of a disastrous war" and declared, "To keep even a residue of a demoralized army in South Vietnam is to invite new disasters like the drug curse." The *Washington Post*'s Flora Lewis added, "If the United States can't successfully fight heroin and Vietnamese Communists at the same time, it shouldn't be hard to choose the worst enemy. There can be no national defense even on this continent if the invasion of drugs is not stopped."[24]

In May 1971, *Newsweek* columnist Stewart Alsop published his "Worse than My Lai" column, in which he argued that the so-called drug "plague" epitomized the degenerate character of the war. Supporting the tenets of Nixon's "Vietnamization" strategy, which sought to shift the burden of fighting to what Alsop characterized as the "pathetically dependent" South Vietnamese army, he stated, "In addition to the 55,000 Americans who have died in Vietnam, there are now many thousands more addicted to heroin who might as well be dead . . . This epidemic reflects the erosion of discipline and morale among our forces in Vietnam and is the worst horror to have emerged from the war."[25] These comments are astonishing in light of the physical devastation wrought by U.S. policies in Indochina—including the creation of over seven million refugees, destruction of large swaths of the countryside through indiscriminate bombing and chemical defoliation, and the killing of at least three million people.[26] They reveal a narrow cultural mind-set all too typical of the American establishment, which placed a primacy on the costs of the war to the United States, while callously ignoring its far more calamitous effects on the population of Vietnam.[27] An ardent anti-Communist with intimate connections to high-level Pentagon officials—like his brother Joseph, who wrote for the *Washington Post*—Stewart Alsop viewed American efforts to establish an anti-Communist bulwark in South Vietnam as honorable. Critical of the government, however, for failing to win the war decisively and tarnishing America's global reputation, he portrayed the spread of heroin as a product of its tainted character, thus accounting for the embellishment.[28]

Alsop was not alone in using morbid analogies surrounding drugs which were reminiscent of the Anslinger heyday. The *Reader's Digest*, for example, likened an opium den frequented by American GIs to "a Nazi death camp, where men little more than skeletons sat staring blankly into space, rising every thirty minutes to buy more drugs." The *Far Eastern Economic Review* editorialized that addicted veterans were as "badly maimed from the war as their visibly crippled comrades." *New York Times* correspondent James Reston meanwhile wrote that the drug crisis "was one of those tragic consequences of the war, where, in Nikita Khrushchev's vivid phrase, the living may envy the dead."[29] These comments epitomize the tone of outrage characterizing the media's response to the drug crisis—in stark contrast to the violence bred by the war itself—and the breadth of their exaggeration in describing its impact. The media in turn helped to promote the popular conception of Vietnam as a war that had been tainted and marred by drugs, with devastating social effect, while cementing antidrug mores in the U.S.

"Heroes and Heroin"
The Army's Last Great Tragedy in Vietnam?

As Alsop's "Worse than My Lai" column exemplified, the wave of media sensationalism reached its apogee during the so-called heroin crisis of the early 1970s. Convenient for Nixon, the timing coincided with mounting antiwar protest, GI revolt, and the ongoing US-ARVN invasion of Cambodia in support of the Lon Nol government, which according to one scholarly observer resulted in "methodical devastation" and the "dismantling of rural society" under conditions "more brutal than those in South Vietnam in 1965."[30] Overshadowing this story, which received scant mainstream coverage and was frequently rationalized as a product of "North Vietnamese aggression," the New York Times printed a barrage of articles on drugs, including a piece by Gloria Emerson on February 25, 1971, documenting the popularity of scag, that highly purified form of heroin that could be smoked.[31] Both the Times and the Washington Post linked the easy availability of scag to the corruption of high-ranking South Vietnamese generals, though they minimized or ignored the critical CIA and Washington connection. On May 16 the New York Times ran a screaming front-page exposé, "GI Heroin Addiction Epidemic in Vietnam," which conveyed alarm at "the ease with which heroin circulated in Vietnam" and at the prospect of addicts returning to American society "craving a drug that costs many times more in the U.S. than in Vietnam." The article continued, "The epidemic is seen by many here as the army's last great tragedy in Vietnam. Tens of thousands of soldiers are going back to the United States as walking time bombs."[32]

These depictions fit into an orientalist discourse in which drugs were associated with the backward qualities of Southeast Asian culture and intended to reflect the corrupting influence of the war on virtuous American youth.[33] On May 24, Newsweek published a photo of a syringe striking a combat helmet as a backdrop to an article titled "The GIs Other Enemy: Heroin." A commanding officer was quoted as stating that "heroin is wrecking the U.S. Army and creating a whole new class of American addicts." On July 5, Newsweek put an emaciated junkie on its cover under the headline, "The Heroin Plague: What Can Be Done?" The lead story was about the spread of addiction from "the back alleys of Long Binh and Saigon" to "Middle-American towns and neighborhoods." The authors editorialized, "Heroin has exploded on us like an atom bomb. Ten years ago, even three years ago, heroin was a loser's drug, an aberration afflicting the blacks and long-haired minorities. Now all this has changed. Nice Jewish boys are coming out of the woodwork as well as Mormon kids, Japanese Americans and all other exemplars of hard-working middle-class ideals." A side article featured the story of Michael Kobler, a formerly clean-cut veteran who had smoked marijuana and opium during his time in Vietnam and remained hooked ever since. Kobler's father told the magazine, "My son is just a dumb dope addict now. He'd lie, but I'd see him coming out of the bathroom rolling down his sleeve. I truly believe there is a concentrated Communist led effort to inveigle these soldiers into drugs."[34]

The sensationalist language in both articles was striking. Like the My Lai and Nazi death camp analogies, the atom bomb reference was a particularly powerful example of the media's role in blowing the scope of addiction out of proportion, while deflecting attention from the physical devastation in Indochina (where it might have been more appropriately applied).[35] The blame placed on the Communists was further indicative of the unwillingness of many Americans to look in the mirror and examine the true roots of the crisis or take responsibility for the human wreckage caused by the war.

Characteristically, in February 1971, Stewart Alsop titled a column "The Smell of Death" and warned that New York City was becoming "infested" with drugs and "killed" by heroin, largely because of the return of addicted soldiers. "Other American cities are on the death list," he remarked, "but New York may be terminal."[36] None of his writings, incidentally, mentioned the far more deplorable conditions in Saigon bred by the U.S. bombings and refugee crisis, nor did they explore the underlying structural variables and abandonment of Great Society programs shaping the breakdown of America's inner cities.[37] In June 1971, *Time* published another superficial piece linking the return of strung-out vets to a "frightening rise" in the nation's crime rate. Alluding to the widely cited case of Dwight Johnson, a Congressional Medal of Honor winner who was shot dead in Detroit when he tried to rob a liquor store, the authors editorialized, "The specter of weapons-trained, addicted combat veterans joining the deadly struggle for drugs in the streets of America is ominous." Quoting Iowa Senator Howard E. Hughes, the article continued, "Within a matter of months in our large cities, the Capone era of the 1920s may look like a Sunday school picnic by comparison!"[38]

In reality, less than one-half of 1 percent of veterans returning to the United States committed any crimes. Generally, returning vets achieved higher education and income levels than their peers.[39] Many had emerged politically awakened by their experience and protested the war as leaders of the peace and justice movement.[40] Feeding into the stereotypes, as Jerry Lembcke demonstrates in *The Spitting Image*, groups like Vietnam Veterans against the War (VVAW) were largely ignored or pathologized in the mainstream press, which created the impression that America's social fabric was being torn apart at the seams by half-crazed and doped-up soldiers from whom nobody was safe. The result was to raise support for Nixon's law-and-order program, while also tarnishing the image of

Vietnam veterans whose courage and sacrifice in resisting an unjust war were quietly swept from public consciousness—much like the fate of Indo-Chinese crushed by the weight of American napalm and artillery.[41]

Television was a powerful medium bolstering popular anxieties about the addicted army and obfuscating the actual facts of the war. Ignoring the revolutionary side almost entirely, as well as the covert wars in Laos and Cambodia that were yielding a devastating effect, the major networks broadcast near daily reports on drugs throughout the early 1970s, blaming them for the military's breakdown and the onset of a domestic crime wave.[42] In January 1971, NBC News aired a two-part series in which an anonymous GI admitted to driving a military caravan while stoned: "There isn't a word big enough to describe the scope of the problem. It is simply out of hand and without restraints." Journalist Phil Brady added, "The drug problem has truly become a commander's nightmare and a disaster for the entire army in Vietnam." On May 26, NBC News aired a story on violence among addicted veterans in which an anonymous GI told investigative reporter Robert Goralski that he snorted heroin almost every day and had cut up a guy with a razor and left him for dead after having hallucinatory flashbacks that he was being attacked by the Vietcong. Another veteran addict spoke about beating a Chinese bouncer in the head with a pipe while stoned on marijuana after being refused entry to a club: "I was yelling at the guy, 'I killed gooks better than you.' To me he looked just like he was from Vietnam and I treated him as such."[43]

Reflecting prevailing cultural norms, the GI's revelation about "killing gooks" and its insights into American military conduct in Vietnam elicited no moral outrage or commentary from NBC, as compared with the use of drugs, which was presented as far more troubling. Other news programs demonstrated a similar myopia. On August 21, 1971, ABC News aired a two-hour special, "Heroes and Heroin," which received special DOD funding and met with approval from the White House in warning that the drug "crisis" in Vietnam represented an ominous threat to national security. Narrator Frank Reynolds spoke with several soldiers addicted to heroin, including Ron Chester, who was serving out a lengthy prison sentence in the United States after robbing a bank to support his drug habit. He stated, "Many guys [from my platoon] were just addicted to it [scag]. They just lay around and slept and got on bad trips and put themselves in danger, you know, just walked around during a rocket attack or something, didn't know what the hell was going on." Another GI, Daniel Kellenbenz, who admitted to heavy opium use in Vietnam, told

Reynolds of a friend who was so stoned that he went to greet a "wave" of enemy combatants with a handshake. Kellenbenz remarked, "The 'gooks' shot him, maybe ten, fifteen times." Kellenbenz later recounted that he himself had fired at an American lieutenant "about 18 times with an assault rifle," thinking "that he was 'a gook' amidst the foggy haze of a protracted heroin high."[44]

Although Kellenbenz's behavior was extreme, the "Heroes and Heroin" special made it seem commonplace and indicated that drugs yielded a crippling military effect in Vietnam. It reserved far greater indignation, predictably, for the use of narcotics among American soldiers than for their exhibition of racist sentiments toward the Vietnamese and the commission of wartime atrocities, which were attributed to drugs, thus absolving U.S. leaders and the high command of responsibility. No wonder the TV special was so well received, then, in official Washington and the directors rewarded with a gushing letter of approval from Egil Krogh.[45]

"How Unrealistic Can You Get!" Media Impact Runs Deep

The media, on the whole, were pivotal in channeling attention away from the acute humanitarian crisis bred by the war, while fostering insular fears over drugs, fears that were divorced from social reality.[46] A June 1971 Lewis Harris Poll found that the American public projected a "much more serious problem" pertaining to the drug crisis in Vietnam than did "veterans who had first hand knowledge of the situation." Civilian approximations for both marijuana and hard-drug abuse in Vietnam exceeded those of soldiers by at least three times. For heroin, public estimates ranged upward from 14 percent, whereas GIs placed the total at no more than 5 percent. Private Michael Longo tellingly declared to reporters, "My parents told me that back in the 'world' [United States in GI slang] people seem to think that 40 percent of GI's are using heroin in Vietnam. How unrealistic can you get!"[47]

In June 1971, as a result of such misimpressions, *Time* reported that 12 percent of Americans viewed the drug problem as the most important political issue facing the country, and more than 50 percent saw it as one of the top three (along with lawlessness and crime).[48] By July, a majority of respondents cited drugs at number one, even though most people admitted having had little to no direct experience with drug abuse. Regional polls recorded similar sentiments, including surveys undertaken by the *New York Times* and the *Boston Globe*, which determined that a majority of respondents viewed drugs as the "foremost problem facing voters." The

Globe found that 83 percent of the people sampled regarded "non-medical drug use" as their "greatest concern for the future of the country."[49] By this time, congressional representatives had become inundated with letters calling for a more vigorous legislative attack against a crisis seen to be "the gravest facing their generation," as one Maine woman put it to Senator Edmund Muskie (D-Maine). Letters to the editor in newspapers across the country—which the Nixon administration carefully monitored—expressed analogous views.[50]

Several parents of American soldiers additionally communicated to their congressional representatives their deep dismay not about the war itself but about their sons being exposed to drugs overseas. Bernard J. Hamik of San Diego wrote to Senator Frank Murphy (D-Calif.), "In World War II, the army was run like it should be. Now all we do is pick up the paper and read about dope. It is frightening to hear how our country is going down. Our son went to Vietnam about six weeks ago and he can't even join a party or join a group as there's nothing but dope parties." In a letter to President Nixon, Mrs. William McMurtry further commented, "I cannot rest a minute knowing that my son is subjected to drugs as well as the enemy. Mr. President, please get him away from the drug experiment that is corrupting him so much."[51]

These letters reflect a fundamental naiveté surrounding the brutality of the war and its Manichean nature. They also exemplify the protracted public alarm bred by the crisis of the so-called addicted army. Some respondents mentioned learning of drug use in private communications, but their attitudes were shaped in large measure by the mass media. Following the news had ingrained in them the perception that drug abuse represented a vital threat to American security interests in Vietnam—as well as a greater hazard to the health and safety of their children than the fighting itself. In this respect, they were not alone.

"Rifles and Reefers Don't Mix"
Congressional Subcommittee Hearings

The specter of "moral panic" engulfing the country was influenced in part by a series of congressional hearings on drug abuse in the military, which provided a key source for many sensationalist media exposés. The hearings evolved from the Committee on Juvenile Delinquency headed by Senator Thomas J. Dodd (D-Conn.), which was designed to broadcast the problem of rising drug-use patterns on college campuses and among "lunatic radicals," as he termed them. Dodd was a vigorous antidrug and anticrime crusader who first made a name for himself in the 1930s as an FBI agent apprehending notorious criminals such as John Dillinger and "Baby Face" Nelson. Throughout his senatorial career, Dodd pushed for criminal justice reforms, including the abolishment of the death penalty and the establishment of special penal facilities for juvenile offenders. He was also a champion of drug rehabilitation and was influential in the passing of the 1966 Narcotic Addicts Rehabilitation Act, a pioneering piece of federal legislation establishing the civil commitment system in which convicted drug offenders could choose between prison and treatment at federally sanctioned facilities.[52] Dodd was ironically reputed to be an alcoholic, who, according to eyewitness accounts, would begin drinking at a bar he kept in his office "first thing in the morning" after arriving "hung over, looking like an unmade bed."[53]

Beginning in 1966, Dodd began to warn about the rise of drug abuse among GIs in Vietnam and called for an extension of existing drug rehabilitation programs in the military.[54] As a prominent member of the Senate Foreign Relations Committee, he had been a powerful proponent of the U.S. intervention—so much so that he once attacked Dean Rusk for Communist sympathies after Rusk had suggested a more moderate escalation of combat troops. Described by colleagues as an "unabashed flag-waver," Dodd also promoted a petition calling for the resignation of UN Secretary U Thant for opposing the war.[55] Fearful that drugs were hindering America's effort to promote "freedom" and "democracy" in South Vietnam, Dodd embarked on a crusade in the Senate to expose the apparent gravity of the situation. He invited John Steinbeck IV to testify, along with addicted soldiers, high-ranking generals, self-acknowledged drug dealers, psychiatrists, journalists, and several NLF defectors.[56]

On the whole, the panel selected by Dodd—as evidenced by the presence of such figures as Steinbeck and Captain Robert Parkinson, who was featured in the *New York Times*—was largely biased. In seeking out witnesses, Dodd searched for individuals who had personal reasons for inflating the scope and evils of drug abuse. Many wore paper bags over their heads as a means of protecting their identity, thus contributing to the largely politicized nature of the hearings and to criminal and subversive implications of drug use in Vietnam. That the hearings were staged before the mass media, including network television, raises added suspicion about their purpose—and helped to maximize their public impact. Roger A. Roffman, who was among the few iconoclasts to testify, commented in a recent interview that "everything down to the choreography was designed to greatly raise public alarm." Frank Bartimo, assistant general counsel for the DOD, complained to Dodd at the time, "Your forum is responsible for some of the bombastic statements in the media. Any incidents involving drugs are isolated and there is no verifiable case where American national security was jeopardized by drugs."[57]

The most sensational hearings were those conducted by Dodd in spring 1970. In his opening remarks he called drug abuse "an evil tide besetting the nation," responsible for causing "excessive troop casualties" and "shocking crimes" such as "soldiers shooting colonels, going partially insane and degenerating to a state where they were totally ineffective." He proclaimed, "Rifles and reefers don't mix." In an attempt to raise added indignation, Dodd read aloud a letter from a young private who stressed that potheads in his platoon threatened his safety during combat missions, and he quoted the commander of an evacuation hospital in Vietnam who asserted that men on marijuana under his watch had "recognized behavioral defects, convulsions and were psychotic-like in nature. . . . Many had become physically unmanageable or had even committed murder."[58]

Although Dodd may have been genuinely alarmed by the proliferation of drugs, he was also an opportunist who had strong incentive to exaggerate the situation for political benefit. His focus on the ravaging effect of drugs served in part to absolve governmental "hawks" like himself from charges of political miscalculation or culpability in the mounting devastation and carnage. The emphasis on drugs was also designed to bolster Dodd's carefully cultivated image as a tireless antidrug and anticrime crusader and to promote the military drug rehabilitation program that he had sponsored. It further helped to deflect public attention from his being censured by the Senate ethics committee (by a vote of 94 to 5) for the misuse of campaign funds, in addition to being charged with receiving illicit corporate payoffs and enriching himself from taxpayer dollars.[59]

At a deeper level, the Dodd hearings exemplified the resonance of antidrug mores and the nationalist ideology of the committee chair, plus his ingrained sense of social and cultural superiority predicated on America's technological and military prowess. Blind like many of his contemporaries to the ideological appeal of Marxist-Leninism in impoverished countries subject to Western imperial exploitation, and to the popularly rooted character of the Vietnamese revolution, Dodd made the setbacks faced by the U.S. military seem contingent upon external variables and influences and not on any fundamental policy miscalculations or institutional shortcomings. Dodd's fixation with drugs further revealed a stark colonialist, or neocolonialist, mentality, epitomized by his failure to recognize that the Vietnamese possessed legitimate aspirations contrary to the American imposed will and the capacity to fend off American military encroachment without the aid of any artificial inducements.[60]

However outrageous in exaggerating the scope of the drug crisis in Vietnam, Senator Dodd was far from unique in his ideological world view and in pinpointing drug abuse as a key factor shaping America's military collapse. In June 1971, Senator Howard E. Hughes (D-Iowa), a recovering alcoholic and proponent of drug rehabilitation programs, fumed before a congressional inquiry that drugs were as available in Vietnam as "chewing gum" and charged the Nixon administration with "sleeping through a tidal wave." "We are fighting a guerrilla war, a war of infiltration in which the ambush and the booby trap figure largely," he stated. "A lapse of vigilance or judgment could easily mean the loss of life." Hughes further warned that addicted soldiers posed a menace to the domestic social order: "We have the hideous picture before us of men, inured to violence and addicted to drugs, returning to civilian society from the war area compelled to use the skills of violence they have learned as soldiers in criminal acts here at home to support their habits. Decisive action to control this [problem] must be taken not only in the interest of our public health, but also in the interest of our national security."[61]

In May 1971, Morgan F. Murphy (D-Ill.) and Robert H. Steele (R-Conn.) released to the Committee on Foreign Affairs their influential report. "The World Heroin Problem," which estimated that between 25,000 and 37,000 (or 10 to 15 percent) of GIs had become addicted to heroin of 96 percent purity. Two months later, after a meeting with Dr. Jaffe and other White House officials, Steele recanted these claims, stating that Jaffe's figures of 3 to 5 percent were "the best available statistics that we have to date." Even though it is possible that Steele was bowing to political pressure, there is no evidence to substantiate his original declaration, which at a minimum conflated drug experimentation with addiction. Murphy and Steele had written without foundation that "in some units, heroin addiction may be as high as twenty five percent. . . . It is ironic indeed that in the last two years of the war, our biggest casualty figures will come from heroin addiction, not from combat." The senators had tried to link the enveloping "drug epidemic," as they termed it, to the corruption of American governmental allies. They claimed, this time accurately, that Royal Lao Air Force general and CIA asset Ouane Rattikone owned a consortium of heroin refineries outside of the Laos capital, Vientiane, which were disguised as Pepsi-Cola bottling plants.[62]

The senators further warned that drugs were following soldiers back to the United States in a Pacific crossing of sorts. They found that over half of the 875 known American military deserters were living in an area of Saigon known as Soul Alley, where they were involved in a myriad of criminal practices including drug trafficking. An African American named William Henry Jackson allegedly operated an opiate smuggling ring out of the Five Star Bar in Bangkok, Thailand. Jackson recruited patrons to work as couriers and to bootleg heroin overseas not only through the military's postal system but also in the coffins of dead soldiers. On April 5, 1971, U.S. customs officials in Monmouth, New Jersey, had confiscated 7.7 kilos of Southeast Asian heroin and later seized 248 more packages of narcotic contraband, most of which was General Ouane's trademark U-Globe brand. Murphy and Steele commented, "The Vietnam War is truly coming home to haunt us. The first wave of heroin is already on its way to our children in high school. . . . The problem is also affecting U.S. industry."[63]

Filled with inflated rhetoric and misinformation, including the insinuation that there was an organized effort by black veterans to flood the country with heroin, the Murphy-Steele report ignited a potent political controversy to which the media devoted sustained attention. On the week of its release, the *New York Times* featured Steele, a former CIA agent, in a blown-up photograph with a vial of heroin in his left hand, which was intended to broadcast the easy availability of the substance and the seminal threat that it represented to Americans. Failing to cover Steele's later repudiation of his original claims about the number of addicted soldiers, the newspaper editorialized that the United States should withdraw its troops from Vietnam immediately to "save the country from a debilitating drug epidemic." One month after the report's release, Jack Anderson accused John Paul Vann, director of Pacification, of destroying incriminating documents linking Ngo Dzu (a high-ranking South Vietnamese general implicated in the Murphy-Steele report) to the drug traffic. Vann responded in a public letter, addressed to nine prominent newspaper editors, charging Anderson with "character assassination" and "slander" and stating that Steele had not produced a "shred of the hard evidence" that he had claimed.[64]

Top Nixon presidential aides were similarly outraged by the Murphy-Steele report and its political ramifications. Jeffrey Donfeld, an assistant to the Presidential Domestic Council who played an active role in shaping federal drug policy, publicly accused Steele of being a liar. After receiving an advanced copy of the report on the eve of its release, Special Counselor to the President Donald Rumsfeld phoned Steele and pleaded with him to moderate his tone before the media. Rumsfeld was particularly concerned about the insinuation of U.S. government complicity in the global narcotics trade, which reflected poorly on the Nixon administration.[65] His actions in turn exemplified the deep political impact of the Murphy-Steele report, which enhanced popular fears about the onset of a drug pandemic that appeared to be intricately tied to the nation's involvement in Vietnam.

In February 1972, Congressman Seymour Halpern (R-N.Y.) issued another inflammatory report to the Committee on Foreign Affairs which exacerbated the sense of nationwide panic over drugs. Calling the influx of heroin "one of the gravest crises ever to face the United States," one that threatened to unleash an "era of social chaos, conflict and repression that would make a bitter mockery of our ideals and aspirations as a people," Halpern lamented that he had been approached over a dozen times by kids as young as eight years old selling drugs on Tu Do Street in the seedy part of Saigon. Failing to note that the majority of these kids sold drugs because of the uprooting of their families, who been made refugees as a result of the U.S.'s raining of bombs on the South Vietnamese countryside, he proclaimed, "The American GI is as liable to die from the needle, as the bullet. . . . What is so scary is that soldiers are bringing back the festering of their contagion to the United States. Society has a terrifying scourge and walking time bomb on its hands."[66] These comments demonstrate the insularity of many in Congress who were more dismayed by the addiction of a small number of American soldiers than the crippling, displacement, and death of millions of Vietnamese. It epitomizes, further, their use of sensationalistic rhetoric, which was the product of deeply held cultural attitudes toward drugs and their function as a political scapegoat. The time bomb and disease metaphors were most striking. By helping to raise public fears, they bred support for an expansion of the federal drug war, while sidelining debate over the injustices of the war and absolving administrative officials of responsibility for their actions.

For their part, the media did a poor job in assessing the biases of the committee chairs and political manipulation of the so-called drug crisis. In their 1989 book *Manufacturing Consent*, Noam Chomsky and Edward S. Herman castigate the media for being overreliant on government sources and uncritically accepting prevailing state ideology and rationalizations for war.[67] With regard to the crisis of the addicted army, this analysis is accurate. With few exceptions, the media neglected to explore in any meaningful depth the underlying roots of addiction, the growth of South Vietman's black market economy or the moral paradoxes of American foreign policy breeding a climate of rebellion in the military. They blamed Vietnamese revolutionaries rather than American allies for selling drugs and mirrored the political establishment in broadcasting the most extreme dimensions. In 1971, a sergeant with the 173rd Airborne Division aptly commented, "Our newspaper reporters are sensationalists— They have to sell a paper or a story, so they are going out and getting one."[68] In conducting their own research, journalists predominantly quoted soldiers who regularly used drugs and were familiar with methods for obtaining them, often in major cities like such as Saigon. Apart from a few notable exceptions, they rarely ventured into rural areas and the jungle "hinterland," where the brunt of the fighting took place and where— according to senior commanding officers, military psychiatrists, and GI recollections—"there was no drug problem."[69]

Most significantly, perhaps, as Dr. Jerome H. Jaffe, special drug adviser to President Nixon, noted in a recent interview, most journalistic commentaries failed to differentiate between drug use and abuse and created the impression that even soldiers who tried drugs only a few times had been rendered drug dependent and incapacitated. The media also utilized hyperbolic analogies—such as comparing drug addicts to the living dead—which distorted the scope of the crisis and obscured the more destructive impact of alcohol abuse. They helped to minimize further the horrendous social ravages of the war itself, which were among the worst humanitarian catastrophes of the post–World War II era.[70]

The media were typically misleading in warning of an impending domestic cataclysm. In February 1980, an op-ed in the *Washington Post* observed, "A decade ago, reports of widespread heroin use by U.S. troops in Vietnam spawned fears that servicemen would come home with their drug habits, leading to a generation of drug enslavement, crime and ruined lives. Today it's clear that those fears were grossly exaggerated."[71] This revelation was profound, coming from a newspaper responsible for having perpetrated some of the most egregious myths surrounding the drug crisis in Vietnam and its domestic ramifications. It came almost ten years too late, however, to alter public opinion or rehabilitate the image of the Vietnam veteran, who had been long since been stereotyped as a psychologically scarred junkie responsible for the collapse of the armed forces and spread of degradation and crime in the United States.

The mass media played a critical role in shaping the sustained "drug panic" of the late 1960s and early 1970s. Influenced in part by governmental subcommittee hearings that aimed for maximal public exposure, newspapers, magazines, and television created the impression that the U.S. Army had broken down because of drugs and that the country was being ravaged by a full-fledged "epidemic." The *Washington Post*'s Jack Anderson and *Newsweek*'s Stewart Alsop were among the most sensationalistic of journalists. Utilizing apocalyptic language and metaphors, they portrayed drugs as a major combat hazard and threat to American security. The *Far Eastern Review* and the *New York Times* meanwhile characterized addicted veterans as being worse off than men crippled and maimed by war—or men whose remains had been shipped home in body bags. Such analogies ultimately made a powerful political impact. They helped to sweep under the surface the crucial sociopolitical factors shaping the war's outcome and the horrific violence meted out by U.S. forces and their proxies (including Thai, South Korean, and Philippine mercenaries responsible for dozens of massacres), while obscuring the social context in which GIs got stoned.[72] They further contributed to the revival of gross public hysteria surrounding drugs to which had been attributed mythic qualities unsubstantiated by scientific evidence. These included the ability to provoke aggressiveness, criminality, and violence and to foster the military's collapse. Harking back to Anslinger's "Reefer Madness" campaigns, these stereotypes helped to create a ripe climate for the growth of the federal drug war during the early 1970s, which was devised by policymakers to counter the crisis of the addicted army.

DECONSTRUCTING THE MYTH

THE GREAT NATIONAL DRUG DEBATE
OF THE SIXTIES AND SEVENTIES

It used to be that an addict was looked upon as a derelict in our society, but today in some quarters, the drug addict is almost placed on a pedestal, or portrayed as a victim of our society.
—General Lewis W. Walt, 1972

The drug "problem" in Vietnam may be therapy in disguise.
—Journal of Psychedelic Drugs, 1971

The past 10 or 15 years has witnessed the development of a national schism on the drug issue, symbolized vividly on the one hand by Dr. Leary's now infamous call to tune in, turn on and drop out and on the other by a never-ceasing parade of news items reporting the seizure of millions of dollars' worth of illicit drugs.
—Dr. Thomas Bryant, Presidential Drug Abuse Council, 1975

In October 1967, countercultural icon Timothy Leary faced off against Dr. Donald B. Louria, president of the New York State Council on Drug Addiction, in a public symposium on lysergic acid diethylamide at Rensselaer Polytechnic Institute (RPI) in upstate New York. Dressed in a white robe to accentuate his newfound persona as a "spiritual holy-man," Leary argued before a packed crowd of students that LSD was a panacea capable of expanding brain capacity and leading the nation's youth on a path of self-discovery. Louria wore a more conventional black suit and bowtie. He countered that anyone who tried LSD outside of medical circles was "insane" and that the drug could lead to uncontrolled aggression, homicide, or suicide.[1]

The forum at RPI brought out the key opposing sides to the great drug debate of the 1960s, which served in many respects as a microcosm of the broader societal rifts of the era. On one side, as epitomized by Louria, was the traditional or "Old Guard" approach, which characterized drugs as dangerous, pathological substances linked to personality disorder, socially aggressive behavior, and paranoia. On the other, a younger generation of "social environmentalists" expressed a belief that drugs were less biologically harmful than had been conventionally thought and emphasized the sociocultural roots of addiction. Influenced in part by Leary's psychedelic research, they challenged the deviance model and claimed that drugs could yield positive therapeutic and spiritual benefits if taken in the right social context. Many psychiatrists came to view Vietnam as a laboratory for the testing and validation of fresh ideas. The crisis there helped to crystallize the heated drug debate of the 1960s, with the Old Guard pointing to the horrors of drug abuse in combat, and the social-environmentalists linking drugs to the war setting and challenging the consensus that they were an antisocial vice linked to the military's collapse. Drowned by the weight of media sensationalism, these latter views ultimately failed to enter the mainstream of public opinion, though proponents raised important philosophical questions about the nature of drug abuse in society and war in Vietnam, and helped to deconstruct the myth of the addicted army.

"Worse than Small-Pox?" The Old Guard Approach to Drugs

Though emotions were particularly high, the great drug debate of the 1960s served to replicate older disputes dating to the late nineteenth century. During the so-called classic era of narcotics control from 1919 through the early 1960s, a reigning consensus emerged as to the hazardous quality of heroin, cocaine, and marijuana, which were subjected to harsh punitive control measures culminating with the notorious Boggs and Daniels Acts of the mid-1950s.[2] Apart from a few iconoclasts, medical specialists generally stressed that drug use was a product of character disorder and psychopathology. Dr. David Ausubel argued in a widely read 1958 book that addicts had an "antisocial" personality and suffered from neurosis, anxiety, depression, and trauma. He felt that marijuana users were particularly narcissistic and focused on instant personal gratification, including that of sex. Dr. Sidney Cohen, chief of psychiatry at Wadsworth Veterans Hospital, who was a pioneer in conducting psychedelic research and served as medical consultant for the U.S. military, referred to drug users as "life's losers" and "emotionally immature, impulse ridden young men who wallow in self-pity." In his 1969 book The Drug Dilemma, he stressed that drugs undermined social ambition and personal self-growth and had an "enslaving effect," resulting in "permanent dependency."[3]

Throughout the 1960s, many Old Guarders advanced a conservative portrayal of hippies as social outcasts and misfits. In *The Drug Scene*, Dr. Louria described drug users as "lost souls" leading "empty lives." Drug users "hate society, reject their family, distrust everyone around them, and are unable to give or accept love," he wrote. "[An individual's] use of drugs is an attempt to forge meaning in his life, but it is all a façade, which cannot change his pervasive pessimism and unhappiness." Characterizing Timothy Leary as a "demagogue" and "irresponsible psychedelic missionary," Louria added in *Nightmare Drugs* (1966), "The addict is playing Russian Roulette every time he injects himself. . . . For those who become hooked, life is a nightmare in which there is no joy, no pleasure, no glory but only physical sickness, decay and all too often, ugly, untimely and unnecessary death."[4]

Dr. Gabriel Nahas, a French émigré and professor of anesthesiology at Columbia University, stressed in *Marihuana—Deceptive Weed* that despite public infatuation with it, marijuana was a pernicious substance that could cause delirium and insanity and, when taken in chronic doses, "eroded the functional reserves of the brain." Dr. Dana Farnsworth, director of Harvard University Health Services, further claimed that marijuana yielded "psychotic effects" and was a "serious hazard to the mental health and stability even of apparently normal people." Dr. Edward R. Bloomquist of the University of Southern California added that when taken in "toxic proportions," marijuana caused "heinous crimes" resulting from "paranoia, megalomania, a lack of moral inhibition, and the release of basic destructive tendencies."[5]

Many specialists of the era subscribed to the disease model of addiction, which viewed drug abuse as a "dangerous social contagion" curable only by "inoculating" addicts through "quarantine" and treatment. Dr. Lawrence Kolb, director of the first federally funded rehabilitation center in Lexington, Kentucky, wrote in a 1962 book that drugs such as opium had an "enslaving effect" that led to "acute mental and moral deterioration." Dr. Victor H. Vogel, another former Lexington director, proclaimed that drug use was "worse than smallpox" and that "addicts spread physical destruction and moral degradation in their wake" and became a "menace to the community." Dr. Marie Nyswander, who helped to develop a groundbreaking treatment facility in New York using a synthetic heroin substitute, methadone, commented in *The Drug Addict as a Patient* that a narcotic substance "ravages the patient, destroys the entire fabric of life, and adversely affects the lives of his family and others close to him. . . .

As in every major disease, the patient is helpless before its destructive inroads and relentless course."[6] While pressing for more humane care and an end to punitive measures, proponents of the disease model resembled the Old Guard through such rhetoric and promoted a biologically determinist outlook that portrayed drug users as products of individual pathology and victims of debilitating chemicals. Both groups demonized drugs as an unmitigated cancer and evil whose eradication should assume top governmental priority.

"They Don't See Killing as a Reality"
The Old Guard and Drug Use in "The Nam"

Old Guarders were at the forefront in warning about a rise in military drug abuse, which most attributed to psychological malfunction—rather than seeing it as a product of the war experience. One doctor concluded that the "Vietnam drug abuse population reflected an inadequate self-concept stemming from a difficult developmental background and insufficient psychological coping skills." Another claimed that the users were "poorly educated, frustrated and had passive-aggressive personalities." In instructional material intended for military commanders, Dr. Sidney Cohen stated that military personnel engaging in drug use were "depressed, tormented and even psychotic," possessing "borderline personality disorder."[7]

Tending to be conservative politically and on the hawkish side, many in the Old Guard feared that drugs would undermine fighting efficiency. They warned about the high level of tetrahydrocannabinol (THC) in Vietnamese-grown marijuana and its capacity to accentuate any normally "hallucinatory" and "psychogenetic" properties of the drug. In testimony before the Dodd committee, Dr. Robert Baird, who treated veterans in New York City, commented, "Marijuana dulls the senses and creates feelings of omnipotence. I am concerned about how our armed boys [under the influence] are vulnerable targets to either bayoneting or shooting by the Vietcong."[8] In a 1971 article, Dr. Joel H. Kaplan, commanding officer of the Ninety-eighth Medical Detachment Neuropsychiatry (KO) Team, located near Da Nang, argued that Vietnamese-grown marijuana produced acute "toxicomania," resulting in grave psychiatric trauma, panic states, and psychosis. Charging that the drug was being sold by Communists as a form of biochemical warfare, he testified before the Dodd committee about a Green Beret who was found naked in front of his living quarters, raving that members of his unit were trying to kill him. Kaplan also recounted the story of a drugged-out soldier who had crossed enemy lines seeking peace, and of a stoned GI who shot his lieutenant after opening fire on his unit in a hallucinatory rage, thinking everyone surrounding him was the enemy. He commented, "In Vietnam, marijuana impaired soldiers' judgment, caused a temporary suspension of his moral standards and values, and led, in a number of cases, to acts of murder, rape and aggravated assault. Chronic users suffered definite psychological and adverse physical effects, and some remain schizophrenic." Kaplan added that if marijuana were legalized in the United States, "all hell's gonna break loose."[9]

Several psychiatrists argued that marijuana was a key factor in the commission of civilian atrocities in Vietnam. Dr. Myron Feld, chief of psychiatry at the Long Beach Veterans Hospital, published a controversial report concluding that many soldiers went insane after smoking Vietnamese marijuana and engaged in reckless behavior that caused unnecessary fatalities. If "soldiers go into battle in a drug induced fog," he stated, "they don't see killing as a reality."[10] Dr. Albert A. LaVerne, a psychiatrist in New York who worked with veterans, testified before the Dodd committee that it was within "reasonable scientific possibility" that the drug had caused the My Lai massacre. LaVerne based this conclusion on his previous casework, and told the story of a young man who had committed dual-generation homicide and matricide, killing his mother and grandmother with an antique sword while high on marijuana. The twenty-five-year-old apparently had no previous criminal record and ordinarily "wouldn't hurt a fly"; under the spell of marijuana, however, he had become psychotic, delusional, and paranoid—a trend Dr. LaVerne concluded had likely repeated itself at My Lai. He stated, "Anyone in the room taking a few puffs would experience abnormal mental affects of the psychic and neurological type that could last from minutes to hours.... Marijuana appears capable of inducing in humans abnormal, uncontrollable, irrational behavioral patterns associated with violence and homicidal tendencies."[11] This testimony epitomized the role of the Old Guard in shaping public hysteria surrounding the "crisis" in Vietnam. While often pursuing their own agenda in exaggerating the scope of the crisis, government officials and media pundits had little basis for contradicting the doctors' claims and relied on their scientific credentials.

From "Stand-up Cat" to "Righteous Dope Fiend"
The Unraveling of the Old Guard Consensus

The Old Guard perspective underwent a concerted challenge during the 1960s by a new generation of scientists who emphasized the social roots of addiction and nuanced character of the drug experience. Many of these researchers were influenced by a burgeoning academic iconoclasm, which drew on a tradition of dissent going back to the Progressive Era.[12] They argued that subcultural and environmental preconditions overrode any innate personal predispositions toward addiction—a synopsis they derived through the incorporation of classic criminological theories. Most notable was Edwin H. Sutherland's differential association theory, which rejected previous scholarly emphasis on biological determinants and examined crime as a learned behavior shaped by social environmental factors and peer influence.[13]

Howard S. Becker of Northwestern University was a pioneer in articulating the social origins of drug use. In a 1951 article, "Becoming a Marijuana User," he stressed that marijuana flourished within the confines of distinctive subcultural milieus where mainstream societal stigmas against the drug were eroded. According to Becker, users learned to enjoy getting high only after developing a series of rituals surrounding its intake, which they passed on through peer networks and more experienced smokers. Over time, marijuana became a vital part of individual users' social identity as outsider or rebel. This in turn hastened their proclivity to engage in further use, partially as a means of flouting governmental moral exhortations.[14]

Becker was a proponent of labeling theory, which argued that social deviance was contingent not on the quality of an act but rather on its public perception. His writings played an important role in stimulating the scholarly emphasis on the social roots of drug use during the 1960s, as did Paul Goodman's book *Growing Up Absurd*; it posited that the rigid social conformism of "organized society" stifled individual capacities for personal exploration and growth, breeding a sense of purposelessness that resulted in rebelliousness and delinquency.[15] In a leading book on the campus drug scene, *The Pleasure Seekers* (1969), Berkeley psychiatrist Joel Fort characteristically argued that rising drug patterns represented a "commentary on *society*. . . . The tweedledums and tweedledees who run for public office (and get elected), and pervasive mediocrity and resistance to change all communicate frustration and hopelessness and foster extremism or pleasure seeking with drugs or sex."[16]

Criminologists studying the concentration of addicts in lower-class urban "ghettos" also pointed to subcultural factors and challenged the assumption that drug users were psychologically maladjusted and withdrawn. Sociologist Harold Finestone argued that drug use represented a subtle form of rebellion among "cats," or individuals living in "achievement blocked" social groups, who, out of frustration and despondency, inverted the norms prized by the larger community. Harvey Feldman postulated that within the defiant, escapist, and thrill-seeking subculture of predominantly lower-class ethnic neighborhoods, "stand-up cats" or, in the black community "bad-ass niggers" were particularly well respected because of their street swagger and toughness. Feldman commented, "Because it was the most dangerous and pleasurable drug, entering the cutthroat game of heroin use became within the context of street life the unspoken route to top prestige."[17]

Feldman's "stand-up cat" (or "bad-ass nigger") was similar to criminologist Allen G. Sutter's model of the "righteous dope fiend" and Herbert Blumer's archetype of "the player," who were portrayed as the most charismatic, socially integrated, and "cool" members of their community.[18] In 1969, criminologists Edward J. Preble and John J. Casey Jr. published an influential article in the *International Journal of the Addictions* emphasizing the resourcefulness of street users, who embraced the drug underworld to avoid work in dead-end menial jobs. They viewed themselves much like successful businessmen in legitimate social circles and displayed pronounced ingenuity in surviving the hustle of street life. Preble and Casey commented, "The quest for heroin is the quest for a meaningful life. It enables [people in the ghetto] to escape the monotony of an existence severely limited by social constraints while gaining revenge on society for the injustices and deprivations experienced."[19]

Preble and Casey's article exemplified the new literature focused on the social and subcultural roots of drug abuse, particularly in its depiction of addicts as rational and innovative human beings intricately shaped by the social world in which they lived. This original perspective would prove to be particularly resonant for academic scholars and public health professionals examining drug patterns in Vietnam, which they felt needed to be contextualized within the distinctive sociocultural milieu of the war.

Drug Set and Setting
Timothy Leary, Antipsychiatry, and the Politics of Ecstasy

Throughout the 1960s a group of health professionals known as the "antipsychiatrists" were at the vanguard in questioning entrenched definitions of social normality and deviancy and in challenging the Old Guard consensus on drugs. Their influence was profound in shaping an alternative understanding of the so-called crisis in Vietnam—which adherents viewed as being symptomatic of a deeper social malaise and the underlying barbarism of the war. Influenced by the writings of R. D. Laing and Erich Fromm, antipsychiatrists lamented the intolerant character of Western society toward social difference and understood mental illness not as a form of human pathology but rather as an adaptive response to particular life circumstances and an increasingly dehumanized social order.[20]

Dr. Thomas Szasz, a German émigré professor of psychiatry at Syracuse University and an icon of the antipsychiatry movement, argued in his classic 1961 study *The Myth of Mental Illness* that scientific definitions of mental illnesses such as schizophrenia and hysteria were bogus and served to stigmatize nonconformist behavior and "the breaking of personal rules of conduct." In 1974, Szasz published *Ceremonial Chemistry: The Ritual Persecution of Drugs, Addicts, and Pushers*, which linked his analysis of the fabrication of mental illness to what he termed the "ritual persecution" of drug users, addicts, and pushers in the United States. According to Szasz, most illicit drugs were less harmful than legally sanctioned pharmaceuticals, including alcohol and tobacco, and had been used by divergent cultures throughout history for medical and spiritual purposes. Health professionals thus had little moral authorization to stigmatize drug use as a "disease"; doing so resembled the spurious use of medical labels to condemn other socially undesirable behavior and had the aim of limiting personal liberties. Szasz viewed the extension of American drug-control efforts in the international realm as particularly coercive: "Like Christians burning mosques to spread the word of Jesus, drug abuseologists are engaged in an arrogant destruction of the culture and custom of people (like the Yao in Laos) for whom opium has long been the best remedy for ills ranging from diarrhea to menstrual cramps to tuberculosis. In my opinion, this pseudo-medical crusade may prove to be more damaging to the cause of human freedom and dignity than have any of the armed conflicts of our age."[21]

Dr. Timothy Leary, a behavioral psychologist at Harvard University who received his doctorate at the University of California, Berkeley, in 1949, was the most notorious proponent of the antipsychiatry movement in the United States to oppose the deviance model of addiction. In 1960 he became convinced of the positive therapeutic and spiritual benefits of psychedelic drugs after reading British philosopher Aldous Huxley's *The Doors of Perception* and experimenting with magic mushrooms while on vacation in Cuernavaca, Mexico. He came to believe that psychedelics had the unique capacity of expanding individual consciousness and facilitating spiritual growth and greater social harmony.[22] Leary tied his embrace of psychedelics to a deep criticism of Western scientific positivism and the social injustice that he saw enveloping American society in its "lousy, class based culture." In a 1966 *Playboy* interview, three years after he had been fired from Harvard for allegedly dispensing drugs to undergraduates, he characterized the United States as a giant "insane asylum," epitomized, he felt, by "the dropping of bombs on native Vietnamese."[23]

Leary's ideological world view was influenced by Herbert Marcuse, a disillusioned Marxist thinker who argued in his classic 1955 *Eros and Civilization* that revolutionary change in American society needed to be accomplished within the realm of individual self-transformation and culture rather than through political ends. Drawing on Freud's *Civilization and Its Discontents*, Marcuse suggested that modern industrial capitalism had caused humankind to stray from its instinctual self by focusing all its creative capacities on labor exploitation and "barbaric" warfare. He advocated an alternative social order based on a removal of sexual inhibition and a return to a life based on "eros"—or the libidinal pleasure principle—where human love and kindness could triumph over material want. Leary embraced a similar vision, with psychedelic drugs being the key variable capable of engendering this transformation and facilitating closer human interrelations and greater psychic awareness.[24]

In spreading their utopian ideology, both Leary and Marcuse inspired the birth of the countercultural movement and popularized the spread of both free love and psychedelics as symbols of nonconformity and resistance. Many hippies adopted Leary's calls to "tune in, turn on, and drop out" from the conventions of society, or what he characterized as the "role playing games to which you have been assigned." Hippie leader Jerry Rubin characteristically referred to drugs as a "cultural detoxicant" whose use "signified the total end of the protestant ethic" and helped to "break the sham and hypocrisy and living death of plastic 9–5 America."[25]

Leary's influence was not confined to 1960s radicals; it helped to shape mainstream scientific attitudes. While still at Harvard, Leary had conducted several significant studies on psychedelics, which determined that their pharmacological properties were not static. Rather, he found that the expectation of the user (or "set," as he termed it) and the social context in which the drug was administered (or "setting") together played a pivotal role in stimulating their physical and behavioral effects. Leary applied this theory in a study at the Massachusetts Correctional Institute in Concord, where he and colleague Richard Alpert (later Baba Ram Dass) administered the psychedelic psilocybin to prison inmates. In order to provide a relaxed social "setting," they brought in Oriental rugs, candles, and soft mattresses. This apparently helped soften even the most hardened of criminals—who began talking of peace, love, and getting in touch with their inner selves—while limiting recidivism rates, according to Leary, by 70 percent.[26]

In retrospect, Leary remains a highly enigmatic figure who became discredited in most intellectual circles for his radical rebuke of academia, which he viewed as promoting "robot-like conformity" with "middle-class, bourgeois values." Leary has been widely criticized for idealizing the use of drugs, taking for granted his privileged class status and urging young people to abandon their education and eschew real-world responsibility. He has been further derided as an egomaniac for claiming the title of high priest of the psychedelic movement, which he cast as a pseudoreligious crusade, and relishing the media publicity that he received. These criticisms may be accurate, but Leary's legacy has been skewed by the negative depictions. His writings and commentaries built on existing scientific and sociological traditions and melded social criticism with demands for liberalization of the social mores surrounding drugs. One drug specialist working in the period commented: "Maybe in the end he burned himself out using too many psychedelics, but Leary's work, as well as that of his colleague Baba Ram Dass, was pioneering in terms of the concepts of set and setting, as were his ideas surrounding the symbolic function of drug taking as a means of 'dropping out of an unhealthy society.' In these respects his influence was profound."[27]

A New Way of Looking at Drugs

Despite his pariah status in the scientific community today, many drug specialists embraced Leary's foundational theories during the 1960s and 1970s, even if some criticized his scientific methodologies and evolvement into a prodrug propagandist.[28] In 1965, Stanford University psychologist Richard H. Blum published *Utopiates*, which refuted claims that LSD caused depression, psychosis, or acts of violence and stressed that users' responses were shaped by their personality and the setting in which they took it. Becker later published a study concluding that marijuana and LSD did not change the basic personality structure of individuals but simply lessened social inhibitions and brought out what was latent in the user's thoughts. They did not, in his words, "evoke responses which would otherwise be alien to him."[29]

In 1972, Dr. Andrew Weil, a former student of Leary's at Harvard, published *The Natural Mind: A New Way of Looking at Drugs and the Higher Consciousness*, which argued that the quest for heightened individual consciousness through artificial intoxication represented a universally innate drive in the human species analogous to the desire for food, sex, and love. Through a crosscultural analysis of indigenous populations in the Brazilian Amazon, Weil contended that drugs held positive transcendental, religious, and therapeutic functions which had not been fully explored in the United States: "I cannot help feeling that what we are now doing in the name of stopping the drug problem *is* the drug problem. Intelligently used drugs can be beneficial in many different ways." Quoting Aldous Huxley, Weil added, "That humanity at large will ever be able to dispense with artificial paradises seems very unlikely. Most men and women lead lives at the worst so painful and at the best so monotonous, poor and limited that the urge to escape, the longing to transcend themselves if only for a few moments is and has always been one of the principal appetites of the soul."[30]

Challenging Old Guard beliefs about "enslaving" effects, Weil's associate Dr. Norman Zinberg of Harvard Medical School stressed that many users of even the hardest narcotics such as heroin carried on productive lives. Danger, in his view, was contingent on the overall health of the individual and on how often heroin was used and in what circumstance (as with all other drugs, including alcohol). In an often cited study he determined that only about one heroin user in ten injected the drug daily—the functional definition of an addict. "Contrary to popular wisdom, occasional heroin users hold jobs, live in stable families in conventional communities and manifest none of the outward signs of social distress associated with the 'junkie addict,'" wrote Zinberg, another student of Leary's.[31]

Both Zinberg and Weil were pioneers in conducting scientific research on marijuana, which they considered to be a benign drug, possessing mystical and curative qualities.[32] In 1971, Dr. Lester Grinspoon, a professor of clinical psychiatry at Harvard, published an exhaustive study, *Marijuana Reconsidered*, which challenged notions that marijuana use led to harder drugs and could provoke mental psychosis and violence. He also emphasized its merits in treating illnesses such as glaucoma and its ability to mitigate the effects, such as nausea, of chemotherapy (as it had done for his teenage son, who had suffered from cancer). Dr. Grinspoon expressed contempt for those who he felt sacrificed their scientific integrity by demonizing drugs such as marijuana primarily for political reasons. He described Dr. Nahas's *Marihuana—Deceptive Weed* as a "work filled with half truths and unverifiable assertions" which promoted a "form of psychopharmacological McCarthyism." Dr. Zinberg characterized Nahas's book as "a piece of meretricious trash done by a man who is solely and cynically interested in picking up a few bucks by playing on the public's enormous concern about drug use."[33] Dr. Joel Fort meanwhile claimed that the Old Guard was responsible for promoting "vicious tripe, misinformation and lies surrounding drugs, which some claim are as dangerous as the hydrogen bomb." He added, "We're moving closer and closer to an Orwellian world of 1984. . . . The tactics of the drug police are indistinguishable from tactics used by Communists and other totalitarians."[34]

These remarks highlight the powerful emotional sway that the drug issue held at this time and the heated nature of the public debate. Members of the Old Guard themselves utilized strong language to condemn their intellectual adversaries. In 1970, Stanley A. Rudin wrote a scathing letter to *Transaction* magazine, which had printed a controversial article by Howard Becker arguing that the best way to solve the "drug problem" on college campuses was for administrators to develop greater tolerance for marijuana smoking and for students to learn to avoid getting caught.[35] Rudin wrote:

> Becker's solution reminds me of an argument I once heard for Murder Inc. If you want someone killed, hire a stranger to do it. Or better still make murder legal then rest assured the murder rate will drop dramatically. There is clear evidence that most of the "mind expanding" drugs either do definite damage to the brain or cause people to do things that are injurious to others. . . . The few addicts I have tested escape reality to an emotional level about that of a three year old child. (Indeed some are stuck at that level and use drugs to stay there). My question is why do we have a nation of teenage infants? And for that matter professors of sociology?[36]

Despite arousing public controversy, social environmentalists, in retrospect, produced an impressive volume of literature counteracting many ingrained public mythologies surrounding drugs, including their link to criminal aggression, mental instability, and violence. Though sometimes walking a thin line between scientific neutrality and social or political advocacy (one clearly crossed by Leary—although the same charge could be applied to Old Guarders and disease-model advocates), they raised important questions about the validity of existing prohibition laws and provoked an impassioned debate surrounding the therapeutic, spiritual, and medical potentialities of specific drugs—a debate that would extend to the crisis in Vietnam.

"It Makes Time Go Away"
Drugs and the Counterfeit Social Universe of "The Nam"

For many public health professionals, the unfolding drug crisis in Vietnam represented a ripe testing ground and, in many cases, validation for new social theories surrounding drugs. Beginning in 1967 the DOD began to commission psychiatric surveys in Vietnam in an attempt to gain a better understanding of the perceived crisis. Most participating psychiatrists were highly critical of the mainstream media and found that social determinants rather than psychopathology were central in shaping relatively high user rates.[37] In linking drug use to the pernicious environment of the war, they also provided a strong critique of U.S. foreign policy and supported the antiwar movement.

Influenced by the subcultural models of criminal deviance, many psychiatrists concluded that an inversion of cultural norms in Vietnam was crucial to the adoption of behavior that would be considered deviant in the United States. Dr. Peter Bourne, who was drafted into the army in 1964 and later became a founding member of VVAW, commented, "In the war zone, there is often the feeling that all usual social mores have been suspended and individuals feel free to engage in behavior both in and out of combat that they would find reprehensible in civilian life. This includes the use of drugs."[38] Dr. Richard Ratner, a psychiatrist from the Bronx working at the Long Binh military stockade, compared GIs in Vietnam to impoverished minorities living in urban slums: "Many have told me they took heroin because of the boredom and hassle of life here," he said. "The soldiers don't want to be here. Their living conditions are bad, they are surrounded by privileged classes, namely officers, and there is accepted use of violence. . . . Like in the ghetto, they take drugs and they try to forget."[39]

Several psychiatrists stressed that drug use was a key factor in minimizing the level of psychiatric casualties in Vietnam, which were approximately one-third below the rate for both World War II and Korea.[40] Dr. Roger Roffman explained, "The objective investigator must consider the possibility that marijuana smoking and other illicit drugs may for some users, perhaps for most, assist with healthy efforts at coping with a hostile environment and reduce the likelihood of mental illness, personality disorder and aggressive or violent outbursts."[41] Norman Zinberg found that heroin's ability to make time pass quickly was appealing for GIs counting down to their Date of Expected Return from Overseas (DEROS). According to soldiers that he interviewed, the drug provided a kind of "blessed oblivion" which helped to "magically remove them" from an "otherwise intolerable situation"—at least for a short time. "Hated by the Vietnamese and hating them," he wrote in a 1972 article appearing in the *Archives of General Psychiatry*, "the American troops were easily attracted to any activity, including drug use, that blotted out the outside world. The user sees his problem as one of getting through a thoroughly unpleasant year. Heroin's remarkable effect in speeding up the time provides him with an ingenious and effective (in one sense) solution to this problem."[42]

Zinberg emphasized further that drug use almost always occurred in a group environment and served as an important bonding mechanism and initiation rite for new recruits (or FNGs—Fucking New Guys—in GI slang). In his synopsis, drug users in Vietnam were not social outcasts, bad apples, or deviant loners, as Old Guarders suggested, but often among the most popular and social members of their units. "The act of gently rolling the tobacco out of an ordinary cigarette, tamping the fine white powder into the opening, and then replacing a little tobacco to hold the powder in before lighting up the O.J. (opium joint) seemed to be followed all over the country," he commented. "Social setting is a predominant factor in heroin use by soldiers in Vietnam, who would fit many people's idea of the healthy all-around American boy, and shows no evidence of character disorder. A cultural taboo of no mean power in Vietnam has been smashed."[43]

Dr. Clinton R. Sanders, who received his doctoral training at Northwestern University under Becker and worked with veterans at a Veterans Administration center in Chicago, concluded that drugs represented a form of "functional self-medication" and "chemotherapy" for GIs, as well as an effective "solution" to the despairing social conditions bred by the war and "vacation" from its horrors. He commented, "While drug use by American soldiers in Southeast Asia is seen as a threateningly illegal activity by military and governmental officials and is indicative of psychopathology, it is defined as a realistic and rational response to the Vietnam experience by the GI user. For him drugs perform certain necessary social and personal functions, and meet a variety of healthy and normal needs." Sanders further pointed to the importance of drug use as a route by which a dispirited soldier could "flaunt those who have authority over him," thereby "tasting the sweet pleasures of rebellion." He quoted one GI who stated: "Guys would come over just out of boot camp talking about cutting off ears and what bad-asses they were. Pretty soon, though, they'd find out that those little 5'2" guys were really big with an AK-47. Then they'd be over with us doing dope, talking about going back to 'the world' and wishing they'd never come over here."[44]

Yale's Robert Jay Lifton, also a committed peace and antinuclear activist, reported that some GIs dreamed up scenarios where they got high together with the NLF and dropped their weapons in mutual amity and affection. One soldier told him, "When I was smoking then I would say it's just a bunch of bullshit. It really is ridiculous, really stupid. . . . Somebody back there in Washington is programming us, and we're just being tools of it." Questioning whether it was the soldiers on drugs who were crazy or the war itself and warmakers, Lifton argued more broadly that drug use helped to "numb" the emotional pain and "guilt complex" of soldiers living in what he termed the "counterfeit social universe of 'the Nam,'" characterized by an omnipresent fear of death, the massacre of Vietnamese, and "absurd" technological destruction.[45]

Captain Larry H. Ingraham of Walter Reed Army Medical Institute accentuated the therapeutic quality of drugs in providing a boost to the cohesiveness and morale of many units. In his view, performance problems usually resulted from withdrawal—not addiction—which caused users to become sick with nausea, aching joints, and fever. In a 1974 article published in *Psychiatry*, he profiled GIs who received awards for outstanding service after switching from alcohol to high-purity heroin. "Soldiers are no fools and know the dangers," he wrote. "They could perform complex tasks, including air traffic control and heavy equipment operations, with distinction while using the stuff in part because they learned how to moderate their level of intake. There is no published report of heroin interfering with combat performance."[46] Writing along a similar vein, Dr. David Smith, director of the Free Medical Clinic in Haight-Ashbury, argued in the *Journal of Psychedelic Drugs* that drugs helped calm the nerves of GIs working under grave distress. He quoted one private who stated, "I was point man for our squad and when you get high, in a way, it calms you down and makes you more alert. You don't miss snake eyes (hidden Vietnamese signs for mined trails) or miss an enemy ambush. You can't do that when you're straight, because you are over-come with fear."[47]

While stopping short of endorsing the positive social merits of drug use in battle, both Ingraham and Smith sought to shed light on the perspective of soldiers taking drugs and their adaptive function, rather than simply demonizing their behavior. They were also intent on challenging the prevailing notion that drugs undermined America's fighting efficiency. Their analysis reflected, in turn, the shifting intellectual and scientific paradigms and was more sensitive than mainstream depictions to the underlying social conditions of war that bred the relatively high user rates.

"We Must Refrain from Sensationalism"
Dispelling Additional Popular Myths

Prominent antipsychiatrist Thomas Szasz was among the most resolute in challenging the myth of the addicted army, arguing in *Transaction* that the government was "scapegoating" addicts for the failure of its war strategy and manufacturing a "pharmacological Gulf of Tonkin." He commented: "Like the Germans after World War I who claimed that their troops were stabbed in the back by pacifists and other 'unpatriotic elements' at home, we claim that our troops are being stabbed in the back by heroin and the pushers responsible for supplying it to them. . . . As we de-escalate against the Vietcong, we will escalate against heroin. No doubt we shall find it easier to control Americans who shoot heroin than Vietnamese who shoot Americans."[48] The drug war in his analysis thus fit a desperate psychological need and was a last-gasp measure undertaken by the ruling establishment to try to preserve its moral authority.

Szasz's colleagues predominantly concurred with his emphasis on political manipulation. Dr. Gordon Livingston, who studied veteran readjustment, commented in a speech before the American Psychiatric Association, "Official statistics about drugs are just like the body count—all lies!" Robert Jay Lifton added that the government had inflated the totals as a means of diverting attention from the "absurd evil of the war."[49]

Building on newly developed sociological theories that not all drug users become addicts, many psychiatrists stressed the casual nature of drug use in Vietnam and were quick to refute media claims that the war had produced a wave of inveterate addicts poised to exacerbate crime and unrest once back in the United States.[50] Lee N. Robins argued that the high recovery rate of veteran addicts served to "dispel popular myths surrounding the persistence and intractability of physiological narcotic addiction." Dr. Jaffe further stated, "The legend has always been that if you get hooked on heroin you never get off. The exception is supposed to be a miracle or mistake. The Vietnam veterans have proven otherwise."[51]

Military psychiatrists were most vocal in challenging the connection between drugs and civilian atrocities, including the My Lai massacre. Lifton stressed that My Lai was a product of the "atrocity-producing environment" of a war marred by racial dehumanization, kill-ratio directives, and the blending of the revolutionary guerrillas into the civilian population that supported them. Other psychiatrists pointed to the sedative qualities of both marijuana and heroin.[52] Dr. Marvin Everett Reed, medical corpsman with the U.S. Navy at Cam Ranh Bay, stated, "When you take marijuana, for instance, you don't want to get up and fight the world. You want to [lie] back and smell the daisies. Marijuana doesn't incite you to riot [or commit crime], it tranquilizes your hostile feelings as a general rule."[53] Dr. John O. Ives, assistant professor of psychiatry at the University of Vermont, who was in Vietnam from 1970 to 1972, added with regard to heroin, "Of the addicts I saw or heard of in Vietnam, I never encountered a case where a heroin addict, either high or in a state of withdrawal, committed a crime of violence. While under the influence they were invariably peaceful, tranquil people. Even in a state of withdrawal, they were more like irritable children than enraged maniacs."[54]

Dr. James Teague, a captain with the 935th Medical Detachment and a psychiatric consultant at Long Binh, detailed a case that appeared to epitomize the danger of drug use in the combat zone. In the *Journal of the American Medical Association* he reported on a nineteen-year-old private who reputedly shot and killed a fellow GI whom he had mistaken for Ho Chi Minh while stoned on marijuana. Sworn statements and a formal judicial investigation revealed that the victim was an African American who had been assigned to guard duty with the private and had introduced him to marijuana. Known as a joker, he had befriended some Vietnamese kids, fired his weapon near them, and claimed that he was Ho Chi Minh, whose name he had inscribed on his T-shirt. The private allegedly became terrified when he saw Ho's name and shot his comrade at point-blank range, then returned to base camp in a confused state and bragged that he had killed Ho Chi Minh. When told the true identity of his victim, he returned to his post with the blood-stained T-shirt. He later experienced severe regret for his actions and was diagnosed by medical officials as being delusional and suffering from acute "toxic psychosis." On the surface, the "Ho Chi Minh killing" appeared to confirm the worst, but

Dr. Teague saw it as a "bizarre anomaly" provoked by the violent social setting of the war and extreme stress-level experienced by the young private: "Marijuana [only] allowed the expression of underlying thoughts or feelings. It is my opinion that environmental stresses may well potentiate, exaggerate or otherwise affect the symptoms of those reactions we have seen [including the Ho Chi Minh killing]."[55]

Dr. Roffman subsequently testified before Congress, "We must refrain from sensationalism, and give up some of our traditional myths and folklore. . . . It is far too easy and dangerous to make the giant and indefensible step [of linking My Lai or other atrocities to marijuana]. Most physicians agree that the individual exhibiting symptoms [of an adverse reaction] must have had an underlying predisposition for [it] to have manifested. From my understanding, there is no greater proportion of marijuana users seeking professional help for emotional problems [than non-users]."[56] Roffman's and Teague's analyses exemplified the prevailing focus on environmental factors as well as the resonance of Leary's concepts of "set" and "setting." These ideas appeared to be particularly relevant to the crisis in Vietnam and in the debate over the roots of military atrocities, which psychiatrists insisted were little affected by drugs.

On the whole, though in some cases overidealizing the use of drugs and sugarcoating their danger, social environmentalists provided a great deal of evidence to back up their analysis, which was based on the viewpoint of the soldiers themselves. A majority of veterans remain adamant today that the drug crisis was overblown in the media and a trivial aspect of the war, far more so than alcohol. Others continue to insist that drugs served various important therapeutic and psychological benefits in a despairing, death-tainted environment. While causing dereliction of duty in select cases, as well, drugs were far from the corrosive cancer that politicians, Old Guard psychiatrists, and the media branded them; rather, they were symptomatic of deeper ills gripping the armed forces. They had an entirely inconsequential role, furthermore, in shaping the outcome of the conflict, which was contingent, as most historians have understood, upon sociopolitical developments and the strength of Vietnamese nationalism.[57] That military psychiatrists and social scientists who engaged in the most systematic study of the crisis both rendered the foregoing conclusions is by no means a coincidence, even if contemporaneous intellectual and scientific currents guided their analysis.

Despite the insightfulness of many of the views it embodied, the social environmental approach did not reign triumphant in the mainstream.

Because of a narrow reach, largely confined to specialized medical and professional journals, it was overshadowed by media and political sensationalism. A large number of Americans as a result remained locked in a scientific time warp, convinced that high-grade Vietnamese marijuana had helped to spur the My Lai massacre and provoked the military's full-scale collapse. The consequence was marked in the shaping of American drug policy, which was premised largely on the Old Guard approach or, at best, the disease model. That approach also helped limit debate about the unyielding brutality of the fighting and devastating consequence of American policy action, which held little regard for Vietnamese popular will and led U.S. soldiers into a hostile environment that drove many to the depths of personal despair. For some, as they saw it, this situation could be mitigated only through the use of drugs.

"A GENERATION OF JUNKIES"

THE ANTIWAR MOVEMENT,
THE DEMOCRATIC PARTY, AND
THE MYTH

It was a cold decision by the State Department. We wanted to remain as paying guests [in Laos] in order to bomb the hell out of a lot of peasants. For that privilege, no price is too high, not even ignoring or formally abetting the dope industry, which hooks our own forces. —James Hamilton-Paterson, 1971

American foreign policy makers have been willing to go to any extreme—even to the extreme of converting a quarter of their fighting force in Vietnam into strung out, haggard "scagheads"—to carry out their schemes of global conquest. —Frank Browning, 1971

The time has come when we have to decide which is more important to our country—propping up corrupt, doggedly anti-Communist governments in Southeast Asia or getting heroin out of our high-schools. —Alfred W. McCoy, 1972

In June 1972, Alfred W. McCoy, a twenty-six-year-old graduate student at Yale University, found himself enmeshed in a hurricane of controversy after writing *The Politics of Heroin in Southeast Asia*. The book accused the CIA of supporting opium warlords in Southeast Asia and provoking the GI drug "epidemic." McCoy had previously appeared before the Senate Foreign Relations Committee and provided documents that had been leaked to the *Washington Post* implicating the South Vietnamese general Ngo Dzu in the drug traffic, along with his father, Ngo Khoung, who had served as a special assistant to President Nguyen Van Thieu.[1] The CIA, not surprisingly, was less than enamored of McCoy's activities and issued a rebuttal to his charges in *Harper's* magazine. Government officials from both major parties were also outraged and questioned McCoy's motivations and character.[2]

The scandal ignited by McCoy's book epitomized the heated political passions provoked by the drug crisis in Vietnam and its link to the deep social divisions brought about by the war. On one side, government spokesmen sought to uphold public belief in the virtuous character of American foreign policy and denied any hint of association with the narcotics trade. Members of the antiwar movement, by contrast, viewed the CIA's complicity as a reflection of the immorality of the war and its imperialist underpinnings. Jumping at the opportunity to expose every layer of intrigue, they exaggerated the scope of the GI crisis and inadvertently helped to enhance the sweeping "moral panic" engulfing the country. They also lent support to an expansion of prohibition efforts, particularly in the international sphere. In his 1968 book *The Betrayal*, Dr. William Corson, a former Green Beret and a U.S. Medal of Freedom winner turned antiwar activist, who saw the war as an act of genocide, went so far as to urge President Nixon to napalm poppy fields in the Golden Triangle to prevent the spread of drugs into the United States. He stated, "The United States routinely napalmed whole villages of women and children. It is hardly extreme to napalm poppy plants and render those fields incapable of producing opium for at least five years."[3]

Corson's comments flew in the face of conventional scholarly interpretations claiming that the conservative New Right had been the sole group driving the growth of the federal drug war.[4] In *Agency of Fear: Opiates and Political Power in America*, political scientist Edward Jay Epstein argued that the Nixon administration manipulated public opinion to promote a law-and-order mandate and expand the police powers of the state.[5] While accurate in its overarching theme, Epstein's analysis ignored the politicization of the crisis in Vietnam and the influence of the antiwar movement in exacerbating public fears over drugs. It also overlooked the support of the Democratic Party and political left for expanded drug control measures—stemming largely from their critique of governmental policy and its tacit alliance with drug traffickers.

"From Tan Son Nhut to Marshall Ky"
The CIA Dope Calypso

During the mid-1960s, several UN and World Health Organization (WHO) studies first suggested that political corruption and the complicity of the American government was fueling a boom in the Southeast Asian drug trade. In his 1969 book *The Pleasure Seekers*, Joel Fort, a WHO representative who had conducted intensive research on the topic, remarked, "The facts are and have been easily available to anyone who really cares to probe beneath the surface. . . . In effect, the United States is covering up and sometimes subsidizing the opium traffic, which it purports to be eradicating. The layer upon layer of duplicity and corruption is rarely surpassed even in modern spy novels."[6]

In April 1968 the *New York Times* obtained leaked information from a Senate subcommittee on foreign expenditures that Nguyen Cao Ky, vice president of the Republic of South Vietnam, had been caught smuggling opium in 1964 while serving on a secret CIA operation that flew agents into North Vietnam from Laos for the purpose of sabotage.[7] Reputable newspapers subsequently began publishing well-researched exposés implicating American government allies in the drug trade.[8] In one revealing piece, *Far Eastern Economic Review* correspondent Don Strock stated that after slipping into an unauthorized military zone, he had witnessed the loading of opium onto T-28 bombers by U.S. crews working in conjunction with Laotian and Thai Special Forces. The *Christian Science Monitor*, meanwhile, documented the arrest of Delbert Fleener, an air force pilot with suspected CIA ties, who was caught smuggling over 500 pounds of opium into Saigon. Fleener had once served as the personal pilot of Ambassador Ellsworth Bunker (1967–1973).[9]

The involvement of high-ranking personnel in the drug traffic captured the attention of antiwar activists working for the left-leaning *Ramparts* magazine. An heir to the muckraking journalistic tradition of the Progressive Era, *Ramparts* had developed a specialty during the 1960s in unearthing the covert activities of the CIA, including its sponsorship of police-training programs in South Vietnam through Michigan State University, and its infiltration of cultural organizations in Western Europe. In a recent interview, Peter Dale Scott, professor emeritus of English literature at the University of California, Berkeley, and former *Ramparts* contributor, commented that "the rumors about the CIA and drugs were floating around the *Ramparts* offices during the late 1960s. Many of us were deeply concerned by the allegations as part of our broader misgivings about the Vietnam War and wanted to know more." In June 1968, *Ramparts* published "The CIA's Flourishing Opium Trade," which accused the agency of flying opium, on behalf of its Laotian clients, "in harmless looking suitcases" on Air America planes to heroin-processing laboratories in Hong Kong. The article also mentioned the corruption of high-ranking South Vietnamese generals, including Ky, whom the magazine referred to, accurately enough, as a "swashbuckling Hitler-admirer."[10]

In the February 1970 issue of *Ramparts*, Scott published "Air America: Flying the U.S. into Laos," which detailed the history of Air America in providing clandestine logistical support for American Cold War operations in Southeast Asia. The airline originally went by the name Civil Air Transport (CAT). It was taken over in 1942 by General Claire Chennault and members of the China lobby loyal to Generalissimo Jiang Jieshi (Chiang Kai-shek) to provide reinforcements for the Guomindang (GMD) in its dual fight against the Chinese Communist Party (CCP) and imperial Japan. During the 1950s, after the "loss of China" and triumph of Mao Zedong's Red Army, Air America continued to provide arms shipment and food supplies to remnants of the GMD in northern Burma and Taiwan that were plotting to reinvade the Chinese mainland. It helped to provide a general cover for the CIA and the suppression of revolutionary insurrections across the subcontinent, including during the Korean War.[11] As the Vietnam War escalated, Scott chronicled the use of Air America to traffic opium for American-backed officials in South Vietnam and Laos (at its peak, it was estimated to have flown 6,000 tons of opium per month—earning the nickname Air Opium). Lacking a firm popular base, both governments appeared to be reliant on black market operations for their political and military survival. Scott wrote: "The use of illegal narcotics networks to fight Communism seems to have been sanctioned inside the United States. With the maturation of both capitalism and third world nationalism, wealthy U.S. interests have resorted systematically to organized outlaws to pursue their operations."[12] Though sensational, Scott's article was well sourced and factually based.

In May 1971, *Ramparts* published another exposé, this one written by Frank Browning and Banning Garrett, which was featured on the magazine's cover under the huge headline "Marshall Ky: The Biggest Pusher in the World?" The authors' answer to this question was, invariably, yes. For them, Ky's involvement in the drug traffic epitomized the corruption of the South Vietnamese government, dating back to Ngo Dinh Diem's rule in the 1950s, during which Diem's sister-in-law, Madame Nhu—popularly known in Saigon as "the grande madame of opium"—was said to have garnered a gross profit of 250–500 million dollars from the trade. Diem's brother Ngo Dinh Nhu, also reputed to be an opium addict, wrested control of major opium syndicates from Binh Xuyen criminal gangsters to finance a repressive state policing apparatus, in conjunction with CIA blood money. According to Browning and Garrett, "Unimpeded by boundaries, scruples or customs agents, the U.S. has—as a reflex of its warfare in Indo-China—built up a support system for the trade in narcotics that is unparalleled in modern history."[13]

Radical academics were among those pointing to the relationship between the U.S. government and drug traffickers, which they tied to a systematic pattern of economic imperialism. Massachusetts Institute of Technology linguist Noam Chomsky, whose first collection of antiwar essays was dedicated to "the brave young men who refuse to serve in a criminal war," wrote in *Ramparts* that Nguyen Cao Ky was so corrupt that his minister of finance "sells drugs to the 'Vietcong.' " In 1972, the Committee of Concerned Asian Scholars (CCAS), an organization composed of young Southeast Asian specialists morally opposed to the war and to intellectual complicity with it, published *The Trail of the Poppy: Heroin and Imperialism*, a pamphlet arguing that the United States was an heir to both the British and French in exploiting Southeast Asia through opium. Because of a cynical quest for open markets and profit, American political and economic elites, wrote the authors, had found a natural affinity with the "criminal gangsters" heading an assortment of regional client-states and were poised to grow rich off the misery and suffering of the ordinary people—as with the waging of the war itself.[14]

The Trail of the Poppy included a profile of Paul Withers, a Green Beret who claimed that he had purchased opium in Laos in 1966 while working for the CIA in order to finance covert military operations. His actions appeared to typify the degeneracy of American Cold War policy going back to its patronage of Jiang Jieshi and the GMD in China in the 1920s and 1930s, which, like Diem in South Vietnam, had established a state monopoly on opium to finance its military activities against Mao and the Communists. The Generalissimos had forged particularly close ties with Du Yuesheng, head of the Green Gang criminal syndicate, whom one scholar referred to as an "Asian Al Capone."[15] "It seems that anything goes if it is in the national interest," the pamphlet read. "The bankrupt policies of counterrevolution have promoted heroin addiction, while rewarding Asian elites for their support of U.S. military goals."[16]

In March 1972 the radical *Earth* magazine devoted an entire issue to the CIA's involvement in the international drug traffic, which it linked to the spread of a "nationwide drug epidemic." Prior to publication, the editors of *Earth* released advertisements broadcasting the photo of a strung-out junkie sticking a needle into his cut-up arm under the caption "The CIA put your brother in Vietnam. CIA heroin traffic turned him on to smack. You are paying the CIA six billion dollars a year for these social

services."[17] The issue itself contained a poem by the famous Beat writer
Allen Ginsberg, "CIA Dope Calypso," dedicated to Peter Dale Scott:

> All through the Sixties the Dope flew free
> Thru Tan Son Nhut Saigon to Marshall Ky
> Air America followed through
> Transporting confiture for President Thieu

> All these Dealers were decades and yesterday
> The Indochinese mob of the U.S. CIA

In another verse, Ginsberg poked fun at the CIA's alliance during the
1950s with Thai chief of police Phao Sriyanon, who had grown rich from
the opium trade while ruthlessly suppressing political opponents through
an elaborate intelligence apparatus funded in part by drug proceeds.
Ginsberg wrote:

> The policeman's name was Mr. Phao
> He peddled dope grand scale and how
> Chief of border customs paid
> By Central Intelligence's U.S. A.I.D.

> The whole operation, Newspapers say
> Supported by the CIA

Ginsberg also satirized the CIA's support for the Hmong (or Meos) in
Laos, who had been molded into a ruthless anti-Communist army and
whose principal cash crop was opium:

> Touby Lyfoung he worked for the French
> A big fat man liked to wine & wench
> Prince of the Meos he grew black mud
> Till opium flowed through the land like a flood

> Communists came and chased the French away
> So Touby took a job with the CIA
> . . . .

> And his best friend General Vang Pao
> Ran the Meo army like a sacred cow
> Helicopter smugglers filled Long Cheng's bars
> In Xieng Quang province on the Plain of Jars

> It started in secret they were fighting yesterday
> Clandestine secret army of the CIA

An idealist at heart, Ginsberg traveled to CIA headquarters in Langley, Virginia, in 1972 after the publication of "CIA Dope Calypso" to confront Director Richard Helms and try to influence a change in policy. He made a bet with Helms, who agreed to sit down for an hour of meditation per day for the rest of his life if the charges could be proved.[18]

Ginsberg's poem was intended as a firm antiwar indictment. He hoped to debunk official propaganda depicting the intervention in Vietnam as a "noble cause" (as Ronald Reagan would later put it) to "save" the South Vietnamese people from "totalitarian Communist aggression." Instead, he argued, like many of his contemporaries, that the war was being waged on behalf of avaricious criminal entrepreneurs with few moral scruples. Ginsberg portrayed drugs as a metaphor for the spiritual corruption of American values in Vietnam. This analogy was somewhat ironic in light of Ginsberg's status as an icon to hippies, during the early 1960s, Ginsberg had even contemplated phoning Mao Zedong, John F. Kennedy, and Nikita Kruschev on a three-way conference call while tripping on LSD to urge them to start smoking marijuana and promote world peace. His desire for a swift end to the war, however, compelled him to portray drugs negatively—especially since the drug in question was heroin, whose use was generally frowned upon by hippies. In *Vietnam Veterans neither Victims nor Executioners,* Robert Jay Lifton wrote that for the antiwar movement, the spread of heroin took on a near "mythic quality" (along with Robert S. McNamara's kill-ratio) as a symbol of the war's depravity: "The fact that American political and military machinations are largely responsible is further evidence of the relationship between the 'heroin plague' (the mass media term) [and] the deeper and profoundly cruel truth about the 'surd evil' we perpetrate in Vietnam."[19]

In 1972 the editors of *Ramparts* published a collection of essays titled *Smack!* which exemplified the left's propensity to embellish the link between drugs and the immorality of the war. The book claimed that CIA support for traffickers helped to precipitate a full-scale societal epidemic in which even "high school football heroes" were turning on, and veterans resembled "Jewish kids about to be incinerated." Smack, or heroin, had made them all "tragic looking." Typical was Augie Schultz, a former all-American type turned heroin addict, who was so mentally disturbed by the war that he allegedly kept a photo of himself eating C-rations over a "pile of dead gooks." His mother stated, "He went in a nice middle class kid and came out a junkie. He's a casualty too. Some boys lose legs and arms. Augie lost his mind."[20]

Smack! concluded with an ominous warning about how "lady smack was winning converts at an unprecedented rate" in small-town America and had become as much a part of suburbia as the "Saturday barbeque." "Like an intercontinental ballistic missile," the authors wrote, "the war has come home—in a silky gray powder that goes from a syringe into America's mainline."[21] The book was generally filled with blown-up rhetoric and analogies—including reference to the Nazi holocaust—which distorted the scope of the crisis. By demonizing drugs and equating them with CIA duplicity and the most horrific elements of the war, it fed into public sensationalism over drug abuse and crime, while paying curt attention to the Vietnamese perspective. The book also helped to advance a pathological image of veterans, similar to that of the mainstream media.

"Vietnam—A Drug Smuggler's Paradise?"
Alfred W. McCoy and the Politics of Heroin

Among antiwar activists, Alfred W. McCoy went to the greatest lengths in exposing the CIA's support for regional drug lords—while also exaggerating the scope of military addiction. McCoy first became interested in the drug issue while editing a volume on the secret war in Laos, which included an essay by Peter Dale Scott on Air America. In 1971, McCoy's editor at Harper & Row suggested that he conduct a study on the roots of the so-called heroin plague in Vietnam. McCoy subsequently traveled to France, where he interviewed retired intelligence officers Roger Belleux and Roger Trinquier, who had become wealthy business executives. Both spoke candidly about establishing an opium monopoly in Vietnam through an operation code-named X, which helped to fund many of their covert military activities. When McCoy asked Trinquier what had happened after the French defeat at Dienbienphu in 1954, he replied, "Your CIA took over."[22]

After his visit to France, McCoy returned to the United States and arranged for interviews with Major Edward G. Lansdale and aide Lucien Conein near CIA headquarters in Langley. The two Cold Warriors welcomed McCoy into their homes and told stories of drug trafficking by Corsican gangsters, French agents, and intimates of Diem, whom they knew. McCoy continued with a string of interviews on the West Coast. He met with Scott in San Francisco as well as a former Green Beret who threatened to kill McCoy if he attributed any information to him by name. McCoy also attended the wedding of a personal friend whose brother had served in Vietnam and told him about Americans being found dead in the field with syringes in their arms. Before traveling back overseas, McCoy met with Ginsberg in New Haven, Connecticut, at a rally to free Black Panther leader Huey P. Newton, who had been imprisoned for killing a police officer.[23] It was over a shared cup of coffee that Ginsberg began to craft his "CIA Dope Calypso" poem. He also provided McCoy with a box of unpublished *Time* and *Life* magazine clippings about the involvement of America's allies in the opium trade. After submitting several overdue term papers at Yale, McCoy journeyed to Saigon and later visited the Golden Triangle, where he continued his often dangerous investigations. At one point, while he was hiking through some poppy fields with an indigenous guide, Laotian soldiers suspicious about his inquiries fired their rifles at him. A CIA operative also threatened to murder his interpreter. McCoy was lucky to survive to tell the tale.[24]

In June 1972, after pulling what he termed "18 hour days in Yale's Sterling library," McCoy completed *The Politics of Heroin in Southeast Asia*. The blockbuster book argued that the CIA actively supported drug-trafficking networks in fulfilling its geostrategic war aims in Indochina. While rarely directly handling opium, the CIA "provided their drug lord allies with transport, arms, cash and political protection," according to McCoy. "It is ironic indeed," he wrote, "that America's heroin plague is of its own making."[25] The "smoking gun" in McCoy's research was an interview that he conducted with General Ouane Rattikone, commander of the CIA-supported Royal Lao Air Force. During his visit to Laos, McCoy convinced Rattikone that he was a correspondent with *Harper's* sent to profile allies of America in its crusade against Communism. He then asked him to comment about allegations that he had stolen money when managing the country's opium syndicate during the early 1960s. Rattikone, in an attempt to deflect these charges, which he attributed to the slander of longtime political rival Phoumi Nosavan, opened up business records showing that he had controlled all drug transactions registered after 1961, when the Laotian government was pressured by the UN to abolish its monopoly on opium. In a forthright manner, Rattikone also divulged his involvement in operating a heroin refinery in the Laotian capital of Vientiane. Masked as a Pepsi-Cola bottling plant, the refinery produced a high-grade substance of 96 percent purity that was marketed under the U-Globe brand label and consumed by American GIs stationed in Vietnam.

Most of the heroin produced in Rattikone's labs, according to McCoy, was originally grown by the Hmong, who served as indispensable allies in the clandestine war waged by the United States against the Communist Pathet Lao. The CIA provided technological and logistical support for the cultivation of opium as a means of gaining leverage among Hmong chiefs Touby LyFoung and Vang Pao.[26] Since the late nineteenth century, opium had served as the main cash crop to the Hmong, whom counterinsurgency specialist Lansdale had termed "splendid fighting men," and who provided the bulk of the American fighting force in Laos. The CIA, according to McCoy, was following in the footsteps of the French, who had recruited the Hmong in hopes of retaining their Southeast Asian colonial empire. Trinquier had told McCoy, "To have the Hmong, one must buy their opium."[27]

McCoy reasoned that the drug trade flourished throughout the Golden Triangle because of America's support for regimes of "total corruption." During the 1950s in Thailand, the United States forged an alliance with Marshall Sarit Thanarat, a cousin to Phoumi Nosavan and a ruthless dictator by almost all accounts, who amassed the huge sum of three billion baht, more than $90 million by today's exchange rate—largely through the opium trade. Sarit was reputed to have had his own opium warehouse where merchants and distributors stored and delivered the drug. General Phao Sriyanon was also notorious in using his control of the regional drug traffic to finance a repressive state policing apparatus and had a close relationship with U.S. intelligence operatives.[28] Following Sarit's death in 1963, the United States allied with Prime Minister Thanom Kittikachorn, whose son Colonel Narong Kittikachorn allegedly headed a nationwide trafficking network along with Phao's successor, Colonel Pramual Vanigbandhu. During this period, the Thai ruling elite greatly benefited from a massive injection of U.S. technical aid, which had helped to "modernize" the drug industry and heighten its efficiency. McCoy wrote, "Modern aircraft replaced mules, naval vessels displaced sampans and well trained military organizations expropriated the traffic from bands of mountain traders."[29]

In South Vietnam, McCoy asserted that Ky and President Nguyen Van Thieu had engaged in a rivalry for control of drug trafficking proceeds, which he estimated at upward of $88 million per year. In the end Thieu won out and purged most of Ky's inner circle. He then ran the country through his own crooked advisers, including Dang Vang Quang, an important CIA "asset" whom McCoy referred to as "the biggest heroin pusher in the world." By the time of Thieu's accession, Tan Son Nhut airport had become what McCoy, quoting the *New York Times*, referred to as a "drug smuggler's paradise," where customs officials were "little more than lackeys to the smugglers" and as "crooked as a dog's hind leg." The ARVN was also deeply corrupt and regularly supplied American troops with high-grade Laotian heroin. One soldier told him, "How do we get the stuff? Just go over there and rap with the ARVN. I look for officers and have even gotten some from as high as captain."[30]

As these comments reveal, the corruption of American governmental allies was open knowledge to most U.S. personnel stationed in Vietnam, even though McCoy's charges today remain a source of continued public controversy. Through extensive interviews and analysis of secret documents, McCoy unearthed a great deal of firsthand evidence implicating high-ranking Vietnamese officials and pointing to a governmental cover-up. His vigorous research provided definitive proof that the rumors circulating around *Ramparts* were no mirage and that the United States and its Cold War proxies bore responsibility for providing U.S. troops with drugs and contributing to the growth of the Southeast Asian heroin industry.

"Vang Pao Made Millions"
Fresh Revelations Confirming McCoy's Charges

McCoy's study, rightfully considered a classic in the field of international narcotic control and "masterpiece of investigative scholarship," has been corroborated by a solid mountain of evidence that has emerged publicly over time.[31] In 1972 an internal CIA study expressed "concern" that "local officials [with] whom we are in contact have been or may still be involved in one way or another in the drug business." The report concluded, "What to do about these people is a particularly troublesome problem in view of its implications for some of our operations, particularly in Laos." Previously, United States Agency of International Development (USAID) agricultural specialist Edgar "Pop" Buell disclosed that he had assisted Hmong farmers in growing opium, which he rationalized as being little different from the cultivation of tobacco in his home state of Indiana.[32] In 1977, Douglas Blaufarb, CIA station chief in Laos during the early 1960s, conceded in his memoirs that "without a doubt" Air America planes transported opium, that the agency turned a "blind eye" to the involvement of the Hmong, and that he was aware of some Americans who took advantage of the opportunity afforded by the availability of both opium and transport. Other former operatives have gone on record confirming that Air America "hauled a lot of dope" and that the CIA and State Department did not give a "rat's ass about smuggling," and took elaborate measures to protect local "assets" from investigation or prosecution, as they had done with Cuban Bay of Pigs veterans linked to the drug traffic and mafia in Miami.[33]

According to insider sources, Vang Pao, head of the CIA's Hmong guerrilla army, ran a drug pipeline with international connections and kept a stash of opium underneath his house for emergency funding and to ensure the patronage of his subordinates.[34] In 1988, legendary CIA agent Anthony Poshepny (aka Tony Poe)—best known for issuing bounties for cut-off enemy ears—told a PBS interviewer that General Vang had made "millions" from the drug traffic. He later admitted to journalist Roger Warner that he had overseen the cultivation of opium and its shipment on civilian cargo aircraft from landing strips built near General Vang's jungle base at Long Tien with CIA and USAID funds. "You could have a war against Communism or a war against drugs," he told Warner, "but you couldn't have both."[35]

U.S. officials stationed in Vietnam made similarly candid revelations. In 1991, Orin DeForest, former chief interrogator for the CIA, published a book in which he stated that "South Vietnamese military and political bigwigs" and their wives "looted the country ruthlessly" and "deposited huge amounts of piasters (Vietnamese currency) in Hong Kong bank accounts," some of which came "from drug sales." In 1974, Father Tran Huu Thanh had led an anticorruption movement in South Vietnam which uncovered the protection provided by President Thieu and Premier Khiem for "intimate friends of theirs" who smuggled drugs into South Vietnam and distributed them to Chinese criminal syndicates. A former high-level South Vietnamese official admitted publicly that the same was true of Diem and his CIA advisers.[36]

Journalist Stanley Karnow wrote in his epic 1983 history of Vietnam that the U.S. mission had thwarted "periodic efforts by American narcotic agents to smash the elaborate smuggling networks in South Vietnam" because a crackdown would have "exposed nearly every prominent member of the Saigon regime." Douglas Valentine, for his 2004 book *The Strength of the Wolf: The Secret History of America's War on Drugs*, interviewed former FBN agents stationed in Southeast Asia who asserted that the principal target of their investigations were high-ranking South Vietnamese, Laotian, and Thai military generals with close ties to American intelligence operatives. Told by the State Department to keep this information secret, they had been prevented from making any arrests. The agents also spoke about widespread police corruption and voiced suspicion about the direct involvement of American military officers thought to be working for the CIA in the regional drug traffic, including a major named Stanley Hobbes, who received a mere $3,000 fine after being caught smuggling fifty-seven pounds of opium on an Air America plane.[37]

Internal FBN, military, and State Department memoranda, mostly on record at the National Archives in College Park, Maryland, provide further verification that the U.S. government actively covered up the participation of its allies in the narcotics trade. The CID, for example, possessed a long file on major general Ngo Dzu, which U.S. military and governmental officials kept secret—until he became a scapegoat for the corruption in Thieu's government and the files were leaked to the press.[38] The CID had information on several additional high-ranking Government of South Vietnam (GVN) officials, which remained classified, and frequently investigated ARVN personnel for selling drugs. In October 1964 an FBN cable to the State Department documented that General Ouane was a primary shareholder in Air Vientiane, a subsidiary of Air America, which was being used to smuggle opium into neighboring Thailand and South Vietnam. An internal survey undertaken by the USAID's Office of Public Safety further found that Lao police under the control of CIA "asset" Phoumi Nosavan "organized vice and the considerable traffic in smuggling into Thailand" as a means of raising money for the carrying out of a wave of repression against political opponents, including mass jailing and executions.[39]

Despite publicly blaming Red China for exporting drugs as a weapon of subversion, FBN chief Anslinger privately conceded that corruption among America's Thai allies was so pervasive that "it comes out of the ears."[40] FBN agent Wayland Speer related in a subsequent communiqué to Anslinger that the State Department in Laos kept a hands-off policy regarding narcotics, because prosecution of top governmental allies would give off "bad publicity." Speer stated, "For Americans to condone or partially close their eyes to bringing the problem out in the open is disappointing."[41] In another frank memo, American consul to Thailand William B. Hussey urged Ambassador Ural Alexis Johnson and the State Department not to press for any counternarcotics enforcement measures in the Golden Triangle, in order to protect their political relationships. From every available indication, Johnson complied. Hussey commented: "With the involvement of the GMD irregulars on the border areas of Burma and Laos and much of the wealth of principal figures from Field Marshall Sarit [Thanarat] down the line based on the sale of opium, tampering by the outside world with this commodity, evil as it may be, would prove politically undesirable. It would result in at minimum severe lip service and at maximum an adoption of an anti-Western posture and strengthening of ties to the East which is not bothered by a moral standard."[42]

Besides a sense of self-righteousness, these observations demonstrate that geopolitical considerations were paramount in shaping American foreign policy in Southeast Asia, which was centered on stopping local insurgencies and the spread of Communism—at whatever the human cost. There is some archival evidence implicating American personnel in the drug traffic. As recently declassified CIA documents reveal, in several cases the BNDD collaborated with the army's CID in arresting U.S.-born Air America employees affiliated with the secret mission in Laos—including two stings in which they seized over eighty kilograms of opium at Tan Son Nhut airport. The employees were later released without trial.[43] One earlier FBN report made specific mention of an American named Willis H. Bird, who worked for a Thai company called Sea Supply, which was later exposed as a CIA front for the training of paramilitary troops along the Laotian border. Bird was suspected of trafficking drugs in cahoots with U.S. governmental allies in order to finance clandestine political operations and attempts to roll back the spread of Communism.[44] Although the truth about the extent to which opium was used to support U.S. foreign policy in Southeast Asia may never be fully known, archival documentation, new anecdotal evidence, and eyewitness testimony confirm that McCoy and his colleagues were far closer to the truth than official government spokesmen, who publicly denied any involvement with drugs while the war was still going on (though privately conceding that the charges were true). However politically motivated the research, the "CIA Dope Calypso" was rooted in fact—like many other biting claims of the antiwar movement.

"Into the Garbage Can of History"
McCoy's Politics and the Politics of Heroin

Apart from proving its controversial thesis and exposing the deep-rooted corruption of American-backed regimes, McCoy's work stands out most for its sociological and political implications. For those aware of the history of the drug traffic in Southeast Asia, the bulk of his findings were unsurprising. Since its spread in nineteenth-century China under the Q'ing Dynasty, opium cultivation was an important economic staple in Southeast Asia, especially for indigenous farmers in the poppy-rich Golden Triangle region, and its use a socially accepted cultural practice.

Because of high demand and the relative ease with which it could be produced, the opium poppy underwrote most military activity in Southeast Asia during the era of rapid social transformation and upheaval following World War II, and it was often exploited by competing sides of conflict.[45] The Office of Strategic Services (OSS) had previously supported Kachin Rangers in Burma who sold opium as a means of funding counterguerrilla operations against Japan. Colonel William R. Peers and Dean Brelis of OSS Detachment 101 wrote: "Our decision to use opium was based on the fact that it would give our troops a certain amount of freedom and buying power. We did not question it as unjust . . . opium was a form of payment there that everybody used. Not to use it as barter would spell an end to our operations.[46] A similar logic prevailed during the Cold War. Duan Xiwen of the Fifth Regiment GMD stationed in Burma commented in March 1967, "We have to continue to fight the evils of Communism, and to fight you must have an army, and an army must have guns, and to buy guns you must have money. In these mountains, the only money is opium." Anthropologist David Feingold, an expert on Southeast Asian culture, added in an essay published three years later: "The French, the Chinese, the Vietnamese north and south, the rightist, neutralist and leftist Lao have all traded and fought over opium. Why should we be any different?"[47]

The tone of McCoy's book ultimately overshadowed its more sustained scholarly insight into the sociopolitical importance of the opium trade in Southeast Asia.[48] Although it does delve into the history of French involvement and its antecedents, McCoy—who served as the national director of the antiwar and antiimperialist CCAS—was bent on tarnishing the prestige of the U.S. government by equating the dirtying of its hands in the narcotics traffic with the depravity of the war.[49] One former CIA agent, who acknowledged the validity of much of his research, told investigative journalist Seymour Hersh that McCoy "is a very liberal kid, and he'd like to nail the establishment." In order to prove a political point, as he would concede in later editions of his book, McCoy exaggerated the scope of military drug abuse. He wrote hyperbolically, "Once large quantities of heroin became available, heroin addiction spread like a plague. Base after base was overrun by these ant-armies of heroin pushers with their identical plastic vials."[50] McCoy added,

World War I produced a lost generation of writers, poets and artists, World War II gave us a generation of collegians and suburbanites. The Vietnam War seems to be fathering a generation of junkies. . . . It will probably be a long time before the memory of the Vietnam heroin epidemic can take its richly deserved place in the garbage can of history, for returning GI addicts have come home as carriers of the disease, and are afflicting hundreds of communities with the heroin virus, spawning a crime wave that has turned America's inner cities into concrete jungles.[51]

Striking features of McCoy's writing were his powerful language and adoption of lurid disease metaphors reminiscent of the worst antidrug scare campaigns of the past. A 1972 *Harper's* article carrying an excerpt from his book characteristically referred to opium as a "flower of evil." One interesting parallel is with Karl Marx, who decried the "free-trade in poison" carried out by British imperialists in China.[52] Stripping addicts of any human agency, McCoy failed to articulate the motives of GIs in turning to drugs and instead portrayed the outgrowth of drug abuse in Vietnam as the inevitable byproduct of CIA manipulation. He actually criticized social environmentalists such as Norman Zinberg for neglecting supply-side variables and focusing on the crisis of morale, which he stated emerged in 1968 after Tet, three years before the onset of heroin abuse. McCoy consequently helped to create the impression that a monolithic network of international traffickers, aided and abetted by the U.S. government, was threatening to destroy American society from within.

This depiction was ultimately little different from that of right-wing conspiracy theorists and government officials who charged that the influx of drugs in America was part of a Communist-devised plot to weaken the nation.[53] The only difference was that in his case, American-inspired duplicity had supplanted Communist evil. McCoy was more on the mark, but both portrayals served to overinflate the scope of addiction and its impact in exacerbating urban crime and jeopardizing national security. They also both placed singular fault with international drug-trafficking conspiracies—which one McCoy reviewer termed a "world-wide octopus of evil"—while ignoring the important underlying socioenvironmental determinants shaping drug usage patterns in both Vietnam and the United States.[54]

"A Black Sheep Gone Astray?"
Raising the Political Stakes of the Drug Issue
Not surprisingly, given its explosive content, McCoy's book aroused bitter acrimony in the government. During his testimony before the Senate Foreign Relations Committee, Gale McGee (D-Wyo.) accused McCoy

of manipulating evidence and engaging in a "McCarthyite witch-hunt" against American political officials. Holding a doctorate in political science himself, Senator McGee facetiously called the author "candidate McCoy," referring to the fact that he had not yet obtained his Ph.D., and told him that an academic committee would have ripped his argument apart. Prior to its publication, the CIA sent lawyer Cord Meyer Jr. to Harper & Row offices to see galley proofs of the book and to offer revisions, which one editor described as "laughable."[55]

Though internally judging the book to be "solidly researched and elaborately documented," as a recently declassified study reveals, the agency went even further in threatening several of his key sources, including a Hmong chief, Ger Yu Sang, who told him that rice aid had been withheld from his village after he refused to send more troops to their clandestine army to be killed, and a Green Beret soldier living in California who had chemicals sprayed into his car as a warning.[56] The CIA additionally conducted an investigation into McCoy's background and the source of his scholarship funding at Yale through the Internal Revenue Service and kept a file on media coverage of the book.[57] CIA bureaucrats wrote several letters to newspapers and issued a rebuttal, which was printed in the October 1972 issue of *Harper's*. In it the agency director, Richard Helms, proclaimed, "It is arrant nonsense that the CIA is somehow involved in the world drug traffic. As fathers, we are as concerned about the lives of our children and grandchildren as the rest of you. As an agency, we are in fact heavily engaged in tracing the foreign roots of the drug traffic." (Ironically, decades later, in an official publication, the CIA admitted to its role in the heroin traffic, which it claimed was "an inadvertent but inevitable consequence of its cold war tactics.")[58]

McCoy's book created the greatest ripple in the State Department. Secretary of State William Rodgers and Nelson Gross, coordinator for international narcotics matters (who was later indicted for tax evasion) wrote to the Foreign Relations Committee claiming that McCoy's charges were "outdated" and that a mere 10 percent of heroin flowing into the United States originated in Southeast Asia.[59] The American embassy in Thailand subsequently circulated a paper stating that even though General Phao "deserved his poor reputation" and "used his position to appropriate vehicles for nefarious activities (i.e., the drug traffic)," Marshal Sarit and his successors were not in favor of "opium profiteering to pay bonuses" and could not be blamed for individual cases of corruption, nor could U.S. officials who did not exercise complete control over items of equipment delivered. The authors added that the Thai were doing their best to police the rugged border with Burma and promote alternative economic activities among the "primitive minority" of hill tribesmen who grew opium and served as a barrier to broader modernization efforts.[60]

The U.S. ambassador to Laos, G. McMurtrie Godley (1969–1974), was irked most by McCoy's book. In a secret memo to Rodgers he wrote, "In deference to the power of the printed word, I will restrain my language, but to get the obvious off my chest, McCoy is a knee-jerk opponent of the U.S. who will use any argument that he can to discredit our foreign policy. It grieves me that he is conducting his propaganda under the auspices of a fine university, Yale. This little black sheep has gone astray." Godley urged Laotian leaders to refute the charges of complicity in the international drug trade.[61] Two days after McCoy's foreign relations testimony, Vang Pao travelled to Washington and gave a public address proclaiming his innocence, despite his having been arrested on smuggling charges in 1963.[62] The former Royal Lao Government (RLG) prime minister Phoui Sananikone, who had been put in power in a CIA-backed coup after the Communist Pathet Lao won a large percentage of seats in the 1958 elections, did the same. Referring to Browning and Garrett's "New Opium War" article in *Ramparts*, of which he had been given a copy, Sananikone declared that while he did not claim to "be perfect," trafficking in narcotics was "not one of his sins." He added that nobody in his family was involved with drugs, though "my family is big and I cannot answer for every last cousin."[63]

Sananikone's remarks, coupled with the CIA's and the State Department's heated rebuttals, testified to the deep political impact of McCoy's book, which sent governmental officials on both sides of the Pacific into a tizzy trying to protect their public reputation. McCoy and the antiwar left ultimately succeeded in utilizing the drug issue to their political advantage and to help breed added public skepticism about the war. They further helped to raise the political stakes of the War on Drugs, which emerged as a key dimension of Nixon's foreign policy, in part to deflect the charges of governmental complicity.

"When Johnny Comes Nodding Home"
Heroin—Tool of the Brass?

By the time McCoy's book was published, the "CIA Dope Calypso" had become a cause célèbre in the antiwar movement. In March 1972 the satirical *MAD* magazine—which had been a persistent critic of the war—pictured on its cover a returning soldier holding a huge needle. The headline read, "When Johnny Comes Marching Home!" Some radicals claimed that the CIA-drugs nexus was a Pentagon plot to stifle social and military dissent. In its July 1971 issue, *The Bond,* an underground newspaper run by antiwar veterans in Berkeley, California, claimed that American soldiers "fighting a criminal war on behalf of wealthy American elites" had been targeted by a conspiratorial network of international traffickers led by the CIA. "The heroin monster has been used as an instrument of the brass and their partners in crime against all oppressed people," author Terry Klug wrote. "The struggle for our rights is also a struggle against the poison they've been filling our veins with in order to keep us down." In its March 19, 1971, issue, *The Bond* published "Heroin: Government Issued?" which pointed to the corruption of top Vietnamese officials in what it termed a "murderous trade." The authors editorialized, "The brass and the moneymen no more want drugs out of Vietnam than they want drugs out of the ghetto. They realize that if the flow of drugs was stopped, all the apathetic stoned GI's would become straight and start looking around to see if they could improve their situation and the atmosphere of death and impending doom."[64]

In 1972, Richard Kunnes, a radical psychiatrist at the University of Michigan, argued in *The American Heroin Empire* that the United States controlled a major heroin empire, replete with "colonies and client states," which served as a microcosm of America's broader imperial dominion. According to Kunnes, American foreign policy was motivated by a desire to expand this empire by incorporating more and more client states, such as Thailand, Laos, and South Vietnam, whose leaders were responsible for supplying "white poison" throughout its fiefdom. In sinister fashion, U.S. leaders worked to ensure the preservation of oppressive social conditions in its colonies, guaranteeing that its subjects would turn to drugs out of despair and become incapable of resisting the mother country's growing imperial hegemony. To bolster his thesis, Kunnes overstated the scope of addiction and its domestic ravages. He claimed that Nguyen Cao Ky operated a brothel-massage-dope complex at An Khe, where GIs could get oral sex and opium for under one dollar, and he profiled a former Purple Heart winner who professed to have relied on his "escape and evasion" training in pulling off fifty successful burglaries to fund his heroin habit. Kunnes also wrote about a crime epidemic in local VA centers where addicts were stealing money from "helpless geriatric patients." He concluded, "As the use of heroin increases in Vietnam and elsewhere, the old war slogans change. It's now when Johnny comes nodding home."[65]

Black Power advocates were among the most vocal in invoking conspiracy theories. They argued that the CIA supported drug traffickers in order to pacify African American soldiers serving as "cannon fodder" and "mercenaries," as Stokely Carmichael (later Kwame Toure) put it, in a "racist, colonialist, honky war."[66] Edward Frazier, an African American soldier, commented, "I have seen the white ghost [as in heroin] turn our black brothers in Vietnam into everything but the new black man." Michael Cetewayo Tabor, a member of the Black Panther Party (BPP), which supported the armed mobilization of blacks to advance the cause of social justice, described heroin as a "poisonous and lethal powdery substance" sold by "depraved money crazy beasts" to black youth as a means of making them "oblivious" to the "abject poverty, disease and degradation that engulfs them in their daily existence." Accusing the government of promoting a form of "cultural genocide" through drugs, he stated, "The plague profiteers threaten to devour an entire generation of our youth." Dr. Michael Rossman, a radical sociologist at the University of California, Berkeley, further proclaimed, "The effect of all this injection of heroin is that the ghetto's people's energies become absorbed internally, turned against itself, undermining all revolutionary impulses against the external colonizing forces and the social conditions they have created."[67]

Rev. James Fracek, who held links to the BPP chapter in Detroit, claimed that the CIA became immersed in the Southeast Asian drug traffic right after that city's notorious 1967 riot, when African Americans had taken up arms against the police. "If you want to control people's minds, it is quite convenient to have them dependent on drugs. . . . Our military involvement in Indochina is as much for the sake of heroin as for tungsten and oil. There is considerable evidence to suggest that heroin is being imported and used by the government [from Indochina] as an instrument of social control in the ghetto." Fracek went on to draw a historical analogy with European colonial exploitation and British foreign policy toward China in the nineteenth century. In both cases, according to his interpretation, the colonial power used social intoxicants as a tool to extend social, economic, political, and cultural domination. In the case of China, Fracek argued, the people rebelled, resulting in the first Opium War, when "the white man declared war on someone who objected to being narcoticized." The same process appeared to be repeating itself in the United States, where black efforts to resist the spread of addiction were being met with renewed force in the form of heightened ghetto policing. Inspired by the writings of Franz Fanon, who argued that violence served as a "cleansing force" for subjugated peoples across the globe, Fracek called on blacks to fight a new Opium War, which this time he felt they could win.[68]

Fracek was far from unique in his views, or in exaggerating the devastation wrought by drugs in order to promote an antiestablishment ideology. The *Black Panther* newspaper, for example, referred to drugs as "poisonous substances" and "evil" and endorsed a strict crackdown against drug dealers, who were portrayed as "lackeys" of the white ruling class.[69] Prominent Chicano nationalists echoed Black Power radicals in portraying drugs as an agent of white "bourgeois" social control. In July 1971, three activists known as Los Tres were arrested for assaulting an undercover narcotics agent, who they thought was peddling drugs in the Pico Gardens housing project in Los Angeles. Outraged by the arrests, activists formed a Committee to Free Los Tres. In a public statement the group made reference to McCoy's writings and proclaimed, "The cultivation of opium, its refinement into heroin and its transportation to the United States have been proven to have the active involvement and assistance of the federal government through the CIA." They added, "Heroin is a major element of America's foreign and domestic policy. [America] is promoting the insidious crime of drug addiction among the people and in the process killing any kind of social consciousness in the Chicano community and subjecting its residents to colonialism, degradation and exploitation."[70] While making many valid points, the above comments typify the vilification of drugs by radical groups, partially for political effect. The rhetoric employed is most interesting and helped to fan the flames of the antidrug hysteria engulfing the country in communities ultimately most affected by the implementation of the War on Drugs.

"The War Is Not Worth a Single Drug-Addicted American"
The Democrats and the Myth

Like the radical left, the Democratic Party was a major force in raising public fear over the spread of addiction and promoting new antidrug legislation, largely because of the crisis in Vietnam. Through the 1960s, most leading Democrats condemned the use of drugs by the student counterculture and advocated liberal reform measures, including educational awareness and treatment programs. They became more strident in maligning drugs in the early 1970s as a result of the CIA connection. This was especially true of leading Democratic "doves" who viewed the addiction crisis as a symbol of misguided governmental policies and the need for withdrawal from the war. Chief among them was 1972 presidential candidate George S. McGovern, who had sponsored several bills, dating back to 1965, calling for the withdrawal of American troops.

A historian by training, McGovern expressed sympathy for the long-standing Vietnamese struggle for self-determination and argued that contrary to popular belief, Ho Chi Minh was no stooge of Moscow but rather a nationalist patriot who had helped to liberate the country from the yoke of Japanese and French imperialism. McGovern believed that America's ill-fated intervention in Vietnam represented a breech of Vietnamese demands for national sovereignty and a violation of the 1954 Geneva Convention. It also served in his view as a betrayal of American ideals of freedom and democracy, particularly in light of the corrupt and brutal nature of successive U.S.-supported regimes in Saigon, which he felt "were not worth the blood of a single American boy." McGovern called the Vietnam conflict the "cruelest and stupidest war in the nation's history," and Nixon's aerial bombardment campaign "the most barbaric action undertaken by any country since Hitler's efforts to exterminate the Jews in Germany during the 1930s and 40s." He added, "I'm tired of old men dreaming up wars for young men to die in, particularly wars of this kind that add nothing to our security."[71]

On September 18, 1972, before a televised audience, McGovern called the War on Drugs a "casualty of the war in Indo-China." He told aides privately that he wanted this charge to "pack a political punch" and went on to say, "Our allies in Laos, Thailand, and South Vietnam are involved in the narcotics trade. The Administration does not crack down on them because it needs air bases in Thailand, Lao mercenaries, and Vietnamese soldiers to fight its war." According to McGovern, America's foreign entanglement was coming back to haunt the nation through the addiction of American soldiers—100,000 of whom, he claimed, used drugs: "I challenge you to explain how the North Vietnamese are a greater threat to our national security than the crime, violence and internal decay caused by narcotics?" He ended the speech with a call to end the war and expand existing drug interdiction campaigns. He stated, "The next president can act to end the war and crack down on the supply of heroin from Southeast Asia. This is the fight America should be pursuing. This is the fight as President, I intend to win."[72]

McGovern was not alone in using the drug issue to promote unilateral withdrawal from the war—and to attack Nixon's drug policy. In a 1971 speech before Congress supporting the McGovern-Hatfield amendment advocating the removal of U.S. troops, the former Diem supporter turned dove, Mike Mansfield (D-Mont.), read aloud a *New York Times* article by Flora Lewis on GIs and heroin, which he termed "chilling."[73] In July 1972, Senator William Proxmire of Wisconsin voiced a similar opinion before Congress, stating, "The drug problem alone is sufficient reason to get us out. The war in Southeast Asia is not worth a single drug-addicted American." In a speech before the New Hampshire Bar Association, Senator Edmund Muskie of Maine further exclaimed, "If it is in the interest of our national security to save the people of Southeast Asia from Communism, it is certainly in our national interest to save our own citizens from the devastation of heroin addiction. The first step for the United States must be to pull our troops out of Southeast Asia by the end of this year."[74]

In promoting a dual anti–Vietnam War, pro-drug-war message, Democrats were often at the forefront in pushing for the internationalization of the War on Drugs. Frank Church (D-Idaho), Walter "Fritz" Mondale (D-Minn.), and Howard E. Hughes (D-Iowa) promoted a $20–25 million increase in funding for international drug interdiction efforts—particularly in Southeast Asia. Senator Hubert H. Humphrey (D-Minn.), the former vice president under Lyndon B. Johnson, stated, "It is time we made known to our friends around the world that we will not permit the cultivation and export of a poison that destroys the lives of hundreds of thousands of Americans and which is responsible for a substantial proportion of American crime. . . . We will find the dope smuggler and put him out of business."[75] Lester Wolff (D-N.Y.), Morgan Murphy (D-Ill.), and Claude Pepper (D-Fla.) urged the repeal of all aid to regimes deemed to be uncooperative in international drug suppression efforts, including South Vietnam, Laos, and Thailand. Calling drug abuse a "Frankenstein-type monster over which we have no control," Pepper fumed, "These governments are *prostituting, perverting our own men who we send over there to help them* and they are sending a stream of opium to contaminate our citizenry back to this country." He added, "In Vietnam soldiers have the benefits of every conceivable technological device of war so sophisticated that they existed only in science fiction novels a few years ago—we seem incapable, however, of helping those very same soldiers from becoming enslaved in a vicious trap of addiction. The Nixon administration and DOD has not assumed the proper burden and this must change."[76]

Promoting myths of national virtuosity even in an antiwar cause and blaming the South Vietnamese government for corrupting ostensibly innocent American boys, Democratic representatives frequently surpassed the media in overdramatization. The tone of their rhetoric was also in many cases more foreboding. In a 1971 speech, Congressman Alan Cranston of California likened the drug crisis in Vietnam to an "infectious disease" capable of engendering "far greater destruction than the war in Southeast Asia itself." Senator John McLellan (D-Ark.) stated that drugs represented an "insidious and deadly enemy" in Vietnam and equally "potent killer to Vietcong bullets." Lester Wolff, who headed a major congressional fact-finding mission on the international narcotics traffic, added that drugs were "more dangerous than an army of murderers because they threaten the American way of life and the American future." Senator Muskie, who, along with Abraham Ribicoff (D-Conn.), had issued a press release demanding Republican accountability for CIA activities, further exclaimed, "The nefarious heroin traffic is infesting our servicemen in Southeast Asia and destroying our cities and towns. Thousands of veterans exposed to heroin in Vietnam are now carrying a horrible curse home. An 'evil white powder' or what Stewart Alsop calls 'the city killer' has invaded our community from the larger world and threatens our children's safety."[77]

Through using such terms as "nefarious," "plague," and "evil white powder," the Democrats helped to demonize drugs, while sidestepping broader debate about the ideological underpinnings of American policy and its consequences for the Vietnamese. Charles Rangel, an African American representative from Harlem, was characteristic in these regards. He likened the import of drugs from Southeast Asia to "an invasion of our shores producing casualties as surely and as horribly as any bullet or bomb." In speaking before Congress, he added, "The problem in a nutshell is that drugs are threatening to kill our cities. New York City is already dying of a malignancy. Other cities are on the death list, but Harlem, which I think reflects what is in store for the rest of the nation, is in the terminal stage." Rangel spoke further about the damaging effects of drugs on the nation's youth in inner-city communities: "In Harlem, young girls shoot up in the locker room, while thirteen year olds buy dope from eighteen year old peddlers. The hope of the black nation used to be that a mom would pray that her son finished high school. Now, she dare not admit her worst fears; that her son's corpse will be found on some rooftop, a needle sticking from his arm."[78]

Rangel stressed that CIA complicity was a root cause of the crisis. In 1972 he invited Secretary of Defense Melvin Laird and CIA Director Richard Helms to testify before a select Senate subcommittee hearing on drug abuse. When both refused, Rangel demanded access to intelligence reports on heroin trafficking in Southeast Asia, which he was further denied. In a public statement widely broadcast in the mass media, Rangel charged the Nixon administration with "bureaucratic bungling" and a "paranoid quest for secrecy," which "helped to cover up for international merchants of death" who flourished at the expense of "black children's lives."[79] While there was truth to his emphasis on the CIA's complicity and the adverse impact of drug abuse on people of color, Rangel's comments were ridden with hyperbole. They helped to enhance mythologies about the monolithic character of drugs in shaping the breakdown of American inner cities such as Harlem, a breakdown in fact equally contingent on structural variables, governmental neglect, and the persistence of poverty amid plenty.[80]

Rangel and his colleagues were ultimately influential in promoting antiwar sentiment, albeit on narrow nationalist grounds. By the early 1970s, elected officials on both sides of the aisle were predicting that Nixon would be forced to withdraw the troops in order to alleviate public concerns about the crisis of the addicted army. In a telling sign of the effect of all the media and political sensationalism and propaganda, Seymour Halpern commented in June 1971 that he was "convinced the American people are more turned off on this war because of the drug problem than for any other reason. They have more fear of their sons becoming drug addicts than being shot. This is reflected by so many parents who come to me as Congressman, who emphasize fears of their youngsters becoming addicts."[81] Senator Jacob R. Javits (R-N.Y.) added that the drug abuse crisis "is the kind of situation that can change everything. The American people can get so fed up that troops will be out of there faster than McGovern, Hatfield, or anyone else ever dreamed up, regardless of consequence. We'll be out of there so fast it'll make people's heads swim."[82] Robert H. Steele (R-Conn.) further stated, "The heroin problem, as it has been revealed, sent an electric shock wave through this country. It will do more to speed up the end of the American involvement in this war than all other demonstrations and all the speeches and all the resolutions we have seen so far."[83]

Indeed, by January 1972, public opinion polls showed that over 75 percent of the country supported withdrawal.[84] Although the degree to which these totals could be linked to the drug panic remains uncertain, the Democratic Party and the antiwar movement proved successful in exploiting it to serve their own political ends. In doing so, they helped to create a ripe climate for the expansion of the federal drug war, to which

Nixon and the Republicans were forced to respond, while ensuring that the human costs of the war for the Vietnamese would remain marginalized in public discourse.

Contrary to the claims of scholars who suggest that the War on Drugs was solely driven by the conservative New Right, the Democratic Party and the antiwar left helped to promote the myth of the addicted army and bolstered public demand for antidrug legislation—lest the country be subsumed by drug-addicted and crime-prone veterans ready to tear up the streets for their next fix. In a 1971 *New York Times* column, James Reston commented, "Both parties, all factions for and against the Nixon policy of 'winding down the war' agree on the human tragedy of drug addiction among the soldiers in Vietnam and the dangers of sending them back home before they are cured." Writing from a different perspective in *Ceremonial Chemistry*, Thomas Szasz observed, "In contrast to the War in Vietnam, which has been condemned by countless Americans and by even more non-Americans, the War on Drugs in Asia (and elsewhere) has received nothing but praise and support. I am not aware of any political party or group having denounced on principle this brutal—and both morally and medically quite unjustifiable—invasion of other people's rights to grow poppy and use opium."[85] Both Reston and Szasz were correct in highlighting the near universal appeal of the federal drug war, which faced minimal societal dissent (apart from that of psychiatrists), in spite of its abuses. The liberal left played a major role in ensuring this trend.[86] While equating drugs with the immoral quality of the war and exposing CIA support for regional drug lords, they helped to demonize drug use and transformed the image of American GIs into that of a victim in the public eye. They further contributed to the process by which public repudiation of the war resulted primarily from its effects on Americans, while playing into the conservative agenda by raising fears about drugs and predominantly supporting the expansion of the War on Drugs.

THE BRASS RESPONDS, PART I
NIXON'S WAR ON DRUGS

In declaring total war against dangerous drugs, our goal is the unconditional surrender of the merchants of death who traffic in heroin. Our goal is the total banishment of drug abuse from American life. —Richard M. Nixon, 1972

It was striking that a federal executive branch dominated by a hard-line lock 'em up and throw away the key attitude turned to a group of reform minded, generally liberal medical experts to handle one of the most politically sensitive issues facing the country at the time. —Dr. Robert L. DuPont, 1978

By the early 1970s, thanks to the spread of misinformation and hyperbole, the myth of the addicted army had become firmly embedded in the American popular consciousness. Former FBN agent John Finlator captured the prevailing mood in comparing the threat of heroin to barbarians menacing the Roman Empire during the fifth and sixth centuries. In a book aptly titled *The Drugged Nation*, he wrote, "The junkman has descended on us like the Vandals upon Rome . . . assaulting an unsuspecting and unprepared people." In *The Stoned Age*, journalist John Rublowsky further proclaimed, "There is panic in the streets that radiates out from our cities. It is as though a new plague has been turned loose on the land. No one is safe. It strikes the rich and the poor, black and white, the city and the country. The specter of drug addiction—the fifth horseman of the Apocalypse—casts a shadow that darkens the lives of all Americans everywhere."[1]

The Nixon administration proved responsive to the sweeping hysteria surrounding drugs. Seeking to discredit liberal social ideologies and eradicate public anxieties over Vietnam, Nixon enacted what was at the time the most expansive antidrug campaign in American history. Building on the precedent set by former FBN chief Harry J. Anslinger, who had similarly inflated the scope of drug abuse to serve political ends, he dramatically increased domestic and international enforcement, leading to a marked increase in imprisonment rates. Despite his "lock 'em up and throw away the key" rhetoric, Nixon also emerged as a major proponent of addiction *treatment*. In June 1971 he hired liberal psychiatrist Jerome H. Jaffe to direct a national rehabilitation program that promoted the use of methadone—a synthetic drug capable of gradually weaning patients off heroin. By the mid-1970s, tens of thousands of addicts were being treated by this method. Through such policies, Nixon was able to portray himself as helping to solve one of society's gravest social crises, as he fed the public mythologies that all the nation's problems—including the horrors of Vietnam—were drug related. In 1975, cabinet member Egil Krogh characterized the drug war policy as a "slam dunk political success."[2] It is difficult to argue with this claim, especially in considering the broader historical context, though in practice Nixon continued to support high-level traffickers and failed to strike a dent in supply rates.

"Those Civilizations Lose Their Spirit"
Drugs and the Conservative Right

The Republicans, to be sure, played an important role in manipulating public opinion and creating the great national drug "scare" of the early 1970s. Discovering an easy scapegoat for deep-seated social problems, they exaggerated the scope of addiction, employing trumped-up rhetoric reminiscent of the Anslinger heyday.[3] Senator Edward Gurney (R-Fla.) characteristically warned that America's "finest men in Vietnam" were becoming "ruined by drugs," which caused "wrecked lives, social deterioration and the potential destruction of our society." Senator Jacob Javits (R-N.Y.) added that 50,000–75,000 addicted veterans, accustomed to the use of weapons, were "being let loose on the streets of our great cities." Nelson Rockefeller, the Republican governor of New York who later served as vice president under Gerald Ford, subsequently proclaimed that "drug addiction represents a threat akin to war in its capacity to kill, enslave and imperil the nation's future. Are the sons and daughters of a generation that survived a Great Depression and rebuilt a prosperous nation that defeated Nazism and Fascism and preserved the free world to be vanquished by a powder, needles and pills?"[4]

Nixon himself provided some of the most inflammatory rhetoric, referring to drug dealers as "slave-traders of the modern era" and "international merchants of death" who should be "hunted to the end of the earth." In a speech delivered in September 1972 he stated that he considered keeping dangerous drugs out of the United States "just as important as armed enemy forces" In perhaps his most sensationalistic address, given before a governors' conference in California, he compared America's fate to nineteenth-century Q'ing China, whose power declined from internal weakness allegedly provoked by the spread of opium. He continued: "Do you think the Russians allow dope? No. It is the enemy of strong societies. . . . When you look at the history of civilization those which turn on a general basis to drugs lose their spirit. They go down. They are destroyed. The question is will it happen to America? There is a national responsibility for the young people of this nation to see that by turning on to drugs they are helping to destroy the national spirit and health."[5]

This analogy reflected Nixon's use of the drug issue to tap into deeply rooted nationalist anxieties surrounding America's declining global status. His rhetoric ironically resembled that of Chinese revolutionary leaders Sun Yat-sen and Mao Zedong, who had exaggerated the ravages of addiction in China because of its status as a symbol of British imperialism and exploitation. In both cases, drugs were cast as imported substances eroding vital societal strength, which needed to be eradicated in order for the nation to reverse course.[6] In the United States, Nixon argued that the spread of drug abuse was symptomatic of a broader crisis provoked by 1960s liberalism, which, in his view, had adopted an overly tolerant or "permissive" attitude toward social deviance, promoting what political scientist Charles Murray would later term a "blame the system" mentality where the onus of responsibility for wrongdoing was placed on society and not on the individual.[7] According to Nixon, this mind-frame helped to inculcate a "decline in respect for public authority and the rule of law," resulting in the spread of drug-inflamed demonstrations, racial rioting, urban crime, and military insubordination. These in turn threatened to render the nation a "pitiful and helpless giant" and "second-rate global power." Nixon commented that during the 1960s "the government napped and the drug scene was tragically and falsely endowed with some sheen of glamour. Now this has become everybody's problem."[8]

Although "viscerally" against drugs, in part as the result of the revulsion he felt toward the counterculture, Nixon and his supporters benefited politically by exaggerating their impact.[9] Turning attention away from the plight of the Vietnamese, attacking drugs aided in their attempts to discredit both liberal governing philosophies and the 1960s social movements, whose far-reaching societal critiques and mobilization

against the war could thus be discarded as the product of a foreign corrupting agent. These attempts were particularly important after efforts to
cast the student left as "Communist infiltrated" and manipulated by Hanoi, Moscow, and Peking had been proved false.[10] Nixon was most egregious in overstating a purported link between drug abuse and the rise in
urban street crime. In public addresses he held addicts responsible for
stealing as much as ten times the value of everything else stolen in the
U.S. over the course of a year.[11] Though statistical manipulation is typical
of most politicians, Nixon inflated drug and crime numbers in a concentrated effort to attract support for his law-and-order campaign, of which
the War on Drugs was a major component. It allowed him and his subordinates, further, to vilify certain groups who could easily be blamed for
America's social ills—including the nation's performance in Indochina—
and thereby to avoid confronting deep-rooted societal inequalities and
injustices, for which they displayed little sensitivity or compassion. They
were also able to advance their agenda of cutting back on Great Society
social programs and restoring what they viewed as traditional values centered on hard work, patriotism, and virtue, which Nixon saw as vital to
America's resurgence from the drug-induced nightmare of the 1960s.[12]

"Different Strokes for Different Folks"
Nixon, Multimodality, and the War on Drugs

Nixon's policy aims had a great deal of resonance, including among
disgruntled middle-class liberals put off by attacks on the perceived integrity of higher education by the student and antiwar movements, and
by the emergence of a new rights-based identity politics that threatened
to empower previously marginalized minority groups while challenging
America's individualist ethic.[13] The proliferation of drug abuse and its
apparent link to the military's collapse in Vietnam was representative for
many, further, of a dangerous erosion of moral values engendered by the
1960s social experiment, which jeopardized the nation's preeminent
global standing. This standing was sacrosanct amid the deep-rooted culture of nationalism and civic pride that had flourished since the end of
World War II.[14]

Inspired by African American jazz culture and the Beat poets, as well
as Timothy Leary, youth of the 1960s from all social classes had experimented with marijuana, LSD, and other drugs as part of a sweeping
generational rebellion.[15] Despite charges of its "liberal bias," the mass
media helped to stigmatize the counterculture by broadcasting its most

extreme dimensions and obfuscating the breadth of its social analysis and criticism. Fitting a longer tradition, drug use was frequently demonized and linked to all kinds of social pathologies and horrors, including an unfounded link to chromosomal damage and psychosis. *Time* magazine was typical in warning in 1966 about a new "disease-epidemic" striking "at the beachside, in beatnik pads, and in the dormitories of expensive prep-schools."[16]

The political backlash began during Lyndon Johnson's presidency. Contrary to Nixon's portrait of a symbiotic relationship with the counterculture, Johnson sponsored congressional investigations into the nature of the "drug threat" and its corrupting influence on American youth, and he increased federal funding for crime control as part of the Great Society. Though stressing treatment for noncriminal addicts, his administration pressed for harsher control measures against the possession and distribution of LSD and did not formally abolish mandatory minimum sentencing laws for traffickers, which had been institutionalized under the 1951 Boggs Act and the 1956 Daniels Act. State legislators at the same time adopted stringent prohibition laws. These were most severe in Texas, where Timothy Leary was sentenced to twenty years in prison for possessing small traces of marijuana while trying to cross the border into Mexico.[17]

Liberal policymakers of the 1960s generally subscribed to the disease model of addiction and gave primacy to public-health solutions for possession offenses.[18] In 1962 the Supreme Court declared in *Robinson v. California* that drug addiction was a disease "comparable to leprosy, insanity and the common cold" and that addicts were "proper subjects for medical treatment."[19] Governor Edmund Brown (D) of California subsequently launched a pioneering civil commitment program that became a model for the national program, in which drug offenders faced a choice between imprisonment and rehabilitation.[20] New York state passed a similar bill one year later, though critics charged that the conditions in state treatment facilities—including the prevalence of barbed wire fences, limited personal freedoms, and armed guards—made them indistinguishable from jails.[21] In 1966, Congress passed the historic Narcotic Addicts Rehabilitation Act, which stipulated that any addict charged with a nonviolent criminal offense could be sent to federally funded rehabilitation centers (or narcotics farms, in popular parlance) in Lexington, Kentucky, or Fort Worth, Texas. These centers, which had been in operation since the mid-1930s, provided drug-aided withdrawals, extensive psychotherapy, and labor projects where inmates were reimbursed with cigarettes. (They also allegedly served as testing grounds for CIA mind-control experiments under Dr. Harris Isbell.)[22]

In one of the great ironies of his presidency, Nixon enacted an unprecedented expansion of the federal treatment apparatus, despite publicly fulminating against liberal social policies. He had come to office riding the wave of a law-and-order slogan, which appealed to so-called middle Americans disillusioned by the specter of student rebellion, urban rioting, and antiwar protest.[23] Because of their symbolic connotation, drug eradication programs came to assume special significance. Nixon first urged greater federal involvement in a July 1969 message before Congress in which he referred to drugs as the "worst sickness in American history," blaming them for "riots in cities, disturbances in colleges and the upsurge in crime reaching unprecedented proportions." In September he initiated a major sting at the Mexican border called Operation Intercept (later aborted because it caused such long customs delays).[24]

The previous February, Nixon had introduced a highly publicized campaign, headed by cabinet appointee Egil Krogh, to crack down on crime in the District of Columbia as a showcase for his law-and-order program. Krogh feared that by arresting more dealers, public authorities were helping to raise the price of heroin, thus causing addicts to commit even more crime.[25] Therefore, at the urging of Dr. Robert DuPont, a graduate of Harvard's medical school who worked with drug abusers in the prison system, he conceived of a program to provide treatment to addicts in order to lessen their inclination to rob and steal.[26] In seeking out models to emulate, Krogh's aide Jeffrey Donfeld was impressed by that of Dr. Jerome H. Jaffe, a pharmacologist at the University of Chicago whose state-sponsored "multimodality" clinic combined methadone treatment with group counseling, psychotherapy, and recreation. Donfeld told Krogh in a private memo that "Dr. Jaffe thinks in broad management terms and is politically sensitive. He is not a dogmatist and believes in trying different strokes for different folks." Recommending that Jaffe be hired to implement a national plan, Donfeld added, "Drug rehabilitation is a virgin yet fertile area for social and political gain."[27]

In January 1970, Congress unanimously passed the Comprehensive Drug Abuse Prevention and Control Act, which increased funding for drug-related research, classified drugs according to their apparent danger, and relegated simple possession offenses to misdemeanor status. It also increased the subpoena powers of the federal government and established a controversial "no-knock" regulation allowing police to conduct warrantless searches if they possessed clear suspicion of illegal activity.[28] Reflecting the bipartisan consensus, Senator Dodd wrote to Senator Muskie, "This is a singular accomplishment in forward-looking law making. Rarely have so many Senators agreed with the opinions of virtually all public and private witnesses of the need for a particular piece of legislation."[29]

Eleven months later, Congress passed the Drug Abuse Education Act, which increased the education budget with a focus on military recruiting centers and high schools. Pointing to the important backdrop of Vietnam in explaining the rationale for the bill, one administrative spokesman pointed out that "the youthful drug abuser of today is the young serviceman tomorrow." Charles "Bud" Wilkinson, a legendary football coach at the University of Oklahoma, was subsequently hired as a special consultant to the president and given the mandate of "deglamorizing drug use."[30] A symbol of bedrock American values, including hard work and patriotism, Wilkinson promoted antidrug curricula and a radio campaign encouraging local disc jockeys to "subtly" counter the spread of the counterculture. He also established a special advertising council and urged television executives to incorporate antidrug plots in their shows.[31] Wilkinson invited Hollywood stars to serve as spokesmen, including Elvis Presley and TV host Art Linkletter, whose daughter Diane had allegedly committed suicide under the influence of LSD. He further enlisted various professional athletes, including Dallas Cowboys quarterback Roger Staubach, who was featured on federally distributed posters under such slogans as "Watch What's Thrown Your Way" and "Lead Your Team in the Right Direction."[32] By promoting clean living through sport, the administration hoped to reinvigorate American youth and strengthen the nation against the ravages of addiction.

"The War Ensured Major Presidential Leadership and Support"
Vietnam and the Expansion of the Medical Drug War

The urgency of Nixon's antidrug agenda was hastened by international developments. Fearful of the mounting insubordination in the armed forces, Henry A. Kissinger, assistant to the president for national security affairs, sent Egil Krogh on a four-day investigative mission to Vietnam in August 1970 along with Secretary of Defense Melvin Laird.[33] Visiting thirteen firebases from the demilitarized zone along the 17th parallel to Bac Lu in the southern tip of the country, the duo witnessed soldiers smoking marijuana and other illegal drugs with great frequency. The boyish-looking Krogh, age thirty-one, was even offered hard drugs by several soldiers who failed to believe that he was a representative of the White House.

Upon return to the United States, Krogh told Nixon, "Mr. President, you don't have a drug problem in Vietnam, you have a condition." He advised Nixon to "more conspicuously associate himself with the War on Drugs" and also to order that military commanders conceal the gravity of the situation from visiting congressional representatives bent on exploiting it for political benefit. In a secret memo to John Ehrlichman—which reflected in part the growing hostility of high-ranking White House officials to domestic political opposition and their growing insecurity about the war—he commented, "My Lai, Con Son and drug abuse are the type of issues which 'radical liberals' will publicize in their efforts to undermine the war. I think the U.S. command in South Vietnam is well aware of these problems created by unlimited disclosure of sensitive, embarrassing information to hostile Congressional types."[34]

In the winter of 1971, Krogh conveyed further alarm about the widespread media attention devoted to the crisis. In a private memorandum he told Donfeld, "The newspaper, magazines and TV have all elaborated the current drug condition. The public is becoming convinced that there is a major problem and we need to take more concerted action." In May, he urged President Nixon to earmark more funding and deliver a televised presidential address vowing to crack down on drug smuggling. In a secret memo, Krogh told Ehrlichman, "The Democrats are beginning to use this issue more and more. We need to take more effective measures, which realistically deal with the problem of drug abuse and develop a mandate for action."[35] Following the release of the hard-hitting Murphy-Steele report, presidential advisers hired a former NBC News reporter, Richard Harkness, as a special public relations representative on the drug issue.[36] Krogh further instructed the State Department and DOD to deny knowledge of the corruption of American allies and to issue a public statement that there were "not sufficient bases to believe that the allegations [outlined in the Murphy-Steele report] were true."[37]

In early June, Nixon received numerous letters from constituents calling for an expansion of federal drug-control initiatives. One correspondent told Nixon that unless concerted action was taken, America could "disintegrate into a nation of mindless escapists." Another stated that drugs represented a "crippling disease threatening the future of America." He added, "In learning the extent to which this blight of drugs has descended on the Armed Forces, I urgently desire the strongest measures be taken. . . . I truly feel this problem is eating away at the moral fiber of our country."[38]

On June 3, at a meeting in the White House with top military and civilian leaders Nixon stated his concern that Vietnam veterans were popularly perceived to be "ruthless killers" and "junkies" and would have trouble finding jobs back in the United States. He told them, "This image must be changed!" On June 10, Krogh summoned Dr. Jaffe for a special meeting at the White House, at which top Cabinet-level executives planned to launch a major national antidrug abuse campaign. One week later, in the face of sweeping domestic protest, Nixon officially declared his War on Drugs, calling drug abuse "public enemy number one in America." The situation, he said, "has approached the dimensions of a national emergency."[39]

The timing of the speech was propitious in that it helped to deflect the barrage of bad publicity coming out of Vietnam.[40] Its aim was to improve Nixon's political image and help sustain the war effort by promoting the impression that the administration was addressing one of the central problems affecting troop morale, while buying time for a shift of the fighting burden to the ARVN. It was thus central to his "Vietnamization" strategy. Tellingly, a centerpiece of the new policy was in the military. For Dr. Jaffe, who assumed the new position of "federal drug czar," Congress appropriated $50 million to establish a urinalysis program in Vietnam for all departing GIs. He made use of new technologies that allowed for assembly-line-like testing, dubbed by the military "Operation Golden-Flow." Soldiers who tested positive were quarantined in special processing centers in order to prevent them from spreading the "contagion of their addiction," as Jaffe termed it.[41] They were then subjected to strip-search and physical examination before being medevaced to Long Binh and Cam Ranh Bay, where they were treated with methadone over a five- to seven-day period. The passage of a congressional bill later resulted in increased funding for improving treatment facilities in Vietnam, which Jaffe had characterized as "primitive."[42]

The military programs coincided with Nixon's creation of a Special Action Office on Drug Abuse Prevention (SAODAP—pronounced Say-oh-dap) to coordinate drug education, rehabilitation, and research.[43] In a recent interview, Dr. Jaffe, who headed the new organization and was known as the "Methadone King," commented, "The Murphy report and media [coverage of the crisis in Vietnam] galvanized the White House's attention and helped to create panic in the streets. . . . Vietnam had a pivotal influence in ensuring major presidential leadership and support [for the War on Drugs]." Jaffe further stressed the importance of Vietnam and the shifting demographics of drug users in shaping Nixon's dedication to treatment: "The great thrust of federal policy up until certainly the 1960s when it began to change a bit was 'once an addict always an addict.' You've got to do anything you can to discourage it, prevent it, because you can't cure it. Now suddenly you have these wonderful heroes (GIs). You have to believe them when they say they can get better."[44]

Seeking to quell public anxieties and show that he was caring for addicted soldiers humanely, Nixon increased the overall treatment budget from $28 to $300 million. He also helped to establish some 2,000 rehabilitation programs and 73,000 methadone treatment slots nationwide, including twenty-eight VA clinics that had previously refused to assist veterans thought to be using drugs.[45] Looking back, Jaffe commented, "Nixon was a pragmatic politician and secret liberal. The Kennedy and Johnson administration talked the talk but Nixon walked the walk. The previous civil commitment program lacked backbone; Nixon worked concretely to expand treatment provisions and put in a national system for the dispensation of methadone."[46]

There were, to be sure, limits to Nixon's liberalism. In 1972, SAODAP had issued a report calling for the decriminalization of marijuana on the grounds that existing penalties were more "harmful than the actual drug." Nixon dismissed these recommendations, however, fearing that they would undercut his tough-on-crime mantra and attacks on the liberal establishment and youth counterculture. In private conversations, he even made reference to the overwhelmingly "Jewish" background of the "soft-headed psychiatrists" responsible for issuing the report, who he asserted were "all on the stuff" and trying to "screw him over."[47] Nixon's demeanor demonstrated that his support for the rehabilitation model went only so far as it benefited him politically. Though enamored of the potential for treatment to curb street crime and public unrest about Vietnam, he was intent on preserving his carefully cultivated image as a champion of law and order and traditional American values.

In addition to disapproval from those on the left who saw through the political facade, Nixon faced criticism from psychiatrists and African American community leaders who felt that methadone was as harmful as heroin, and that the conditions in federal treatment facilities violated the Eighth Amendment to the U.S. Constitution prohibiting "cruel and unusual punishment" by holding patients against their will in an oppressive institutional setting. Noting high recidivism rates, they argued that drug abuse should be addressed as a social problem in communities where it took root, not as a medical condition to be treated with pharmaceuticals. Dr. Roger Smith, a criminologist at the University of California, Berkeley, commented, "We're increasingly placing our faith in chemicals, gadgets and technology to control behavior which we define as deviant. The primary focus on the national level seems to be the imposition of more and more social control."[48]

Despite these views, the methadone boom took off throughout the country. Between 1971 and 1972 the number of cities housing treatment facilities increased from 54 to 214.[49] In New York, Mayor John Lindsay agreed to a contract with Dr. Vincent Dole for the founding of a major detoxification center in the Tombs prison in Manhattan, which was filled to 200 percent of intended capacity.[50] Below the Mason-Dixon Line, Georgia's Governor Jimmy Carter took on responsibility for coordinating regional cooperation among southern states. In 1971 he launched the Georgia Narcotics Treatment program under the directorship of Dr. Peter Bourne, which included a treatment facility in the Atlanta penitentiary. According to Carter, the presence in Georgia' of some of the nation's largest military bases enhanced the importance of providing adequate rehabilitation: "Heroin is growing rapidly among our troops in Vietnam as part of a problem of morale, discipline and leadership, and we can expect many of the 71,500 Georgians who served to bring their habits home when they return. We need to take seriously our responsibility for treatment."[51]

Carter's response reflected the sweeping popular concern provoked by the crisis emanating out of Vietnam and its link to the expansion of the drug war at the state and local levels. During the early 1970s, school boards began to establish antidrug programs and supported Project DARE (Drug Abuse Research and Education), an organization founded by Dr. Thomas Ungerleider in Los Angeles to encourage teenagers to take the lead in promoting education and abstinence among their peers.[52] Church organizations and charity groups began creating recreation programs to prevent drug abuse and also subsidized halfway houses and detoxification centers.[53] Many private treatment facilities sprang up and adopted the "therapeutic community" approach, which was modeled after Alcoholics Anonymous in staffing recovering addicts as counselors.[54] Dr. Joel Fort established a center that abolished distinctions between doctors and patients and provided services such as art and music therapy, legal support, educational classes, and tutoring as well extensive vocational help. He also encouraged local community activism. The 3H-O Foundation in Los Angeles, another novel organization, promoted yogic meditation and natural herbal remedies as the cure for heroin addiction.[55]

The proliferation of rehabilitation centers, when developed in a noncoercive fashion, was a positive development shaped by the social circumstances of the time. Although it would have benefited from a more concerted attack against poverty and the social conditions that bred rising drug-use patterns, it demonstrated the civic-mindedness of medical doctors and community leaders, who banded together to help tens of thousands of addicts through cutting-edge sociological and medical methods. The success of many treatment facilities remains lost on conservative drug warriors today who remain fixated on the enforcement end, even at the local community level.[56] During the 1970s, however, drug treatment was equally prominent—in part because of political exigencies surrounding the crisis of addicted soldiers in Vietnam and the fear spawned by their return to the "mean streets" of the United States.

"The Pusher Should Live behind Bars"
Growth of the National Drug Police

Nixon's focus on treatment coincided with the expansion of the federal enforcement apparatus. In 1970, he dramatically increased funding for the BNDD (formerly FBN), which hired nearly 800 new agents and began to work in coordination with the IRS to target mid- and high-level street dealers.[57] In June 1971, Nixon created the Office of National Narcotic Intelligence (ONNI) within the Department of Justice to collect and disseminate narcotics intelligence to local officials. Circumventing congressional control by reporting directly to the president, the organization served an ulterior function in bolstering the surveillance and policing capabilities of the executive branch, which used the cover of narcotic control to increase its spying programs on political adversaries and "subversive" organizations such as the Black Panthers, whom it also investigated for drug-related activities. It was no coincidence that many key Cabinet officials later indicted in the Watergate scandal, including G. Gordon Liddy, Krogh, and Howard E. Hunt, ran the surveillance network responsible for a litany of constitutional abuses.[58]

In January 1972, Nixon established the Office of Drug Abuse Law Enforcement (ODALE), a national antidrug police force headed by Myles J. Ambrose, a former New York attorney general nicknamed "Bulldog" for his tough approach to crime. Krogh later admitted that ODALE was created largely for political reasons and to "stress federal involvement in the drug war on the local level going into an election year." Excelling at undercover work, in its first seven months it claimed to have made more than 1,400 arrests and contributed to a near doubling of the seizure rate for marijuana and quintupling for heroin.[59]

ODALE became mired in controversy after its forces were charged with unlawful break-in-and police brutality. In one notorious incident, agents nearly killed an Illinois boilermaker named Herbert Giglotto and terrorized his wife before discovering that they had entered the wrong house. Ambrose later issued a public apology, though he initially had told the press, "Drug people are the vermin of humanity. Occasionally we have to adopt their dress and tactics."[60] Ambrose was eventually forced to resign after it was discovered that he had close ties to a Texas rancher indicted in a weapons- and drug-smuggling conspiracy along with members of the Gambino crime family. Government and police corruption, including incidents of bribery, extortion, theft, and the illegal sale of narcotic contraband by law enforcement personnel, generally remained significant throughout much of the early 1970s—especially in Ambrose's home state of New York—hindering domestic policing efforts.[61]

In 1973, following Ambrose's ignominious resignation, Nixon disbanded ODALE and formed the DEA, a superagency given the mandate of coordinating all drug intelligence gathering, customs interdiction, and federal policing efforts and of rooting out corruption.[62] Its first director, John Bartels Jr., was forced to resign too after being accused of fraud, although critics speculated that he was railroaded for trying to oppose CIA infiltration and the protection of key governmental assets, including Cuban Bay of Pigs veterans linked to the drug traffic in Miami. Jack Anderson later revealed that over sixty-four CIA employees worked for the DEA, which served as a staging ground for covert foreign policy operations in Latin America.[63]

The enforcement budget for narcotics under Nixon increased overall from $65 million in 1969 to $719 million in 1974. In spite of all the paradoxes, arrest rates escalated nearly tenfold, leading to the clogging of court dockets and increased overcrowding of the penal system, particularly with poor minority youth from overpoliced ghetto neighborhoods. Many local districts developed specialized narcotics courts. Charles E. Wyszanski, a Massachusetts district judge, commented, "Over 50 percent of my cases have to with drugs. It's as if we're back in the days of prohibition." In an act of defiance, some local judges began to decline to prosecute minor drug charges. They also refused to enforce heavy sentencing provisions, particularly in New York state, where the notorious Rockefeller laws called for a mandatory minimum of fifteen years for drug trafficking and thirty years for second-time offenders. Third-time offenders were mandated life sentence without the possibility of parole.[64]

New York City was generally at the epicenter of the heroin "panic." In breeding support for the draconian new measures, the media charged that drugs were turning large swaths of Manhattan into what *Newsweek* columnist Stewart Alsop characterized as an "unlawful jungle" and "hell on earth" where "no sane person would want to live."[65] Toward the end of his tenure, Nixon tried to pass new regulations modeled after the Rockefeller laws, imposing national mandatory minimum sentences and stricter bail regulation. They never gained passage, despite fervent support from leading Democrats. Nevertheless, Nixon's drug programs proved to be a watershed in American history and helped to create an elaborate drug war bureaucracy that would endure for decades, despite many shortcomings and Nixon's inability to reduce the rate of either supply or demand, which experienced "no appreciable decline," as one analyst aptly phrased it.[66]

"Hunting 'em to the End of the Earth"
Nixon and the International War on Drugs

Nixon's drug war, with all its contradictions, left its greatest mark internationally. The global emphasis was of pivotal significance in trying to lessen public fears about the influx of drugs entering the country and to inspire greater confidence in the military's fighting capabilities, thus allowing for the prolongation of the Vietnam War. It was also conceived of as a means to help reassert America's global credibility and power and to allow for the forging of meaningful diplomatic alliances consistent with the aims of the Nixon Doctrine.[67]

Since the beginning of the twentieth century, the United States had been at the vanguard among Western nations in promoting global drug control efforts by diplomatic means as well as through the UN, largely as an extension of its domestic policing program. From 1930 until his retirement in 1962, Harry J. Anslinger was particularly influential as head of the FBN in making drug control an important aspect of American national security policy and in increasing the presence of drug-control agents overseas.[68] In 1962 the Kennedy administration began to train foreign police in narcotics control at the newly created International Police Academy in Washington, D.C. Through USAID, Kennedy also provided Mexico with $500,000 worth of helicopters, light planes, jeeps, and rifles for a special narcotics destruction campaign targeting marijuana and opium growers.[69] These programs were expanded by Lyndon Johnson and reached new levels under Nixon in response to the crisis of the so-called addicted army.

In April 1971, Nixon characteristically extended the mandate of the CIA to include the gathering of narcotics intelligence—which a House committee later concluded to be ironic, since the agency itself "supported the prime movers [in the narcotics traffic]," particularly in Southeast Asia. Nixon also formed a Cabinet-level Committee on Narcotics, which worked through the UN to bolster the enforcement capacities of global police organizations such as the International Criminal Police Organization (INTERPOL).[70] The committee further endorsed some zany initiatives: it funded scientists within the Department of Agriculture to invent a special worm capable of destroying opium and marijuana crops; it signed a contract with the National Aeronautics and Space Administration (NASA) to develop space satellites capable of surveying drug cultivating areas around the world; and, most controversially, it proposed creating covert assassination squads under the direction of legendary CIA operative turned DEA intelligence specialist Lucien Conein (aka "Black Luigi") to "terminate" 150 key international traffickers. Among the kingpins suggested was General Manuel Noriega of Panama, who, unknown to most committee members, had been on the CIA's payroll since 1959.[71]

In May 1971, Nixon sent aides Donald Rumsfeld and Robert Finch on a mission to eleven European countries to "emphasize the President's personal concern about the drug problem." In a private memo, Rumsfeld told Krogh, who headed the Cabinet committee, "We were instructed to say that the President has elevated the problem of drugs into the foreign policy area. That says a lot. It's a major change in U.S. attitude."[72] On June 14, Nixon summoned the American ambassadors to Turkey, Mexico, Luxembourg, Thailand, and South Vietnam to a White House conference to promote bilateral interdiction. He further appointed special narcotic control advisers in all foreign embassies and expanded federal assistance to mobile training teams, which provided instruction to more than 6,600 drug-control officers in some sixty countries.[73] Overall, Nixon increased funding to over $43 million per year for USAID's Office of Public Safety

(OPS), which trained foreign police in drug enforcement, in addition to counterinsurgency, and provided technical aid for crop substitution. A major focal point for OPS activity was in the Golden Triangle region, where the aim was to curb the supply of drugs reaching American troops.[74]

In February 1972, after promoting a crackdown on organized crime in Italy (which was ironic, because the CIA had previously supported organized criminal networks as a bulwark against Communism), Attorney General John M. Mitchell signed a bilateral agreement ensuring France's cooperation with American interdiction efforts in Marseille—a major pipeline for heroin trafficked into the United States.[75] In the Middle East, Nixon strengthened cooperation with Iranian dictator Shah Mohammed Reza Pahlevi, whose own family members reputedly lined their pockets with narcotics contraband; and pressured Prime Minister Nihat Erim of Turkey to enact a poppy ban in return for the promise of $35 million in technical aid for law enforcement and crop substitution.[76]

In Latin America, Krogh brokered bilateral agreements with Venezuela and Brazil and signed a treaty with Colombia whereby the United States promised $6 million over four years to create a special antinarcotics unit within the national police (which was already heavily U.S.-subsidized for counterinsurgency purposes).[77] In August 1972 the State Department threatened to cut over $10 million in foreign assistance to Paraguayan dictator Alfredo Stroessner if he did not allow for the extradition of Auguste Ricorde, a Corsican trafficker with links to organized crime and high-ranking government officials.[78] Ricorde had fled to Latin America after World War II because of his ties to the Nazis in Vichy, France, and was characterized by the BNDD as "among the most important sources of U.S. imported heroin."[79]

Nixon pushed most vigorously for a strengthening of drug-control efforts in Mexico, which, according to DEA estimates, was the source of 80 percent of American-imported heroin and marijuana.[80] After the failure of Operation Intercept in September 1969, the White House launched "Operation Cooperation," in which the United States helped to train some 500 Mexican police officers in narcotics enforcement and supplied special military helicopters and aerial surveillance equipment to aid in the detection of poppy fields.[81] Between October 1969 and 1974, American assistance was crucial in the destruction of 20,000 opium cultivation sites, as well as 18,000 marijuana fields, largely by means of spraying herbicidal defoliants. An internal State Department study later determined that nearly 60,000 hectares of nontarget vegetation were also affected by these operations, causing pronounced health and environmental damages, including skin corrosions, the contamination of grazing cattle and natural drinking water, and a devastation of the natural habitat of various endangered animal and fish species. The Catholic Church charged that chemical defoliants destroyed the food crops of impoverished Indian farmers, who represented the "weakest and most socially fragile link of the drug chain," according to sociologist Ricardo Vargas, and were "driven as a result to hunger."[82]

The dire humanitarian consequences of the defoliation campaigns, which included the possibility of long-term cancer, appeared to be of little importance to the architects of the drug war policy in Washington, who remained singularly fixated on protecting American national security from a perceived dangerous foreign menace. As in Indochina, these men viewed themselves as being accountable above all else to the American citizen and voter—and tailored their policies accordingly, without regard for international consequences or the plight of Third World farmers and the environment.

Governmental and police corruption—extending to the highest reaches of power—proved to be a major barrier to effective interdiction. In December 1972, a top army general, Humberto Marillen, was arrested in a swank Paris apartment with 132 kilograms of heroin. John Ingersoll, head of the BNDD, noted that he had frequently smuggled drugs through Mexico City, where he "had no fear of customs due to his high-rank." A congressional staff report revealed that in spite of the provision of millions of dollars of technical aid, including military aircraft equipped with sophisticated radar systems and remote night-sensing vision, the drug war in Mexico did not yield the arrest of a "single major drug trafficker" and was plagued by a "massive misappropriation" of governmental funds and phony police statistics.[83] DEA personnel themselves referred to the aerial eradication program as a "fraud" targeting "poor dirt farmers" instead of major trafficking syndicates, with most U.S. helicopters aiding President Luis Echeverria (1970–1976) and the ruling Partido Revolucionario Institucional (PRI) in waging a "dirty war" against student protesters in Mexico City, as well peasant activists in the Guerrero province, who were subjected to napalm attacks.[84] After initiating a special eradication campaign in the Sinaola, Durango, and Chihuaha regions, DEA-trained forces were subsequently accused by 567 prisoner witnesses of extorting millions of pesos and torturing illegally detained peasants and youth, sometimes to the point of amputation and death. DEA chief Peter

Bensinger conceded to a *San Diego Union* reporter that "our agents are instructed to leave the room when the torture begins."[85]

These remarks exemplified the tendency of high-level American officials to try to wash their hands clean of human rights violations through a reliance on proxy forces. They also conveyed the willingness of the United States to endorse repressive behavior so long as it was perceived to benefit American security interests.[86] In Argentina, drug-war aid served as a funnel for ongoing counterinsurgency programs aimed at crushing the left-wing Montoneros guerrillas. Between 1973 and 1974, Nixon increased the State Department's counternarcotics budget from $3,000 to $347,000—the same total, not coincidentally, that Congress had cut from USAID police training programs because of their support for methods of "selective torture" and "assassination." In a televised press conference, Argentina's Social Welfare Minister Jose Lopez Rega, who was ironically later forced into exile amid charges that he funded death squad operations through wholesale cocaine trafficking, openly proclaimed that American funding intended for drug-war purposes would "be used in the anti-guerrilla campaign as well."[87] The State Department expressed few objections to this announcement, despite the egregious human rights violations and brutalities associated with the latter efforts.[88] As this case makes clear, Nixon's international drug-control policy was often embedded in Cold War geostrategic aims and served a broader diplomatic agenda, including the bolstering of "friendly" regimes of an often repressive character and the rooting-out of social subversion deemed threatening to American hegemonic interests.[89]

Though lacking the backbone that its architects claimed, the international drug war was expanded by Gerald Ford following Nixon's resignation. Tapping into deeply engrained nationalist sentiments and the media's insular focus on the domestic costs of the Vietnam War, Ford claimed to target the spread of narcotics as part of a broader effort to "heal the nation" from its "inner-wounds." Ford's drug war was most controversial for sanctioning the use of the herbicidal spray known as 24-D, developed by scientists at the Department of Agriculture, which was used on a "massive scale" in Mexico, according to political scientist Richard D. Craig, and was later linked to adverse health effects and crop poisoning.[90] In 1976, Secretary of State Henry Kissinger brokered an accord with Bolivian dictator Hugo Banzer Suarez (1971–1978) promoting a $45 million crop substitution program for coca in the highlands region. In spite of the regime's brutality and the link of close Banzer associates to the growing cocaine industry, Kissinger promised another $8 million to help create a special police narcotics brigade, which became known as the Leopardos. Much like their Mexican counterparts, the Leopardos developed a reputation for corruption, torture, and cruelty—sometimes terrorizing whole villages on the slightest of pretexts. Their rogue character exemplified the destructiveness of the American antinarcotics crusade, which combined with broader foreign policy initiatives to promote major human rights violations.[91] Those most affected, including Latin American farmers whose crops were destroyed and who were subjected to torture by American-trained police, had scant knowledge of the U.S. domestic political considerations that promoted an expansion of global interdiction efforts. Nor were they aware of the crisis of the addicted army, to which their fate was intricately tied.

The drug crisis in Vietnam and its political reverberations helped to shape the expansion and internationalization of the modern War on Drugs. Nixon was politically shrewd in capitalizing on the antidrug hysteria pervading the country, which he in part helped to manipulate, and in enacting major international and domestic campaigns. Even while he was mired in the Watergate scandal, Nixon's record would remain for him an intrinsic source of pride. During the 1972 election campaign, he bragged that he had "brought the frightening spread of drug abuse, crime and anarchy to a standstill" and that the nation had "turned the corner on drug abuse." In 1973 he further declared, "Three years ago, the global heroin epidemic was raging completely out of control and time was running out for an entire generation. But we launched a crusade to save our children and the nation, and now we're moving from defense to offense and rolling up victory after victory. The sources are drying up."[92]

In reality, these claims were largely illusory. Despite enormous expenditure and political rhetoric, federally commissioned studies concluded that drug rates for marijuana and heroin remained largely static throughout the early 1970s and increased thereafter, with cocaine experiencing a particular boom. DEA officials admitted that they were intercepting as little as 15 percent of all drugs crossing the border. Egil Krogh candidly told reporters that enforcement efforts were "like squeezing a balloon. You squeeze it in one place and it will bulge out in another." Dr. Judianne Denson Gerber, executive director of the treatment center Odyssey House in New York City, further commented, "Talk about drying up the sources is for the birds. Heroin and other hard drugs are readily available on practically every street corner as almost any addict knows. . . . The optimistic statements by people in Washington frankly make me sick."[93]

The Nixon administration exhibited particular neglect in failing to address the underlying causes of addiction—including rising youth unemployment and the spread of poverty amid plenty, which the cutting of Great Society programs helped to exacerbate.[94] Nixon's drug war was least effective in the international realm, where corruption was a major problem and aid was siphoned off for counterinsurgency operations that resulted in gross human rights violations—a reality neglected by drug-war scholars such as David F. Musto and Michael Massing, who offer a favorable assessment of the president's performance based largely on the partisan views of top Nixon officials themselves.[95] From a public relations perspective, Nixon's campaign was considerably more successful than it was in practice. It helped to deflect attention from the human costs of the war in Indochina and to quell public demands for withdrawal by making it appear that he was addressing the problem of troop morale. Nixon's policy gave further credibility to the conservative pledge for law and order, which was highly resonant among middle Americans. The hiring of Dr. Jaffe and support for multimodality was a particular stroke of political genius. It ensured bipartisan support for the War on Drugs, while conveying Nixon's apparent flexibility in responding to a crisis many viewed as among the gravest confronting the nation.

THE BRASS RESPONDS, PART II

FROM COUNTERINSURGENCY TO NARCO-INSURGENCY IN SOUTHEAST ASIA

If we have found we cannot be the world's policeman, can we hope to become the world's narc?—H. D. S. Greenway, 1972

Never in his wildest dreams could Bill Hart have envisioned himself running a heroin clinic—especially in Vietnam. On July 4, 1971, however, the colonel found himself in just that position as the head of a newly created drug treatment center at the Long Binh military stockade. At 9:30 p.m., Hart phoned Dr. Tom Robbins of the Walter Reed Medical Center in Washington, D.C., to report on the clinic's progress. Displaying a brief level of candor, he asked Robbins, "Did you ever think that you would be doing this?" Robbins replied with a curt "No," and the two men continued with their routine.[1] Hart's revealing question reflected the frustration of an officer trained in the art of modern warfare but forced to play the role of drug specialist. It also epitomized the significance of the military's drug war pledge, which came to consume enormous resources—while causing more than a few gray hairs.

The military first became vigilant in policing drugs during the mid-1960s when rumors of an addicted army first became manifest. The State Department stepped up efforts to immobilize trafficking networks in South Vietnam and the poppy-rich Golden Triangle region and trained local police in narcotics suppression techniques. As public hysteria intensified, the Nixon administration authorized aerial surveillance and chemical defoliation, as well as crop substitution and alternative economic development projects in opium-growing regions—in addition to the urinalysis program and funding for rehabilitation. All these initiatives, which lay at the heart of Nixon's international drug policy, were designed to cut the supply of drugs reaching American troops, assuage the specter of moral panic, and bolster the prestige of the armed forces, which had reached a nadir in their history. They were also intended to silence charges of government complicity in the international drug traffic, while limiting public dissent over Vietnam. The Southeast Asian drug war ultimately served as a watershed in U.S. foreign narcotics policy in its breadth of federal commitment and the scope of its programs. It also came to expose the limits of American international policing and the nation's universal approach to foreign policy more broadly, arousing popular animosity and resistance but failing to curb supply rates.[2]

"Stifled by the CIA?"

Origins of the Vietnamese Drug War

During the mid-1950s, the FBN first established bureau posts in Southeast Asia because of an interest in curbing the sources of drug supply. Following the French defeat at Dienbienphu in 1954, FBN agents began to investigate the involvement of the Communist Vietminh in trafficking opium from Thailand and Laos, which, according to French colonial sources, had provided an "appreciable" source of income for the purchase of arms since the declared formation of the Democratic Republic of Vietnam in 1945. They found more evidence, however, about the corruption of American strategic allies in the region, which consular officials had been warning about since the late 1940s.[3] On January 1, 1955, with American prodding, Bao Dai, the former French puppet emperor and newly designated ruler of South Vietnam below the 17th parallel, issued a decree banning the government monopoly on opium as a means of bolstering his political image. Government advisers from Michigan State University, nevertheless, remained suspicious about his continued links with the Binh Xuyen criminal network.[4] After being taken on a tour of an abandoned opium refinery, Dr. Wesley Fishel, who oversaw the creation of the South Vietnamese police, articulated his fear to the American embassy that the refinery was being used to process drugs clandestinely at night. He urged Bao Dai's successor, Ngo Dinh Diem, to make drug enforcement a top priority in order to promote law and order and legitimize his political rule.[5]

Despite this plea, FBN field agents working out of Thailand came to suspect that GVN police under the command of Diem's brother, Ngo

Dinh Nhu, were continuing to receive regular payments from gambling and the smuggling of opium.[6] Nhu's forces had worked to violently crush the Binh Xuyen, which posed a threat to the government's power base, and were ostensibly using profits from the opium trade to fund what historian Marilyn B. Young termed a campaign of "state terror" against suspected Vietminh cadres, who had led the liberation struggle against the French.[7] The campaign intensified following the formation of the NLF under the leadership of Nguyen Huu Tho in 1960, when the GVN passed a law allowing for the trial and execution of political opponents within a period of three days. Consisting of an amalgamation of dissenting groups, the NLF had declared a strategy of armed resistance to Diemist repression, with the support of Ho Chi Minh and the Hanoi leadership.[8]

In November 1963 the Diem brothers were murdered in an American-supported coup d'état led by General Tran Van Don. Following a brief power struggle, General Duong Van "Big" Minh took power. Corruption in his government remained rampant—in part as a product of the influx of American consumer goods on a hollow economic base and privatization schemes that rewarded local elites. After sending American troops to strengthen the ongoing counterinsurgency against the NLF, American officials began to worry about the prevalence of drugs throughout the country. In 1964 the State Department pressured General Duong to declare cannabis illegal. In 1965 the Agency of International Development's OPS, whose police training and prison construction programs were pivotal to American "nation-building" efforts in South Vietnam and enhanced the scope of state repression, began providing full-time advisory assistance in the suppression and control of illegal drugs. Having taken over from the Michigan State advisers and CIA, OPS also provided technical aid, including radios and laboratory equipment, to detect contraband.[9]

In June 1966, General Lewis Walt, commander of the III Marine Amphibious Force, wrote to USAID representatives that opium and marijuana were being sold in Danang and Hoa Phat village near American military bases and that enforcement was lax. James E. McMahon, public safety adviser for USAID in Danang, responded by setting up a meeting with the district chief of police, Tran Minh Cong, who assured him of his "personal interest in taking action on this matter." Secretary of State Robert S. McNamara further called for a monthly report from the FBN on all drug abuse cases under investigation, while USAID officials were instructed to promote alternative crop development in regions where marijuana was grown.[10]

In August 1966, federal narcotics agent Albert Habib, who had been stationed in Bangkok, met with Colonel Ngo Van Luan, chief of the Saigon municipal police, and prodded him to step up local enforcement efforts. Colonel Luan had told Habib that marijuana cultivation was expanding because of the demand created by "Negro-American" soldiers. The main distributors, according to Luan, were members of the Hoa-Hao religious sect, who were loosely allied to the GVN. Because of a desire to maintain the political support of the Hoa-Hao, Colonel Luan stated that he was willing to tolerate their actions. Nevertheless, he agreed to work with Habib and the FBN in attempting to halt the flow of narcotics from the Golden Triangle and conducted a wave of raids on local opium dens.[11]

In 1967, as rumors of drug abuse grew stronger, FBN officers lobbied the State Department to expand Colonel Luan's campaign.[12] The OPS subsequently extended advisory assistance to the South Vietnamese police and established a special narcotics bureau to coordinate intelligence and a "buy program" to stop the flow of marijuana into U.S. troop areas. Extortion and kickbacks by local chiefs, however, who often had ties to organized crime, and a lack of will in enforcing the new laws hindered its effectiveness. The CIA sometimes staffed the bureau with counterterror specialists, who used the guise of narcotics control to initiate covert programs such as Operation Phoenix: "hunter-killer" squads working to decimate the political infrastructure of the NLF through targeted assassination. It was far from coincidence that Lucien Conein, chief assistant to CIA special operative Edward Lansdale, appeared on one of the counternarcotics training teams in the early 1970s.[13]

Despite this ulterior function, which exemplified a historical link between U.S. counternarcotic and intelligence agencies, one hundred national policemen were brought to Saigon in 1967 for formal drug training. Between 1967 and 1971, 1,254 members of the national police received specialized eighty-hour courses of instruction in the investigation and enforcement of narcotic laws.[14] In 1968 alone, they claimed to have made 18,498 arrests, mostly in the province of Danang, although there was suspicion that they and their American advisers used the narcotic contraband to line their own pockets and fund state-terror operations.[15]

In 1968, the FBN merged with the Department of Justice's Treasury Division to form the BNDD. After being appointed director, former Oakland police chief and criminologist John E. Ingersoll traveled to Vietnam and hired Fred T. Dick as the first full-time federal narcotics agent stationed in Saigon.[16] Bureau insiders questioned why Dick's appointment had not occurred sooner—particularly in considering that Assistant Commissioner Wilbert Penberthy had requested a full-time officer to "work on actual cases" as early as March 1967. They also held misgivings about the involvement of CIA "assets." According to one agent, the American ambassador, Henry Cabot Lodge, suppressed investigation of the National Police chief, Nguyen Nguyen Ngoc Loan, and customs director, Nguyen Vinh Loc, who were loyal to Prime Minister Nguyen Cao Ky and oversaw the selling of confiscated opium through the back door of a warehouse.[17] Lodge's successor, Ellsworth Bunker, subsequently dismissed the recommendations of an ad hoc committee to "stop burying our hands in the sand like ostriches" in the face of rampant governmental corruption. He stated that "pressures which are too well known to require enumeration" prevented him from taking action, despite the "unmitigated evil" associated with the drug traffic.[18]

Bunker's position reflected a long-standing conflict, particularly marked during the Vietnam War, between international drug enforcement efforts and American foreign policy interests.[19] Although neither the CIA nor the State Department necessarily promoted the drug traffic as official policy, they nevertheless appear from these private testimonials, as well as previous investigative scholarship, to have done everything in their power to protect regional proxies who used drug trafficking proceeds to bolster the state security apparatus (as well as, perhaps, their own personal fortunes). Secretly harnessing trafficking networks, or at the very least suppressing public knowledge of their existence, the State Department meanwhile engaged in persistent efforts to present an image of proactive behavior in the face of the mounting threat of addiction among American soldiers. These efforts were primarily waged for public relations purposes. Because of political expediencies as well as sheer greed, GVN officials had little genuine interest in suppressing the drug traffic, despite public proclamations to the contrary. American political officials were well aware of this attitude, it appears, but did little to reverse it.

"Two Wars in Vietnam—Against the VC and Mary Jane"

By the late 1960s the public reputation of the U.S. military had reached rock bottom and was being compared to that of the French following humiliating defeats at Dienbienphu and Algiers. General Creighton "Fighting Abe" Abrams expressed prevailing sentiments in an outburst to one of his subordinates: "What the hell is going on! I've got white shirts everywhere—psychologists, drug counselors, detoxification specialists, rehabilitation people, social workers. Is this a goddamned army or a mental hospital? Officers are afraid to lead their men into battle and men won't follow. Jesus Christ what happened?"[20]

Beginning in 1967, in an attempt to bolster the military's waning public image, the Pentagon initiated a campaign to minimize the scope of drug abuse. Attributing sensational charges in the press to "Communist propaganda," high-ranking generals conducted a press conference claiming that John Steinbeck IV's allegations that 75 percent of soldiers smoked marijuana were "ridiculous" and that drugs were "not a catastrophe but at worst a damn nuisance."[21] They further began to bolster internal policing efforts. Ever since American troops had first been caught smoking marijuana in the early 1900s, while helping to oversee the building of the Panama Canal, the military's legal code had maintained strict prohibitions against drugs. In Vietnam, throughout much of the war, drug offenders could face dishonorable discharge or hard labor at the Long Binh military stockade. As unofficial punishment, however, unit commanders often employed what one former sergeant termed "local justice": either physical beating or forced labor regimentation, intended to convey a lesson to other unit members to stay "clean."[22]

In 1968, in the aftermath of the Tet offensive, the CID developed a special antinarcotics brigade, trained in undercover work and intelligence gathering by FBN agents stationed in Thailand. The DOD simultaneously instructed all unit commanders to "conduct an aggressive program to combat the threat of drug abuse."[23] In response, John H. Cushman, commanding officer for the Delta Regional Assistance Command, characteristically ordered shakedown inspections of all soldiers under his authority, declared cities and towns to be off limits, and mandated checks on all vehicles entering or leaving military installations. In select instances, unit commanders allowed Vietnamese prostitutes—"local national guests," as they were sometimes referred to—into military barracks in order to dissuade soldiers from using drugs. Hannah Browning, the outraged wife of a marine, wrote to her congressional representative, "I don't want my husband living in a brothel, nor to think of the commanding general as a pimp—horrible but logical."[24]

In 1969, with drugs increasingly considered a national security threat, the OPS launched a marijuana destruction campaign in collaboration with the BNDD, local village chiefs, and the Vietnamese national police.[25] Even though it served in some instances as a pretext to unleash chemical weapons on "guerrilla-infested" areas and to force villagers into strategic government-controlled "hamlets" by ravaging their food crops, the general aim of the program was to eradicate the growth of marijuana at the source. American helicopters began to conduct flyover missions, predominantly in the Mekong Delta region, with pilots assigning kill-ratios to the number of crops destroyed.[26] According to OPS records, they wiped out 504,795 marijuana plants (or 27,770 pounds). In most cases, USAID officials paid farmers one piaster (less than one U.S. cent) for each plant targeted. Journalist Richard Boyle wrote, "The United States is now waging two wars in Vietnam; one against the VC [Viet Cong] and the other against Mary Jane."[27]

The military quickly realized, however, that it couldn't sustain this two-front war. Fighter pilots encountered sustained resistance from farmers who profited from the black market economy and sought to protect their vegetation and water buffalo from the imprecision of the chemical attacks. As with the broader crop destruction program, pilots reported having to abort several missions after being shot at. Besides confronting open popular defiance, the aerial interdiction campaign faced eventual political constraints.[28] In May 1971, Director of Pacification John Paul Vann sent a memo to senior OPS advisers warning them not to spray marijuana-growing fields in the Chau Doc, An Giang, and Se Dec provinces controlled by the Hoa-Hao sect. He feared alienating the sect's members and driving them into the hands of the NLF, which had capitalized on the brutality of previous relocation efforts.[29] Vann viewed the marijuana program as a bane to broader pacification efforts designed to win over the "hearts and minds" of the South Vietnamese people.[30] Though considering the smoking of marijuana to be a "major command problem," he advocated a "more restrained" crop substitution program, which was eventually abandoned because of what Ingersoll termed "higher combat priorities."[31]

Coinciding with the collapse of the marijuana destruction campaign, the DOD began to enforce more stringent guidelines for custom inspections and initiated a program to train specialized dogs to detect the scent of marijuana and, later, opium. The dogs were used to check all packages leaving Vietnam via mail, to search all GIs leaving for and returning from R&R, and to scrutinize all vehicles entering military bases. They also searched the sampans (boats) of local Vietnamese thought to be trafficking in contraband.[32] The vigorous policing tactics and growth of the CID's antinarcotics brigade led to a near tenfold surge in arrest rates, with approximately 6,500 soldiers being court-martialed for drug-related offenses in 1971 (compared with fewer than 1,000 in 1968, for example). Some 110,000 marijuana cigarettes were also confiscated.[33] By 1972 the military court system was jammed with drug cases.[34] Henry Aronson of the Lawyers Military Defense Committee, which provided civilian counsel to accused soldiers, commented, "Drug cases have become to the judicial system here [in Vietnam] what automobile accidents have become to the civil courts at home."[35]

Faced with overcrowded courts and an overburdened criminal justice apparatus, the DOD implemented an extensive advertisement campaign in military newspapers and radio "to turn [GIs] away from drugs and instill in them a love of country." In the *Army Reporter* the corpse of a dead soldier was pictured lying in a morgue under the headline "Drugs: A Great Way to Get Away from It All." A label on his foot stated that he had died from a heroin overdose.[36] In January 1970, in line with attempts to liberalize the military's code of ethics amid a crisis of insubordination and to limit the number of dishonorable discharges, a novel amnesty program was adopted granting prosecutorial immunity and the promise of rehabilitation to soldiers who admitted using drugs.[37] (Lieutenant General Robert Gard commented in retrospect, "If we had discharged everybody who smoked marijuana, we wouldn't have had much of an Army left.") During the first three months, 3,600 marines took advantage of this policy—though many distrusted the military's pledge that their permanent records would be unaffected, often with good reason.[38] They also came to resent conditions at a newly developed drug-abuse wing at the Long Binh jail, where inmates were purportedly treated like "caged animals" and confined to "vermin- and rat-infested" cells, as in the prison at large.[39]

In the winter of 1970, MACV established a telephone line that GIs could use to get help for drug-related problems and report any drug "tips" to the police. It also developed its own drug library, which included books such as Donald Louria's *Nightmare Drugs* and Gabriel Nahas's *Marihuana—Deceptive Weed*. Sergeants were ordered to lecture incoming soldiers on the dangers of drug abuse and to distribute a series of pamphlets, one of which warned, "Don't let drugs be your 'bag' or you may go home in one!" The military later modified its approach—in response to rumors that soldiers were rolling joints with the pamphlet's pages—by encouraging more open dialogue and sensitivity among officers to the sociocultural transformations in the United States.[10] As another preventive measure the military upgraded several state-of-the-art recreational facilities, including one at Vung Tau off the South China Sea, where GIs could go to the beach and enjoy a luxurious whirlpool and sauna. They also invited many top Hollywood entertainers to Vietnam, including Sammy Davis Jr., who was urged to mix a distinctive antidrug theme with his music.[41]

Smashing an Epidemic?
Operation Golden-Flow and the Military Heroin War

In June 1971 the public relations fallout surrounding the addicted army in Vietnam reached a high point. On June 3, after an urgent meeting with military leaders, Nixon sent a memo to Secretary of Defense Melvin Laird stating that heroin addiction in the armed forces had reached "intolerable proportions" and urging the DOD to initiate a major eradication campaign. Krogh also issued a directive to Westmoreland's successor, General Creighton Abrams, to make the suppression of heroin a "number one command priority." On June 18, after declaring a national state of emergency surrounding drugs, Nixon enacted the urinalysis testing program for departing soldiers known as Golden-Flow. Within a year the DOD began to administer tests to randomly selected units and extended them to troop displacements in South Korea, Thailand, Japan, and West Germany, where White House officials warned that institutional lethargy toward drug abuse was helping to create a "European Vietnam."[42] By the end of 1972, Dr. Jaffe boasted that an improvement in rehabilitation was responsible for limiting the scope of heroin abuse to under 2 percent and that in utilizing special technologies to detect positive samples he had made a contribution to science equivalent to the discovery of the X-ray and a cure for tuberculosis! Assistant Secretary of Defense Richard S. Wilbur proclaimed before Congress that he and Jaffe had helped to "smash the gravest disease epidemic in modern military history—virtually overnight!"[43]

Not everyone shared in this enthusiasm. Lee N. Robins concluded in a comprehensive study that there was no "evidence for the effectiveness of treatment in the Army, either in Vietnam or since."[44] Dr. A. Carl Siegel resigned his officer's commission to protest the urinalysis tests, believing that they violated the civil liberties of troops, especially those forced into a week-long "cure" which was no more than a brutal incarceration.[45] Sociologist Paul Starr documented a deep culture of resistance among GIs placed in rehabilitation centers against their will, in part because the centers were run by the same authorities as those responsible for prosecuting the war. Despite official efforts to promote humane standards, most saw the centers as "ineffective, badly run, based on a simplistic view of drug use and designed to 'save political face.'" Soldiers often refused to participate in therapy sessions and attempted to defy the system through acts of insubordination and violence. The culprits were placed in tiny solitary confinement cells where ventilation was poor and "rat bites" allegedly common.[46] They were eventually forced into handcuffs on the plane ride back to the United States in a vivid reflection of the deep internal divisions plaguing the armed forces at this time. One soldier remarked, "Everybody is cynical. The people running the programs are not hip; they come out with old-fashioned rhetoric and don't have any idea what a 'grunt' drug culture is like, much less a larger drug culture."[47]

As these comments make evident, from the perspective of those it was designed to assist the rehabilitation system was not nearly as successful or enlightened as Jaffe and his backers claimed. They lacked the foresight to recognize that the only plausible solution to the drug problem was the unilateral withdrawal of American troops, given how wedded drugs were to the social environment of the war. Dr. Norman E. Zinberg commented, "Unfortunately, the possibility that going home is more effective therapy [for the GI] than any treatment program now available is scarcely considered"—perhaps, he added, "because then no agency or class of professionals could claim him as their success."[48]

Whatever its shortcomings, which were legion, Golden-Flow was characteristic of its time. It reflected shifting ideological mores surrounding drugs and the triumph of the disease model of addiction. The emphasis on rehabilitation was also based on political contingencies. In a recent interview, Egil Krogh stated, "Our greatest fear was that if we didn't detect and offer some treatment in Vietnam, people that had become addicted in Vietnam would return to the United States and be compelled to commit crimes to maintain their habit." Dr. Peter Bourne added, "It was politically unacceptable for Nixon to attack military people fighting in a war zone for their country as moral reprobates. He had to treat them in a humane way. As such he determined that a public health approach was necessary."[49]

Nixon faced pronounced criticism for being aloof to popular sentiment and trying to hijack the reigns of government for his own self-interest. His response to the GI drug crisis in Vietnam, however, reveals that, keenly conscious of public opinion and shrewd in using the drug issue to deflect attention from his prolonging the war, Nixon was willing to adopt flexible tactics in response to political pressure. He was also willing to show sympathy toward drug addicts, even if those on the receiving end, perhaps rightfully, did not necessarily think of it in those terms.[50]

"Vietnamization" of the War on Drugs

For Nixon, Vietnam was always a sideshow that detracted from his grander ambition of easing Cold War tensions through détente and gaining international acclaim for promoting world peace. In the face of mounting protest against the war, including from his own troops, Nixon crafted the "Vietnamization" strategy, which called for shifting the fighting to the ARVN and a renewal of "nation-building" programs. It was designed to help salvage U.S. credibility without sacrificing any U.S. strategic interests, while also minimizing public dissent. Unrecognized by many historians, Nixon's escalation of the international War on Drugs was central to Vietnamization, the primary aim of which—besides bolstering the reputation of the armed forces and easing public anxieties about the return of addicted vets—was to improve the image of the South Vietnamese government so as to allow for its political sustainability.[51] Nixon was fighting an uphill battle because of revelations of widespread human rights abuses and systematic torture—in addition to the connection with drug trafficking exposed by *Ramparts* and eventually the mainstream press.[52]

In mid-1970, Nixon had begun applying diplomatic pressure on President Nguyen Van Thieu to crack down on the drugs problem, which congressional opponents of the war likened to an "infectious cancer."[53] Following the release of the Murphy-Steele report in May 1971, Congress included a provision in the Foreign Assistance Act requiring the president to cut off military and economic aid to any country determined to be uncooperative in narcotics control and to petition international development organizations, including the World Bank, to deny monetary assistance.[54] In a secret meeting, under Nixon's urging, Ambassador

Ellsworth Bunker, John Ingersoll, and General Abrams threatened to break ties with Thieu if he did not comply. Bunker told Thieu, "In all frankness, no one can assure that the American people will continue to support Vietnam or [that] the Congress will vote the hundreds of millions required for economic assistance next year and in the following years, if this situation continues." The ambassador added, "You are well aware that the American press is now filled with articles about the heroin traffic in Vietnam and the involvement of high officials. A more concentrated effort is required by your government as a whole to penetrate the upper level of the narcotic trafficking organizations."[55]

After being issued this ultimatum, Thieu launched a sustained anti-drug offensive under the leadership of Admiral Chung Tan Cang, a former classmate of his at the Merchant Marine Academy, who replaced twenty-five police chiefs throughout the countryside and ten out of eleven precinct commanders in Saigon.[56] Admiral Chung further issued an order to have over 300 corrupt officers dismissed from the Tansonhut airport and fired several prominent officials publicly linked to the drug traffic—including the former commander of Military Region II, Ngo Dzu; Vice-Premier Tran Thanh Khiem (head of Operation Phoenix); and former Lower House Deputy Pham Chi Thien, who was sentenced to seven years in prison after being caught smuggling 4.6 kilos of heroin out of the country.[57] Critics viewed these actions as a public relations ploy designed to protect more powerful members of Thieu's inner ruling circle from exposure and to destroy his political rivals. Tran Van Tuyen, a deputy in Thieu's cabinet who led an anticorruption drive, cynically commented, "Eradication of corruption and graft was done with reluctance [by Thieu] in order to gag the press so that he and a group of protégés could continue to exploit the anti-Communist struggle to get rich upon the toil and blood of the people."[58]

Irrespective of the purges' true motive, Admiral Chung thereafter created a special Joint Narcotics Investigation Division (JNID) to coordinate all police interdiction in conjunction with former CIA operative Byron Engle, head of the OPS. In the fall of 1971, sixty-seven JNID officers were sent to the United States for intensive counternarcotics training. Upon return to Vietnam, they were outfitted with modern law enforcement equipment, including offshore patrolling boats capable of intercepting Thai fishing trawlers, which regularly smuggled heroin into the country, and testing kits capable of "on the spot" identification of narcotic substances.[59] In total, the OPS extended over $2 million to the JNID, whose officers were known for their ruthlessness and use of the water torture method to gain confessions. Many reputedly participated in the Phoenix program, for which the counternarcotic mandate served as a cover (Engle's involvement was highly suspicious, as was that of other former CIA operatives).[60] Marred by continuous corruption and extortion, which was legendary among the South Vietnamese police, they nevertheless nabbed several high-profile traffickers, including portly Saigon financier Tap Vinh, and, according to U.S. data, seized 14,269 marijuana cigarettes and 23,656 vials of heroin, while contributing to a 70 percent increase in the arrest rate for narcotics. The street price of heroin subsequently rose from $1.50 to $9 per gram.[61]

One unforeseen problem was an exacerbation of prison overcrowding. South Vietnamese prisons already harbored upwards of 30,000 political prisoners, many of whom were detained without charge. Inmates were usually crammed into tiny, rodent- and fly-infested cells where they were forced to sleep standing up, subjected to torture, and had to use a honey bucket as a toilet. Diseases like beriberi and tuberculosis were widely reported. Hygienic conditions were so deplorable that one American inspector wrote that "the stench was so nauseating" as to make him sick. Unmindful of the consequences, on June 17, 1971, Thieu initiated a "Vi-Dan campaign to eradicate social evils," which included a major focus on narcotics. He instructed his military chief of staff to remove addicted soldiers and provide them treatment, and he instigated a propaganda campaign on South Vietnamese radio and television. One ad declared, "Narcotics weaken the body and the will. Shun them as you would shun death." Local village representatives loyal to Thieu contributed to the Vi-Dan campaign. A group of concerned citizens in the Ninh Tuan province established a drug rehabilitation center headed by Dr. Doan Trinh to treat an estimated 400 addicts. In Phu-Bon, located in II Corps, provincial chiefs organized a massive parade to celebrate the commemoration of a special Antinarcotics Day in which banners were raised depicting the evils of drugs and speeches made denouncing them as the "first enemy of the South Vietnamese nation." In a symbolic act, local residents burned in effigy a dummy labeled "heroin" in the town center.[62] The ceremony reflected in part popular concerns surrounding the spread of heroin in Vietnamese communities as a product of the black market economy and desperation bred by the war. It also showed that popular derision for American policies and the Thieu government was not uniform throughout the country.

On August 12, 1972, Thieu issued a decree mandating a life sentence for the importation of opium, morphine, or heroin and the death penalty for members of organized trafficking syndicates. The new laws were promoted in a public relations campaign funded by the OPS. One poster pictured a sad man sitting in a tiny and decrepit jail cell under the headline "One day in jail equals 1000 days in freedom. Don't sell Heroin to American GIs."[63] Thieu sought to portray himself through these ads as a champion of drug prohibition—ready to dole out swift justice to anyone caught selling heroin. Reliant on U.S. military support and foreign aid for survival—as his vice president frankly conceded in a 1977 interview—Thieu had few alternatives.[64] The State Department had come under intense public pressure to clean up the image of American allies and curb the spread of drug abuse in the military as a precondition for implementing its "Vietnamization" strategy and preserving the war effort. It was also desperate to smooth over the CIA scandal, which the South Vietnamese drug war was designed to counteract.

"The Internationalization of American Criminal Justice"
Narco-Insurgency in Thailand

For political and security reasons, the State Department extended its antidrug campaign into the notorious Golden Triangle, which was a key source of most of the opium imported into South Vietnam. The United States enjoyed a particularly close relationship with the Thai ruling dictatorship, which agreed to cooperate with the War on Drugs and allow for air bases in return for aid in suppressing its political opponents and the Thai Communist Party.[65] The Thai government had officially abolished the sale and smoking of opium in 1959, but corruption in government remained rampant. In the mid-1950s, CIA operative Edward Lansdale had been sent to northeast Thailand to organize hill tribesmen into paramilitary militias who mounted armed incursions into North Vietnam. Funding was in part obtained through the sale of opium poppies. The CIA encouraged the Border Patrol Police (BPP) to refrain from enforcing antidrug edicts, because it would deny the hill tribes their traditional source of income. In subsequent years, the OPS began advisory training of the seventh subdivision of the Thai national police in narcotics enforcement and intelligence gathering and formed a police aerial reinforcement unit to enhance customs and border patrol.[66] It also provided a camouflage for CIA operations into neighboring Laos and Vietnam, which some suspect was funded by narcotic contraband resold on the black market (a charge that received added credence after a CIA asset and DEA employee responsible for training the police, Puttaporn Khramakruan, was arrested at Kennedy Airport with fifty-nine pounds of pure heroin).[67]

As the drug crisis in Vietnam intensified, Nixon increased the number of federal narcotics agents in Thailand from five to eleven. On August 4, 1971, Egil Krogh visited with Thai officials and issued a memo to the State Department calling for an "all out war to disrupt those supplying American troops." He expressed further fear that traffickers from Thailand would set up a pipeline to the United States after the Vietnam War ended. On September 28, 1971, the American ambassador, Leonard Ungar, helped broker a pact whereby the United States agreed to send Huey helicopters to bolster the enforcement capacities of the Royal Thai police, which had received previous U.S. monetary assistance under OPS programs for what it termed domestic "security purposes."[68] By 1974 the modernized police were receiving upward of $12 million per year from the DEA for counternarcotics purposes, though a congressional investigation uncovered that much of the technical aid continued to be directed toward political ends, with the police implicated in spot executions, torture, and the massacre of student protesters.[69]

In October 1971, Prime Minister Thanom Kittikachorn fired the director general and the deputy commander of the Thai national police, Pramual Vanigbandhu and Paesert Ruchirawongse. Both had been publicly linked to drug-trafficking networks in a series of articles appearing in the *Bangkok Daily Post*. Pramual later turned up at Walter Reed Hospital in Washington, D.C., where he claimed to be suffering from mental problems; he was eventually sentenced to twenty-five years in prison for bribery and extortion.[70] In 1972, Kittikachorn collaborated with the State Department in establishing a chain of radio-linked narcotics-suppression stations and a mobile counternarcotic task force to crack down on drug smuggling in loosely policed zones along the Burmese border and in the northern part of the country. Within a few months the force had a total of thirty-seven officers on active duty and seized upward of 4,720 kilograms of opiates. It also landed several high-profile arrests, including William Henry Jackson, the veteran smuggler cited in the Murphy-Steele report, and the Burmese warlord Lo Hsing-Han, whom senior U.S. narcotics adviser Nelson Gross once termed "an international bandit responsible for a growing proportion of Asia's and America's drug caused miseries." The CIA proclaimed Lo's capture a "major step forward in the War on

Drugs." In reality, it simply enabled rival Khun Sa (aka Chiang Chi Foo) to take over the market and emerge as the most powerful opium warlord in the Golden Triangle—with minimal effect on supply.[71]

Crop substitution, an important element of the drug war in Thailand, was linked to broader economic development and relocation programs. These were designed to inculcate pro-American sentiments among the indigenous population and, in theory, improve living conditions, though they were often implemented coercively. As part of the 1971 agreement, Ambassador Ungar pledged to donate $5 million to encourage the growth of maize, corn, peaches, and kidney beans as replacements for opium. The U.S. Department of Agriculture later established a specialized research center at Chiang Mai and, with UN backing, two fruit and nut experimental centers on opium-growing sites in the Doi Suthep Mountains.[72]

In July 1972 the State Department brokered a resettlement program for GMD soldiers under the command of General Li Wen-Huan. The GMD had become major opium traders after losing financial support from the CIA following a failed Bay of Pigs–style invasion of the Chinese mainland during the early 1960s. In return for land, citizenship, and 20.8 million baht (over $1 million), they agreed to burn twenty-six tons of opium in a ceremony witnessed by two State Department envoys and a forensic chemist. It was later discovered that General Li had substituted horse fodder for opium and retained his control over large parts of the Golden Triangle trade. This fiasco exemplified the ineffectiveness of American drug-control efforts in Thailand, which nevertheless endured through the reinstitution of democracy in 1973 and the bloody U.S.-supported 1976 Kittikachorn countercoup.[73]

"Poppies, Pipes, and People"
A War on Heroin in Phnom Penh, Philippines, and Vientiane

Because of its strategic location bordering Vietnam, Cambodia was an important venue for the extension of America's antidrug campaign. Throughout the 1960s, Prince Norodom Sihanouk headed a neutralist government, which possessed a monopoly on all opium profits. In 1970 a U.S.-backed coup opened the border and increased the flow of drugs into South Vietnam—in addition to destabilizing the country and sparking a long reign of violence.[74] Synonymous with broader nation-building efforts, the State Department began conducting advisory training of Cambodian police in drug suppression techniques. In May 1972, President

Sirik Matak signed an agreement calling for the establishment of a special narcotics enforcement unit as well as inspections of all aircraft departing the Pochtong airport in Phnom Penh. Matak later appointed Van Houth to head the new drug unit of the national police and as a delegate to the UN on drug-control policy. Van helped to engineer several high-profile raids on local opium dens and the shutting-down of various clandestine heroin labs. His unit continued to operate until the triumph of the Khmer Rouge revolution in 1975, when it was disbanded and its members likely killed in the ensuing genocide.[75]

In the Philippines, which had long been an American protectorate, OPS advisers established a special section of the constabulary for narcotics control and an antismuggling center. Their main objective was to curb the supply of marijuana reaching American troops stationed at the Clark and Subic Air Force Bases, which served as important launching pads for bombing raids into Vietnam, though they also arrested critics of Dictator Ferdinand Marcos, sometimes torturing them to death.[76]

The State Department enacted one of its most sustained drug-control programs in Laos, which served as a "conduit nation" for the heroin utilized by American soldiers in Vietnam. In 1967 the OPS had helped to establish by ministerial decree a local narcotics bureau to enforce antiquated French antidrug laws but managed to seize only 93 kilograms of opium in four years of operation. Ambassador William Sullivan (1964–1969) conceded before a congressional committee that the American-backed RLG army was "engaged in transport and commerce in raw opium," thus hindering prohibition efforts.[77] FBN operatives have since revealed that they had been discouraged by the State Department from even entering the country.

In 1963, the FBN's Bowman Taylor identified Hmong chief Touby Lyfoung as a direct participant with General Phoumi in a transaction involving 100 kilograms of opium and arrested General Vang Pao, head of the CIA's clandestine Hmong army, after an undercover buy. Taylor stated that he was subsequently thrown out of Laos, while Vang Pao was given a brief respite by the CIA in Miami before returning to his jungle base in Long Tien. In 1967, FBN agent Albert Habib began to investigate a series of heroin laboratories in the province of Luang Prabang, controlled by high-ranking government officials including Ouane Rattikone. According to Habib, Ambassador Sullivan halted his queries and sent a memo to Secretary of State Dean Rusk asking to have Habib recalled. Rusk denied the request. Sullivan, however, forced Habib to limit his narcotics investigations to American personnel not working for the CIA. Referring to the RLG, Sullivan allegedly stated, "Don't forget they're fighting a war for us."[78]

By the early 1970s, political pressures forced the State Department to take a harder line on narcotics. Embarrassed by evidence implicating General Ouane in the heroin traffic, it considered ways to minimize the public relations fallout. In November 1971, after a visit by Krogh to Vientiane consular officials pressured the RLG to enact a decree making illegal the importation of acetic anhydride, an essential element in the production of heroin from raw opium. They further implemented a law banning the production, sale, and consumption of opium—known locally as *khai*, or flower medicine—with older addicts being allowed to smoke but only under police supervision. The new bills sparked vocal opposition and were highly unpopular because opium had been for centuries an important cash crop in Laos and was used for medicinal, spiritual, and holistic purposes.[79]

To show that they meant business, Lao officials carried out several widely publicized burnings of confiscated opium crops.[80] The BNDD simultaneously worked with OPS advisers in training over 273 Lao police and creating a special narcotics control unit which claimed to have confiscated over 3,000 kilograms of acetic anhydride. In August 1972, American-trained teams headed by the chief of intelligence conducted raids of refineries in Ban Houei Sai, in Luang Prabang, and in Vientiane, the capital.[81] They also provided customs officers with jeeps, boats, and walkie-talkies and organized a vigorous system of cargo inspection at the Wattay airport in Vientiane. In a significant policy shift, two private American charter airlines under contract to the mission, Air America and Continental Air Service, were instructed by the U.S. embassy to cooperate with Lao authorities to prevent trafficking on the aircraft. During the first six months there were thirty-five seizures totaling a relatively insignificant 22 kilograms of opium. Rumors of Air America's support for the drug traffic, meanwhile, persisted.[82]

Overall, the Nixon administration spent upward of $2.9 million on the Laotian drug war, some of which was diverted toward pure military and counterinsurgency ends. Part of Nixon's budget went to the development of a drug rehabilitation program to treat Lao heroin addicts, including soldiers, whose condition resulted from the growth of the refinery industry and dislocations bred by the fighting and its horrors.[83] In 1972, USAID funded two major clinics in Wat Tham Ka Bok and Vientiane, providing methadone treatment to addicts, mixed with Buddhist spirituality and prayer. Dr. Jaffe later advocated that USAID turn all opium parlors into methadone centers.[84] These programs were intended to serve as a last-ditch effort at nation-building by policymakers who saw them as a means of promoting goodwill. They also exemplified the interplay between foreign and domestic policy and the missionary-like drive of the "methadone king" and his contemporaries to curb the global "scourge" of drug abuse through the latest scientific innovations—notwithstanding the contradiction that the spread of heroin in Laos was a direct byproduct of American foreign policy and the social ravages of war.

The public health model espoused by Jaffe was generally overshadowed by more widely publicized eradication efforts. In March 1972 the State Department contemplated bombing an opium refinery near Ban Houei Sai; it was later destroyed in a mysterious fire that embassy officials claimed was set by the CIA. One agent pointed out that "with bombing everyone would have known that we did it. With a fire, people are not sure. It may be a business rival."[85] Such comments testify to the balancing act performed by American embassy officials, who hoped to placate American public opinion by promoting prohibition while minimizing Laotian popular dissent. The State Department likely leaked the fire plot to the press for public relations purposes and to help exonerate the CIA of complicity in the international drug trade.

In 1972, U.S. forces began systematically to relocate Hmong families to northern Laos to "protect them" from Pathet Lao insurgents while promoting alternative crop development. This was a part of a broader "cluster village" resettlement program modeled after the Strategic Hamlet initiatives in South Vietnam. In February 1973, USAID opened an agricultural center in the Phu Pha Dang province headed by community development specialist Gary Alex, where it trained Lao opium producers in vegetable, livestock, and fish production. Given the high profitability of opium and its deep-rooted cultural acceptance, the Hmong were resentful and reluctant to endure further displacement because of the war and removal from their ancestral lands.[86]

Ambassador G. McMurtrie Godley, who had been a fervent supporter of the "cluster village" program, worried about the political ramifications of crop substitution. In a secret memo to Secretary of State Rodgers, he suggested that "crop substitution will cause the loss of livelihood, which will hurt us in an attempt to redress the losses caused by the war." Godley nevertheless began to target opium fields as part of what was likely the most concentrated bombing campaign in history, one that caused thousands of civilian casualties, immense environmental wreckage, and the systematic destruction, according to one observer, of "the material basis of the civilian society in enemy held territory."[87] In 1973, after lobbying by two International Voluntary Service workers, Fred Branfman and Walter Haney, Senator Edward Kennedy (D-Mass.) chaired a congressional committee on the scope of the humanitarian crisis. Pointing to the leveling of villages and people being burnt alive by white phosphorus and napalm, refugees testified that at least fifteen people had been poisoned to death by the chemical herbicides and defoliants sprayed on their opium crops by American military aircraft. Residue from the spraying had allegedly infested local livestock, papaya plants, and vegetables, thus contributing to the spread of disease.[88]

Ambassador Godley vehemently denied these allegations, though the affidavits appeared convincing and consistent with the deployment by the United States of over 80 million liters of chemical agents during the war (in addition to displaying parallels with similar initiatives in Latin America). Because of a lack of federal oversight, Laos had generally served as a "laboratory" for American counterinsurgency operations and the testing of high-tech machinery and weapons. By spoiling their crops, threatening their livelihood, and causing more senseless fatalities, the opium eradication campaign ultimately served as another source of both anxiety and peril for the Laotian population and added to the colossal devastation yielded by the American "secret" or executive war undertaken in violation of the 1962 Geneva Accords.[89]

"There Is No Underworld Stigma"
The Failure of Prohibition

While exacerbating human rights atrocities, the drug war failed to make a dent in the flow of heroin. Even after passage of the new laws, a mere 30 percent of all aircraft departing the Wattay airport faced inspection. In a 1974 meeting with the minister of justice, Godley expressed deep dismay over the "lack of actual sentences and trials in narcotics cases." One U.S. official stationed in Vientiane commented, "[The United States] will never make any headway against the illegal drug traffic [in Southeast Asia] until they break the back of the Laotian Air Force's involvement in it." A USAID official further observed, "Despite our campaign in Laos being among the most aggressive in the world, there is no control of aircraft movement and the narcotics enforcement machinery cannot challenge senior generals or military politicians wishing to engage in narcotics trafficking. Nothing could prevent them." In February 1972, Prince Sopsaisana, the newly appointed ambassador to France, was arrested at D'Orly Airport in Paris with over 60 kilograms of pure heroin that had been refined in a laboratory at Long Tien, the CIA's headquarters. Deported back to Laos, he was retained as vice president to the assembly and remained a popular political figure and socialite, immune from any sort of prosecution. The same was true for Mua Su, a prominent Hmong assemblyman who was arrested using one of General Vang Pao's vehicles to transport opium.[90]

Beyond corruption, the shortcomings of the counternarcotics campaign in Laos was predicated on similar factors shaping the overriding failure of U.S. foreign policy: namely, its inability to "win over the hearts and minds" of the indigenous population. The State Department and federal enforcement agencies faced grave difficulties in adapting to local circumstance and persuading the native population to give up profiting from the drug trade in a depressed wartime economy. Chao La, Yao chief of the opiate-growing Nam Keung province bordering Thailand and a CIA "asset," told an American reporter that "what the Protestant ethic of American society sees as corrupt, others see as fair game. . . . It is hard for my people to understand why they should stop growing opium because they are told that it affects Americans thousands of miles away in a strange country." Ambassador Godley similarly observed that there was "no underworld stigma attached to any of the local principals or fetch and carry men who transported drugs through Luang Prabang [in Laos]." In a memo to Washington explaining the difficulty of U.S. drug-control efforts, he recounted an incident that he termed "pathetic": Laotian municipal officers had given opium to several men they had arrested on drug charges out of fear that they would develop painful withdrawal symptoms. The police chief subsequently told Godley, "We had to find opium for them to smoke, otherwise, because of a strong craving for the drug they would scream, cry or raise a hue."[91] Such comments epitomize the barriers plaguing American drug-control efforts with their apparent unnaturalness to the setting and the broader peril of trying to export Western ideals in an often coercive fashion.

The spread of heroin in Laos actually underwent a substantial decline *after* the U.S. mission was terminated, as an internal State Department report detailed. Following their consolidation of national power, the Communist Pathet Lao initiated "drastic" antidrug measures similar to those of Premier Pham Van Dong in Vietnam, including harsh penalties for traffickers and the imposition in state-run facilities of treatment regimens for addicts combining martial arts, acupuncture, and Buddhist meditation. Because of a growing association between heroin and the degrading sociocultural influence of Western imperialism, the end of the war, and the flight or imprisonment of corrupt government ministers, the programs proved to be more successful in limiting supply and demand rates than those run by the American embassy, though they likewise frequently showed little regard for civil liberties.[92]

Although Laos may have been at the extreme end, the ineffectiveness of the U.S.-imposed drug-control program there epitomized the program's broader failure across Southeast Asia. A June 1972 CID staff report tellingly proclaimed that in spite of all the new measures, drugs were "so abundant [throughout the subcontinent] and the distribution through local nationals so pervasive, that efforts to cut off the supply, even within the military compounds, are like trying to imprison the morning mist."[93] In Thailand, despite State Department pressure, a joint CIA-BNDD intelligence report in 1972 concluded that "officials of the Royal Thai army and Customs at checkpoints along the route to Bangkok are usually bribed and protection fees prepaid by the smuggling syndicates. The Thai government has little desire or power to stop this."[94] A DEA officer later confided to Alfred W. McCoy that top-ranking generals loyal to Thanom Kittikachorn and his successors controlled "nation-wide trafficking networks" and received a "share of all narcotic profits," which "turned his stomach." Lester Wolff (D-N.Y.), chairman of a Foreign Affairs Subcommittee investigating the international drug traffic, complained before Congress, "The trade [in Thailand] has got so much protection in high places that the administration is afraid they'll take our air bases out if we put too much pressure on them."[95]

In Vietnam, the massive social dislocation bred by the war, rural to urban exodus from the bombings, and high profitability of the black market economy amid an influx of Western luxury goods were major factors shaping the ineffectiveness of Nixon's narcotic war. Corruption and graft continued to permeate even among prison wardens who regularly sold narcotic contraband to addicts convicted under Thieu's enforcement program.[96] Admiral Chung, the chief of prohibition, reportedly himself profited from the opium traffic and had been removed from his military command in 1965 for selling refugee relief supplies on the black market following a devastating typhoon in central Vietnam.[97] Despite embassy pressures, U.S. narcotic agents suspected that high-ranking military personnel and JNID officers were skimming the profits of all drug seizures, which, as one OPS adviser concluded, "presents a major problem in narcotics investigations." When asked by a *New York Times* reporter whether or not he had confidence in the ability of his new staff at the Tansonhut airport to curb smuggling, Colonel Cao Van Khanh promptly replied "No." In 1973, Ingersoll resigned as head of the BNDD because of the perceived futility of existing drug-control efforts. Having previously admitted that planes owned by Air America had been used in the transport of opium in Southeast Asia, he told a congressional committee that "a cultural problem" in Indochina was involved and "entire cultures are not changed overnight."[98]

These comments conveyed a patronizing attitude toward Southeast Asian cultures, which lay at the root of the failure of American drug-control programs, as well as a universal belief in the not necessarily transcendent utility of narcotics control. They also display a disregard for the social circumstances of the war which fueled the durability of the black market economy and spread of corruption, trends that were magnified at the end of the war as government officials (and no less than a few of their American advisers) stashed money in overseas bank accounts in the hope of preserving their luxurious lifestyle in exile.[99]

The War on Drugs was considerably more successful politically than it was in practice. It helped to bolster the drug- and crime-fighting image of the Nixon administration. In August 1971, Krogh furnished a public list of Indo-Chinese officials removed or shifted as a result of investigations in drug trafficking, a list intended to counter charges of government complicity in the international traffic. In October 1972, Nixon gave a campaign speech providing a point-by-point rebuttal to George McGovern's charges that the War on Drugs had become a "casualty of the War in Indo-China."[100] Nixon frequently boasted further about the vast resources that his government was committing to halt the drug "epidemic" in Vietnam and about its positive results. He hoped to promote renewed confidence that he was doing everything in his power to protect American interests and to "contain" the drug crisis in Vietnam from expanding to uncontrollable levels, much like the broader Communist virus, which government officials continued to link it to. In both regards, these efforts were largely symbolic and meagerly attentive to the social and political realities of Southeast Asia—though the American public was led to believe otherwise.

"A Concerted Campaign of Genocide?"
Fighting the Pushers and Insurgents in Burma

Realpolitik played a major role in limiting the success of the War on Drugs in Burma (not yet called Myanmar), which was an important source of heroin in the Golden Triangle. In the late 1960s, enforcement agents expressed increasing concern about the part played by Burma in fostering the addiction of American soldiers in Vietnam. The State Department felt it could do little about it, however, because of the political isolationism of General Ne Win (Thakin Shu Maung), chairman of the Burmese Revolutionary Council. Having acceded to power in a 1962 coup d'état, Ne Win espoused a mixed Buddhist, socialist and anti-Western political ideology. Faced with a mounting ethnic and Communist insurgency, however, he gradually warmed to the idea of accepting American military and economic assistance. In January 1972, Nelson Gross of the State Department secretly met with the general, who agreed to a crop substitution program and the dismantling of the local militias that regularly smuggled opium in order to finance their campaigns against the Burmese Communist Party. In April 1973, Burmese military forces destroyed several morphine and heroin laboratories owned by Shan rebels in Tachilek across the Thai border. They also attempted to curb the opium-smuggling caravans of rebel insurgent groups, although critics charged that they themselves seized the profits.[101]

In September 1973 the State Department reached a controversial deal in which it agreed to provide an extensive foreign aid package to General Ne, including eighteen Huey helicopters, to be used for narcotics suppression purposes. Several congressional representatives, including Lester Wolff (D-N.Y.), worried that the helicopters would be utilized solely to fight ethnic guerrillas seeking regional autonomy and urged the State Department "not to repeat errors of the past when military supplies were covertly channeled to the South Vietnamese under the guise of police equipment."[102] In 1977, General Bo Mya, commander in chief of the Karen People's National Liberation Army, wrote to Wolff that American helicopters had been used as combat transport by Ne Win's forces in Wankha along the Thailand border in what he termed a concerted "campaign of genocide" against the Karen. General Bo stated, "The helicopters given to the Burmese government by your state with the full understanding for use in narcotics suppression is nothing but a farce and misused gift of honor that is being used to destroy my people." According to an internal State Department report, these charges were not groundless: U.S. military equipment was indeed used to burn rice fields and livestock and to strafe villages as part of Ne Win's scorched-earth campaign against the rebellious hill tribes—modeled after American operations in both Laos and Vietnam.[103]

American policy advisers justified their actions by proclaiming that the insurgents controlled the Burmese drug trade and that Ne Win had the sole force capable of suppressing the heroin traffic, even if not all U.S. assistance was used at this task. On September 1, 1973, Kenneth Rush, acting secretary for the Domestic Counsel, wrote to USAID officer John Hannah in a private memorandum: "We are well aware that the Burmese might not confine the use of equipment exclusively to narcotics control activity and to accept the likelihood that aircraft would be used against dissident groups not directly involved in the drug business, including Communist insurgents. . . . However, the Burmese Armed Forces are the only resource around for the job [of suppressing the drug traffic] and there is an increasing sense that drugs threaten vital Burmese security interests."[104]

Before this bargain was made, American policymakers had been faced with a peculiar dilemma, as Shan insurgents offered to sell a large portion of their opium harvest for $12 million plus American support in brokering a truce with the Rangoon government. The Shan, who had historically cultivated opium for medicinal purposes and as a profitable cash crop, invited the DEA to conduct inspections of the territory for intelligence gathering. They further promised to allow UN helicopters to conduct aerial surveillance of opium-growing regions and to undertake "search and destroy missions," as well as herbicidal sprayings. State Department officials rejected the deal, along with another similar Shan proposal in 1975, citing the failure of the "preemptive buy" strategy in Thailand.[105]

Congressional drug warriors, including many Democrats, expressed outrage over these decisions; Wolff went so far as to proclaim that he would be "willing to deal with the devil" to root out the "drug evil" and save America from an "invasion of Asian heroin."[106] Blind to the oppressive social circumstances fueling the rebels' use of arms and the brutality of the Burmese military, as his "devil" reference made explicit, Wolff was most dismayed by the perceived deference of the War on Drugs to broader diplomatic concerns. On this latter account, he was largely correct: despite Ne Win's appalling human rights record, the State Department valued him as an ally, like many other global leaders, because he promoted domestic stability and stood as a bulwark against threatened Communist expansion. American policymakers furthermore held deep mistrust for insurgent groups, partially for historical reasons, including the triumph of revolutionary forces in Vietnam, Laos, and Cambodia. They feared that another "falling domino" in Southeast Asia would sound the death knell of American power and influence in the region and allow the Shan rebels to breed regional instability. Even though drugs had been elevated to an issue of primary national security concern, they had not come to supersede Communist or revolutionary containment as the principal motivator of American foreign policy action.[107] By promoting the illusion that the war on guerrilla insurrection and drugs were one and the same, American policymakers nevertheless were able to preserve their image as public servants committed to the antidrug mission and to deflect oppositionist criticism that the War on Drugs was a political artifice riddled with contradiction.

The drug crisis in Vietnam played a central role in shaping the massive expansion of the American international drug war and its extension into Southeast Asia. Fearful of the consequence of skyrocketing military addiction rates, American foreign-policy-makers initiated a sustained prohibition campaign in South Vietnam and neighboring countries, utilizing an array of novel methods and approaches that would become staples of America's global antidrug crusade. These included the development of specialized police-training programs, rehabilitation, aerial surveillance, chemical defoliation, crop substitution, and urinalysis. In terms of the breadth and diversity of programs as well as the embrace of a universally demonized conception of drugs, the American War on Drugs in Southeast Asia served as a microcosm the broader federal prohibition campaign. One unique aspect was the skilled use of regional allies to fulfill American political aims, which testified in part to the power of U.S. diplomatic leverage, as well as the dependent character of the regimes involved.

Yet in spite of all the expended energies and resources, the drug war in Southeast Asia ultimately fell short of its stated goals, primarily because of economic and cultural factors as well as geopolitical constraints. Convinced of the moral righteousness of their cause (as in other realms of their foreign policy), American government officials failed to account for the localized antipathy and resistance that their policies bred, including such attitudes among members of their own armed forces. They also failed to recognize or address the sociopolitical factors and wartime conditions fueling the high rates of both supply and demand. The War on Drugs was least successful in Laos, where American officials faced the greatest sociopolitical and cultural barriers. From a political standpoint, the failure of the international drug war and the myriad abuses that it spawned were less important than the public illusion of success. Nixon's number one priority was the projection of an image of proaction in countering the drug "threat" emanating from Southeast Asia. The political climate surrounding drugs in the United States and crisis of the addicted army had necessitated this trend.

"GET UP YOU DOPED UP BASTARD!"

THE MYTH IN HOLLYWOOD AND POPULAR TELEVISION

In World War II films, the All-American GI Joe kissed their sweethearts goodbye, fought the noble war and came home to cheers. They were heroes. But Vietnam vets are alienated. They're militarily undisciplined and uncaring towards everyone around them. They always seem to be druggies. In Apocalypse Now *they're even tripping.* —Vietnam veteran, 1980

You know, the Vietnam War, we imagine it's this thing that happened to us [America], when in fact, the Vietnam War is this thing we did to them [Vietnam]. —William D. Ehrhart, 2002

In the 1973 Columbia Pictures film *The Stone Killer*, a black veteran named Gus Lipper appears to be out of control. Scarred by the brutality of the war and its apparent purposelessness, he is arrested for selling heroin and holds up a policeman at gunpoint. When taken into custody, he is gunned down by a team of assassins, who are also Vietnam veterans, competing for his share in the drug trade. During the investigation into the killing, a prison psychologist tells the detective, "We tend to count the victims from the war among the dead, but after carrying out the burning of children we have nothing left but the psychopaths. Vietnam doesn't make heroes, it makes a generation of Lippers!"[1]

Reflecting a fixation on the domestic costs of the war, *The Stone Killer* was characteristic for the time in demonizing Vietnam veterans, who appear "mentally and spiritually infected by the senseless genocide," as one analyst put it, rather than being politically awakened. They are caricatured as psychopathic killers and junkies responsible for the spread of social degradation and crime in the United States. In 1977, President Jimmy Carter proclaimed that we "owe Hanoi no reparations" or "debt" because "the destruction from the war was mutual." He continued: "We went into Vietnam without any desire to capture territory or impose American will on other people. I don't feel we ought to apologize or castigate ourselves or assume the status of culpability." These remarks were met with outrage by Vietnamese; a professor at the University of Hue likened them to a "rapist claiming his victims hurt him as much as he hurt them." They were nonetheless part of a sustained political effort, later accentuated during the Reagan era, to conceal the devastation wrought by U.S. policies and to absolve Americans of responsibility for the violence inflicted.[2]

Popular cultural representations can be seen to have contributed immeasurably to the institutionalization of a revisionist view and helped to sanitize the American record in the conflict, at the same time that they promoted nostalgia about the past and misgivings about how the nation wielded its global power.[3] As a result of nationalist blinders and orientalist stereotypes, Hollywood and television were replete with misrepresentations and neglected any sort of Southeast Asian perspective. They focused instead ad nauseum on the psychological torment of American GIs, often through their symbolic addiction to drugs, and on the cataclysmic domestic legacies of the war. This focus helped to enhance a mythic belief in America's victimization and bred a rising intolerance for drugs, which were blamed for a host of social ills—including the misconduct of American soldiers during the war (ironic since some directors embraced countercultural attitudes toward drugs).[4] The plight of the Indo-Chinese meanwhile was forgotten as the United States strove for internal self-regeneration through the late 1970s and 1980s, while imposing further economic sanctions on Vietnam and denying the ravaged country reparations aid.[5]

"Pitiful Victims of a Hated War"
The Myth of the Addicted Soldier on the Big and Silver Screens

As Julian Smith best noted in the aptly titled *Looking Away*, Hollywood largely avoided Vietnam throughout the long duration of the war in order to avoid political controversy. John Wayne's *The Green Berets* (1968) was one notable exception, although the film fit the paradigm of the World War II genre in its glorification of war and was animated, as one critic put it, by an "unashamed fascination with violence and themes of Anglo-Saxon racial superiority, leavened only by sentimentality." Brian DePalma's 1968 low-budget *Greetings* was the first film to criticize U.S. foreign policy and to portray drug use as a metaphor for the tainted character of the conflict.[6] Though set in Korea, *M*A*S*H* followed suit with a similar theme in 1971, making subtle references to the wide prevalence of marijuana-smoking in Vietnam.

A majority of films of the early 1970s focused little on the war itself and more on its corrosive spiritual impact *within* the United States—often through the spread of drug addiction and crime.[7] The 1972 20th Century Fox production *Welcome Home, Soldier Boys* traced the cross-country journey of four returned Green Berets who rape a woman passerby and lay siege to a tiny town in New Mexico with the use of bayonets and rifles. Pretending they are back in Vietnam, they assume platoon formation when confronted by the National Guard and wind up killing dozens of officers and blowing up a helicopter before being either arrested or killed. Prior to the final blowout scene, the men pass around a joint and get stoned together, replicating their experience in Vietnam and symbolically conveying a link between drug use and the perpetration of criminal aggression and violence, in both the United States and Vietnam. In 1972, two University of Illinois sociologists completed a study, *Wasted Men,* which concluded that in spite of comparatively low psychiatric casualty rates and overwhelming antiwar sentiments, veterans were thought of as "dehumanized killers and drug addicts, pitiful victims of a hated war to be avoided and shunned."[8] Much like the popular and radical press, *Welcome Home, Soldier Boys* helped to shape these stereotypes, while diverting public attention from the consequences of the war in Vietnam itself.

Television was as influential as Hollywood throughout the 1970s in typecasting veterans as psychopathic criminals and junkies—and distorting public memory of the war. The hit ABC series *The Streets of San Francisco* aired several segments in which detectives Mike Stone (played by Karl Malden) and Steve Keller (played by Michael Douglas) pursue ex-GIs responsible for robbing banks, dealing drugs, and even, in one episode, killing a former war deserter.[9] Many crime capers of the era featured similar protagonists. One viewer noted that "the networks had discovered a marketable villain. No grade-B melodrama was complete without its standard vet as a psychotic heroin addict or rapist."[10] Cultural critic Julian Smith proclaimed in January 1974 that she "turned on *Columbo* and within three minutes a hired killer tells his employer not to worry about a murder contract, 'I fragged a couple of hundred in 'Nam.' . . . Last night, tired of struggling to compress the sheer bulk of veteran sagas into meaningful shape, I turn on *Hawaii Five-O* in time to catch a returned hero blow up himself, his father and a narcotics lab."[11] In 1979, a disgruntled veteran commented, "If I acted according to what I have seen on television in the last six months or so, I should probably be harboring extreme psychopathic tendencies that prompt me to shoot up heroin with one hand while fashioning explosives with the other as my drug crazed mind flashed back to the rice paddy where I fragged my lieutenant."[12]

Helping to demolish deeply held conceptions about the omnipotence of American power, such portrayals were echoed in Elia Kazan's *The Visitors* (1972), Martin Scorsese's *Taxi Driver* (1976), Hal Ashby's *Coming Home* (1978), and Harry Jaglon's *Tracks* (1976), where veterans were stereotyped as mentally deranged killers, spousal abusers, and rapists shattered by the war and their apparent betrayal by society to the point of no return. In *Black Sunday* (1977), Bruce Dern's character plots with a Palestinian terrorist (also typecast in this role) to blow up the Super Bowl. In the *Dirty Harry* series (1972–88) starring Clint Eastwood as a vigilante cop, ex-GIs join with hippie extremists in turning San Francisco into a cesspool of lawlessness and violence—lending support to the conservative tough-on-crime mantra.[13]

All these films bear an interesting contrast to the less publicized documentary *Winter Soldier* (1972) which portrayed politically conscious veterans gathering at a motel in Detroit to denounce U.S. war crimes and military aggression in Vietnam. Based on personal experience, the vets recount how the My Lai massacre was no aberration but institutionally rooted in dehumanized boot camp training and racial contempt for the Vietnamese people. Invoking Thomas Paine, they see it as their patriotic duty both to expose the true facts of the war, to help put an end to it, and to change the system that created it.[14] Another documentary of the period, *Only the Beginning* (1971) shows decorated combat veterans, many in wheelchairs and on crutches, hurling their medals over a fence at the Capitol as part of Operation Dewey Cannon III, the code name for a previous military incursion into Laos. Epitomizing the transformation of the antiwar movement into an antiimperialist and even revolutionary movement, an African American explains that he is returning the awards given him by "the power structure" because it adopts "genocidal policies against non-white people of the world." A white veteran subsequently points to the Capitol and proclaims, "We don't want to fight anymore, but if we do it'll be to take these steps."[15]

Because of its controversial character, mainstream popular cultural representations shunned the GI resistance movement, which would have made for engrossing drama, instead casting veterans in the familiar role of crazy villain and junkie. The consequences were profound in that the public at large quickly forgot about the antiwar vets and their revelations, while often blaming civilian antiwar activists for denigrating their military service. If recognized at all, veteran dissent was usually dismissed as another marker of psychopathology, the stories of atrocities and substantive political criticism hence invalidated in the public's eye.[16] The emergent discourse of post-traumatic stress disorder (PTSD) only aided in this process, which helped to ensure that public unease surrounding America's role in the world became largely detached from an underlying anti-imperialism and consciousness about the destructive capacities of United States military power.[17]

"What's It Like Over There?"
The Strung-out Vet and Search for the Real War in Seventies Hollywood

The year 1973 was important in the Hollywood mythmaking process with *The Stone Killer* and the "blaxploitation" feature, *Gordon's War*. Directed by civil rights activist Ossie Davis, the latter film starred Paul Winfield as a heavily decorated Green Beret officer who returns from Vietnam to find his wife dead of a heroin overdose. Pained by this tragedy and the devitalizing drug subculture engulfing Harlem, he recruits a team of veterans to serve as a vigilante force against regional pushers and pimps, whom they either arrest or kill. Using sophisticated military surveillance techniques, they trace the source of the heroin, symbolically, to a group of greedy white businessmen with ties to the Indochina traffic. Though antiestablishment, *Gordon's War* failed to promote any meaningful insights about the experience of black soldiers in Vietnam, including their involvement in antimilitary resistance. The film also fit the mold in depicting drugs as a social evil linked to the war, rather than as a product of structural inequalities, and suggested that drug-crusading efforts like those undertaken by Winfield were necessary in salvaging heroin-infested inner-city communities from ruin.[18]

The 2007 Universal studios release *American Gangster*, about the life of drug lord Frank Lucas, replicated many of the themes of *Gordon's War*, linking the so-called drug epidemic in Harlem to American involvement in Vietnam. Ignoring structural and political contingencies, director Ridley Scott depicts Lucas as making a fortune smuggling heroin from Bangkok through the coffins of dead soldiers in an exaggerated and probably fictional way, as DEA agents have attested. The film on the whole demonstrates a continuity in ideas from the 1970s and the institutional-ization of Hollywood-constructed myths that ultimately contributed to the spread of a superficial public memory of the war.

Ted Post's 1976 film *Go Tell the Spartans* was the first to link drugs directly to American military ineffectiveness. Set in 1964 when Vietnam was "still a little war, confused and far away," it focuses on the futile efforts of an American advisory command unit under the helm of Captain Asa Barker to seize the deserted village of Muc Wa, an abandoned outpost of the French legionnaires. The campaign ends in miserable failure, with Barker commenting, "This war is a sucker's tour, going nowhere, round and round in circles."[19] The use of drugs exemplifies the growing disillusionment of GIs and facilitates various tactical disasters. In one telling scene, a medic named Abraham Lincoln gets high while on guard duty. He begins to hallucinate and envisions himself as his famous namesake, bellowing out the Gettysburg address and thus giving away the American position. The watchtower is shot down, and Lincoln is wounded, though not fatally. A superior officer chews him out, yelling, "Get up you doped up bastard—We've got 'gooks' on our hands." Lincoln's character is intended to represent American national virtue, and his addiction to drugs, its spiritual corruption. The film's setting in the early stages of the war is further significant: it suggests that if drugs were undermining America's position in 1964, the impact in later years was more acute. The failed siege at Muc Wa, after all, was only the beginning.

The Boys in Company C (1978), which traces the journey of a close-knit unit from boot camp, was another film to exaggerate the scope of drug abuse in Vietnam, linking it to the venality of America's South Vietnamese allies. The plot centers on a corrupt ARVN general named Trang, who plans to smuggle heroin to the United States in the body bags of dead soldiers. He seeks the assistance of Tyrone, a black gangster from Chicago, who is pictured bragging to his friends back home about the riches of the Asian market. Trang asks Tyrone if it bothers him that heroin could endanger the lives of American troops. When Tyrone answers "No," Trang responds, "It doesn't bother me either!" Tyrone ultimately reneges out of a sense of disgust with the ARVN soldiers—who are stereotyped as being greedy, lacking in ideological conviction, and using children as human shields. Emerging as group leader, Tyrone subsequently helps his comrades defy command orders and discourages a southerner, Billy Ray, from using drugs sold by General Trang. His efforts are intended to reflect what one reviewer termed "unremitting nobility and unmitigated righteousness unseen on the big screen in recent years."[20]

On the whole, the film provides yet another example to contradict the belief promoted by conservatives and some contemporary scholars that Hollywood universally glamorized drug use throughout the 1970s and 1980s, while enhancing the notion that drugs undermined America's fighting resolve.[21] There is little attempt to come to terms, meanwhile, with the devastation caused by U.S. foreign policy in Vietnam, or with the political calculations leading to war. The story of the Vietnamese revolution and the basis for its grassroots appeal is also suppressed.

Michael Cimino's 1978 Academy Award–winning epic *The Deer Hunter* was among the most influential films helping to transform the image of American soldiers from legions of empire (as many came to see themselves) and resisters to anguished victims. Devoid of any human-ized Vietnamese characters, the film traces the fate of three working-class draftees from small-town Pennsylvania who are either physically maimed or psychologically ravaged during their tour of duty.[22] After es-caping from NLF captivity, where they are badly tortured in what critics have noted to be an inversion of the war's reality, Christopher Walken's character Nicky is left particularly demoralized.[23] He stays in Saigon playing a sadistic game of Russian roulette run by wealthy Western profiteers and becomes addicted to heroin, eventually killing himself. Besides stigmatizing veterans and obscuring the carnage bred by the war, there is also a subtle orientalist theme running through the film. Not only do the Vietnamese exist in caricature; the American soldiers are portrayed as having been irrevocably corrupted by the Asian envi-ronment, largely to the point of no return, with drugs serving as a central metaphor. America's virtue, meanwhile, is reaffirmed at the end as Nicky's family and friends commemorate his death by singing "God Bless America."[24]

Though more critical of U.S. foreign policy, *Who'll Stop the Rain* (1978) was another film to promote an array of mythologies, focusing on the domestic costs of the war through the symbolic lens of drugs. The 1979 United Artists' release was based on Robert Stone's acclaimed novel *Dog Soldiers*, which one scholar termed "the best book about the corrupting spiritual effect on the United States of the war it fought in Vietnam."[25] Emphasizing the irrationality of American strategy, as epit-omized by the dropping of bombs on a convoy of elephants, both the book and the film center on the efforts of a disenchanted photojournalist, John Converse, to smuggle two kilograms of heroin from Southeast Asia to Berkeley, California, with the help of his bookish wife, Marge, and a battle-hardened marine, Ray Hicks. The drugs represent, in the words of one critic, "a historically apt and symbolic poison, a metaphor for the cultural disease America contracted in Vietnam." This disease included the proliferation of violence, social instability, and national purposelessness, as well as what historian Christopher Lasch character-ized as a superficial preoccupation with self-gratification and instant pleasure.[26] Tellingly, at the end of the film, Marge is forced to flee from two veterans seeking to steal the heroin supply and sends their children to live in Canada in order to keep them safe. She begins using heroin herself out of despair while living in an abandoned hippie commune, and she attends a dinner party where the guests get high and sexually abuse young women. The volatile Hicks eventually dies in a fight over the drugs, reflecting the shattered dreams of a generation left despon-dent by drug abuse and war, and by a society whose morals have ostensi-bly been denigrated in the war's wake.

"Charlie Don't Surf"
Drugs and Historical Distortion in *Apocalypse Now*

Francis Ford Coppola's *Apocalypse Now*, which won top prize at the prestigious Cannes festival and whose 1979 debut was referred to by the *New York Times* as a "cultural event," was most celebrated in portraying drugs as a metaphor for the tainted character of the fighting and limits of American global power. Coppola envisioned it as the definitive Vietnam War film, remarking, "My film is not about Vietnam. It *is* Vietnam. It is what it was really like. It was crazy. We were in the jungle, there were too many of us. We had access to too much money and too much equipment and little by little we went insane."[27]

An adaptation of Joseph Conrad's *Heart of Darkness*, *Apocalypse Now* centers on the secret mission of an American captain, Benjamin Willard (played by Martin Sheen), to kill Colonel Walter E. Kurtz (Marlon Brando) on behalf of military intelligence. Having been groomed for a top posi-tion in the CIA, Kurtz has been driven insane by the conditions in Viet-nam and comes to command a rogue group of indigenous Montagnards (natives of the central and southern Vietnam highlands), who engage in sadistic rituals and torture. A previous assassin who has defected to this private army has been reported to his family as MIA (thus reinforcing the myth about a cover-up surrounding the fate of missing soldiers).[28]

Drugs symbolize the madness of the war and futility of missionary efforts to export Western-style democracy. At Kurtz's compound his followers smoke marijuana and other psychedelic intoxicants, as does a renegade photojournalist played by countercultural icon Dennis Hopper. Willard's crewmate, Lance, undergoes a dramatic transformation from naive and innocent all-American surfer to battle-weary soldier and junkie. At the beginning, he appears clean-shaven and participates reservedly in the assault on a Vietnamese village by a zealous lieutenant named Kilgore, who serves, in the words of one critic, as a "caricature of an unadulterated love of war and killing." By the end, Lance has grown his hair long and gets high at every chance; he dons war paint and has lost all inhibitions toward killing. In the film's penultimate scene, Lance blends in with the Montagnards trained by Kurtz and participates in many of their tribal ceremonies, including the ritual intake of psychedelic mushrooms. He is depicted as having gone "native," so to speak, like Hopper's character and Kurtz, and to have transmogrified into the very "backward" being he was attempting to civilize.[29]

Coppola's primitive depiction of the Montagnards is the most culturally condescending aspect of the film. Running wild and naked through the forest with painted faces, they appear as the apotheosis of human savagery—as epitomized by the ingestion of psychedelic drugs—and serve as a prejudicial reference for America's descent into moral barbarism, which is linked to a degenerating environmental influence.[30] Events generally appear to be irrational and insane, as epitomized in the mass proliferation of drugs, without historical context and meaning or calculated intent on the part of the United States. The inclusion in the 2001 redux edition of a scene involving French plantation owners belatedly creates an important historical connection that is lacking in the original film. The agency of the Vietnamese and strength of revolutionary nationalism is further discounted, with the Vietcong stereotyped—like the Montagnards—as violently sadistic—evidenced in their cutting off the arms of child soldiers whom Kurtz's special forces have inoculated for polio (an act Kurtz himself had come to admire).[31]

Synonymous with these broader misrepresentations, Coppola overstates the scope of drug abuse for symbolic reasons—leaving viewers with the false impression that it helped to shape the military's unsavory conduct and collapse. Lance's drug habit is shown to jeopardize the crew's safety and provokes unnecessary violence and the reckless use of force. In one emblematic scene he is pictured waterskiing from a rope at the back of the boat while tripping on acid. He lights up a purple flare and, in reference to a Jimi Hendrix song celebrating drug use, screams out, "Purple Haze, man!" The smoke triggers a sense of panic among neighboring Montagnards, who fire at the boat with bows and arrows and kill a crew member named Clean.

In a previous scene, the crew gets high together and becomes paranoid and jittery. During a routine search and seizure of a commercial fishing boat, they overreact when one of the women refuses to open a basket carrying her puppy. A trigger-happy Clean unloads a burst of gunfire, killing everybody on board; stoned, Lance and Chef contribute to the mini–My Lai–style massacre by emptying their own machine guns on the boat; and Willard later shoots the woman in the head in order to put her out of her misery. The insinuation is that the drugs and their effect in clouding the soldiers' judgment are as much responsible for the atrocity as the institutionalized structure of the war and American military policy.

Drug use contributes to further unnecessary casualties in a scene involving the destruction of a bridge near the Cambodian border. Upon arrival, Willard and the crew are flabbergasted to find American soldiers operating in what he terms "the asshole of the world" without any senior commanding officers. Stoned on marijuana, they begin firing recklessly at another American unit. Lance joins the fray while tripping on acid and fires several indiscriminate rounds into the abyss. He later witnesses with awe the pyrotechnic display unleashed by the collapse of the bridge, commenting, "This is better than Disneyland!"

Through characterizations like these, *Apocalypse Now* fostered a shallow public understanding of the war by exaggerating the impact of drugs to the neglect of deeper sociopolitical variables. In this respect, it was typical of its genre, though ultimately more influential because of its wide popular acclaim and Coppola's delineation of it as the "definitive" Vietnam movie.[32]

"We Gon' Get High, High Tonight!"
The Reagan Era and Beyond

During the 1980s, American popular culture became increasingly infatuated with Vietnam and echoed President Reagan in recasting the war in a more favorable light, promoting the theme of a need for national reconciliation and healing from trauma.[33] Many films, including *Rambo: First Blood Part II* (1985), put forward the stab-in-the-back myth that treasonous antiwar protesters and a weak-willed government were responsible for losing the war and betraying the troops. As the archetypal disturbed vet, Rambo achieves symbolic redemption by rescuing POWs and defeating America's enemies after being sent back to Vietnam free from bureaucratic constraint.[34]

Fitting with the shifting national mood, American soldiers were generally depicted as tragic victims of misguided policies or an unreceptive homecoming, worthy of the recognition and compassion they purportedly never received.[35] Lawrence Kasdan's blockbuster 1983 hit *The Big Chill* was characteristic in this regard. The film features the reunion of a group of college friends from the 1960s, following the death of one of their classmates. William Hurt's character, Nick, the lone Vietnam veteran of the crowd, remains traumatized by his experience, sexually impotent, and addicted to hard narcotics. Unlike real-life counterparts who engaged in solidarity work with marginalized peasant communities in Central America who had been subjected to Vietnam-style pacification by U.S.-backed forces at this time, he leads "an aimless, rootless life supported by drugs."[36] There are emblematic signs of hope at the end: with encouragement from his friends and the revival of an old love relationship, he appears ready to straighten up and integrate into the middle class.

In *Lethal Weapon* (1987), edgy veterans are both the cops and the robbers. Mel Gibson's loose-cannon character symbolically absolves himself of past sins by thwarting the plot of an ex-general to flood Los Angeles with heroin. The deranged man has gone so far as to induce the suicide of his own daughter to protect himself from arrest. In Oliver Stone's Academy Award–winning *Platoon* (1986), drugs serve as a metaphor for the transformation of lead Chris Taylor (played by Charlie Sheen) from jejune Ivy League conscript to hardened, battle-tested warrior. Taylor, who mirrors Stone himself, is first introduced to marijuana laced with opium by one of his fellow platoon members following a long day digging trenches. Taking a break from work, he sits back and gets high just as the sun is setting. Through initiation into the socialized ritual of drugs, Taylor has officially become one of the working-class warriors stripped of both his youthful naiveté and his privileged class pedigree.

Stone portrays drug use as an emblem of American military divisiveness and failure. The platoon becomes divided between "juicers," or alcoholics, loyal to commanding officer Bob Barnes (played by Tom Berenger), and "heads," loyal to Staff Sergeant Elias (played by Willem DaFoe). In one telling scene, the "heads" gather in the barracks for a "groovy" drug party where they pass around opium-laced joints, listen to black soul music, and use a rifle butt as a bong. The "juicers" meanwhile get drunk in separate quarters and display contempt for the "heads." One black private, Junior, alludes to the influx of drugs as a "gook plot" to put chemicals in the grass and "make us pacifist." He states that drugs helped to "keep the black man down" by having him "smoke that shit." In a drunken state, Barnes orders an end to the party and physically abuses several of the men. He later kills Elias after threatening him with court-martial for massacring Vietnamese civilians. When most of the platoon is eventually wiped out in a brutal firefight, Taylor proclaims, "We did not fight the enemy, we fought ourselves. The enemy was within us."

Although breathtaking in its visual imagery and poignant in chronicling the war from a grunt's perspective, Stone's film, as various critics have noted, was characteristic in its parochial neglect of the Vietnamese. And his contention that America fought and defeated itself did a profound disservice to the ability of huge sectors of the Vietnamese population to mobilize in defeating the most technologically advanced power in history; it ignored the complex sociopolitical factors shaping the war's outcome.[37] Besides helping to skew public memory of the war, the film demonized drugs and could be seen to support a conservative antidrug agenda focused on ensuring that they should never divide the nation again, whether in war or in peace–this, ironically, despite Stone's own liberal politics and outspoken criticism of the War on Drugs and of Nancy Reagan in particular, whom he characterized in a 1988 *Playboy* interview as a "phony."[38]

Stone's 1989 film *Born on the Fourth of July* was more historically accurate in showing the connection between veterans and the antiwar movement, though it also exaggerated the scope of addiction by showing vets shooting up heroin in the back room of a rundown VA center. Adrian Lyne's *Jacob's Ladder* (1990) helped to preserve the myth of the addicted army into the 1990s. The film is set in the Mekong Delta during the late 1960s, where Jacob Singer (played by Tim Robbins) and his platoon mates experience hallucinatory visions and fire at their own men after smoking some potent marijuana. Singer dies, hit on the head by a bayonet, though the film flashes forward to his imaginary postwar life in New York City, where he sets out to prove that the Pentagon laced the drugs that he and his comrades smoked with chemicals designed to make them go insane. The film ultimately served to reinforce the notion that drugs were a divisive social factor during the war, breeding fratricidal violence and self-destruction, with soldiers serving as guinea pigs and victims of wrongheaded policy. It fit right into the popular mood of the late 1980s, which cast the Vietnam era as a nightmarish epoch blighted by drugs.[39]

Roger Spottswood's *Air America* (also 1990) conveyed a similar theme. Starring Mel Gibson (Gene) and Robert Downey Jr. (Billy Covington), the film focuses on the escapades of a group of hard-living Air America pilots in Laos who become disillusioned after unwittingly flying opium for a key U.S. ally, Lu Soong. Covington soon discovers that General Lu owns a major heroin refinery near the capital with the support of the American ambassador and the CIA. He tells his buddy Gene, "I never committed any crimes until working for my own government. They've turned me into a dope smuggler." He continues, "We're getting our American GIs strung out by delivering this stuff. We might as well be dropping *rattlesnakes in a schoolyard*. Tell me, doesn't this bother you in your soul?" Covington eventually decides to take matters into his own hands and blows up one of General Lu's heroin labs. Asked the next day if he feels satisfied, Covington replies with a smile, "Hell yes."

In focusing on drugs as the most immoral element of America's involvement in Laos, *Air America* helped to obscure the true devastation wrought by the "secret war," which the *New York Times* referred to as "the most appalling episode of lawless cruelty in American history." According to Alfred W. McCoy, who remains one of the best chroniclers of these events, the United States dropped at least 2.1 million tons of bombs (more than the total U.S. bombs dropped during World War II), mostly on the Plain of Jars region, which was designated as a free-fire zone.[40] Farmers living in that area were forced to seek shelter in underground caves, as USAID reports confirm, and could emerge only at night to plow their fields. Their cattle and livestock were often depleted by the bombs and the spraying of chemical defoliants, including white phosphorus and napalm. As in Cambodia and the rest of Indochina, countless villages were leveled or destroyed, and thousands of civilians were wounded and killed, a fact toward which Ambassador G. McMurtrie Godley and Henry A. Kissinger, responsible for ordering the attacks, expressed cold indifference.[41] By the end of the war a large portion of the Laotian countryside resembled, in the words of journalist T. D. Allman, a "wasteland" and "lake of blood" where, according to another observer, "civilized society had ceased to exist."[42] Upward of 40,000 Hmong recruited by the CIA as a proxy army also lay dead. With nearly the entire mature-adult population wiped out, Americans began to conscript prepubescent boys as young as ten years old to fight the Pathet Lao and face, in the words of one agent, "certain slaughter" and a "one way copter ride to death."[43] The CIA and its Air America subsidiary meanwhile sustained few casualties.

In a telling reflection of Hollywood's inversion of history, Gibson's and Downey's characters are portrayed as heroes not only for torching General Soong's heroin lab but also for saving Laotian refugees under assault by the Pathet Lao, the lone political group that in reality had any indigenous base of popular support. They had been thrust underground following the CIA's subversion of elections in which they won a majority of seats. No mention is made of this, nor of the terrible humanitarian ramifications of the real-life bombing sorties, which were responsible, according to U.S. government documents, for the creation of more than a million refugees. The cruel fate of the Hmong, who were decimated, uprooted, and eventually forced into exile, is also overlooked. In ignoring these trends, *Air America* ultimately contributed to what historian George Herring characterized as America's "self-conscious collective amnesia" surrounding the social brutalities of the Indo-China war and the perpetration of wartime atrocities, while in the process helping to promote a resonant antidrug message.[44]

"That Sucker Is Going to Get Somebody Killed!"
Television and the Extension of the Myth

Like Hollywood films, television shows played a significant role in preserving the myth of the addicted army throughout the Reagan and Bush I eras and revising the history of the war to cast Americans as its primary victims. The CBS hit series *Magnum PI* featured numerous episodes where Vietnam veterans and demonic Asian Communists were cast as criminal drug traffickers; playing on the worn theme that the war had come back to haunt the United States through the proliferation of drugs. The show's pilot in December 1980, "Please Don't Eat the Snow in Hawaii," focused on the efforts of lead investigator Thomas Magnum, an emotionally scarred Vietnam veteran, to clear the name of a former platoon member named John Cook, who was found dead with ten pounds of cocaine in his stomach. Magnum discovers that Cook was framed by their former sergeant, who had gone insane after the war ended. While solving the mystery, he encounters a Hmong princess known as "Snow White," who was said to control the major trafficking networks from the Golden Triangle. The woman had allegedly killed her husband, General Nhu Trang, a former CIA asset and drug lord, to gain her position.[45] The broader implication of the episode remained clear in stereotyping drugs as a product of the degrading influence of Asian culture and linking America's drug problem and the decay of its inner cities to the psychopathology of veterans.

In the episode titled "All for One," which upheld the POW myth and falsely associated the Khmer Rouge genocide with the Communist revolutionary victory in Vietnam, Magnum is sent to Cambodia to save a missing comrade from captivity, as well as a democratic "third force alternative" presidential candidate, who is referred to as the country's "George Freakin' Washington." Before the heroic rescue scene, Magnum is detained by Communist cadres who have been forced by their Vietnamese backers to grow and export opium as a means of financing a ruthless police-torture state. (Many viewers likely were unaware that the Vietnamese Communists had actually fought a war against the Khmer Rouge, who received indirect support from both China and the United States, or that American allies frequently ran vicious police states too.)[46]

The NBC cop series *Miami Vice* placed primary blame for the influx of hard narcotics on American streets not with evil Communists but with the CIA. In a 1985 episode titled "Golden Triangle," which depicts the region as a "lawless frontier" in need of being "civilized" through American-style law enforcement, a wealthy Laotian General, Lao Le, receives protection from the CIA for political reasons and is linked to the free flow of heroin into Miami. Another episode, "Back in the World," featured flashback footage to Vietnam and focused on the reunion of detective Sonny Crockett with a fellow veteran named Ira Stone, who had investigated the drug trade as a military news correspondent and uncovered a plot in which heroin was smuggled in the coffins of dead GIs. Stone tells Crockett of his suspicion that the drugs had been kept in storage for ten years and were recently re-released to the market laced with methanol, causing several apparent overdoses. After conducting his own inquiry, Crockett determines that a lieutenant with CIA connections, whom he had admired for his courage during the war, is behind the scheme and controls a major drug trafficking syndicate out of the Golden Triangle. Crockett also finds that Stone has lied and is implicated in the plot, in part to support his debilitating addiction to heroin. In stereotyped fashion, Stone's character is psychologically scarred by the war—as evident in a scene where he envisions that Vietcong sappers have invaded Miami Beach—and has turned to drugs as a solace.[47]

The CBS hit *Tour of Duty*, which aired from August 1987 to early 1991, followed the norm in advancing popular stereotypes about drug use in

Vietnam while distorting other aspects of the war. Sponsored by the DOD, the series focused on a multiracial platoon fighting out of the central highlands of South Vietnam beginning in 1967 (racial tensions are idyllically minimized). The Vietnamese revolutionaries are cast as savages and the ARVN soldiers, in paternalistic fashion, as seeking "guidance" from their American advisers or as being incorrigibly corrupt (in contrast to the virtuous Americans, whose intentions are always pure). As in countless Hollywood films, there is no broader analysis of the role of ideology or history in shaping the character of the war. In the pilot episode, Captain Zeke Anderson uncovers a drug-smuggling ring among corrupt ARVN officers while training a group of Montagnards deep in the jungle. Captain Zeke later finds a platoon member dead in an opium parlor in Saigon.[48]

In March 1988 the "Blood Brothers" episode opened with the declaration, "By 1970, it is estimated that 10 to 15 percent of all U.S. troops serving in Vietnam were addicted to one form of heroin or another." These totals were derived from the Murphy-Steele report, which was actually not issued until May 1971, and which Steele himself later repudiated. The show featured the arrival of a young Puerto Rican private named Alvaro who becomes addicted to heroin. Contrary to the findings of military psychiatrists, who depicted drug use being undertaken collectively as a social activity to vent frustration with the military brass and as a symbol of resistance, Alvaro gets high only in isolation and becomes a pariah in the platoon.[49] After catching him shooting up in the barracks (itself a rarity in Vietnam—heroin was usually smoked), a Latino soldier, Alberto Ruiz, tells him, "You want to mess with that crap you do that on your own ground, brother. Here you're risking guys' lives." While out on patrol the next day, Alvaro becomes delusional and fires his gun wildly into the air, alerting the Vietcong. He then steps on a land mine and is instantly killed. Captain Zeke blames himself for not recognizing the problem, commenting, "It's like a spider on a hot stove going into battle. . . . I've seen it happen before. A whole unit got wiped out earlier in my tour because of one guy using drugs."

Bent on cutting off the source of supply, Zeke travels with Ruiz to a seedy area around Tu Do Street in Saigon known as "sin city," where GIs are depicted shooting "smack" in the bathroom of a rundown bar. In an interesting juxtaposition, a black soldier and his friends get drunk at the same bar and later visit the brothel next door, where they solicit Vietnamese prostitutes. These activities are portrayed as completely natural to the war setting and not at all inappropriate or immoral, in stark contrast to the portrayal of drug use. The show ends with a Western-style gunfight in which a wounded general named Exeley, who was the one selling drugs to fellow American soldiers, is killed. He has been referred to by Ruiz as a "low-life bastard."

During *Tour of Duty*'s third season, another platoon member, Purcell, becomes addicted to heroin as a result of his disillusionment with the war. He has previously been depicted as an all-American type, having beat up a Stanford undergraduate who arrogantly told him about writing his senior thesis on American imperialism (in yet another example of the denigration of the antiwar movement in popular culture and construction of an adversarial relationship with enlisted men). In "A Necessary End," Purcell's heroin supplier gets high before going into battle. Much like Alvaro in the "Blood Brothers" episode, he becomes jittery when entering a village and participates in a My Lai–style massacre of civilians at Phu-An, which the senior command covers up. Purcell is forced to reevaluate his life and undergoes rehabilitation after Zeke saves the day once again by rescuing him from a dank Saigon opium den.[50] This plot conveyed the well-worn theme that drugs provoked civilian atrocities (which were portrayed as aberrations carried out by "bad apples" and not systemic to the war), while casting drugs as dangerous social substances responsible for jeopardizing American war aims. It further valorized the actions of antidrug crusaders like Zeke, thus lending support to their real-life incarnations.

NBCs *China Beach*, which was set at a military recreational and medical facility off the coast of Danang, promoted a strong antidrug message similar to that of *Tour of Duty*. In an episode titled "Cherry," a nurse named K.C. becomes addicted to heroin as a means of coping with the death of a close friend in combat, and she plots with another disgruntled soldier to smuggle heroin back into the United States. In "One Giant Leap," one of the hospital staff, Boonie, begins dispensing marijuana joints and opiates to wounded patients in order to lift their spirits. He plans a party in the hospital, where drugs flow freely. Chief Nurse Colleen McMurphy is not amused and, when passed a joint, puts it out. She tells Boonie. "If these guys get addicted and go out in the field stoned, they could get killed!" With an air of moral indignation, she continues, "Guys come in eighteen, nineteen, addicted to opium, heroin—they're just kids!" After the party McMurphy is confronted at gunpoint by a deranged veteran named Everett who had previously asked her to forge medical documents so that he could be sent home. High on heroin, Everett rants about being surrounded by enemy forces and alleges that McMurphy is part of a conspiracy to send him back to the front lines to get killed.[51]

The "One Giant Leap" episode concludes when Boonie nearly dies after letting Everett drive his jeep while still high from the party. Metaphorically speaking, this incident reinforced the link between drugs, unnecessary casualties, and the breakdown of military discipline. It also helped to promote moral outrage at the use of drugs—though not any other aspects of the war—while sidestepping deeper political analysis and engagement. Everett's character generally provides for an interesting comparison with McMurphy, who is portrayed as a heavy drinker and retreats to the local bar to drown out her sorrows following the party. Reflecting the producers' bias, there is never any suggestion that alcohol exerted a negative effect on McMurphy's work or was a problem in Vietnam. In this respect, *China Beach* was little different from most other popular-cultural representations.

Rather than presenting either a realistic or a romanticized view of the Vietnam War, Hollywood and television created a demonic picture of a nation—the United States—shaken to its core by drug abuse among its fighting men. By the late 1980s, together with the spread of other cultural myths, Americans had become saturated with the image of a country whose very survival was threatened by the curse of addiction. The impact should not be underestimated. Taking hold among a wide public audience, this impression helped elevate drugs to an issue of central political importance and bred support for heightened drug-control measures. It also contributed to an erasure from public memory of the intricacies of the war itself, making it seem, as veteran and acclaimed poet W. D. Ehrhart noted, that "Vietnam was something that happened to us [in America], when in reality it was something that we did to them [the Vietnamese]." Instead of questioning the fundamental tenets of U.S. foreign policy and empire, a majority of Americans consequently came to embrace domestic policy reform as a means of revitalizing the nation, with the War on Drugs designed as a pivotal measure to help fulfill this end. The devastating scope of America's aerial bombardment campaign and the suffering of the Southeast Asian people, meanwhile, were cast aside as U.S. leaders embarked on new imperial interventions in Central America and elsewhere, placed a crippling embargo on Vietnam, and re-armed for future wars.[52]

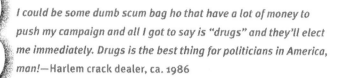

THE CRACKDOWN

THE REAGAN REVOLUTION
AND THE WAR ON DRUGS

I could be some dumb scum bag ho that have a lot of money to push my campaign and all I got to say is "drugs" and they'll elect me immediately. Drugs is the best thing for politicians in America, man!—Harlem crack dealer, ca. 1986

In 1989, journalist Jefferson Morley smoked a rock of crack cocaine and wrote about his experience for the *New Republic* in "What Crack Is Really Like." Though Morley was known to indulge in recreational drug use, the piece held deep political significance: it was written as a parody of the sweeping drug sensationalism that he saw pervading the country. Morley concluded that crack was not instantaneously addictive, as it was portrayed in the media, but produced a mere mild euphoric high followed by a brief hangover the next day. "If all you have in life is bad choices," he wrote, in attempting to highlight the structural variables of race, class, and socioeconomic background that shape addiction patterns, "crack may not be the most unpleasant of them."[1]

Besides selling magazines and earning the ire of presidential drug policy adviser William Bennett, who called the author a "defector in the drug war," Morley's journalistic stunt captured the zeitgeist of the late 1980s. This was best described in the title of a book by Mike Gray, *Drug Crazy.*[2] By mid-decade, public opinion polls showed that a majority of Americans viewed drugs as among the worst social problems and national security threats plaguing the nation; they were supporting renewed prohibition policies in ever greater numbers.[3] The Reagan administration made drug control central to its broader mandate of reviving the nation's prestige and eradicating the "culture of permissiveness of the 1960s," which stood guilty, Reagan said, of "contaminating the larger society."[4] Though not always explicitly, Vietnam and the enduring myth of the addicted army had an important impact on social attitudes toward drugs in the 1980s and on the determined character of the Reagan anti-drug crusade. Reagan officials frequently claimed that "narco-guerrillas" and "terrorists" in Latin America deliberately trafficked drugs into the United States as an act of warfare and sabotage. This claim harked back to similar accusations made against Communist traffickers earlier and tapped into deep-rooted anxieties surrounding the ramifications of drug use in post–Vietnam America, including its purported link to the spread of violence, crime, and an erosion of national strength and power. Reagan's War on Drugs was designed to address these problems. It also sought to revive public confidence in American social institutions, including the military, purportedly ravaged by drugs during the 1960s and '70s.

Misreading Public Opinion
The Carter "Failure"

The political underpinning of Reagan's drug war was partially tied to the shortcomings of predecessor Jimmy Carter, who had left himself susceptible to attack by failing to placate popular concerns over drugs. Commissioner of Customs William Von Raab characteristically commented that before 1981, "fighting the drug war was sort of like being with the Brooklyn Dodgers. It was sort of wait until next year." Carter saw himself more as part of a winning tradition and had increased federal drug control programs, placing an emphasis on supply-side interdiction.[5] With the Middle East supplanting the Golden Triangle as a major source of heroin, Carter boosted federal aid to UN crop substitution and rural development programs in Turkey, Iran, Pakistan, and Afghanistan's Upper Helmond Valley, and he supported the formation of an antidrug unit in the Afghan national police. He also expanded military and police assistance in the Andes, in response to the growing export of cocaine, and backed a major eradication campaign in Peru's Upper Huallaga Valley (UHV) in which American-trained security forces were given broad powers of search and seizure and detention.[6] In Colombia, Carter tripled the foreign aid budget and signed an extradition treaty with President Julio Turbay Ayala mandating the deportation of high-level traffickers. In Mexico, he simultaneously helped coordinate what journalist Jack Anderson characterized as a Vietnam-style war involving search-and-destroy missions and aerial defoliation campaigns—including flights over marijuana fields—that soiled the land.[7]

Domestically, Carter's administration boasted about the arrest of several prominent traffickers, including Harlem kingpin Leroy "Nicky" Barnes, who had been featured on the cover of the *New York Times Magazine.* Carter also proved to be a major benefactor of rehabilitation, distributing over $135 million in federal aid grants per year in support of the Federal Bureau of Prisons' opening twenty-three treatment units in twenty institutions.[8] In 1977, Carter appointed Dr. Peter Bourne as his director of a newly created Office for Drug Abuse Prevention (ODAP). A product of the 1960s intellectual generation and a social environmentalist, Bourne endorsed marijuana and cocaine decriminalization and the harm-reduction model used in the Netherlands, which called for the controlled dispensation of narcotics by specialized clinics in gradually reduced doses. In 1974, Bourne wrote an article titled "The Cocaine Myth," which argued that the drug was more or less harmless when taken in moderate doses and was a minimal public health risk, especially compared with legally accepted drugs such as nicotine and alcohol. He nevertheless supported the international drug war, albeit more modestly than his successors, and opposed an amendment put forward by Senator Charles Percy (D-Ill.) calling for the banning of herbicidal sprays.[9]

Based on Bourne's advice, Carter endorsed an easing of punitive sanctions for marijuana, commenting that the "penalties for possession of a drug shouldn't be more damaging to an individual than the use of the drug itself." By 1980, ten states including New York had adopted decriminalization laws. Carter's association with marijuana decriminalization would backfire politically and made him susceptible to charges of being "soft on crime." Polls showed that 50 percent of the public feared walking on their own streets alone at night and that 66 percent thought drug use a "major problem," particularly among high school–aged students.[10] The media had helped to exacerbate public fears by airing such specials as the 1978 CBS documentary "Reading, Writing and Reefer," which featured fifteen-year-old heroin addicts and twelve-year-old middle school students from affluent suburbs who skipped class and smoked upward of five marijuana joints per day.

Local parent organizations, including the Parents Resource Institute for Drug Education (PRIDE) in Georgia, had begun to lobby at this time for greater government vigilance in the fight against drug abuse. Journalist Peggy Mann gave them inspiration in a series of *Reader's Digest* and *Ladies' Home Journal* articles warning about a "lost generation" of American youth being corrupted by drugs. She quoted favorably from the writings of Dr. Gabriel Nahas, author of *Marihuana—Deceptive Weed*, who was voted PRIDE's "Man of the Decade" for the 1980s, as well as from those of Dr. Sidney Cohen, who warned that the spread of cocaine threatened to create a generation of "coke whores" mired in a vicious form of "human bondage."[11]

Prominent intellectuals, including James Q. Wilson of Harvard's Kennedy School of Government, had since abandoned the scholarly emphasis on environmental factors, attributing the proliferation of drug abuse and crime to individual choices, intelligence, physiological factors, and cultural upbringing. In a widely read 1977 book, *Thinking about Crime*, Wilson wrote, "I have yet to see a root cause or to encounter a government program that has successfully attacked it."[12] Wilson promoted the concept of the "career criminal," who was considered to be incorrigible because of a long history of criminal activity and who could be deterred only through the threat of harsh punishment. He supported strict drug-control measures, including the public quarantining of addicts, whom he likened to sufferers of smallpox. Wilson's writings encapsulated a rising disenchantment with the Great Society liberalism that had pervaded the United States during the late 1970s, and a perception that liberal social programs had wrought an ugly harvest of social disorder and criminality—as embodied in the perceived explosion of drug abuse—which furthered the demand, in turn, for the revival of harsh punitive measures.[13]

In 1978, Robert DuPont joined the antimarijuana bandwagon and later published *Getting Tough on Gateway Drugs*, which recommended that parents keep a number of collection bottles in the home so that "if a question of drug use arises, a urine sample can be taken promptly." In 1979, in his last action as director of the NIDA, DuPont supported the publication of an antidrug diatribe by Marsha Schuchard, *Parents, Peers, and Pot*, in which she recounted horror stories of studious and athletic kids falling prey to drug addiction. In her synopsis, the Carter administration had been shortsighted about the dire consequences of the "drug epidemic" and had failed to assert the necessary moral leadership. This charge was given added credence when in 1978 Peter Bourne was accused of snorting cocaine at a Christmas party for the National Organization for the Reform of Marijuana Laws (NORML) and of writing a phony drug prescription for one of his secretaries, charges that forced him to resign.[14] Several months later, Carter's chief of staff admitted to a cocaine problem, as did his national campaign manager. These scandals did irreparable damage to Carter's public image and played into the hands of

Ronald Reagan, who proved successful in tapping into social anxieties remnant from the Vietnam era and in exploiting the drug issue for political benefit.

"We Do Not Want a Recurrence of Vietnam"
Nimitz and the Renewed Panic

Carter's failure to engender confidence in his drug policies was echoed by the military's similar failure. Reflecting their flag-waving sensibilities and parochial focus, the media continued to claim that drug abuse represented a perilous legacy of the Vietnam War and a recurring security threat. In November 1978 the *Washington Post* published a characteristic article, "Drug Abuse Casts Shadow on Army's Readiness," which detailed the case of a stoned GI who nearly caused a major collision between a truckload of Hawk antiaircraft missiles and an oncoming tank. "The guy just wasn't right," Sergeant Charles Smith stated. "A guy on heroin is of no use." A *New York Times* editorial had previously concluded, "Drug use in the military is accelerating at such a rapid pace that it threatens to reach the epidemic levels of the Vietnam years when many American troops in Asia dropped out and found heroin a bitter solace to the war. This trend bodes ominous for the future."[15]

Politicians drummed up similar fears in reinvoking the myth of the addicted army. Congressional representatives visiting military bases in Germany, for example, referred to the proliferation of drug use as a "chilling phenomenon" that threatened national security. In testimony before Congress, Lester Wolff (D-N.Y.) commented, "We all recall seeing pictures of open opium parlors in Vietnam and hearing reports suggesting the My-Lai incident may have been influenced by marijuana. What developed in Vietnam—the degradation that took place in the efficiency of our forces as a result of the ready availability and subsequent abuse of narcotics—was one of the elements that undermined the U.S. effort in Vietnam. We certainly do not want a recurrence of those events."[16]

A helicopter crash on the aircraft carrier USS *Nimitz* in May 1981, in which six of the ten dead flight crewmen were found to have traces of marijuana in their system, amplified fears of a repeat of Vietnam. In the six months before that crash, which caused $150 million in property damage and left forty-eight soldiers wounded, a Senate investigation determined that there had been 124 formal cases of court-martial or nonjudicial punishment against the *Nimitz* crew solely for drug abuse. Drugs, it was found, had even been sent to some crewmen via first-class mail.

Joseph P. Addabo (D-N.Y.), who investigated the crash, commented, "The use of drugs was tantamount to a death sentence for those in the aircraft as well as for those on the flight deck."[17]

The *Nimitz* crash helped to prolong existing fears surrounding the erosion of American power and to heighten public anxiety that like Vietnam, the Cold War was being lost—in part by drugs. Even though the Soviet Union was on the verge of collapse, public opinion polls showed that an overwhelming majority of Americans (as high as 93 percent in some polls) were alarmed by the threat of Communist expansion and felt that a strengthening of national defense capacities should be the president's number one priority.[18] Congressman Robert R. Dornan (R-Calif.) commented, "If I were a Soviet commander, I'd be licking my chops at the prospect of taking on soft American kids who are only interested in getting high." He added, "The Soviets are well aware of our drug abuse problem and planning on banking on it as an additional benefit to them in combat situations. They're expecting to blow their way to the North Sea, the English Channel in a matter of days, not weeks, because Western civilization is so decadent and that decadence has transposed itself to the military."[19]

Dornan's comments typified the revival of fears about the use of drugs in the military, which American enemies, it appeared, were bent on exploiting. The backdrop of Vietnam helped shape this outlook, as did the toppling of American clients in the 1979 Nicaraguan and Iranian revolutions.[20] In a July 1979 speech which, pundits charged, marked the death knell of his presidency, Carter declared that America was gripped by a "crisis of confidence" that "strikes at the very heart and soul and spirit of our national will." He warned, "The erosion of confidence in the future is threatening to destroy the social and political fabric in America."[21] Carter's policies—both domestic and international—ultimately did little to alleviate public fears about America's declining global prestige.[22] The failure of his drug war policy, in many respects, represented this trend.

Morning in America?
The Reagan Revolution, the War on Drugs,
and the Politics of Symbolism

Though disparaged by critics as intellectually hollow and aloof, with policies catering to an upper-class constituency, Ronald W. Reagan remains one of the more popular presidents in American history. As historian Robert Dallek best expressed it in a book published shortly before the 1984 reelection campaign, Reagan's acclaim was largely predicated on a politics of "symbolism" and an ability to satisfy psychological rather than material needs.[23] This ability was embodied in his domestic policies, which garnered widespread backing despite resulting in a cutback of vital social services, in budgetary deficits, and in an increase in economic inequality. Reagan further enacted a dangerous arms buildup to counter a crumbling Soviet empire, while sponsoring rogue forces such as the Nicaraguan contras and Uniao Nacional para a Independencia Total de Angola, which terrorized civilians in crushing liberation movements that had few established links to Moscow.[24]

A large element of Reagan's symbolic appeal was his ability to promote nostalgia for the past and renewed confidence and pride in being American, in part by associating himself with traditional values such as hard work, religious adherence, and patriotism.[25] Predominantly ignored by chroniclers of his presidency was the importance of the War on Drugs. In a 1986 public address, Reagan stated, "Drug abuse is the repudiation of everything America is. The destructiveness and human wreckage mock our heritage." He added that America was "threatened by an epidemic of drug abuse that was growing in intensity since the 1960s. By 1980, illegal drugs were every bit as much a threat to the United States as enemy planes and missiles. The plague was fueled by an attitude of permissiveness, both public and private. America was losing its future by default."[26] In order to counter these tendencies, Reagan increased funding to the DEA and FBI, helped to establish a nationally coordinated border control system, and signed an executive order authorizing the CIA to produce intelligence on drug trafficking. In 1982 he formed the South Florida Task Force under Vice President George Bush to facilitate cooperation between state and local law enforcement officials in cracking down on organized criminal activity and smuggling.[27]

Reagan's enforcement mandate was strengthened by the rise of the Colombian Medellín cartel, headed by the infamous Pablo Escobar Gaviria, which had pioneered the bulk shipping of cocaine into the United States through Miami during the late 1970s and early 1980s.[28] The media became filled with sensational pieces depicting the harrowing violence unleashed by Escobar's henchmen in an effort to control the lucrative market from Cuban exiles (many of them Bay of Pigs veterans) and other organized criminals.[29] A 1981 *Miami Herald* editorial proclaimed, "If the War on Drugs is the Vietnam of law enforcement, then South Florida is its Khe Sanh—isolated, besieged, almost overrun." Invoking a similar Vietnam analogy, Senator Claude Pepper of Florida declared, "We're seeing a Tet offensive in South Florida. 18,000 flights per year are smuggling narcotics and the influx of cocaine is having a horrifying effect on our communities, with people turning into walking zombies. You pick up the paper and read about a drug related murder every day."[30]

Attempting to calm public anxieties, Reagan pushed Congress into amending the Posse Comitatus Act of 1878 so that military forces could be used to assist civilian officers in the enforcement of drug laws.[31] This was important symbolically in conveying that the addicted army of the 1970s was now doing everything in its power to fight the spread of drugs. By the mid-1980s the DOD had come to employ some of its most sophisticated weaponry, such as Black Hawk assault helicopters and Blue Thunder speedboats, for prohibition purposes. The Coast Guard also began to program high-tech satellites to detect smuggling routes from the Caribbean. Reagan simultaneously promoted stricter punitive sentencing through the 1984 Comprehensive Crime Control Act, which included a "drug kingpin law" elevating the maximum penalty for drug traffickers to life imprisonment without the possibility of parole.[32] In a shrewd public relations maneuver, the president enlisted the support of the first lady, Nancy Reagan, in the antidrug crusade after she had received bad press for spending taxpayer dollars on fancy White House china. Nancy became highly influential in organizing various antidrug conferences involving first ladies from around the world, and in promoting international antidrug education. She further helped to promote grassroots antidrug efforts among America's youth, which epitomized the important nationalistic underpinnings of the Reagan drug war.[33]

In 1983, a *U.S. News & World Report* article, "How Drugs Sap the Nation's Strength," linked drugs to a decline in worker productivity and a 40 percent decline in SAT verbal and math scores since the 1960s. Black community leader Jesse Jackson commented that drug abuse had swept across the nation's schoolyards with a "fervor rarely matched. Demosthenes said 'whom the gods would destroy, they first make mad.' Our young are being driven mad with drugs." Texas Governor Jim Wright added, "Our elementary schools are functioning like fast breeder reactors for future junkies. This is the fountain from which we must draw our science, our leaders. The young are being enslaved through drugs and ruining their whole lives."[34]

In response, the Reagan administration developed the "Just Say No" campaign, which was inaugurated by Nancy during a visit to an elementary school in Oakland, California. Some 10,000 clubs were eventually formed to sponsor public parades, rallies, local drug hotlines, and a national walk against drugs. In California in 1986, more than 8,000 young people gathered in the Rose Bowl to read in unison their Just Say No drug pledge. Displaying the intrinsic patriotic message of the campaign, they released thousands of red, white, and blue balloons bearing antidrug slogans. The youth were meant to represent the bright future of an America unsullied by drugs. Reagan pleaded, "To the young people out there, our country needs you and it needs you to be clear eyed and clear minded. Please when it comes to drugs, Just Say No."[35]

Much like Nixon's, Reagan's administration enacted a massive media campaign directed at America's youth. In March 1983 the White House Drug Abuse Council sponsored a made-for-television film, *Cocaine—One Man's Poison,* about a man who destroyed his family life and career as a result of addiction. Drug policy adviser Carleton Turner called the show a "perfect vehicle for deglamorizing drugs." In a 1986 letter signed by more than 300 members of Congress, Reagan subsequently pleaded for the collaboration of the major television networks in waging an "unprecedented, coordinated offensive against the culture that encourages the use of dangerous drugs."[36] The White House's Office on Drug Abuse Policy subsequently aired a string of ads through the Media-Advertising Partnership for a Drug Free America, which had been established with network subsidies to help "unsell" illegal drugs. Many ads featured prominent celebrities; others, the McGruff crime dog ("Take a bite out of crime"), a creation of Reagan publicists which was highly popular among kids.

With government prodding, prime-time programs also adopted antidrug themes. In one episode of the hit show *Punky Brewster,* Punky formed a Just Say No club at her school after being pressured by her friends to try drugs. At the end of the NBC broadcast, Soleil Moon Frye, the real-life Punky, elaborated on the dangers of drug use. Nancy Reagan later appeared as a guest star on the NBC hit *Different Strokes* to decry the pernicious influence of drugs at the school of lead character Arnold (played by Gary Coleman). The prominence accorded the antidrug message in these shows and the scope of the advertising campaigns demonstrate how the Reagan administration was able to sway the content being presented in the media and popular culture, more shrewdly than Nixon had, while helping to solidify antidrug mores in the United States. The mandate of the old Oklahoma football Coach Charles "Bud" Wilkinson of trying to repudiate the spread of the 1960s counterculture was at long last being fulfilled.

Operation Golden-Flow Redux and Reagan's War on Drugs in the Military

The legacy of Vietnam was central in the revival of a protracted antidrug campaign in the military. Commenting that "an alert mind in battle free of drugs can mean the difference between life and death," Reagan commissioned the DOD to ensure stricter enforcement and to expand recreational facilities on military bases, where boredom was seen to be a root cause of rising addiction.[37] He also promoted drug education for new recruits and revived the mandatory urinalysis testing system from the Nixon-Jaffe era. After the withdrawal of American troops from Vietnam, urinalysis had been temporarily halted because of complaints that it violated individual civil liberties. In 1979 the American Civil Liberties Union (ACLU) filed a successful lawsuit on behalf of a lieutenant named Antonio Giles, claiming that the tests were unconstitutional because soldiers were not told that they could decline participation. In 1980, however, a new court injunction proclaimed future tests legal so long as individual military personnel were aware of their right to refuse. The White House subsequently mounted "Operation Clean-Sweep," which was similar in scope to Golden-Flow. Because of a technological breakthrough, the army was able this time to detect cannabis as well as opiates. Those found with traces of either substance faced likely discharge or punishment (but not rehabilitation, which was a lower priority).[38]

As a result of the new regulations, Reagan was able to boast in 1986 that drug use had declined by 67 percent in the armed forces during his presidency. He portrayed this as a symbol of the resurgence of American military power—particularly in light of Operation Urgent Fury in Grenada, where the military overthrew a Marxist regime in less than a week (in a mission which, one analyst noted, "the NYPD could have carried out.")[39] Throughout the mid-1980s, public opinion polls documented that nearly 70 percent of Americans approved Washington's delivery of a "stronger national defense." Reagan proclaimed, "Restoring America's strength has been one of our administration's highest goals. We've turned a desperate situation around."[40] The War on Drugs appeared to be pivotal in facilitating these ends and helped to promote public assurances that the drug-tainted war of Vietnam was in the past.

"Narco-Guerrillas" and the Expansion of the International Drug War

Reagan's War on Drugs was most vigorous in the international realm, where he built on the programs institutionalized in Southeast Asia. In April 1986, at the urging of a House Select Committee on Narcotics Abuse and Control, which pushed incessantly for the militarization of the War on Drugs, Reagan signed a national security directive identifying drug production and trafficking as threats to American national security. He subsequently brokered bilateral interdiction agreements with twenty-three countries that pushed for crop substitution and alternative development projects. The most ambitious efforts undertaken were in Turkey, Thailand, and Burma, as well as Peru, where USAID provisioned $26.5 million to help reduce coca cultivation in the UHV region, and paid farmers $300 per hectare of coca destroyed.[41]

The State Department simultaneously expanded provisions for the establishment of special counternarcotics police and army regiments in Latin America in programs modeled after the OPS initiatives of the 1970s in Southeast Asia.[42] Most of the advisory instruction was conducted at the U.S.-run School of the Americas in Fort Benning, Georgia, which served as a center for the training of elite officers—including some of the continent's most notorious murderers and torturers—in counterinsurgency strategy. As in the past, the narcotic subsections sometimes served as a front for CIA agents and the waging of counterguerrilla warfare and were staffed by state security forces linked to major human rights violations, including a notorious death squad operator in El Salvador, Dr. Hector Regaldo. They helped to bolster the policing powers of repressive regimes and were implicated in extrajudicial kidnappings and torture. Stan Goff, a former Special Forces officer in Colombia who headed a counternarcotic training team, explained, "The training that I conducted was anything but counter-narcotics. It was updated Vietnam-style counter-insurgency, but we were told to refer to it as counter-narcotics should anyone ask. This was a clear cover."[43]

In 1986, Congress passed a special law calling for the certification of American allies based on their commitment to the antidrug crusade as a precondition for their receiving foreign assistance. Critics charged that the screening was done in a discretionary way and served a dual agenda by enabling the State Department to intensify cooperation with the policing and intelligence networks of allied regimes engaged in the suppression of social movements deemed threatening to American interests.[44] Throughout Central America and the Andes, military equipment—including B-52s, helicopters, and assault rifles for drug suppression purposes—was utilized in direct strikes against insurgents and their civilian supporters, strikes legitimized on the grounds that they were harboring narcotics manufacturers and distributors.[45] The parallel with Burma in the 1970s and elsewhere in Southeast Asia was explicit.

In trying to justify its actions, the State Department claimed that Latin American "narco-guerrillas" or "narco-terrorists" had plotted to undermine American national security through the export of drugs.[46] According to customs commissioner William Von Raab, "What we're seeing is the development of what I call the Siamese twins of death and destruction—international terrorism and narcotics smuggling. Drugs have become the natural ally of those who would choose to destroy the democratic societies in our hemisphere through violent means." The terms "narco-guerrilla" and "narco-terrorist" had been first employed by Lewis Tambs, the American ambassador to Colombia, to promote congressional support for the war against the Fuerzas Armada Revolucionario de Colombia (FARC)—a pro-Castro guerrilla organization intent on redistributing national wealth through land reform and expelling American private investment.[47]

The resonance of the narco-guerrilla metaphor in the United States drew in part on the legacy of Vietnam and the ingrained perception of drugs as a security threat and weapon of foreign subversion. As in the past, few were able to recognize that this threat was more imaginary than real. According to the DEA and regional specialists, FARC's involvement with drugs actually paled before the deeper corruption of government forces and was predominantly limited in this period to the taxing of coca farmers living under their domain. Most criminal traffickers deplored left-wing political ideologies and amassed vast personal fortunes, including lavish mansions, professional sports clubs, and even their own petting zoos.[48] Bolivian drug baron Roberto Suarez Gomez was so rich that he offered to pay off Bolivia's foreign debt on the condition that his nephew be released from prison. The Medellín and Cali cartels allegedly contributed upward of $10 million to the Nicaraguan contras, an amalgamation of U.S.-trained paramilitary organizations dedicated to destabilizing the popularly backed Sandinista government. Suarez meanwhile allied himself with the right-wing Garcia Meza regime in the early 1980s.[49]

In Colombia in 1981 the M-19 guerrilla group, which adopted a radical nationalist and socialist philosophy, kidnapped the daughter of Cali king-pin Jorge Luis Ochoa, leading to the eruption of violence between the two groups. The Colombian cartels subsequently formed paramilitary "hunter-killer" squads to assist the state security apparatus and military in targeting the *guerrilleros* and their followers with CIA assistance, even after the declaration of a cease-fire.[50]

Despite the drug war's frequent subordination to broader foreign policy objectives, the DEA did play an aggressive role in countering the transnational spread of narcotics. In 1984 it launched a major sting operation in the Andes, dubbed Pisces. Later it helped to set up Operation Intercept II in Mexico, which resulted in the closing of the border for eight days and the arrest of several notorious underground operators, including the murderer of DEA agent Enrique "Kiki" Camarena. On March 10, 1984, the DEA worked in collaboration with the Colombian national police to destroy the Medellín cartel's main cocaine-refining complex at Tranquilandia in the Amazon rain forest. The operation forced the cartel to develop mobile refining plants as well as to increase use of extortion and violence, culminating in the murder of Justice Minister Lara Rodrigo Bonilla, who had sanctioned the raid. In 1985 the DEA launched Operation Condor in conjunction with Rural Mobile Police Patrol Units (UMO-PAR), the special counternarcotics brigade of the Peruvian national police. The mission consisted of joint military strikes and air raids on cocaine-processing laboratories in Tingo Maria, the capital of Peru's "cocalandia" in the UHV. Using Bell 214 and fixed-wing C-123 helicopters donated by the U.S. military, as well as special power trimmers capable of cutting coca bushes from the air, Condor resulted in the demolition of forty coca labs, the disabling of forty airstrips, and the destruction of 725 metric tons of coca leaf.[51]

In 1986 the U.S. based another four-month mission in Bolivia on the model of Condor. "Blast Furnace," a joint collaboration of 160 U.S. military troops, sixteen army helicopters, and Leopardo antinarcotics police, conducted 256 raids and blew up twenty-one cocaine-processing laboratories in the Chapare region (though these were later found to have been empty). Touching off widespread public outcry against the violation of national sovereignty, the operation also resulted in the murder of well-known botanist Noel Kempff and two other men after they mistakenly landed their plane near a drug-processing facility targeted for attack. Nevertheless, a year later, the DEA launched Operation Snowcap, where U.S.

Special Forces wearing camouflaged uniforms assisted Bolivian military officers in laying siege to regional refineries and in destroying thousands of hectares of coca-cultivating fields.[52] The House Foreign Affairs Committee later warned against the direct use of American personnel in drug operations for fear of their "dying an excruciating death on an isolated jungle floor." It instead advocated that the DEA train "local military forces" to carry out America's drug control mandate—just as the State Department was promoting greater reliance on proxy forces to fight revolutionary insurrections throughout the so-called developing world.[53]

In the Caribbean the Reagan administration launched a joint policing effort to deny use of the Bahamas for aircraft refueling and as a staging area for smuggling.[54] It also intensified herbicidal sprayings in Jamaica, where neo-liberal structural adjustment programs and the debt crisis made many farmers dependent on growing drug crops and was a boon to the nation's underground economy, coinciding with a massive fumigation program across Latin America. In 1981, Congress repealed the Percy amendment banning the use of chemical defoliants, which Pentagon officials and Vice President Bush viewed as "the most effective means" of destroying drug crops on a large scale. In the Golden Triangle the DEA worked in collaboration with specially trained police forces to destroy over 40,000 acres of opium through this method.[55] The DEA enacted similar heavy-handed efforts in marijuana- and coca-growing regions in Mexico, the Andes, and Central America. In Colombia and Peru, chemical spraying was incorporated into increasingly brutal military pacification efforts and helped to drive farmers away from guerrilla territory into strategic government-controlled zones—much as in Vietnam. In Guatemala, aerial fumigation was part of a scorched-earth campaign in which government militias under the command of American-trained Generals Efrain Rios Montt and Hector Gramajo razed over 400 villages and killed more than 100,000 civilians—mostly Mayan Indians loosely linked to M-13 and Guerrilla Army of the Poor rebels.[56]

Apart from contributing to a rising tide of state-sponsored terror, chemical defoliation helped to destroy the livelihood of farmers who had largely been driven to narcotic cultivation by external market forces, poor regional infrastructure, and neoliberal free trade policies undermining local agricultural production. The sprayings further accelerated the process of deforestation, forcing Quechua Indian *cocaleros* in Bolivia and Peru to move deeper into the rain forest, where they practiced slash-and-burn agricultural techniques damaging to the soil. As in Mexico, the defoliants themselves caused protracted health and environmental damages, helping to turn part of the Andean landscape into what political scientist Cynthia McClintock aptly termed a "toxic waste dump."[57]

Unmindful of humanitarian ramifications, as in other realms of its foreign policy, the Reagan administration forged a pact with Peruvian president Alan Garcia in 1988 to supply the military with a potent chemical herbicide called Tebithurion (or "Spike") deemed capable of wiping out the regional coca crop. Garcia approved the quid pro quo arrangement because of his reliance on the United States to pay off the country's national debt and to help fight the left-wing Sendero Luminoso (Shining Path) and Tupac Amaru (MRTA) insurgencies. Human rights organizations later uncovered the fact that Eli Lilly, the pharmaceutical company that had manufactured Tebithurion, had refused to sell to it to American enforcement agents because it was thought to emit fumes capable of causing birth defects and cancer and to leave a residue in neighboring crops, plants, and water systems for up to five years. Yet despite protest from Congress and the resignation of Walter Gentner, the State Department's chief herbicidal scientist, the deal went forward. The sale of Tebithurion ultimately backfired politically by forcing many *cocaleros* to seek the protection of Sendero guerrillas, who had the military capabilities to shield them from future chemical attack (the same was true with FARC in Colombia).[58]

One of Reagan's most publicized initiatives was the ratification of existing bilateral extradition treaties with the Andean countries. In 1987 this policy led to the deportation of ten major Colombian traffickers, including Carlos Rivas Lehder, a flamboyant leader of the Medellín cartel, who was sentenced to life imprisonment without the possibility of parole. In a speech before the Hartford County Bar Association, Vice President Bush bragged that Lehder "now sits to rot and languish in a Jacksonville jail for the rest of his miserable life."[59] Lehder's imprisonment was given particular prominence because of his support for left-wing guerrilla movements in Latin America and espousal of an anti-American political ideology. In the early 1980s, Lehder had formed his own political party, Movimiento Latino Nacional, and hoped to use his public stature to wage an all-encompassing attack against the Colombian oligarchic leadership, which he considered to be "hopelessly dependent on North American economic and financial support." In 1985, Lehder appeared on Colombian television calling for an alliance of Marxist revolutionaries and military officers to join him in "the cocaine bonanza, the Achilles heel of

American imperialism and the arm of the struggle against America." He also placed a bounty of $350,000 dollars on the killing of American DEA agents.[60]

Though Lehder's case was presented as the sign of a left-wing conspiracy, his politics were in fact an anomaly and publicized in order to deflect attention from the corruption of key government allies. These included Gulbuddin Hikmatyar of the Islamic mujahadin in Afghanistan, Zia Al-Huq in Pakistan, high-ranking contra operatives in Nicaragua, and military officers throughout Latin America who were supported by U.S. military intelligence in using narcotics to fund counterinsurgency and terrorist activities.[61] This fit a long-standing pattern of American complicity in the global drug trade, with the former chief of the DEA's international intelligence unit, Dennis Dayle, admitting on the record that almost all his key targets of investigation in a thirty-year career "invariably turned out to be working for the CIA."[62] In 1983 the U.S. ambassador to Honduras, John Negroponte, suspiciously closed the DEA office in the capital, Tegucigalpa, allegedly to protect members of the corrupt ruling oligarchy—including death squad operator Gustavo Alvarez Martinez—who had established training camps for contra operatives waging war on their home country.[63]

Reagan had previously reestablished diplomatic relations with Panamanian dictator Manuel Antonio Noriega, after he agreed to provide air bases for the contras. A longtime CIA asset trained at the School of the Americas, Noriega was implicated in arms-for-cocaine deals with Colombian cartels that operated processing labs in the Panamanian jungle. Noriega presided over what John Kerry (D-Mass.) termed a "narcokleptocracy," implying that he pilfered all funds from drug sales to bolster his own personal fortune.[64] In 1987, Norman Bailey, a special assistant to President Reagan, resigned from his position on the National Security Council because of Reagan's ties to Noriega. In an internal memorandum, he stated, "It saddens me to think that successive administrations, both Democrat and Republican, all conspired for years to protect a group of despicable international outlaws."[65] Senator Joseph D'Amato (D-N.Y.) further charged that the War on Drugs was "nothing more than rhetoric," which did little to "combat tin-horn dictators who hide behind puppet presidents and have turned governments into criminal drug enterprises."[66] These comments, echoing similar ones made by Democratic Party representatives and the antiwar left during the Vietnam era, exemplified the continued political explosiveness of the drug issue in the United States. They also reflected an ingrained belief that drugs constituted a continuing security threat. On their part, top administrative officials did their utmost to conceal their support for known drug-trafficking entities, such as Noriega, who served America's broader strategic objectives.

Indigenous Resistance and the Failure of Prohibition (Again)

As with the Asian drug war, besides failing to limit the supply of drugs entering the United States and contributing to extensive human rights abuses, American prohibition efforts yielded pronounced animosity and resistance—particularly in Latin America. In Colombia, farmers subjected to spraying allied with the guerrillas for protection, while the cartels declared "absolute and total war" on the government with the support of paramilitary networks and hired teenage killers (known as *sicarios*)—thus instigating an orgy of violence from which the country has yet to recover. When the United States refused to rescind its extradition treaty following a peace proposal in 1985, the cartels took two dozen judges and parliament representatives hostage, leading to violent military counterreprisals and the destruction of the Palace of Justice. They later assassinated liberal presidential candidate Luis Carlos Galán. Through the end of the decade, many traffickers were able to operate with impunity because of the fear they spawned. In 1987 the Colombian government released Ochoa from custody in an act that U.S. Attorney General Edwin Meese termed "a shocking blow to international law enforcement." One DEA agent commented, "There isn't a cop that will arrest [traffickers], a judge that will try them or jail that will hold them out of fear for being killed."[67]

Elsewhere in Latin America, resistance was nearly as fervid, if only slightly less socially destructive. In Mexico, farmers often fired back at military helicopters trying to defoliate their fields, and high-level traffickers assaulted and murdered antidrug officers and other so-called drug-war collaborators, provoking a malicious wave of government reprisals. Following the launching of Operation Intercept II, over 60,000 demonstrators took to the streets in protest against the militarization of the drug war and the continued presence of the DEA on Mexican soil, which they tied to a policy of American unilateralism and hegemonic encroachment.[68] In Bolivia, Operation Blast Furnace undermined the presidency of Victor Paz Estenserro, a popular figure in the country's 1952 revolution, and helped to stoke strong anti-American sentiments. The Bolivian labor federation under the leadership of its future president, Evo Morales, mobilized coca farmers as well as workers and peasants in the Chapare and Yungas regions to demonstrate against USAID-enforced crop substitution and aerial defoliation programs and to conduct acts of civil disobedience in the form of rail and road blockades. U.S. Secretary of State George P. Schultz was later the target of an attempted bombing, as the movement radicalized.[69] In Peru, coca-growing farmers banded together to ambush DEA convoys in response to brutal eradication campaigns that drove some to suicide, and Sendero guerrillas declared an all-out war against "government genocide and eradication," which it thought to be analogous. In 1988, Sendero cadres conspired with local *cocaleros* to murder thirty-two UMOPAR officers, while also waging terrorist-style attacks against known DEA collaborators.[70]

Because coca was a profitable economic commodity and chewing it a socially accepted practice with deep historical roots, by the late 1980s Latin Americans of all political persuasions had come to view the DEA and other narcotics officers with both suspicion and disdain.[71] The broad resistance to American interdiction efforts reflected the deep shortcomings of America's foreign drug policy. Although heavy on rhetoric and, in some cases, action, American policymakers failed to consider the local terrain in which they were operating, or to address the underlying factors shaping the expansion of the international drug traffic, just as they failed to address the social problems—such as rising economic inequality, spiritual despondency, and community breakdown—breeding the high rates of demand at home.[72] The Reagan administration also failed to consider the protracted human costs of the War on Drugs, which became increasingly high as the 1980s progressed and contributed to escalating cycles of violence. As in the past, human rights issues or root causes appeared to be thought less important than the political dimensions of the drug-war policy. In this respect, little had changed since the pioneering international drug programs of the 1970s in Southeast Asia.

Casual Drug Users as Accomplices to Murder?
Crack and the Late Eighties Drug Frenzy

The 1980s antidrug crusade in America reached its zenith during the last three years of Reagan's presidency. This was due in large measure to the spread of crack, a cheap form of cocaine that could be smoked. In June 1986, Len Bias, a prominent basketball star at the University of Maryland, died of a cocaine overdose after being selected as the second overall pick in the National Basketball Association entry draft. His death helped to spawn a media frenzy, which was further provoked by DEA lobbying.[73] In May of that year, CBS aired the documentary *48 Hours on Crack Street*, which attracted over fifteen million viewers and depicted in graphic detail the workings of the New York City crack trade. Host Dan Rather proclaimed, "Tonight, CBS takes you to the streets, to the war zone, for an unusual two hours of hands-on horror." The same month, ABC anchor Peter Jennings declared crack to be "instantaneously addictive" and "the most dangerous drug known to man."[74] In June, *Newsweek* compared the spread of crack to a "medieval plague" and editorialized, "In 1941, the Japanese bombed Pearl Harbor and we went to war, and today, little white packets are invading our country."[75] While criticized by the likes of Jefferson Morley, who tried to demystify the drug and minimize its harmful effects, the media were, in retrospect, quite shrewd in serving their interests. By exaggerating the threat of crack and linking it to issues of national security, they were able to capitalize on deep-rooted Vietnam-era fears surrounding drugs and to sell more copies or garner higher ratings in the process.

Tellingly, in 1987 the DEA issued a private report blaming the media for "distorting the public perception of crack," which it characterized as a "secondary rather than primary problem in most areas." NIDA concluded that less than 1 percent of young adults used crack, which was "not instantaneously addictive." Its survey also found that cocaine-inspired fatalities were "markedly" fewer than those caused by alcohol and nicotine.[76] Adam Paul Weissman of the *Washington Post* later admitted in the *New Republic* that he had become a "drug-hype junkie," and the *New York Times* editorialized that the media had "discovered crack and overdosed on oratory."[77] In a 1989 public opinion poll, nevertheless, 64 percent of respondents cited drugs—more specifically, crack—as the top national security threat confronting the nation. By this time, congressional representatives had become flooded with letters demanding increasing vigilance in the face of a national epidemic. One woman, who expressed support for the death penalty for traffickers, wrote to Charles Rangel (D-N.Y.) that "drugs were killing America and jeopardized American freedom."[78]

As during the Vietnam era, government officials were at the vanguard in drumming up fears over drugs. In 1988, First Lady Nancy Reagan characterized casual drug users as "accomplices to murder."[79] John Kerry stated that Latin American traffickers had "aimed drugs at the U.S. like an atom bomb" and "threatened to destroy civilized society as we know it."[80] Mayor Ed Koch of New York City advocated strip searches of all travelers entering the country from Southeast Asia and Mexico and the bombing of Medellín, Colombia. Arthur Ravenal Jr. (R-S.C.) called for the military to shoot down on sight any aircraft suspected of smuggling drugs.[81] Illinois Congressman Henry J. Hyde was even more radical, suggesting before the House Foreign Affairs Committee that "maybe a firing squad would be suitable punishment for federal agents caught collaborating with drug traffickers." He said, "It wouldn't bother me, I tell you. It's my kids or your kids." William Bennett, secretary of education under Reagan and later director of the Office of National Drug Control Policy, added that he'd have no moral problem if all drug dealers were "beheaded."[82] Even though his own son, Lowell Scott, had been at one time addicted to drugs, Chief Daryl Gates of the Los Angeles Police Department offered the most extreme prescription: he told a *Los Angeles Times* journalist that "casual drug users ought to be taken outside and shot." Reflecting the intrinsically nationalistic aspect of the drug war, and the ideological importance of drugs as a symbol of social subversion continued from the 1960s, the inventor of the Special Weapons and Tactics (SWAT) team also called drug use a form of "treason."[83]

Gates's comments exemplified both the intense emotional sway that the drug issue held during the late 1980s and its political resonance. The 1986 midterm and 1988 federal elections were both characterized by candidates challenging their opponents to urine tests.[84] In 1986, Congress unanimously passed the Omnibus Anti–Drug Abuse Act, granting $6 billion to the drug war over three years.[85] "The bill is out of control, but of course I'm for it," said Congressman David McCurdy of Oklahoma wryly. Patricia Schroeder, a Democrat from Colorado, further commented, "There's a mob mentality in there. In football there's a thing called piling on. I think that's what we're seeing here right before the election." Claude Pepper added, "We're close to the point now where you could put an amendment through to hang, quarter and draw drug dealers."[86]

Besides stiffer sentencing, the 1986 Anti–Drug Abuse Act called for a six-pronged strategy of attack and mandated urine testing for workers in "sensitive" jobs, including all federal employees and law enforcement officials. Mandatory minimum sentencing regulations were also imposed for possession and dealing of all illicit drugs, including marijuana. In 1988 another major antidrug bill increased federal funding from $4.1 billion in fiscal year 1988 to $7.9 billion in 1990, 75 percent of which was appropriated for supply-side interdiction.[87] As in the 1986 Omnibus act, drug enforcement and policing were prioritized over treatment. In 1987, in an attempt to reduce the national deficit, Reagan had mandated a $200 million cut in federal funding for drug rehabilitation programs. This caused the closure of multimodality clinics and therapeutic community centers established during the Nixon era and led to the chronic underfunding of local treatment facilities in many American cities.[88] It also epitomized the shift away from the 1970s public health approach to addiction.

Reagan's legislation promoted particularly harsh penalties for crack. Under the terms of the 1986 Anti–Drug Abuse Act, possession with intent to sell five grams or more carried a mandatory minimum five-year sentence. Because crack was largely a phenomenon of the inner cities, social activists and scholars charged that these sentencing stipulations were racist, particularly in light of the fact that the mandatory minimum sentence for similar amounts of cocaine was just ten to thirty-seven months. They documented that the discrepancy in sentencing coupled with over-policing in ghetto communities contributed to the so-called darkening of America's overbloated prison system, which experienced a 98 percent rate of growth between 1980 and 1988. Dubbed the "gulag state" by critics, America in the mid-1980s surpassed both the Soviet Union and apartheid South Africa as, proportionately, the leading prisoner state in the world. By the end of the decade, over one million inmates were incarcerated in federal or state facilities—58 percent having been convicted on drug charges.[89] In total, despite its proclaimed fiscal conservatism, the Reagan government is estimated to have spent more than $23 billion in the drug war, with three-fourths going toward law enforcement. Drug arrests increased by an average of 60 percent in major urban areas, including New York City, where 88,641 people were indicted on drug charges in 1988, compared with just 18,521 in 1980. Approximately 70 percent of convictions were for felonies.[90]

These totals would increase even further under President George H. W. Bush. He expanded the drug war to new heights in response to continued public hysteria and as a means of advancing the conservative emphasis on punitive law enforcement over social welfare programs for the poor. Bush became notorious for inflating the threat of crack when he claimed in a national address to have purchased the drug in a park across the street from the White House; in reality, it had been sold to the DEA in a prearranged buy.[91] His administration also utilized the end of the Cold

War as a pretext to pursue the full-scale militarization of the War on Drugs, exemplified by its Andean strategy and the invasion of Panama to overthrow Manuel Noriega in an operation that claimed the lives of several thousand innocent civilians.[92]

As in the 1970s, the main opposition to the drug-war policy came from intellectuals.[93] Among these were libertarian conservatives such as University of Chicago economist Milton Friedman, an adviser to Reagan, who stated in a public editorial: "Every friend of freedom must be as revolted as I am by the prospect of turning the United States into an armed camp, by the vision of jails filled with casual drug users and of an army of enforcers empowered to invade the liberty of citizens on slight evidence. A country in which shooting down unidentified planes 'on suspicion' can be seriously considered as a drug war tactic is not the kind of United States I want to hand to future generations."[94]

The dissent pervading the American intellectual establishment was largely mooted, however, by the political climate of the times. Though the expansion of the War on Drugs had become based on contemporary political contingencies, the enduring legacy of Vietnam had remained salient. Hollywood's connection of drugs with American military collapse in Vietnam contributed to their continued vilification and characterization as a national security threat. The perceived link between drug abuse and rising domestic crime rates was also remnant from the Vietnam period and a solipsistic culture that measured the costs of the war only to America. Federal drug control efforts during the 1980s generally built on the organizational structure of Nixon's policy, despite Reagan's lessening support for treatment. The Nixon model was particularly influential in shaping U.S. international drug policy, which maintained an emphasis on bilateral diplomacy, aerial interdiction, crop substitution, and the training of indigenous police forces. These programs had become institutionalized in spite of the overriding failure of the Southeast Asian drug war, whose lessons American policymakers of the 1980s and '90s had failed to heed.

CONCLUSION THE MYTH ENDURES

Rarely is history predictable. From the late 1940s through the early 1960s, American policymakers were consumed with the Cold War and preventing the spread of "falling dominos" in Southeast Asia. By first extending financial support for nation-building projects in South Vietnam and then committing American ground troops, they hoped to create a bastion of American influence and check the spread of what they perceived to be an international Communist movement. By the early 1970s, after extending the war into Laos and Cambodia and utilizing the entire arsenal of American technological might, short of nuclear weapons, those hopes had been dashed, in part because of the powerful political mobilizing skills of the Vietnamese revolutionary leadership, and the lack of popular legitimacy of the U.S.-sponsored Saigon regime. Besides causing pronounced human devastation and suffering and fundamentally transforming the social and political dynamic of the "wasted nations" of Indochina, the Vietnam War had a huge and unforeseen impact in the United States. It bred cynicism and mistrust toward the government and created deep social divisions, which conservatives exploited to their political advantage. Through the spread of powerful cultural mythologies, which helped to preserve the nation's vision of self-righteousness and allowed it to evade responsibility for the carnage inflicted, the war further elevated the drug issue to the forefront of public attention and led to the internationalization and expansion of the modern drug war.

During the late 1960s and early 1970s, a wave of media reports based on congressional subcommittee hearings created the perception that drug use was endemic in Vietnam and linked to a breakdown in military discipline and fighting efficiency. Turning attention away from the escalation of U.S. atrocities and the ravaging of the Vietnamese countryside, the media also promoted widespread fear that addicted soldiers returning to the United States would exacerbate domestic crime rates and disorder. The apparent involvement of the CIA in supporting drug trafficking networks in Southeast Asia enhanced the political sting of these charges and catapulted the Nixon administration into action. In June 1971, following the release of the Murphy-Steele report, Nixon orchestrated a massive effort to quell the spread of addiction in Vietnam through Operation Golden-Flow, in conjunction with a major escalation of domestic policing and treatment programs. Attempting to legitimize his "Vietnamization" strategy and prolongation of the war, he further pressured America's Southeast Asian allies to crack down on drug-related corruption and extended American financial and advisory assistance for narcotics suppression. Despite numerous contradictions and shortcomings, Nixon's policies would become institutionalized during the late 1970s and '80s, albeit with a declining emphasis on treatment. The legacy of Vietnam remained potent, partly because of the influence of popular cultural media in preserving the myth of the addicted army and in distorting public memory of the war by recasting American GIs in the role of drug-addled victims.

Capitalizing on a shifting public mood, which he helped to manipulate further, Ronald Reagan made the drug war a central aspect of his platform of revitalizing American social institutions thought to have been corrupted by drugs during the Vietnam era. The military served as a major focal point in these efforts. Domestically, Reagan continued the Nixon precedent of expanding federal enforcement capabilities and bolstered the power of the DEA. As part of a comprehensive repudiation of 1960s liberalism, though, he broke course in abandoning treatment. On the supply side, Reagan was the first to use American military troops in international drug interdiction efforts, and he procured millions of dollars in federal assistance for chemical spraying and the training of foreign police, particularly in Latin America. As in the past, these initiatives were largely unsuccessful and often yielded devastating consequences, including a rise in anti-American sentiment, environmental damage, and the escalation of political repression and violence. Fixated on protecting American interests from the perceived dangerous influx of drugs, U.S. policymakers were insensitive to these developments. They had been caught up in a political frenzy that demanded a proactive international policy, regardless of the social cost.

During the 1990s the myth of the addicted army remained resonant in shaping the continued political scapegoating of drugs and the intensification of federal prohibition. The myth accorded well, further, with a triumphalist spirit surrounding the end of the Cold War, which saw a flourishing of post hoc justifications for U.S. policy in mainstream commentary and scholarship and a minimized emphasis on the scale of American-backed atrocities.[1] By the end of the decade, when kids of high school and college age were asked about the number of Vietnamese casualties, the average response was one-thirtieth the real total. Few students knew at all that the United States had even waged covert proxy wars in

Laos and Cambodia which killed tens of thousands of civilians—let alone that they were the most heavily bombed countries in human history.[2] While serving as chief federal drug policy adviser under President Bill Clinton (1992–2000), General Barry R. McCaffrey made frequent references to the corrosive impact of drug abuse in Vietnam, reinforcing the false belief that it was among the greatest "tragedies" to have emerged from America's participation in the conflict. In 1996, reflecting on his days as a young commanding officer, McCaffrey commented, "The U.S. army that I was a part of and so loved was almost destroyed by illegal drugs in the 1970s. Up to two thirds of our battalion was using drugs all the time or some of the time, and the impact on our discipline, on rape, violence, spiritual loss of focus, physical health was just atrocious."[3] As drug "czar," McCaffrey proclaimed his public intent of achieving "total victory" over the "drug cancer" in order to mitigate the pernicious legacy of Vietnam and ensure military readiness for future operations. The cornerstone of his effort was "Plan Colombia"—a $1.3 billion military assistance program in the Andes authorizing the destruction of over 100,000 acres of drug crops in order to cut off the source of supply reaching American youth, and giving a boost to counterinsurgency efforts against the FARC.[4]

McCaffrey's deep patriotic disposition—evident in a speech to his troops in Vietnam urging them to "go out and kill for God and country"—exemplified the dominant nationalist undercurrent shaping the War on Drugs through the 1990s.[5] This same impulse remained powerful through the presidency of George W. Bush, which based its drug policy on the premise of a benevolent superpower being besieged by a foreign corrupting agent. "Radical nationalists" in the administration, many of whom had served in high positions under Reagan, persisted in portraying drugs as a seminal national security threat and linked the antidrug crusade to the broader "War on Terror," whose own legitimacy was sustained by a belief in aggrieved national innocence and virtue shaped in part by lingering cultural myths about Vietnam—including that of the addicted army.[6] The War on Drugs retained its symbolic significance as a mechanism for eradicating the seemingly "permissive culture" of the 1960s and overcoming the "Vietnam syndrome." This task took on added primacy with the emergence of renewed anxieties over America's declining global status—a repercussion of the War in Iraq, which was increasingly referred to as another Vietnam after it became clear that the mission was not accomplished.[7]

Drug eradication efforts continued to be most vigorous in Latin America, where Bush II bolstered police training and defoliation efforts (some of which were subcontracted to private mercenary forces), resulting in an enhancement of the state of military siege engulfing most drug-cultivating regions.[8] Domestically, militarized SWAT teams raided homes on the slightest suspicion, sometimes killing innocent civilians (even a ninety-two-year-old woman in Atlanta), and Bush passed stringent laws against medical marijuana use.[9] He also developed a concerted public relations campaign in which radio and television ads promoted the most ludicrous claims of the Old Guard—including a long-discredited link with mental insanity and murder.[10] As war festered in the Middle East, meanwhile, Bush adopted a zero-tolerance approach in the military designed to ensure that drugs would not undermine America's fighting resolve, as they ostensibly did in Vietnam (particularly in the Hollywood version).[11] All the while, his government turned a blind eye to the involvement of brutal U.S.-backed warlords and top Karzai regime officials in the Afghan opium trade, resulting in a major boost in local production, thus fitting a long-standing precedent. This trend repeated itself in Iraq, where amid the wreckage of war and occupation, impoverished farmers turned to the opium poppy, which is controlled by Sunni Arab militias linked to organized crime.[12] Evidence also suggests that despite official government denials, dwindling morale and a flourishing black market economy resulted in a "surge" in military drug-abuse rates among psychologically distraught soldiers, in addition to increases among the local civilian population.[13]

On the whole, the drug issue remains as politically contentious and charged as ever. As Hollywood churns out new films linking the drug "epidemic" in Harlem to the Indochina drug traffic and war, the revived antiwar movement (possessing many holdovers from the 1960s, including a now aging Alfred W. McCoy and Peter Dale Scott) has undertaken new efforts to expose the hypocrisy of governmental rhetoric and hollowness of the so-called War on Drugs.[14] Dissolving the responsibility of U.S. leaders for the death of tens of thousands and for carnage on the ground, moreover, the solipsistic media have begun to produce a barrage of stories on the addiction of Iraq War veterans to hard narcotics, which they compare with reports from Vietnam and depict as among the gravest consequences of a failed crusade.[15] On the basis of secondhand hearsay, some correspondents have even blamed the Haditha massacre, in which marines killed twenty-four Iraqi civilians, on the use of amphetamines.[16] The impact of this remains uncertain; the legacy of Vietnam in shaping contemporary drug debates and broader policy initiatives nevertheless remains powerful, as recent developments suggest.

In 1977, journalist Michael Herr ended his acclaimed book *Dispatches* with the refrain: "Vietnam, Vietnam, Vietnam, we've all been there."[17] He meant to imply that the nation bore collective responsibility for what had unfolded during that war and had been irrevocably transformed in the process. Decades after the fall of the Saigon government, Herr's words remain true, in ways both he and his contemporaries could have hardly envisioned. With nearly 350,000 souls currently imprisoned in what McCaffrey of all people termed America's "drug gulag," and billions of taxpayer dollars committed to another futile war that has helped to terrorize poor Latin American farmers, America's participation in the Vietnam War has come back to haunt in yet another way.

ABBREVIATIONS USED IN THE NOTES AND BIBLIOGRAPHY

AIDNC   Development Project Files Related to Narcotics Control
AMHI   U.S. Army Military History Institute, Carlisle Barracks, Pa.
ANC   Alternative Newspaper Collection, Thomas J. Dodd Research Center,
          University of Connecticutt Storrs
BNDD   Bureau of Narcotics and Dangerous Drugs (formerly FBN), National Archives
CIB   Criminal Investigation Branch, U.S. Army
CID   Criminal Investigation Division, U.S. Army
CORDS Civil Operations for Rural Development Support, National Archives
CTF   Carleton Turner Files, Ronald Reagan Presidential Library, Simi Valley,
          Calif.
CWP   Charles Wilkinson Papers, National Archives
DAF   Thomas J. Dodd Research Center, University of Connecticutt Storrs
DEA   Records of the Drug Enforcement Administration, Washington, D.C.
DEAL   Drug Enforcement Administration Library, Pentagon City, Va.
DP&P   Drug Programs & Plans Branch, National Archives
EJE   Edward J. Epstein Papers, Howard Gottlieb Research Archive, Boston
          University
EKP   Egil Krogh Papers, National Archives
EMP   Edmund Muskie Papers, Bates College, Lewiston, Maine
FFP   Frances Fitzgerald Papers, Howard Gottlieb Research Archive, Boston
          University
GSP   Geoffrey Shepherd Papers, National Archives
IMF   Ian McDonald Files, Reagan Presidential Library, Simi Valley, Calif.
JFK   John F. Kennedy Presidential Library, Boston, Mass.
LEN   Nixon Presidential Files/Materials, National Archives
M&W   Morale and Welfare Branch, National Archives
MACV   Military Assistance Command Vietnam
MPD   Motion Pictures Division, National Archives
NA   National Archives, College Park, Md.
NSA   National Security Archive, George Washington University, Washington, D.C.
NSC   National Security Council Files, Ronald Reagan Presidential Library, Simi
          Valley, Calif.
NSF   National Security Files, Ronald Reagan Presidential Library, Simi Valley,
          Calif.
OF   Office Files, National Archives
OPS   Office of Public Safety, National Archives
RDS   Records of the Department of State, National Archives
RFK   Robert F. Kennedy Papers, JFK Presidential Library, Boston, Mass.
USAID   Records of United States Agency of International Development
USAV   Records of United States Army Vietnam

NOTES

INTRODUCTION

Epigraphs

Szasz, "Scapegoating Military Addicts," 5.

House Select Committee on Crime, *Drugs in Our Schools* (1972), 914.

Paul Starr, "Drug (Mis)treatment for GIs," *Washington Post*, July 16, 1972, B1.

1 Abramsky, *American Furies.*

2 See, for example, Alsop, "Smell of Death," and "GI's Other Enemy."

3 "Excerpts from President's Message on Drug Abuse Control," *New York Times,* June 18, 1971, 22; Nixon, "Special Message to the Congress," 744.

4 Gravel, *Pentagon Papers.*

5 Cortright, *Soldiers in Revolt*; Moser, *New Winter Soldiers.* For polling data on Vietnam and support for withdrawal, see Gallup, *Gallup Poll*, 93, 153.

6 Featured in Geiger, *Sir! No Sir!*; Meyrowitz and Campbell, "Vietnam Veterans and War Crimes Hearings," 138; *Washington Evening Star*, April 23, 1971, A3.

7 See Kerry and Vietnam Veterans Against the War, *New Soldier*; Wells, *War Within*, 495.

8 E.g., Staneford Garellek to President Nixon; Raynard I. Jameson, President B'nai Brith, to Nixon; "Drug Letters," Memo for Bob Haldeman, Chuck Colson, Bud Krogh, June 18, 1971. All in LEN, OF, box 12, folder July 1971.

9 See Nixon, *Real War.*

10 See Dallek, *Partners in Power*, 145; Perlstein, *Nixonland.*

11 Richard M. Nixon, speech to Republican National Committee, September 17, 1968, and "LEN 13-3, Staff Papers on Drug Abuse," NA, box 12, folder 4.

12 Roszak, *Making of a Counter Culture.*

13 "President's Proclamation on Drugs," *Philadelphia Bulletin*, May 25, 1970, collected in "Off the Press—Drug Abuse News Excerpts from the Nation's Press," June 4, 1970, CWP, box 35, folder 5.

14 Senate Committee on Labor and Public Welfare, *World Heroin Problem* (1971), 39–86.

15 Michael Parks, "CIA Reported Shifting Attention in Laos from Communists to Opium," *Baltimore Sun*, March 13, 1972; Johnson and Wilson, *Army in Anguish*; Musto, *American Disease*, 91, 246.

16 Steinbeck, "Importance of Being Stoned"; Steinbeck, *In Touch.*

17 Steinbeck, *In Touch*, 4, 71.

18 Stanton, "Drugs, Vietnam and the Vietnam Veteran"; Roffman and Sapol, "Marijuana in Vietnam."

19 Slotkin, *Gunfighter Nation*, 6.

20 E.g., Marilyn B. Young, *Vietnam Wars*; Kahin, *Intervention.*

21 The classic expression of the quagmire view is Halberstam, *Making of a Quagmire.* For an effective criticism, see Franklin, *Vietnam and Other American Fantasies,*

42; Chomsky, "Responsibility of Intellectuals"; and among general histories of the war, Kolko, *Anatomy of a War.*

22 Franklin, *M.I.A. or Mythmaking in America*, 7: Lembcke, *Spitting Image*, 3; Kimball, "Stab-in-the-Back Legend, 433–58"; Jeffords, *Remasculinization of America*, 18. A recent variation of the stab-in-the-back myth promoted by right-wing historian Mark Moyar blames liberal journalists David Halberstam and Neil Sheehan for reporting about Diem's political repression and hence creating public doubt about American involvement in Vietnam; see Moyar, *Triumph Forsaken*, xvi.

23 See Chomsky, "Visions of Righteousness."

24 E.g., Alvin M. Shuster, "GI Heroin Addiction Is Epidemic in Vietnam," *New York Times*, May 16, 1971, 1, 20; Malloy, "Harvest Home." For the historical precedent, see Courtwright, *Dark Paradise*, 76; Dikotter, Laamann, and Xun, *Narcotic Culture*, 98.

25 Alsop, "Worse Than My Lai"; "Heroin Plague: What Can Be Done?"; Barbara Campbell, "Ex GI's Report Vietnam Drug Use," *New York Times*, March 21, 1970, 26.

26 Robert M. Smith, "Senators Told GI's in Song-My Unit Smoked Marijuana Night before Incident," *New York Times*, March 25, 1970, 14; "My Lai Drug Question Raised," *New York Times*, March 16, 1970, 24; Parenti, *Lockdown America*, 9.

27 "Remarks in Introducing Omnibus Narcotic and Dangerous Drug Control and Rehabilitation Act of 1969," in Senate Committee on the Judiciary, *Narcotics Legislation* (1969), 2. See also Dodd, *Freedom and Foreign Policy.*

28 Berman, *No Peace, No Honor*; Morris, *Uncertain Greatness*; Dallek, *Partners in Power*, 111; Hersh, *Price of Power.*

29 Quoted by Chomsky in Caldwell and Tan, *Cambodia*, x.

30 See Shawcross, *Sideshow*; Kiernan, *How Pol Pot Came to Power*, xxiii; Owen and Kiernan, "Bombs over Cambodia." On the hideous U.S. record in Laos in particular, see Branfman, *Voices from the Plain*; McCoy and Adams, *Laos.*

31 Kimball, *Nixon's War*; Valentine, *Phoenix Program*; Zinberg and Robertson, *Drugs and the Public*, 29–30.

32 See Goode and Ben-Yehuda, *Moral Panics*, 7; Glassner, *Culture of Fear.*

33 Browning and Garrett, "New Opium War," 41.

34 On a GI viewing himself as an "agent of imperialism" see Ehrhart, *Passing Time.*

35 Lifton, *Vietnam Veterans*, 125–26.

36 On the right's particular brand of populism, see Kazin, *Populist Persuasion*, 245–66; and Greenberg, *Nixon's Shadow*, 6.

37 See Appy, *Working-Class War*, 309; Helmer, *Bringing the War Home*, 150. On the effects of the devastation, see Browning and Forman, *Wasted Nations.*

38 See Podhoretz, *Why We Were in Vietnam*; Norman Podhoretz, "Proper Uses of Power," *New York Times*, October 30, 1983, E19; Chepesiuk, *Hard Target*; Rosenblatt, *Criminal Injustice*; Austin and Irwin, *It's About Time*, 1, 2.

39 Hogan, *Cross of Iron*; Sherry, *In the Shadow of War*, 475; Lieven, *America Right or Wrong.*

40 On the fabrication of the "narco-guerrilla" term by government officials, see Marshall and Scott, *Cocaine Politics*, 1,2; Lee, *White Labyrinth*.

41 This term comes from John Kaplan, *Marijuana*.

42 See, as an emblematic title, Johns, *Power, Ideology and the War on Drugs*.

43 Lusane, *Pipe Dream Blues*.

44 Bourgeois, *In Search of Respect*; Jones, *Dispossessed*, 288; Chomsky, *Year 501*.

45 Carpenter, *Bad Neighbor Policy*; Lee, "Perversely Harmful Effects," 187; Stokes, *America's Other War*.

46 Youngers and Rosin, "Drugs and Democracy in Latin America," 5, online 1–2.

47 E.g., Trebach, *Great Drug War*; Bertram et al., *Drug War Politics*.

48 Musto and Korsmeyer, *Quest for Drug Control*; Inciardi, *War on Drugs*.

49 Epstein, *Agency of Fear*; Reinarman and Levine, *Crack in America*; Baum, *Smoke and Mirrors*; Beckett, *Making Crime Pay*.

50 Baum, *Smoke and Mirrors*, 104.

51 For other works exploring this theme, see Bender, *Nation among Nation*; Dudziak, *Cold War Civil Rights*; Sherry, *In the Shadow of War*.

52 Wyant, "Addiction in Vietnam"; DuPont, "Drug Abuse Decade," 175.

53 The most egregious cases include Jonnes's *Hep-Cats, Narcs, and Pipe-Dreams*; Allison, *Military Justice in Vietnam*, 121; and Torgoff, "Next Stop Is Vietnam," 192, in which the author claims that drugs were an "enemy more formidable than the 'Vietcong.'" Though more measured in their analysis, Herring's *America's Longest War* and Karnow's *Vietnam* also employ exaggeration and ignore the broader social implications of the so-called drug crisis.

54 McWilliams, *Protectors*, 74–80; Courtwright, *Dark Paradise*, 155–56; Musto, *American Disease*, 210, 229, 231. The Marijuana Tax Act outlawed marijuana, while the harsh punitive laws of the 1950s included mandatory minimum sentencing provisions and the death penalty for selling heroin to a minor.

55 William Walker, *Opium and Foreign Policy*, 132–217; Douglas Kinder, "Bureaucratic Cold Warrior."

1. "THE PRESS HAS DONE A TREMENDOUS DISSERVICE"

Epigraphs
Steinbeck, "Importance of Being Stoned," 37.
House Committee on Armed Services, *Inquiry into Alleged Drug Abuse in the Armed Services* (1971), "Statement of William Mack," 1273.

1 "GI's in Vietnam High on Hope's Jokes," *New York Times*, December 23, 1970, 2.

2 Hope once went so far as to call the U.S. bombing raids on North Vietnam "the best slum clearance project they ever had." Quoted in Aptheker, *Mission to Hanoi*, 65–66.

3 Colbach and Willson, "Binoctal Craze."

4 "Pentagon Explains GI's Get Pep Pills to Diet and Survive," *New York Times*, March 7, 1968, 16; Thornton interview.

5 See Polner, *No Victory Parades*, 116; Herr, *Dispatches*, 4–5.

6 Steinbeck, *In Touch*; Verrone and Calkins, *Voices from Vietnam*, 186–87.

7 "Monthly Drug Abuse Report," Edward G. Lurie, Colonel, MPC, Deputy Provost Marshall, January, 1972, USAV, DP&P, box 4, folder 12; "Marijuana in Vietnam," Major Anthony Pietropinto, Chief Mental Hygiene Consultation Services, Cam Ranh Bay, Vietnam, Drug Abuse, DP&P, box 4.

8 "Fresh Disclosures on Drugs and GIs."

9 Roffman, "Survey of Marijuana Use," 1118; Roffman and Sapol, "Marijuana in Vietnam" (1970), 15–16, and "Marijuana in Vietnam" (1969).

10 House Committee on Armed Services, *Inquiry into Alleged Drug Abuse in the Armed Services* (1971), 1277; Roffman interview.

11 Stanton, "Drug Use in Vietnam"; Stanton, "Drugs, Vietnam and the Vietnam Veteran"; Robins, Helzer, and Davis, "Narcotic Use in Southeast Asia."

12 Fischer, "Preliminary Findings," 389–461; Treanor and Skirpol, "Marijuana in a Tactical Unit," 29–37; Roffman and Sapol, "Marijuana in Vietnam" (1970), 15–16.

13 See Black, Owens, and Wolff, "Patterns of Drug Use"; Postel, "Marijuana Use in Vietnam"; Fischer, "Preliminary Findings," 417–19; "Drug Abuse" C6—4th Infantry Division, Pleiku, RVN, Unclassified 1-141, LMG5416 0060937-0000-RIMAVA, DP&P, box 5, folder 4.

14 Janecek, Casper, and Martinelli, "Marijuana in Vietnam," 69; "Testimony of John K. Imahara," in Senate Committee on the Judiciary, *Drug Abuse in the Armed Forces* (1968), 6422–23; Senate Committee on the Judiciary, *Drug Abuse in the Military* (1966–70), 1201; Lembcke interview.

15 "Correspondence Col. Bill Hart and Dr. Tom Robbins," Walter Reed Medical Museum archives, Washington, D.C., audiotape 102-7; House Committee on Armed Services, *Inquiry into Alleged Drug Abuse in the Armed Services* (1971), 47; Thomas G. Rame, Vietnam Company Command, Oral History Project, AMHI, box 27; Zinberg, "Heroin Use in Vietnam and the United States"; "Introduction of Heroin in Vietnam by Thai Soldiers," January 1970, PSD, Records of the Agency of International Development, OPS, East Asia Branch, NA, box 111, folder 1.

16 Holloway, "Epidemiology of Heroin Dependency"; Rae, Forman, and Olson, "Drug Usage," 43; Robins, *Vietnam Drug User Returns*; Appy, *Working-Class War*, 284.

17 Richard S. Wilbur, "A Follow-Up of Vietnam Drug Users," Press Conference, April 23, 1973; Levine and Grimes, "Pulmonary Edema and Heroin Overdose"; Memo for the Record, "Civilian/Military Drug Exchange Programs," May 1, 1971, AMHI, Drug Abuse UN, folder Narcotics; "Correspondence Col. Bill Hart and Dr. Tom Robbins," Walter Reed Medical Museum archives, audiotape 102-7.

18 Carol Kilpatrick, "New Drug Chief Finds GI Addiction below Estimates," *Washington Post*, July 18, 1971, 1; "Results of Urinalysis Screening," in Senate Committee on Armed Services, *Drug Abuse in the Military* (1972); "Figures on Heroin in Vietnam Differ: New Tests Cut the Number of GI Users by a Third," *New York Times*, September 5, 1975; "Imprecision of Urinalysis Is Admitted," *Wash-*

ington Post; October 30, 1971; Ralph Yarborough, "Urinalysis Losing Credibility," *Drug Education Summary*, December 2, 1971, AMHI, box MACV, folder Drug Abuse.

19 Robert Reinhold, "Army's Drug Testing Program Stirs Sharp Dispute," *New York Times*, June 2, 1972, 1; Helmer, *Drugs and Minority Oppression*, 144; Ashley, *Heroin*, 9.

20 On the accuracy of the tests, see Pike and Goldstein, "History of Drug Use," 1125; Stanton, "Drugs, Vietnam and the Vietnam Veteran," 285. Jaffe quoted in Jane Sims, "House Probe Told How Returning GIs Cheat on Dope Test," *Washington Post*, August 3, 1971, A3, Jaffe interview. For GI perspectives on the deterrent quality of the tests, see Ackerman, *He Was Always There*, 203.

21 See Paul Starr, "Drug (Mis)treatment for GIs," *Washington Post*, July 16, 1972, B1.

22 E.g., Ursano, USARV to USAV, September 26, 1970, CIB, NA, box 1; Department of Defense, *Drug Abuse: Game without Winners*.

23 Senate Committee on the Judiciary, *World Drug Traffic and Its Impact* (1972) 58, 125–26; Weimer, "Drugs as Disease," 273; "Interview with Lewis W. Walt," *CBS News*, September 14, 1972 (transcript); "Narcotics Suppression," Chief of Staff, October 4, 1968, MACV Command, Historians Collection, AMHI, Drug Abuse—UN, folder Drug Abuse.

24 Senate Subcommittee to Investigate Juvenile Delinquency, *Drug Abuse in the Military* (1966–1970), 9; Westmoreland, *A Soldier Reports*.

25 Stanton, "Drugs, Vietnam, and the Vietnam Veteran," 567; Ackerman, *He Was Always There*, 194; Verrone and Calkins, *Voices from Vietnam*, 187; Ebert, *A Life in a Year*, 229; Fischer, "Preliminary Findings," 41; Pierson interview.

26 Postel, "Marijuana Use in Vietnam"; "Interview with Mike Davison," in Dorland, *Legacy of Discord*, 22; "Senate Study Finds Drug Abuse by GIs a Rarity in Combat," *New York Times*, April 2, 1971, 10.

27 Herr, *Dispatches*, 88; "Interview with Malvin Handy," Vietnam Company Command, Oral History Project, AMHI, box 16. Davis quoted in Solis, *Marines and Military Law*, 104; Interview with Pvt. Marvin Matthiak, Vietnam Archives, Douglas Pike Virtual Vietnam Archive, Texas Tech University, Vietnam Company Command, Oral History Project, www.texas.tech.edu. Also, Rodriguez interview; "Interview with Neal J. Delisanti," Vietnam Company Command, Oral History Project, AMHI, box 10.

28 Sanders, "Doper's Wonderland," 71–72; Ebert, *A Life in a Year*, 229; Levy interview; Appy, *Working-Class War*, 284.

29 E.g., Caputo, *Rumor of War*; Appy, *Working-Class War*; Burchett, *Vietnam Will Win*.

30 Helmer, *Bringing the War Home*, 190; Ruybal, *Drug Hazed War*, 2; Linden, "Demoralization of an Army," 13; Kashimba, "Uncle Sam, Pusher."

31 Steinbeck, "Importance of Being Stoned," 36; Kolko, *Anatomy of a War*, 363; Bourne quoted in Starr, *The Discarded Army*, 119.

32 Bourne, "Vietnam Veteran"; Stanton, "Drugs, Vietnam and the Vietnam Veteran," 112; Senate Committee on Labor and Public Welfare, *Drug and Alcohol Abuse in the Military* (1970), 34.

33 Senate Committee on Armed Services, *Staff Report on Drug Abuse in the Military* (1971), 7; "All Skyed Up and Coming Down Slow," *The Army Reporter*, March 22, 1971, 4; Zinberg, "Rehabilitation of Heroin Users"; Ingraham, "Sense and Nonsense," 61; Davison quoted in Johnson and Wilson, *Army in Anguish*, 25; Lindsey quoted in Arturo Gonzalez, "The Vietcong's Secret Weapon."

34 *U.S. Appellate v. Michael Posey*, no. 24, 254, U.S. Court of Military Appeals, February 18, 1972, CMA Lexis 830.

35 "Serious Incident Report," February 16, 1972, Records of the United States Forces in South East Asia, HQ, USAV, Protective Services Division, CIB, NA, box 3, folder Drug Abuse Suppression Programs.

36 Leary interview.

37 Bentel and Smith, "Drug Abuse in Combat," 27, "When 30,000 GIs Are Using Heroin," 94; "Report on Peter Lemon: Congressional Medal of Honor Winner," *CBS News*, June 21, 1971, MPD.

38 "Playboy Interview—Oliver Stone," 57; Appy, *Patriots*, 256.

39 E.g., Earlywine *Understanding Marijuana*; John Kaplan, *Hardest Drug*, 24; Zimmer and Morgan, *Marijuana Myths*.

40 Interview with Neal J. Delisanti, Lt. Col. Ronald Gornto, AMHI, box 14; Olson interview; Fischer, "Preliminary Findings," 41; Herbert, *Soldier*, 158; Leary interview; "Testimony of Keith Carney," in House Committee on Armed Services, *Alleged Drug Abuse in the Armed Services* (1970), 1302, and "Testimony of Lieutenant General Keith B. McCutchem," 1345; Berry, *Those Gallant Men*, 37; Levy interview.

41 Roffman interview; Levy interview; Talbott and Teague, "Marihuana Psychosis," 300–301; Gibson, *The Perfect War*, 223.

42 See Fischer, "Preliminary Findings," 41; Ingraham, "Sense and Nonesnse," 65; "Drinking Behavior by Pay Grade Officer," in Senate Committee on Armed Services, *Review of Military Drug and Alcohol Programs* (1973), 27; Robins, Helzer, and Davis, "Narcotic Use in Southeast Asia."

43 "Memo to Army Chiefs of Staff: Subject: Alcohol Program," in Senate Committee on Armed Services, *Review of Military Drug and Alcohol Programs* (1973), 24; "Army Criminal Investigation Division Staff Report" October 1970, CIB, NA, box 5.

44 Interview with Gonzalo Baltazar, Vietnam Archive, Texas Tech University, March 23, 2001, by Steve Maxner; Douglas Pike Archive, www.vietnam.ttu.edu.

45 Fussell, *Wartime*, 99; Rose, *Myths and the Greatest Generation*, 38; Pike and Goldstein, "History of Drug Use in the Military," 1133.

46 R. W. "Johnny" Apple, Jr., "4 GI's Held in Vietnam as Drug Inquiry Is Begun," *New York Times*, January 26, 1966, A4; Maclear, *Ten Thousand Day War*, 144; "USARV Regulation 210-65," November 6, 1970, DP&P, box 34, folder 2; Terry Anderson, "GI Movement," 114; "Testimony of David K. Tuck, Specialist 4th

Class with the U.S. 25th Infantry Division in Vietnam," in Duffet, *Against the Crime of Silence*, 406.

47 Roffman interview.

48 E.g., "Drunk While on Duty," Summary of Non-Judicial Punishment, October 18, 1971, CIB, NA, box 36, folder 2; Cecil, *Herbicidal Warfare*, 87; House Committee on Government Operations, *Evaluating the Federal Effort to Control Drug Abuse* (1973), part 3, 774.

49 Brush, "Higher and Higher"; Verrone and Calkins, *Voices from Vietnam*, 186; Pierson interview; Randle interview; Levy interview.

50 Pham interview. On the institutional lethargy of the ARVN, see Brigham, *ARVN*.

51 Bourne, *Men, Stress and Vietnam*, 73; Huffman, "Which Soldiers Break Down," 344–45; Colbach, "Marijuana Use," 206.

52 Bey and Zecchinelli, "GI's Against Themselves," 226.

53 Senate Committee on the Judiciary, *Drug Abuse in the Armed Forces* (1968), 6415.

54 Currey, *Long Binh Jail*, 44; *U.S. v. Smith*, 44 C.M.R. 292, 1971 CMR LEXIS 816 (A.C.M.R. Mar. 26, 1971); see Appy, *Patriots*, 160–61, for a similar incident, in which a "piss drunk" soldier, who was a veteran of the Korean War, killed a fellow comrade in a "drunken rage."

55 Roth, "Psychoactive Substances"; Roffman interview.

56 Johnson and Wilson, *Army in Anguish*, Cortright, *Soldiers in Revolt*, 19; Terry Anderson, "Counter-Culture," in *The Movement and the Sixties*, 245. For an early dissenting voice, see Duncan, "I Quit."

57 Stapp, *Up Against the Brass*; "CIA Ordered Nazi Style Massacre in My-Lai," *The Bond*, December 16, 1970; "GIs United against War in Indochina," *Bragg Briefs*, Special Spring Offensive, 1971; all in ANC.

58 *Sir! No Sir!*, directed by Geiger; Gabriel and Savage, *Crisis in Command*, 45–46; Gioglio, *Days of Decision*; Waterhouse and Wizard, *Turning the Guns Around*; Moser, *The New Winter Soldiers*; "A Deserter Raps: Outasight in Saigon—How to Scram in the Nam," *Berkeley Barb*, February 11–17, 1972, 2.

59 Heinl, "Collapse of the Armed Forces," 30–31; Appy, *Working-Class War*, 246; Franklin, *Vietnam and Other American Fantasies*, 64.

60 See *The Bond*, July 24, 1971, and "Lifers Dig War . . . It Makes Them Rich," *The Ally*, November 1969, both in ANC; Halstead, "The New Anti-War Army"; Linden, "Demoralization of an Army," 13.

61 Cortright, *Soldiers in Revolt*, 19; Rinaldi, "Olive Drab Rebels"; Starr, *Discarded Army*, 23, 36; Terry Anderson, "GI Movement," 104; Cline quoted in Moser, *New Winter Soldiers*, 63.

62 Ingraham, "'The Nam' and 'The World,'" 123, Lembcke interview; Moskos, *American Enlisted Man*, 35, 148–52, 164.

63 See "How Nazi Brass Run Long Binh Jail," *The Bond*, October 21, 1970, ANC; Currey, *Long Binh Jail*, 50.

64 See Sherrill, "Justice, Military Style"; "Fresh Disclosures on Drugs and GIs"; Willard W. Hawke, "Report of Inquiry concerning Allegations Made in *Playboy*

Magazine about the USARV Installation Stockade," February 24, 1970, Army Criminal Investigations Branch, CID, NA.

65 See Westheider, *Fighting on Two Fronts*; Terry, *Bloods*; Cortright, *Soldiers in Revolt*, 39; Gerald Gill, "Black Soldiers' Perspectives," 174.

66 Sanders, "Doper's Wonderland," 68; "Black Power Group in Vietnam Fights the Enemy Within: Heroin Addiction," *New York Times*, August 12, 1971, A3; Graham, *Brothers' Vietnam War*, 110.

67 This was my impression of Musto and Korsmeyer, *Quest for Drug Control*, 50.

68 "Statement of Charles West, Chicago, Illinois," in Senate Committee on the Judiciary, *Drug Abuse in the Armed Forces* (1970), 6291, Dodd quoted on 6260; Robert M. Smith, "Senators Told GI's in Song-My Unit Smoked Marijuana Night Before Incident," *New York Times*, March 25, 1970, 14; "My Lai Drug Question Raised," *New York Times*, March 16, 1970, 24.

69 Roffman interview; Robert M. Smith, "Marijuana Link Denied," *New York Times*, March 26, 1970, 14; Goldstein, Marshall, and Schwartz, "My Lai Massacre"; Hersh, *My Lai 4*; interview with Ronald Ridenhour, 1994, in Baum, *Smoke and Mirrors*, 40.

70 Citizens' Commission of Inquiry, *Dellums Committee Hearings*, 55; Herman, *Atrocities in Vietnam*; Appy, *Working-Class War*, 203–4.

71 Chomsky, *At War with Asia*, 25; Chomsky and Herman, *Political Economy of Human Rights*, 1:313.

72 "Alleged Incident Involving Fourth infantry Division Troops on February 1, 1968" (January 17, 1970), "12-year-old Vietnamese Boy Killed, An Bang Hamlet," "Alleged ROK Massacres," "100 Montagnard Villagers Shot," and "Soldier Trying to Smuggle Vietnamese head," CIB, NA, boxes 34–36; Nicholas Turse and Deborah Nelson, "Civilian Killings Went Unpunished: Declassified Papers Show U.S. Atrocities Went Far Beyond My Lai," *Los Angeles Times*, August 6, 2006.

73 Quouted in Appy, *Patriots*, 77.

74 "Colonel Says Every Large Combat Unit in Vietnam Has a My Lai," *New York Times*, May 25, 1971.

75 Robins, *Vietnam Drug User Returns*, 8; Helmer, *Drugs and Minority Oppression*, 142–43; Robins, Helzer, and Davis, "Narcotic Use in Southeast Asia"; John W. Finney, "Veteran Addicts Few, Army Finds," *New York Times*, April 24, 1973; Michael, "Investigation of the Substance Abuse Behavior"; William Claiborne, "GI Drug Use Figure Raised, But Few Are Still Addicted," *Washington Post*, April 24, 1973, *Washington Post*, A1; Robins, "Interaction of Setting and Predisposition"; Nurco, Hanlon, and Kinlock, "Heroin Use in the United States," 16.

76 Richard Wilbur, "Study Confirms that Vietnam Veteran Drug Abuse at Low Levels," Office of Assistant Secretary of Defense (Public Affairs), April 23, 1973, AMHI.

77 "Interview Egil 'Bud' Krogh," *Front-Line Drug Wars*, www.pbs.com.

78 "Employees of Chase Manhattan Bank Arrested at Pattaya Beach," *Bangkok Post*, March 31, 1971, RDS, Office of Thai and Burma Affairs, 1963–1975, box 8, folder Narcotics; "Public Safety Directorate," MACV, June 30, 1972, CIB, NA,

box 1; Senate Committee on Armed Services, *Drug Abuse in the Military* (1972), 268. For the testimony of DEA agent Carl Lutz, stationed in Bangkok, see Chepesiuk and Gonzalez, *Superfly*, 96. Lutz insists that there was never any concrete evidence of major smuggling rings out of Thailand and no major arrests for smuggling heroin in the coffins of dead soldiers as was claimed by drug dealer Frank Lucas in a 2000 interview in the *New York Times Magazine*. This claim was the basis for his portrayal in the 2007 film *American Gangster*.

79 Johnston, *Illicit Drug Use*; Gallup, *Gallup Poll*, 98; Beschner and Friedman, *Youth Drug Abuse*, 353.

80 Wald et al., *Dealing with Drug Abuse*; Hunt and Chambers, *Heroin Epidemics*, 10; Epstein, *Agency of Fear*, 174–75; Bruce D. Johnson, "Once an Addict"; John Kaplan, *Hardest Drug*, 38; Peele, *Diseasing of America*, 23; Regus, *Drug Addiction Business*; Dikötter, Laamann, and Xun, *Narcotic Culture*, 98.

81 See, for example, Fort, *Alcohol*; Barkan, *Criminology*, 158; Gottschalk, *Prison and the Gallows*, 24; Chambliss, *Power, Politics, and Crime*, 35–42; Silberman, *Criminal Violence*, 81.

2. CREATING THE MYTH OF THE "NAM JUNKIE"

Epigraph
Stanton, "Drugs, Vietnam and the Vietnam Veteran," 41.

1 Lee Israel, "Turn On, Tune In and Fire Away," *Washington Post*, February 9, 1969, 23; "A New GI for Pot," 24; "Short-Timer GIs Deep Into Drugs," *Washington Post*, August 20, 1971, A18; "Marijuana—The Other Enemy in Vietnam."

2 Szasz, "Scapegoating Military Addicts," 5.

3 E.g., Raymond W. Apple Jr., "4 GI's Held in Vietnam as Drug Inquiry Is Begun," *New York Times*, January 26, 1966, A4; "Marijuana Termed Big Problem among U.S. Troops in Vietnam," *New York Times*, October 26, 1967; "Mary Jane in Action," 40.

4 Roffman interview; Anslinger and Cooper, "Marihuana," 18; Anslinger and Oursler, *The Murderers*.

5 McWilliams, "Through the Past Darkly," 387. While Lacata was under the influence of marijuana when he killed his family, he was also deemed to be "criminally insane" by psychiatrists, and suffered from "dementia praecox." He was committed to a Florida mental hospital following the murder, and hanged himself in December 1950.

6 "Playboy Panel—The Drug Revolution," 11.

7 See W. R. Conklin, "Asia Reds Accused of Making GIs Narcotic Addicts," *New York Times*, July 18, 1954; "Anslinger Tells Senate Group Japan, Korea, Communists Debauch Americans," *New York Times*, July 18, 1954, A1; Anslinger, "The Red Chinese Dope Traffic," *Saturday Evening Post*, September 17, 1960.

8 Anslinger and Tompkins, *Traffic in Narcotics*, 95.

9 "The Troubled U.S. Army in Vietnam," 29; Nicholas Von Hoffman, "Even the MPs Smoke Pot at Ft. Head: Soldiers Use over 400 Pounds a Month," *Washington Post*, July 4, 1968, A1.

10 Von Hoffman, "Even the MP's Smoke Pot at Fort Head," A1; and Darrel Garwood, "Marijuana Use by Vietnam Troops Increases," *Washington Post*, February 16, 1968, A15.

11 "Foe of Marijuana Says GI Threw Grenade at Him," *New York Times*, August 19, 1970, 16.

12 See Haynes Johnson and George C. Wilson, "Our Strung Out Troops and the Big O," *Washington Post*, September 14, 1971, A1; Aronson, "Media and the Message."

13 See Iver Peterson, "Vietnam: How Do You Turn Off the Turned On Troops," *New York Times*, January 17, 1971, E6; "Former Servicemen Testify on Drug Use," *New York Times*, August 20, 1970, 71; Murray Shumach, "Court Hears Story of a Soldier's Life with Drugs," *New York Times*, September 9, 1971, 32.

14 Peter A. Jay, "TV Report on Marijuana No Surprise in Vietnam," *Washington Post*, November 16, 1970, A14. "The CBS Marijuana Smoke-in at Fire Base Aires," in House Committee on Armed Services, *Inquiry into Alleged Drug Abuse in the Armed Services* (1970), 2205.

15 E.g., Arturo Gonzalez, "Vietcong's Secret Weapon"; Stanton-Candlin, *Psycho-Chemical Warfare*.

16 Nashel, *Edward Lansdale's Cold War*, 164–65. On the credibility of William C. Westmoreland and Victor H. Krulak as sources, see Sheehan, *A Bright Shining Lie*.

17 Senate Committee on Foreign Relations, *Post-War Southeast Asia* (1976), 9; "Drug Abuse Report," MACV to Chief of Staff, Franklin M. Davis Jr., January 25, 1968, MACV, Historians' Collection, AMHI, Drug Abuse—UN, folder 3; "Indications of Communist Forces Involvement in Vietnam Narcotics Traffic," Records of the Agency of International Development, OPS, East Asia Branch NA, box 111, folder 1; Goscha, *Thailand and the Southeast Asian Networks*, 201–4, Henry A. Giordano to James A. Reed on "The Opium War in Vietnam," translated from a Japanese newspaper, June 1, 1965, BNDD, box 164, folder Vietnam.

18 "Marijuana Termed Big Problem among U.S. Troops in Vietnam," *New York Times*, October 26, 1967, 4; Appy, *Working-Class War*, 203–4; Herman, *Atrocities in Vietnam*, 10; Cronkite cited in Pach, "The War on Television," 135.

19 "Viet Opium Planted by Peking: Zhou," *Washington Post*, October 24, 1971, A3; "China Drug Plot Seen to Incapacitate GIs," *Washington Post*, October 31, 1970, A16.

20 On this theme, see Robin, *Making of the Cold War Enemy*; Hallin, *Uncensored War*.

21 See, among emblematic works, Race, *War Comes to Long An*; Kolko, *Anatomy of a War*; Elliot, *Vietnamese War*.

22 Jack Anderson's articles, "GI Drug Abuse Hushed Up," *Washington Post*, August 9, 1970, 42; "Combat Dangers of GI Drug Use Told," *Washington Post*, June 5, 1971, D13; and "GI Drug Report Kicks Up a Storm," *Washington Post*, February 3, 1971, B11. See also "Okinawa Mata Hari reports," in House Committee on

Armed Services, *Inquiry into Alleged Drug Abuse in the Armed Services* (1971), 2207.

23 Lindesmith, *Addict and the Law*; Lindesmith, "'Dope Fiend' Mythology," 199. On Jack Anderson's views towards the war, see his *Peace, War and Politics*.

24 Marquis W. Childs, "Vietnam's Drug Traffic," *Washington Post*, July 15, 1971, A17; and "Drug Problems of Vietnam GI," *Washington Post*, April 30, 1971, A27; Flora Lewis, "Facts Surface on the Heroin War," *Washington Post*, June 14, 1971, A6.

25 Alsop, "Worse than My Lai."

26 On the human and environmental toll, see Schell, *Village of Ben Suc*; Environmental Conference on Cambodia, Laos, Vietnam, "Long-Term Consequences of the Vietnam War," 43–44, www.nnn.se/vietnam/ethics.pdf.

27 The Pentagon Papers certainly give this impression. See Chomsky, *For Reasons of State*, 3–171.

28 On Alsop's views on Vietnam, see, e.g., Merry, "Stewart and Vietnam"; interview with Stewart Alsop, July 15, 1969, Lyndon B. Johnson Oral History Collection, www.lbj.lib.utexas.edu/johnson/archive.hom/oralhistory.hom/alsop-s.

29 "Heroin: A New and Growing Threat"; Malloy, "Harvest Home"; James Reston, "Nixon, Drugs and the War," *New York Times*, January 2, 1971, 41.

30 Jean Claude Pomonti and Serge Thion quoted in Caldwell and Tan, *Cambodia*, x.

31 Gloria Emerson, "GIs in Vietnam Get Heroin Easily," *New York Times*, February 25, 1971, 39. For a review of media coverage of the "decade of genocide" in Cambodia and how coverage of atrocity picked up only when Communist Khmer Rouge forces were the perpetrators, see Chomsky and Herman, *Political Economy of Human Rights*, 2:31.

32 E.g., "Saigon Airport: A Smuggler's Paradise," *New York Times*, April 22, 1971, 1; Alvin M. Shuster, "GI Heroin Addiction Is Epidemic in Vietnam," *New York Times*, May 16, 1971, 1, 20.

33 See Said, *Orientalism*.

34 Alsop, "GI's Other Enemy"; "Heroin Plague: What Can Be Done?" See also "White, Suburban, Middle Class," 28.

35 Bernard Fall characteristically wrote that Vietnam had been "threatened with extinction" after the countryside was literally pounded to bits by the largest military machine ever unleashed on an area of this size. "Vietnam Blitz," 19.

36 Alsop, "The Smell of Death." For similar sensationalistic prose, see Barbara Carlsen, "Now the Needle's Hitting Home," *Hartford Courant*, July 4, 1971, A1; Adrian Peterson, "Junkie Comes Marching Home," *National Observer*, June 1971, 1 and 16.

37 Herr said wartime Saigon resembled "the insides of a poisonous flower— fucked at its root," *Dispatches*, 120.

38 "New Public Enemy No. 1," 20. For other sensationalist pieces, see John O'Neill, "The Ones Who Came Back," *New York Times*, September 1, 1972; Jon Nordheimer, "From Dak Tho to Detroit: Death of a Troubled Vietnam Hero," *New York Times*, May 26, 1971, A1.

39 See Starr, *Discarded Army*, 23; Dean, *Shook Over Hell*, 12; Harris and Associates, *Myths and Realities*, 185; and with caution, Burkett and Whitley, *Stolen Valor*, 72–73.

40 See Wilbur J. Scott, *Politics of Readjustment*; Hunt, *The Turning*.

41 Lembcke, *Spitting Image*, 114. For an emblematic article quoting counter-demonstrators who question their credibility, see "Veterans Discard Medals in War Protest at Capital," *New York Times*, April 24, 1971, 1.

42 "Report on Heroin Addiction among Troops," April 19, 1971; "Report on Drug Addiction Among Troops in Vietnam," May 17, 1971; and "Phil Jones on Soul Alley," June 15, 1971, *CBS News*; "Report on Drugs in the Mekong Delta," *ABC News*, June 25, 1971; "Report 30,000 Addicts in Vietnam," *NBC News*, June 15, 1971; all in MPD.

43 "Phil Brady Reports on Drugs," *NBC News*, January 24 and 25, 1971; MPD; "Robert Goralski Reports on Violence among Drug Addicts" *NBC News*, May 26, 1971, MPD.

44 "ABC News Presents . . . Heroes and Heroin," *ABC News*, August 21, 1972; Westin and Schaffer, *Heroes and Heroin*, 25.

45 Schaffer to Krogh, "Heroes and Heroin," August 23, 1971, EKP, box 13, folder, 2.

46 On how the media helps to set the public policy agenda by prioritizing specific issues, see McCombs and Shaw, "Agenda-Setting Function of the Mass Media."

47 Harris and Associates, Inc., "The Drug Problem," June 1971, LEN, White House Central Files, GSP, box 2, folder Drugs; Louis Harris and Associates, Inc., "Drugs, Military," *Washington Post*, February 21, 1972, E1; Longo quoted in Stuart R. Carlin, "Mass Urinalysis Started," *Army Reporter*, October 25, 1971, 3.

48 "New Public Enemy No. 1," 21.

49 Zinberg and Robertson, *Drugs and the Public*, 29–30; Wald et al., *Dealing with Drug Abuse*, 52.

50 Miss Jacky Fortin to Senator Edmund Muskie, November 22, 1971, Senate Office File, EMP, box 1789, folder 11; and, e.g., Harry J. Davis, "Action on Drug Abuse," *Washington Post*, October 19, 1971, A15.

51 Bernard J. Hamik, "Letter to Senator Murphy," Canoga Park, Calif., November 12, 1970, DP & P, box 7, folder Drug Abuse; Mrs. William McMurtry, "Letter to President Richard M. Nixon," January 25, 1971, DP&P, box 7, folder Drug Abuse.

52 "Senator Dodd Reports to the People of Connecticut," *Washington Report*, and Dodd, "Speech before the Political Science Department, University of Connecticut," both in DAF, box 216, folder 5997.

53 Anderson and Pearson, *Case against Congress*, 58; Hamilton-Paterson, *Greedy War*, 234.

54 Senate Committee on the Judiciary, *Drug Abuse in the Military* (1966–1970), 25.

55 Dodd, *Freedom and Foreign Policy*; "Senator Dodd Addresses Pro Vietnam Rally," DAF, box 203, folder 6540; "The Most Dangerous Fallacy of the McGovern-Hatfield Amendment," DAF, box 216, folder 5997; "Senator Dodd Presents Peti-

tion for President Nixon," DAF, box 216, folder 5997; Anderson and Pearson, *Case against Congress*, 52–58.

56 "Testimony of John Steinbeck IV," in Senate Committee on the Judiciary, *Drug Abuse in the Armed Forces* (1968), 4639.

57 E.g., "Testimony of Jon Steinberg," in Senate Committee on the Judiciary, *Drug Abuse in the Armed Forces* (1970), 6376; Jon Steinberg, "Pot Is #10," *Pacific Stars and Stripes*, October, 19, 1969; "Former Servicemen Testify on Drug Use," *New York Times*, August 20, 1970, 71; Roffman interview; "Senate Panel Told Users Mainly Experiment," *New York Times*, August 21, 1970, 9.

58 "Another Check-Up on Drug Use by GIs," 33; Senate Committee on the Judiciary, *Drug Abuse in the Armed Forces* (1970), 6260, 6356.

59 "Senator Dodd introduces Military Bill to treat hooked GI's," and "Senator Dodd—Speech before the Political Science Department, University of Connecticut," both in DAF, box 216, folder 5997; Roffman interview; Anderson and Pearson, *Case against Congress*, 62–97; Hamilton-Paterson, *Greedy War*, 234.

60 See Latham, *Modernization as Ideology*; Adas, *Dominance by Design*; Said, *Culture and Imperialism*.

61 "Comments of Senator Harold E. Hughes," in Senate Committee on Labor and Public Welfare, *Military Drug Abuse, 1971*, 1, 185; *Congressional Record*, April 20, 1971.

62 "Shrinking the Drug Specter," 21; Senate Committee on Labor and Public Welfare, *World Heroin Problem* (1971), 60; McCoy, *Politics of Heroin: CIA Complicity*, 1991 ed.

63 Senate Committee on Labor and Public Welfare, *World Heroin Problem* (1971), 45.

64 Michael Getler, "U.S. Vows Crackdown on Heroin Flow to GIs," *Washington Post*, May 28, 1971, A14; Alsop, "Worse than My Lai"; Felix Belair, "House Team Asks Army to Cure Addicts, *New York Times*, May 28, 1971; "When 30,000 GI's Are Using Heroin," 98; Letter, John Paul Vann, Director Regional Assistance, Senior Advisor, MACV, to Editor, *Washington Post*, September 23, 197, FFP, box 13, folder Vann; "Mr. Vann Replies to Anderson's Charges," *Washington Post*, October 9, 1971, A15.

65 Donfeld quoted in Musto and Korsmeyer, *Quest for Drug Control*, 51; Memorandum for Bud Krogh to Donald Rumsfeld, the White House, May 25, 1971, EKP, box 32, folder 6.

66 Seymour Halpern in House Committee on Foreign Affairs, *The International Narcotics Trade* (1972), 6; Senate Committee on Labor and Public Welfare, *Military Drug Abuse, 1971*, 14.

67 Chomsky and Herman, *Manufacturing Consent*, Hallin, *Uncensored War*; Aronson, "Media and the Message."

68 House Committee on Armed Services, *Inquiry into Alleged Drug Abuse in the Armed Services* (1971), 2174.

69 See Solis, *Marines and Military Law*, 104; Roffman and Sapol, "Marijuana in Vietnam," 615.

70 Jaffe interview; Senate Committee on the Judiciary, *War-Related Civilian Problems in Indochina* (1971).

71 Spencer Rich, "Fear of Narcotics Wave among Vets Exaggerated," *Washington Post*, February 25, 1980, A3.

72 For example, Gerald Waite, "Outsourcing a War: What You Get for your Mercenary Dollar," paper presented to the Conference on the Impact of Culture, Ethnicity, Race and Religion on the Vietnam War, Vietnam Center, Texas Tech University, March 24, 2007; Chomsky and Herman, "The 43+ My Lai's of the South Korean Mercenaries," in *Political Economy of Human Rights*, 1:321–22.

3. DECONSTRUCTING THE MYTH

Epigraphs

Senate Committee on the Judiciary, *World Drug Traffic and Its Impact on U.S. Security* (1972), 135.

Bentel and Smith, "Drug Abuse in Combat," 26.

Senate Committee on Government Operations, *Federal Drug Enforcement* (1975), 81.

1 "The Campus Debate—Religion versus Reality," The Attack on Narcotic Addiction and Drug Abuse (October 1967), EJE, box 13, folder 1.

2 See Musto, *American Disease*.

3 See Acker, *Creating the American Junkie*; Ausubel, *Drug Addiction*; Cohen, *Drug Dilemma*, 1–2, and *Beyond Within*.

4 Louria, *Drug Scene*, 28–29, and *Nightmare Drugs*, 10, 17.

5 Nahas, *Marihuana*, 35, 249; Farnsworth quoted in Wakefield, "Hallucinogens," 66; Edward R. Bloomquist quoted in John Kaplan, *Marijuana*, 23; Bloomquist, *Marijuana*.

6 De Alarcón, "Spread of Heroin Abuse"; Kolb, *Drug Addiction*, 5; "Testimony of Dr. Victor H. Vogel," U.S. Treasury, *Interim Report of the Joint Committee*, 94; Nyswander, *Drug Addict as a Patient*, 1; Wakefield, *Addict*, 20.

7 Treanor and Skirpol, "Marijuana in a Tactical Unit"; Camp, Marshall, and Stretch, *Stress, Strain, and Vietnam*, 82; Siegel, "Heroin Crisis"; Sidney Cohen, "Instructional Unit on Drug Abuse in Vietnam," Department of Army Headquarters, DP& P, box 4, folder 2.

8 Senate Committee on Labor and Public Welfare, *Military Drug Abuse, 1971*, 6495.

9 Joel Kaplan, "Marijuana and Drug Abuse: Does Our Army Fight on Drugs?" in Senate Committee on the Judiciary, *Drug Abuse in the Military* (1966–1970), 6263, 6287–89.

10 See Stuart Auerbach, "Doctor [Feld] Blames Viet Marijuana for Needless Killings by GIs," *Washington Post*, May 11, 1970, A1.

11 "Testimony of Dr. Albert LaVerne," in Senate Committee on the Judiciary, *Drug Abuse in the Armed Forces* (1970), 6345.

12 See Roszak, *Dissenting Academy*.

13 Sutherland, *Professional Thief* and *White Collar Crime*.

14 Becker, *Outsiders*, 35–78; Clark, *Autobiography of a Girl Drug Addict*.

15 Among works bearing Goodman's influence, see Jock Young, *The Drug Takers*.

16 Fort, *Pleasure Seekers*, 218–19.

17 Finestone, "Cats, Kicks, and Color"; Feldman, "Ideological Supports"; Feldman, "Origins and Spread," 112.

18 Blumer et al., *World of Youthful Drug Use*, 56; Sutter, "World of the Righteous Dope Fiend." Sutter was a co-author of Blumer's study.

19 Preble and Casey, "Taking Care of Business."

20 Laing, *Sanity, Madness and the Family* and *Politics of Experience*; Fromm, *Sane Society*, for example the chapter titled "Can a Society Be Sick?"

21 Szasz, *Myth of Mental Illness*; *Ceremonial Chemistry*, 48; and "Ethics of Addiction."

22 Leary, *Flashbacks* and *The Politics of Ecstasy*, 35.

23 "Interview with Timothy Leary," 101; Morcuse, *Eros and Civilization*.

24 Leary, "Politics, Ethics, and Meaning of Marijuana."

25 Jerry Rubin, "Liberty or Death," Letter to the Editor, *The Village Voice*, April 18, 1968, 4; Jerry Rubin, "An Emergency Letter to My Brothers and Sisters in the Movement," *New York Review of Books*, February 13, 1969, 27.

26 Leary, Litwin, and Metzner, "Reactions to Psilocybin"; Lee and Shlain, *Acid Dreams*, 75.

27 Sanders interview. On Leary's influence as a drug specialist and social critic, see Stevens, *Storming Heaven*, 154; Zinberg, *Drug, Set, and Setting*.

28 E.g., David E. Smith, "Lysergic Acid Diethylamide"; David Solomon, *LSD*.

29 Becker, "History, Culture and Subjective Experience."

30 Weil, *Natural Mind*, 27.

31 Zinberg, "Search for a Rational Approach," 57; Zinberg and Hunt, *Heroin Use*, 162.

32 Zinberg and Weil, "Comparison of Marijuana Users." For their views on cocaine, see United States v. Jose Castro, No. 74, CR 556, U.S. District Court of Illinois, Eastern Division, February 12, 1975, Lexis 13873.

33 Grinspoon and Zinberg quoted in Thomas Gleaton, "Gabriel Nahas: PRIDE Man of Our Time," National Parents Resource Institute for Drug Education, July 1985, CTF, box 7, folder 2; Grinspoon, "Marijuana in a Time of Psychopharmacological McCarthyism."

34 In "Playboy Panel—The Drug Revolution," 1970. See also "Testimony of Joel Fort, School of Social Welfare, University of California, Berkeley," in House Select Committee on Crime, *Crime in America—Illicit and Dangerous Drugs* (1969), 5.

35 Becker, *Campus Power Struggle*, 137–51.

36 Quoted in in Becker, *Campus Power Struggle*, 147–48.

37 Holloway et al., "Drug Abuse in Military Personnel," 1200.

38 Bourne, "Vietnam Veteran."

39 Ratner, "Drugs and Despair," 15; also quoted in Halstead, "The New Anti-War Army," 28.

40 Bourne, *Men, Stress, and Vietnam*, and *Psychology and Physiology of Stress*, 226–31.

41 "Testimony of Roger Roffman, PhD Candidate, University of California, Berkeley," in Senate Committee on the Judiciary, *Drug Abuse in the Armed Forces* (1970), 6476; Roffman interview.

42 "Testimony of Dr. Norman E. Zinberg," "Drug Abuse Prevention and Control," in Senate Committee on Armed Services, *Drug Abuse in the Military* (1972), 356; Zinberg, "Heroin Use in Vietnam," 488, "Rehabilitation of Heroin Users," and "GI's and OJ's."

43 Zinberg, "Rehabilitation of Heroin Users," 263–66.

44 Sanders interview; Sanders, "Doper's Wonderland," 66, 71–72.

45 Lifton, *Home From the War*, 101, 129, 171; and *Death in Life*.

46 Ingraham, "'The Nam' and 'The World,'" 118; and "Myth of Illicit Drug Use," 19.

47 Bentel and Smith, "Drug Abuse in Combat."

48 Szasz, "Scapegoating Military Addicts."

49 Quoted in Nicosia, *Home to War*, 179.

50 Stanton, "Drug Use in Vietnam"; Roffman and Sapol, "Marijuana in Vietnam" (1970), 15–16.

51 Robins, Helzer, Hesselbrock, and Wish, "Vietnam Veterans Three Years after Vietnam"; Harris and Jaffe, "As Far as Heroin Is Concerned," 71.

52 Lifton, *Home from the War*, 41, and "The 'Gook Syndrome'"; Mirin and McKenna, "Combat Zone Adjustment," 480–82.

53 "Testimony of Master Chief Hospital Corpsman Marvin Everett Reed," in House Committee on Armed Services, *Alleged Drug Abuse in the Armed Services* (1970), 1426.

54 Ives, "Profiles in Disaster."

55 Talbott and Teague, "Marihuana Psychosis"; "Testimony of Dr. James W. Teague," in House Committee on Armed Services, *Alleged Drug Abuse in the Armed Services* (1970), 6311.

56 "Testimony of Dr. Roger A. Roffman," in House Committee on Armed Services, *Alleged Drug Abuse in the Armed Services* (1970), 6327, 6386.

57 E.g., Elliot, *Vietnamese Wars*.

4. **"A GENERATION OF JUNKIES"**
Epigraphs
Hamilton-Paterson, *Greedy War*, 242.
McCoy, *Politics of Heroin in Southeast Asia*, 362.

1 George C. Wilson, "General Linked to Drug Ring in South Vietnam," *Washington Post*, June 2, 1972, A16.

2 "Heroin and the War," *Washington Post*, July 26, 1972; Seymour M. Hersh, "CIA Aides Assail Asia Drug Charge: Agency Fights Report," *New York Times*, July 22, 1972, A1.

3 Kunnes, *American Heroin Empire*, 35; Corson, *Betrayal*, 71. Corson tellingly commented, "This was not and is not war, it is genocide."

4 E.g., Baum, *Smoke and Mirrors*.

5 Less radical than Epstein, Massing's *The Fix* is another work characteristic in its focus on the conservative movement.

6 Joel Fort, "Drug Addiction in Asia—A Study of 16 Asian Countries," World Health Organization, Summer, 1963, LEN 12-19, NA, box 11, folder 3; Fort, *Pleasure Seekers*, 61–62.

7 "CIA Once Ousted Ky, Report Shows: Senate Study Charges He Flew Opium on Mission," *New York Times*, April 19, 1968, 11.

8 Hans J. Spielmann, "The South-East Asian Connection," *New York Times*, May 17, 1972, 47; "Saigon Airport: A Smuggler's Paradise," *New York Times*, April 22, 1971, 1; "The Wonderland of Opium."

9 Strock, "No News from Laos"; John Hughes, "Four Lane Drug Highway," *Christian Science Monitor*, June 16, 1970, 6.

10 Hinckle and Scheer, "University on the Make," 14; Scott interview; "The CIA's Flourishing Opium Trade," 8. Ky had indeed given an interview to a European journalist stating that he admired Hitler for strengthening and bringing order to Germany during the depression.

11 For more recent scholarly corroboration, see Schaller, *U.S. Crusade in China*, 65–85; William M. Leary, *Perilous Missions*.

12 Peter D. Scott's analysis on this count drew from prominent revisionist histories of the period including Williams's seminal book *The Tragedy of American Diplomacy*. In the case of China, Scott argued that corporate sponsorship of the CAT typified the close business relationship between American corporate executives and influential members of Jiang's regime, including wealthy financiers T. V. Soong and H. H. Kung. Peter D. Scott, "Air America," and *War Conspiracy*, 212–13.

13 Browning and Garrett, "New Opium War."

14 Chomsky, "Editorial Statement on Vietnam," and *American Power*; Haseltine et al., *Trail of the Poppy*, 64. Harvard-educated historian Mark Selden, author of a favorable account of the Chinese revolution, *The Yenan Way in Revolutionary China*, was the among the principal authors.

15 On Jiang's corruption and relationship to Du Yuesheng, see Slack, *Opium, State, and Society*; Martin, *Shanghai Green Gang*; Marshall, "Opium and the Politics of Gangsterism."

16 Haseltine et al., *Trail of the Poppy*, 64.

17 *Ramparts*, January, 1972, 21; "Earth News," *The Sound*, March 1972.

18 Scott interview; "Sparks or Sputters."

19 See Ginsberg, "First Manifesto"; Leary, *Flashbacks*, 144; Lifton, *Home from the War*, 125–26.

20 Editors of *Ramparts* and Browning, *Smack!*, 50, 80.

21 Ibid., 29.

22 McCoy and Adams, *Laos*; McCoy, *Politics of Heroin: CIA Complicity*, 2003 ed., ix. Trinquier later wrote to Harper & Row expressing approval of McCoy's book and its factual accuracy.

23 Newton claimed to have been targeted by the police for selective assassination. See Keating, *Free Huey*.

24 DeRienzo, "Interview with Alfred McCoy"; McCoy, *Politics of Heroin: CIA Complicity*, 2003 ed., ix; Amy Goodman, "Interview with Alfred McCoy."

25 McCoy, *Politics of Heroin: CIA Complicity*, 2003 ed., 385.

26 As McCoy noted, the United States exploited an internecine rivalry between the Lo and Ly clans of the Hmong and garnered the support of the Ly Hmong (led by Touby LyFoung). The Lo Hmong clan, headed by Lo Faydang, meanwhile fought for the Communist Pathet Lao. See Lyfoung, *Authentic Account*.

27 See Lansdale's *In the Midst of Wars*; Currey, *Edward Lansdale*; Nashell, *Edward Lansdale's Cold War*.

28 On this connection, see Lobe, *U.S. National Security*.

29 McCoy, *Politics of Heroin: CIA Complicity*, 2003 ed., 191. On the U.S.–Thai military alliance, see Fineman, *A Special Relationship*, 134–36.

30 The CIA assisted General Dang in escaping to Canada after the war and provided him with financial support. He was later deported because of continued involvement in criminal activity and drug trafficking; McCoy, *Politics of Heroin: CIA Complicity*, 2003 ed., 237.

31 For a favorable assessment of McCoy, see Weir, *In the Shadow*, 208.

32 Senate Select Committee to Study Governmental Operations with respect to Intelligence Activities, *Final Report* (1974), 57, 229–31; Prados, *Safe for Democracy*, 359; Schanche, *Mister Pop*, 120.

33 Blaufarb, *Counter-Insurgency Era*, 151; Corn, *Blond Ghost*, 148–50; Robbins, *Air America*; Kwitny, *Crimes of Patriots*, 43–53; Kruger, *Great Heroin Coup*, 141–48.

34 "Guns, Drugs and the CIA," *PBS Frontline*, May 17, 1988; Jonathan Mirsky, "Heroin, Laos and the CIA," *New York Review of Books*, August 16, 1990; Prados, *Lost Crusader*, 169. Prados quotes former National Security Council staffer Michael Forrestall to this effect from a 1988 interview.

35 Warner, *Backfire*, 254. For more disclosures, see Weldon, *Tragedy in Paradise*, 184–85; Robbins, *Air America*, 237. These stories have been confirmed to me through personal interviews (off the record) with USAID and former CIA operatives at the Texas Tech Vietnam Center in Lubbock, Texas.

36 Deforest and Chanoff, *Rise and Bitter Fall of American Intelligence*, 205; Father Tran Huu Thanh, "Indictment #1: The People's Front against Corruption, For National Salvation and for Building Peace," Letter from Hue, Vietnam, September 8, 1974, Douglas Pike Archive, Texas Tech University, Vietnam Center, www.vietnam.ttu.edu.; Prados, *Lost Crusader*, 245; Tran Van Khiem, letter to the editor, *Washington Star*, July 20, 1972.

37 Karnow, *Vietnam*, 440; Valentine, *Strength of the Wolf*, 335.

38 E.g.,"Discussion with Minister of Justice on Narcotics," American Embassy, Vientiane, to Secretary of State, May 1974; USAID, H.Q. East Asian Bureau, AIDNC, NA, box 1, folder 4; "Narcotics Suppression," November 1972, Records of the United States Forces in South East Asia, CIB, NA, box 2, folder 2; "Major Ngo Dzu's Involvement in the Drug Traffic," CID, Investigative Report, filed May 1971, Records of the United States Forces in Southeast Asia, CIB, NA, box 9, folder 6.

39 E.g., "MACIG Report of Inquiry concerning Alleged Corruption in the Qui Nhon Area of the Bin Dinh Province," CIB, NA, box 9, folder 5; "Memo for files

Re: Lien Ching Chao," Charles D. Casey, Narcotics Agent to District Supervisor, at Bangkok, DEA, BNDD, box 164, folder Vietnam, 1953–1967; Walton, Skuse, and Motter, *Survey of the Laos National Police*, vi, 1.

40 Harry J. Anslinger to Gilbert Yates, February 25, 1959; also Gilbert Yates, Director Division Narcotic Drugs, to Harry J. Anslinger, February 20, 1959; Bowman G. Taylor to Honorable Leonard Ungar, American Ambassador, December 30, 1963. All in BNDD, box 164, folder Vietnam.

41 Wayland Speer to Harry J. Anslinger, "Opium Smuggling in Vietnam," January 14, 1957, BNDD, box 164, folder Vietnam.

42 U. Alexis Johnson, American Consulate to State Department, June 13, 1958, BNDD, box 164, folder Vietnam.

43 "2 baggage handlers dismissed . . . ," CIA declassified documents, NA; Walter Morris to District Supervisor, "Vietnam—Dope Smuggling Mission Contract Plane," William H. McKeldin, October 18, 1956; Bowman G. Taylor to Honorable Leonard Ungar, American Ambassador, December 30, 1963; "CIA Disclaims Knowledge of Arrested," John Enright to Rexell Moore, February 23, 1967. All in BNDD, box 164, folder Vietnam.

44 "Officials Involved in Opium Running," American Embassy, Bangkok, to Department of State, July 7, 1958, AIDC, box 1, folder 5; Scott interview. On Sea Supply, see Fineman, *Special Relationship*, 223.

45 Trocki, *Opium, Empire and the Global Political Economy*; Lintner, "Golden Triangle Opium Trade."

46 William Walker, *Opium and Foreign Policy*, 162; Peers and Brelis, *Behind the Burma Road*, 64.

47 *London Weekend Telegraph*, March 10, 1967, 6; Lintner, *Burma in Revolt*, 236; Feingold, "Opium and Politics in Laos"

48 See McCoy, "Heroin as a Global Commodity."

49 On CCAS, see Douglas Allen, "Scholars of Asia and the War"; Cobrun, "Asian Scholars and Government"; McCoy, "Subcontracting Counterinsurgency."

50 Seymour M. Hersh, "CIA Aides Assail Asia Drug Charge," *New York Times*, July 22, 1971, 1; McCoy, *Politics of Heroin in Southeast Asia*, 181–82.

51 McCoy, *Politics of Heroin in Southeast Asia*, 1.

52 McCoy, "Flowers of Evil"; Marx, "The Opium Trade."

53 Particularly egregious cases include Turnbull, *Chinese Opium Narcotics*, and Stanton-Candlin, *Psycho-Chemical Warfare*.

54 Flora Lewis, "Heroin and the CIA."

55 "Viet Heroin Book Author Is Criticized," *Washington Post*, June 3, 1972, A6; "Statement of Alfred W. McCoy," in Senate Foreign Relations Committee, *Hearings before the Senate Committee on Foreign Relations*, June 2, 1972: 699; Richard Lingeman, "The CIA as Book Reviewer," *New York Times Book Review*, September 3, 1972, 23; "Harper Proceeding on Drug-Trade Book Despite CIA View," *New York Times*, August 9, 1972, 14; Lawrence R. Houston, General Counsel, CIA, to Mr. B. Brooke Thomas, Harper & Row Publishers, July 5, 1972, CIA declassified documents, NA.

56 McCoy, *Politics of Heroin: CIA Complicity*, 1991 ed., xxi; Ahern Jr., *Undercover Armies*, 458; Scott interview. Scott bore witness to the chemical burning incident and later wrote about it in his poem *Coming to Jakarta*, about the brutality of U.S. methods in Indonesia during the mid 1960s, where the CIA and State Department were proven to be complicit in the genocidal activities of General Suharto in liquidating the Indonesian Communist Party (PKI). Scott wrote: "That clean morning in Palo Alto/ the former Green Beret / who just the night before said he would talk to us / about opium in Laos / showing us the sharp black hole / in his M.G.'s red steel door / the floorboards hardly scorched / and saying that a hot thermal charge / must have come from old unit / and if not from such terror / we each acknowledge / we are not normal / in this world where / we live by forgetting."

57 "William Colby to Mr. Joseph Pullitzer," *St. Louis Dispatch*, July 17, 1972.

58 William E. Colby, "Letters to the Editor—The CIA Responds," *Washington Star*, July 5, 1972; "The Agency's Brief"; McCoy, "The Author Responds." Ahern Jr., *Undercover Armies*, 458.

59 "Nelson Gross to William Proxmire," June 8, 1972, reprinted in *Washington Daily News*, June 29, 1972; Richard Phalon, "Federal Drug Traffic Figures Contested," *New York Times*, June 10, 1972, 29.

60 The paper went on to compare the hill tribes to American Indians in their acting as a barrier to modernization: M. J. W. Pevoy and J. M. Wilkinson, "References to Thailand in Mr. McCoy's book," 1972, State Department Records, Subject Files, Offices of Thai and Burma Affairs, 1963–1975, NA, box 5, folder Narcotics.

61 "Narcotics: McCoy's Testimony before the Senate," memo from G. McMurtrie Godley, American Embassy, Vientiane, to Secretary of State, June 5, 1972, OPS, Laos, box 113, folder 3.

62 Valentine, *Strength of the Wolf*, 365.

63 "Narcotics—Presidential Assembly Will Push New Law," American Ambassador, Vientiane, to Secretary of State, July 1971, RDS, Laos, box 3075, folder 1. After coming to power in the CIA-backed coup, Sananikone perpetrated a major purge of suspected Communist elements, killing many people and thrusting the Pathet Lao underground. This may have been one of the sins to which he was referring. See McCoy and Adams, *Laos*, 289–90.

64 Terry King, "Heroin—Tool of the Brass," *The Bond*, July 24, 1971, 3, and "Heroin: Government Issued?," *The Bond*, March 18, 1971, 4, both in ANC.

65 Kunnes, *American Heroin Empire*, 77, 83, 133.

66 Carmichael, "Speech at the University of California." The term *mercenary* to Carmichael implied "hired killer."

67 Frazier quoted in Graham, *Brothers' Vietnam War*, 110; Haseltine et al., *The Opium Trail*, 14; Michael Rossman, "Politics of the White Drug Plague," *Liberation News Service*, August 7, 1971.

68 Frazier quoted in Kunnes, *American Heroin Empire*, 102. See also Fanon, *Wretched of the Earth*.

69 "Daley's Dope Dealing," *Black Panther*, July 1, 1972, 3, and "Heroin Is King But Methadone Is the Emperor," *The Black Panther*, June 24, 1972, 7, both in ANC; "Black Power Group in Vietnam Fights the Enemy Within: Heroin Addiction," *New York Times*, August 12, 1971, A3.

70 "The Government Drug Conspiracy in the Case of Los Tres," cited in Chavez, *Mi Raza Primero!*, 102. For a Chicano perspective, see Ybarra, *Vietnam Veteranos.*

71 Contact Indochina, August 26, 1970, no. 3, Harry J. Norr Anti-War Collection, Healy Library, University of Massachusetts Boston, box 11, folder 3; Knock, "Come Home America, 116; "McGovern, $500 plate dinner," Waldorf, New York, October 2, 1972, EKP, box 84, folder 3.

72 "McGovern Calls War on Drugs a Casualty of the Indo-China War," September 18, 1972, EKP, box 32, folder 3; See also McGovern, "Toward an End to Drug Abuse," 1; Howard E. Hughes, "Position Paper of Senator McGovern on Southeast Asia Narcotics Traffic," *Congressional Record*, September 26, 1972, 323–57.

73 Mike Mansfield, "GIs and Heroin," *Congressional Record*, July 13, 1971; Flora Lewis, "GI's and Heroin: The Facts of Life," *New York Times*, July 11, 1971, A1.

74 William Proxmire in *Congressional Record*, July 26, 1972; Edmund Muskie, "A War against Heroin," speech before the New Hampshire Bar Association, Bretton Woods, N.H., June 18, 1971, EMP, box 1891, folder 7.

75 "Humphrey Urges CIA Hunt Down Heroin Smugglers," *Fresno Bee*, February 1, 1972.

76 House Committee on Foreign Affairs, *Foreign Assistance Act of 1971*, 296; Pepper quoted in House Select Committee on Crime, *Narcotics Research, Rehabilitation and Treatment* (1971), 1, 350.

77 Cranston quoted in Weimer, "Drugs as Disease," 274; "Testimony of John L. McLelland," in Senate Committee on Government Operation, *Drug Abuse Prevention and Control* (1971), 2; "Testimony of Lester Wolff," in Senate Committee on Labor and Public Welfare, *Narcotics Situation in Southeast Asia* (January to February 1973), 2; Muskie, "A War Against Heroin," EMP, box 1891, folder 7; Statement of Senator Abraham Ribicoff, *Congressional Record*, June 18, 1971, in Senate Committee on Government Operations, *Drug Abuse Prevention and Control* (1971), 74; "Release from Senator Abraham Ribicoff," September 24, 1971, EKP, box 32, folder 4.

78 "Statement of Charles Rangel," in Senate Committee on Foreign Relations, *Hearings before the Senate Committee on Foreign Relations* (July 1971), 58; Rangel quoted in Kunnes, *American Heroin Empire*, 83–84.

79 "Charge CIA Covers up Drug Traffic," *Daily World*, July 12, 1972, NA.

80 See Bourgois, *In Search of Respect.*

81 Halpern quoted in Senate Committee on the Judiciary, *Drug Abuse in the Military* (1966–1970), 98.

82 "Javits Says Drugs May Speed Pullout," *Washington Post*, June 8, 1971; "Statement of Jacob Javits," in Senate Committee on Government Operations, *Drug Abuse Prevention and Control* (1971), 5.

83 Steele quoted in Senate Committee on Armed Services, *Drug Abuse in the Military* (February to April 1972), 99.

84 See Gallup, *Gallup Poll*, 93, 153. On the impact of the antiwar movement in shaping public policy, see Small, *Johnson, Nixon and the Doves*; Wells, *War Within*.

85 James Reston, "Nixon, Drugs and the War," *New York Times*, June 2, 1971, 41; Szasz, *Ceremonial Chemistry*, 48.

86 Gottschalk, in her excellent book *The Prison and the Gallows*, notes this trend for the broader war on crime, pointing to the power of victims' rights lobbies supported by feminist groups on the left in bolstering the conservative social agenda.

5. THE BRASS RESPONDS, PART I

Epigraphs

Nixon quoted in H. D. S. Greenway, "Drug Dealing Nations to Lose Aid from United States," *Washington Post*, September 19, 1972.

DuPont, "Drug Abuse Decade," 175.

1 Finlator, *Drugged Nation*, 8; Rublowsky, *Stoned Age*, 1.

2 Interview with Egil Krogh, EJE, box 9, folder 1.

3 E.g., Bruce Winters, "Agnew Warns of Impending Drug Doom," *Baltimore Sun*, June 24, 1970.

4 "Statement of Edward Gurney," in Senate Committee on Government Operations, *Drug Abuse Prevention and Control* (1971), 5; "Statement of Jacob Javits," ibid., 5; Rockefeller quoted in Finlator, *Drugged Nation*, 37.

5 Richard M. Nixon, "The Global Battle against Drug Abuse," Address to the International Narcotics Conference, September 18, 1972, USAID, NA, Vietnam, box 29, folder 7; Garnett Horner, "Nixon Warns of Aid Cut to Drug Dealer Nations," *Washington Star*, September 18, 1972; Richard M. Nixon, "Remarks before Governors' Conference," December 12, 1969, EKP, box 13, folder 2.

6 See Dikotter, Laamann, and Zhou, *Narcotics Culture*; Yongming, *Anti-Drug Crusades*.

7 Murray, *Losing Ground*.

8 Nixon, "What Has Happened to America?" 50; Nixon, *Real War*; Nixon, *No More Vietnams*, 17; Presidential Remarks, Drug Abuse Fight: 2nd draft, March 31, 1972, EKP, box 32, folder 3.

9 "Interview with David F. Musto," PBS, May 1, 2007, www.pbs.org.musto.html.

10 Wells, *War Within*, 448, 459. These charges had been long adopted by J. Edgar Hoover and the Johnson administration but never had any credibility, although some Nixon officials, including Henry Kissinger, remained convinced. On the home-grown nature of the student movement, see Terry Anderson, *The Movement and the 1960s*.

11 Baum, *Smoke and Mirrors*, 69; Epstein, *Agency of Fear*, 71.

12 See Mason, *Richard Nixon and the Quest for a New Majority*.

13 Ehrenreich, *Fear of Falling*; Hodgson, *World Turned Right-Side Up*; Franklin, *Vietnam and Other American Fantasies*, 111–30.

14 See Bennett, *De-Valuing America*; Englehardt, *End of Victory Culture*.

15 Hunter S. Thompson, "The Hashbury Is Capital of the Hippies," *New York Times Magazine*, May 14, 1967, 14; Lee and Shlain, *Acid Dreams*.

16 See Gitlin, *The Whole World*; Glass and Henderson, *LSD*. *Time* quoted in Stevens, *Storming Heaven*, 155.

17 Musto and Korsmeyer, *Quest for Drug Control*, 18, 21, 23; Greenfield, *Timothy Leary*. Leary later escaped from prison with the help of the Weather Underground.

18 See "Drug Addiction: Crime or Disease?" and "Drugs Are Medical Problem," RFK Senate Papers, subject file, 1968, RFK, box 31, folder LSD.

19 Brown, "Treatment and Rehabilitation"; "Supreme Court of the United States v. Lawrence Robinson," June 26, 1962, no. 554, in House Committee on Labor and Public Welfare, *Federal Drug Abuse and Drug Dependency Prevention, Treatment and Rehabilitation Act of 1970*, 55.

20 Presidential Advisory Commission on Narcotics and Drug Abuse, Final Report, November 1963, RFK, box 40, folder Narcotics.

21 For a critical discussion of what he terms New York's "uncivil commitment program," see Ashley, *Heroin*, 179.

22 O'Donnell, *Narcotic Addicts in Kentucky*; White, "Trick or Treat," 137–39.

23 Massing, *The Fix*; Flamm, *Law and Order*.

24 Nixon, "Message before Congress," 515; Kate Doyle, "Operation Intercept: The Perils of Unilateralism," Electronic Briefing, NSA, www.gwu.edu/~nsarchiv. Intercept was cancelled after three weeks because lines at the Mexican border were extending more than six miles, delaying tourists and curtailing trade flows.

25 "Testimony of Egil Krogh," in Senate Committee on Government Operations, *Federal Drug Enforcement* (July 1976), 10:; Krogh interview, EJE, box 9, folder 1.

26 Robert L. DuPont, Nicholas J. Kozel, and Barry S. Brown, "A Study of Narcotic Addicted Offenders at the D.C. Jail," District of Columbia, National Treatment Association, report no. 1, 1970, EJE, box 14, folder 4; DuPont, "Heroin Addiction Treatment."

27 "Washington D.C. Methadone Maintenance Program," John Ehrlichman to Egil Krogh, January 1971, EKP, box 3, folder 5; Jerome H. Jaffe, "Multimodality Approaches to the Treatment and Prevention of Opiate Addiction," paper presented at the Symposium of the American Federation of Clinical Research, May 1971, EJE, box 14, folder 3; "Different Strokes for Different Folks," White House Memo, Jeffrey Donfeld to Egil 'Bud' Krogh, June 9, 1970, EKP, box 32, folder 2; Massing, *The Fix*, 106.

28 The bill further abolished mandatory minimum sentencing for most offenses. "Remarks of the President upon Signing H. R. 18583, The Comprehensive Drug Abuse Prevention and Control Act of 1970," CWP, box 28, folder 2; Musto and Korsemeyer, *Quest For Drug Control*, 57, 68.

29 Thomas J. Dodd to Edmund Muskie, February 2, 1970, EMP, box 1813, folder 11.

30 Drug Abuse Education Act, in *Hearings before the Special Subcommittee on Alco-holism and Narcotics* (1970), 1. On the broader administrative strategy in this period, see, e.g., John Ingersoll, "The Search for Credibility in the Narcotics and Dangerous Drugs Area," delivered to the 31st Annual Meeting on the Problems of Drug Dependence, National Academy of Sciences, Palo Alto, Calif., February 25, 1969, CWP, box 27.

31 "Project Straight Dope," Mrs. Ralph Falk II to Charles B. Wilkinson, April 11, 1970, CWP, box 31, folder 2; "Drug Abuse Prevention Week," June 22, 1970, White House Memorandum to James Atwater, Special Assistant to the Presi-dent, CWP, box 31, folder 4; "The Administration's Drug Abuse Campaign, Memo from Bud Wilkinson to Bud Krogh," February 26, 1970, CWP, box 27, folder 1; "Memo for the President via John Ehrlichmann, From Egil 'Bud' Krogh: Meeting with Sammy Davis Jr.," September 12, 1971, CWP, box 31, folder 1; "Poi-soned Snow," *Streets of San Francisco*," CBS, September 11, 1975, and "Mer-chants of Death," *Streets of San Francisco*, CBS, November 20, 1975, UCLA Film and Television Archive.

32 Statement of Art Linkletter, House Select Committee on Crime, *Crime in America—Illicit and Dangerous Drugs* (1969), 145; "NFL Stars Line Up"' Nixon, "Remarks to Athletes," 563.

33 "The Drug Problem in the Armed Forces," Henry A. Kissinger, White House Memo to Secretary of Defense, June 1, 1970, LEN, box 807.

34 Krogh, "Heroin Politics and Policy," 39; "RN's Identification with the Drug War," Egil Krogh to Jeb Magruder, and "Vietnam," Egil Krogh to John Ehrlich-man, September 15, 1970, EKP, box 3, folder 1. On the broader point, see Hersh, *Price of Power.*

35 White House Memo, Egil Krogh to Jeff Donfeld, "Drug Abuse Suppression Programs, Vietnam," January 6, 1971, EKP, box 4, folder 1; "Drugs," Egil Krogh to John Ehrlichman, May 14, 1971, EKP, box 32, folder 2.

36 "Heavy Media Coverage," John Huntsman to Bud Krogh, June 8, 1971, Anno-tated News Service, NA, box 33, folder Ray Price; "Drug Letters," memo for Bob Haldeman, Chuck Colson, and Bud Krogh, June 15, 1971, LEN, box 12, folder July 1971; Baum, *Smoke and Mirrors*, 70.

37 "Meeting August 3, 1971, Request for Executive Session Appearance of the At-torney General, Alleged Involvement of South Vietnamese Officials in Drug Traffic," EKP, box 32, folder 2.

38 William Mendelsohn and Ray Price to Honorable Richard M. Nixon, June 7, 1971, Weekly Mail Sample, OF, box 12, folder 7; William Simmons, Executive Secretary of the National Association of Retail Druggists, to Nixon, June 18, 1971.

39 "Summary—Narcotics Meeting, State Dining Room, June 3, 1971," EKP, box 11, folder 3; Nixon, "Special Message to the Congress," 744.

40 E.g., Staneford Garellek to President Nixon; Raynard I. Jameson, President B'nai Brith, to Nixon; Drug Letters, Memo for Bob Haldeman, Chuck Colson, Bud Krogh, June 18, 1971; all in OF, box 12, folder July 1971.

41 "Drug Abuse Fighter, Jerome Herbert Jaffe," *New York Times*, June 18, 1971, 22; Stuart R. Carlin, "Mass Urinalysis Started," *The Army Reporter*, October 25, 1971, 3; "10,000 GI's Checked Daily For Heroin Addiction in Viet," *Pacific Stars and Stripes*, June 3, 1972, 7; Jaffe interview. This language typifies Jaffe's support for the disease model of addiction.

42 "Medical Activities Report United States Army Drug Treatment Center Long Binh," June 28, 1972, Department of the Army, DP&P, box 7, folder 6; Baker, "U.S. Army Heroin Abuse Identification Program"; "Drug Center Opens at Long Binh," *The Army Reporter*, October 18, 1971, 4; House Committee on Armed Services, *Inquiry into Alleged Drug Abuse in the Armed Services* (1971), 7543.

43 Richard M. Nixon, "Draft Statement on Drug Abuse," January 27, 1972, NA, Nixon Presidential Speech File, box 73, folder 1; "Memo Jeffrey Donfeld to Egil Krogh: SAODAP," October 28, 1971, GSP, box 1, folder 4.

44 Jaffe interview; Jaffe quoted in Musto and Korsmeyer, *Quest for Drug Control*, 91.

45 Goldberg, "The Federal Government's Response to Illicit Drugs, 1969–1978"; Wilbur, "Battle against Drug Dependency," 27; Veterans Administration, *Drug and Alcohol Dependency Program*.

46 Jaffe interview; "Drive to Curb GI Drug Use in Vietnam," *Washington Post*, February 2, 1971, A17.

47 National Commission on Marihuana and Drug Abuse, *Marihuana: A Signal of Misunderstanding*; "Oval Office Tapes," September 9, 1971, 3:03 PM–3:34 PM, Conversation No. 568–64; "Nixon Tapes Show Roots of Marijuana Prohibition: Misinformation, Culture Wars and Prejudice," *Common Sense for Drug Policy Research Report*, March 2002, 2.

48 Alfred R. Lindesmith to Robert F. Kennedy, October 9, 1962, Records of the Presidential Advisory Commission on Narcotics and Drug Abuse, JFK, box 1, folder Narcotics; Senate Committee on the Judiciary, *Methadone Use and Abuse* (November 14, 1972), 221; see also Szasz, *Ceremonial Chemistry*, 8–9; Bourne, *Methadone*.

49 House Select Committee on Crime, *Narcotics Research, Rehabilitation and Treatment* (1971), 782; "Statement Milton Shapp, Governor Pennsylvania," in Senate Committee on Labor and Public Welfare, *Hearings before the Senate Subcommittee on Alcohol and Narcotics* (Philadelphia, 1973), 102.

50 Dole, "Detoxification."

51 "Testimony of Jimmy Carter," in Senate Committee on Government Operations, *Drug Abuse Prevention and Control* (1971), 303, 570.

52 "Statement Dr. Thomas Ungerleider, Director Drug Abuse Research and Education (DARE)," Los Angeles, Calif., in House Select Committee on Crime, *Drugs in Our Schools* (1972), 177; "National Survey of Health Related Drug Abuse Education Programs," CWP, box 5, folder 1.

53 Galvin and Taylor, "Drug Education in Massachusetts," 411; "Testimony of Father Paul Shanley—Counselor to Runaways," in Senate Committee on Labor and Public Welfare, *Federal Drug Abuse and Drug Dependence* (1970), 809.

Shanley was later imprisoned on charges of child molestation in a highly publicized case.

54 Denson-Gerber, *We Mainline Dreams*; Yablonsky, *Tunnel Back*; Meyer, *Guide to Drug Rehabilitation*.

55 "Testimony of Dr. Joel Fort, Director Center for Solving Special Social and Health Problems," in Senate Committee on the Judiciary, *Methadone Use and Abuse*, November 14, 1972; Fort, "Social Problem of Drug Use"; William L. Claiborne, "Heroin Treatment: Garlic Juice, Yoga," *Washington Post*, March 22, 1972, C2.

56 This is a central point of Massing's *The Fix* (1998).

57 George M. Belk, "International Narcotics Control Programs," U.S. Department of Justice, October 1972, DEAL, International Control Folder, 1961–1976; "Goals for Treasury's IRS Narcotics Traffickers Program," GSP, box 1, folder 3.

58 McWilliams, "Through the Past Darkly," 22.

59 "Drug Law Enforcer: Myles J. Ambrose," *New York Times*, January 28, 1972, 8; "Testimony of Egil Krogh," in Senate Committee on Government Operations, *Federal Drug Enforcement* (1976), 774; "Office for Drug Abuse Law Enforcement, Myles J. Ambrose," in U.S. Attorney General, *1972 Annual Report of the Attorney General of the United States*, 37; "Big Gains in Drive to Cut Off Narcotics," 32; "Gains in the War on Drug Smugglers," 60. The agency also set up a heroin hotline, which was discontinued after it was realized that most of the calls it received were crank.

60 See Browning (of *Ramparts* fame), "American Gestapo," 79; Epstein, *Agency of Fear*, 17–19; untitled article, *Newsweek*, May 14, 1973, 27; "Statement of Myles J. Ambrose," in Senate Committee on Government Operations, *Federal Drug Enforcement* (July 1975), 888.

61 Martin Tolchin, "Ambrose Quits as Nixon Advisor and Drug Enforcement Chief," *New York Times*, May 22, 1973, 12; Peter D. Scott, *Deep Politics*, 79–80; James R. Markham, "Narcotics Corruption Appears Easy and Common," *New York Times*, December 23, 1972, 26; Fred J. Cook, "How Deep Are the Police in the Heroin Traffic," *New York Times*, April 25, 1971, E3; "Corruption Confirmed," *New York Times*, August 15, 1972, 34; "Police as Pushers," *New York Times*, December 26, 1972, 32.

62 Nixon, "Message to the Congress Transmitting Reorganization Plan 2 of 1973"; Bartels, "The Mission Before Us" and "Nation's War on Drugs."

63 The DEA, as internal documents reveal, suspected that up to one-eighth of Bay of Pigs veterans were "dope peddlers." See Kruger, *Heroin Coup*, 195; Grinspoon and Bakalar, *Cocaine*, 53; "Ex-Cuban Government Official in Cocaine Arrest," *New York Times*, August 25, 1973, 92; Jack Anderson, "Closer Look at CIA-Dope Link," *San Francisco Chronicle*, February 19, 1975.

64 *Congressional Quarterly*, September 24, 1973, 516; Parenti, *Lockdown America*, 20; "Jail No Answer to Drug Problem," *Buffalo Evening News*, December 27, 1972, 11; "Points from the Message by Governor Rockefeller," and Leslie Gelsner, "Governor's Drug Plan Draws Anger," *New York Times*, January 4, 1973.

65 Alsop, "City Killer" and "Smell of Death." For another sensationalist piece, see Thomas A. Johnson, "Heroin Epidemic Hits Schools," *New York Times*, February 16, 1970, 1.

66 David Burnham, "State Investigator Links Corrupt Police to Heroin," *New York Times*, April 6, 1971, 1. For reliable data, see Hunt and Chambers, *Heroin Epidemics*, 1–10.

67 On the Nixon doctrine, see, e.g., Bundy, *Tangled Web*.

68 See William Walker, *Drug Control in the Americas*, 95–96; Kinder and Walker, "Stable Force in a Storm."

69 Records of the fourth Meeting, Interagency Group, April 30, 1963, Records of the Agency of International Development, OPS, NA, box 8; Records of the Presidential Advisory Commission on Narcotics and Drug Abuse, box 1, JFK; Craig, "La Campaa Permanente."

70 *Boston Globe*, October 3, 1977; Kruger, *Great Heroin Coup*, 173; *Department of State Bulletin*, no. 1737 (October 1972): 401–15, and Statement of John E. Ingersoll, United States Mission Information Service, Geneva, Switzerland, September 28, 1970, both International Narcotics Control files, 1961–1975, DEAL.

71 Marshall, "White House Death Squad"; Epstein, *Agency of Fear*, 105; McWilliams, "Through the Past Darkly," 22. On the worm idea, see Jeffrey Donfeld, Nixon Presidential File, Meeting held Thursday, June 10, 1971, EJE, box 14, folder 7. Nixon joked that the special worm was a "screw worm" because the main one tested died after having intercourse; Seymour M. Hersh, "U.S. Aides in 1972 Weighed Killing Officer Who Now Leads Panama," *New York Times*, June 13, 1986, A1.

72 "Donald Rumsfeld to Egil Krogh," White House memo, June 21, 1971, GSP, box 1, folder 7.

73 Cabinet Committee on International Narcotics Control, *World Opium Survey, 1972*; Senate Committee on the Judiciary, *The Mexican Connection*, Feburary 10, 1978; "DEA International Training Program."

74 USAID, Public Safety—Philippines, NA, Box 9; "Breaking the Connection," Gordon Liddy to John D. Ehrlichman, November 10, 1971, NSF, box 1025, folder 1; Senate Committee on Foreign Relations, *Heroin: Can the Supply Be Stopped?* (Spong), 15.

75 Takashi Oka, "French-United States Tie Tightens Vise on Drug Trade," *Christian Science Monitor*, February 24, 1972; Senate Committee on the Judiciary, *Poppy Politics* (1975), 12; Flanders, "Heroin Labs of Marseille." On the CIA's alliance with the mafia in Italy, see Peter D. Scott, *Deep Politics*, 176.

76 Epstein, "Incredible War"; "Drug Smuggling and Visit of BNDD to Turkey," Henry A. Kissinger to John E. Ehrlichman, White House memo, April 26, 1971, EKP, box 32, folder 4.

77 Bagley, "Columbia and the War on Drugs," 77.

78 Nadelmann, *Cops Across Borders*, 273–74; Jack N. Anderson, "The Drug Traffic in Paraguay," *Washington Post*, May 24, 1972, B15; Paul H. Lewis, *Paraguay Under Stroessner*, 135–37.

79 See Collins, "Traffic in Traffickers," 445; Newsday, *Heroin Trail*, 153. Ricorde eventually served a twenty-year sentence at Rikers Island in New York.

80 For the view that these totals were deliberately inflated to serve political ends, see Kruger, *Great Heroin Coup*, 173.

81 Department of Inter-American Affairs, telegram, November 14, 1969, *Country Analysis and Strategy Paper*, Department of State, NSA, *Operation intercept*, document 18; Senate Committee on the Judiciary, *The Mexican Connection* (1978).

82 State Department, Bureau of International Narcotics Matters, *Narcotics Control in Mexico*; Klare and Aronson, *Supplying Repression*, 38–39; Vargas Meza, *Democracy, Human Rights, and Militarism*.

83 House Committee on Foreign Affairs, *U.S. Narcotics Control Programs Overseas* (1985), 37–38; Marshall, "CIA Assets"; Astorga, "Mexico," 90–91; Mills, *Underground Empire*, 359–60; "American Embassy to Department of State," December 8, 1972, OPS, Mexico, box 89, folder Narcotics.

84 Marshall, *Drug Wars*, 22; M. J. McConahay, "Mexico's War on Poppies—and Peasants," *New York Times*, September 3, 1976, 33–38.

85 Peyes, "Legal Murders," 13; "La Operacion CONDOR: Letania de Horrore," *Processo*, Mexico, October 9, 1978, 6–8; Klare and Aronson, *Supplying Repression*, 39; Marshall, *Drug Wars*, 22.

86 E.g., Schoultz, *Human Rights and United States Foreign Policy*; McCoy, *Question of Torture*; Chomsky and Herman, *Political Economy of Human Rights*, vol. 1.

87 In McSherry, *Predatory States*, 74–75; Klare and Aronson, *Supplying Repression*, 28–29; Lernoux, *Cry of the People*, 338–39; Marshall and Scott, *Cocaine Politics*, 44.

88 For more on the U.S.–Argentina connection, see Gareau, "Washington's Support."

89 See Schoultz, *Beneath the United States*.

90 Ford, "A Message to the Congress of the United States," 17, and *A Time to Heal*; Kendrick, *Wound Within*; Craig, "La Campaa Permanente."

91 "Testimony of Mathea Falco, Special Assistant for International Narcotics Control," in House Select Committee on Narcotics Abuse and Control, *Southeast Asian Narcotics* (July 12–13, 1977); Goti, "Reinforcing Poverty, 67, 81; Lebedur, "Bolivia," 148.

92 Robert B. Semple, Jr., "Nixon Says He Kept Vow to Check Rise in Crime," *New York Times*, October 16, 1972, 1; Finlator, *Drugged Nation*, 320.

93 Hunt and Chambers, *Heroin Epidemics*, 1–10; "Testimony of Thomas E. Bryant, M.D., President Drug Abuse Council," in Senate Committee on Government Operations, *Federal Drug Enforcement* (1975); O'Donnell et al., *Young Men and Drugs*, 59; "U.S. Losing Smuggler War," *Chicago Daily News*, June 7, 1975; "President Will Cut Off Aid to Nations in Drug Traffic," *New York Times*, August 28, 1972, A1; Finlator, *Drugged Nation*, 320.

94 See Currie, *Reckoning*.

95 The humanitarian ramifications go ignored as well in volumes of scholarship on Nixon-Kissinger diplomacy that exonerate human rights violations in the "Third World" and the commission of major war crimes. With regard to the

drug war, though I agree with those authors that there were progressive developments associated with the treatment programs, I would argue that these were to a large degree dwarfed by the consequences of the international (and domestic) enforcement campaign.

6. THE BRASS RESPONDS, PART II
Epigraph
Greenway, "Book the CIA Couldn't Put Down."

1 "Correspondence Col. Bill Hart and Dr. Tom Robbins," Walter Reed Medical Museum archives, Washington, D.C., audiotape 102-5, July 4, 1971.

2 See McMahon, *Limits of Empire*; Latham, *Modernization as Ideology*.

3 "The Narcotics Traffic in Indo-China," American Embassy, Saigon, to Department of State, May 18, 1954, DEA and BNDD, 1916–1970, NA, box 164, folder Vietnam; Wayland Speer to Harry J. Anslinger "Red China and the Narcotic Traffic—Vietnam, Laos, Cambodia," July 7, 1954, BNDD, folder Vietnam; Goscha, *Thailand and the Southeast Asian Networks*, 201–44. On the growing stature of the FBN in this period and paradoxes of U.S. foreign narcotics policy, see Kinder and Walker, "Stable Force in a Storm"; William Walker, *Opium and Foreign Policy*, 180.

4 Smuckler et al., *Report on the Police*, 19. U.S. officials had previously tolerated Bao Dai's control of the opium trade under French auspices for political reasons.

5 Wesley R. Fishel, "Notes on Visit to Opium Factory Operated under the Direction of the Director General of Customs, Vietnam," February 19, 1955, BNDD, box 164, folder Vietnam; Ernst, *Forging a Faithful Alliance*.

6 E.g., "Thomas Tripodi, Narcotic Agent to LeRoy Morrison, Agent in Charge," October 3, 1962, and "Merton D. Perry, Saigon to Stanley Karnow, Hong Kong, 'The Opium Business in Vietnam'," both in BNDD, box 164, folder Vietnam.

7 Marilyn D. Young, *Vietnam Wars*, 70–72; McCoy, *Politics of Heroin in Southeast Asia*, 229; Ngo Vinh Long and Noam Chomsky, "Thirty Year Retrospective on the Fall of Saigon," MIT Public Forum, April 30, 2005. According to Ngo, now a reputable scholar of the Vietnamese war, who served briefly for U.S. intelligence before becoming an antiwar activist, American advisers often posed as malaria specialists and conducted house surveys while covertly gaining intelligence on suspected Vietminh. Those fingered were later rounded up by Nhu's forces and imprisoned, tortured, or "disappeared."

8 See Brigham, *Guerilla Diplomacy*.

9 See Schulzinger, *Time for War*, 118–22; McCoy, *Politics of Heroin: CIA Complicity*, 1991 ed., 231; "Narcotics in Vietnam," November 15, 1967, BNDD, box 164, folder Vietnam; Resources Control, National Police of Vietnam, Public Safety Division, Summary of Counterinsurgency Projects, NA, March 1965, 40–41.

10 Lewis W. Walt to Marcus J. Gordon, Regional Representative, USAID, July 1, 1966; "Narcotics Matters Abroad Affecting the United States," James L. McMahon to Mr. Robert Lowe, USAID/Saigon, July 9, 1966; and Marcus J. Gordon, Regional Director, USAID/Danang to Lt. General Lewis W. Walt, Commanding

General III Marine Amphibious Force, Danang, RVN, July l9, 1966, all in BNDD, box 164, folder Vietnam.

11 "Narcotics in Vietnam," and Albert Habib, Narcotics Agent, to Wilbert Penberthy, District Supervisor, "Meeting with Colonel Luan, Chief Saigon Municipal Police," August 19, 1966, and "Status of Investigation Involving 300 Kilograms of Opium," Habib to Penberthy, April 21, 1967, all in BNDD, box 164, folder Vietnam.

12 Penberthy, to Commissioner of Narcotics, November 30, 1967, BNDD, box 164, folder Vietnam, 1953–1967; "Marijuana," John D. Enright, Assistant Commissioner, Department of Customs, to Lawrence Fleishman, Assistant Commissioner, Investigations, Bureau of Customs, March 21, 1967, both in BNDD, box 164, folder Vietnam.

13 "Business of Marijuana," Lt. Van Ngu, Head Police Office, Quang Tri, to National Police Service, Quang Tri, October 6, 1968, OPS, Vietnam Division, Narcotics, box 110, folder 5; Hougan, *Spooks*, 123–38; Valentine, *Phoenix Program*, 300.

14 For historical precedents of covert operations co-opting narcotics control efforts and collaboration between counter-intelligence operatives and the FBN, see Block, "Anti-Communism"; "Historical Narrative—PSD Support of Narcotic Control," Michael G. McCann, Director OPS, to John Maopoli, Chief Vietnam Division, OPS, Office of the Assistant Chief of Staff, Records of CORDS, USAV, Personnel Policy Division, Drug Abuse Programs, box 286, folder 2.

15 U.S. Embassy, Saigon, to Secretary of State, OPS, Vietnam Division, Narcotic Control, box 112, folder 3; "Updating of Narcotics Control Action Program," OPS to American Embassy, Saigon, July 1971, OPS, AIDNC, Vietnam, box 113, folder 6; Narcotics Suppression Campaign, March 30, 1968, AMHI, Drug Abuse—UN, Narcotics Suppression; Valentine, *Phoenix Program*, 300, 409.

16 "Testimony of John Ingersoll," in House Select Committee on Crime, *Narcotics Research, Rehabilitation, and Treatment* (1971), 348; Review of Advisor's Monthly Report—Bureau of Narcotics, Frank E. Walton to Jon Weiss, November 7, 1969, OPS, Vietnam, Narcotics, box 110, folder 2. Ingersoll also had a background in military intelligence.

17 Penberthy to Commissioner, Washington, D.C., March 14, 1967, BNDD, box 164, folder Vietnam; Valentine, *Strength of the Wolf*, 335, 420. On Loan's involvement in other corrupt practices, see Hamilton-Paterson, *Greedy War*, 191.

18 See George Roberts, Report to R. Johnson, Public Administration Ad Hoc Committee on Corruption in Vietnam, November 29, 1967, cited in McCoy, *Politics of Heroin: CIA Complicity*, 1991 ed., 213–14, nn. 63–64.

19 William Walker, *Opium and Foreign Policy*, 162.

20 "Annotated News Summaries—May 1971," LEN, White House OF, box 33, folder May 1971; Boyle, *Flower of the Dragon*; Abrams quoted in Olson and Roberts, *Where the Domino Fell*, 34.

21 See Ward Washington, "Steinbeck Keeps Pot Boiling," *Washington Post*, December 28, 1967, A1; Thomas Corpora, "Use of Marijuana by GIs in Vietnam Being Studied Up," *Washington Post*, October 1, 1967, A10; "Marijuana Termed

Big Problem among U.S. Troops in Vietnam," *New York Times*, October 26, 1967, 4.

22 Pike and Goldstein, "History of Drug Use in the Military"; Siler, "Marijuana Smoking in Panama"; Peterson interview; Hannon interview.

23 "Drugs in Vietnam," Provost Marshall Briefing, USAV, DP&P, box 4, folder 2; Howard McLendon, "Illegal or Improper Use of Drugs," Department of the Army, June 1, 1968, DP&P, box 9, folder 6.

24 "Drug Suppression Program in MR4," September 11, 1971, and "Major General John H. Cushman, Letter to be read to each serviceman in the Delta" June 28, 1971, Records of the U.S. Forces in South East Asia, HQ, USAV, Protective Services Division, CIB, NA, box 5, folder 1; Hannah Browning to Jerry Pettis, January 27, 1972, USAV, M&W, box 6, folder 1; also "Legalized Prostitution: Brass' New Weapon against GIs and Vietnamese Women," *The Bond*, January 27, 1972, ANC.

25 Walter Sears, Enforcement, Security, and Investigations to Joint Chiefs, "Narcotic Suppression Campaign," February 4, 1969, AMHI, Drug Abuse—UN.

26 On chemical defoliation, see Chomsky, *For Reasons of State*, 159; Dean Rusk, "Memo to the President—Defoliation Operations in Vietnam," November 24, 1961, Papers of President Kennedy, Meetings and Memoranda, JFK, box 332, folder Defoliation Operations in Vietnam; "Narcotic Destruction Report, Public Safety Division," July 6, 1971, OPS, Vietnam Division, Narcotic Control, box 112, folder Marijuana Destruction Program; B. Drummond Ayres, "Helicopters and Television in Suppression Drive," *New York Times*, September 21, 1969, 1; "Marijuana Suppression," MACV, OPS, Vietnam Division, Narcotics, box 111, folder Intelligence.

27 Richard Boyle, "U.S. Escalates War against Pot-Heads," *Overseas Weekly, Pacific Edition*, August 30, 1969, 7–8.

28 E.g., "Cancellation of Rewards for Marijuana Plant Destruction Program," B. Harry Wynn to Leigh M. Brilliant, June 9, 1971, Minutes of CORDS/Public Safety Narcotics Meeting, September 25, 1972, OPS, Vietnam Division, AIDNC, box 112, folder Marijuana Destruction Program.

29 See Russo, *Statistical Analysis*; Race, *War Comes to Long An*.

30 See John Paul Vann, "Harnessing the Revolution in South Vietnam," September 10, 1965, FFP, box 9, folder Vann; and Sheehan's brilliant biography, *A Bright Shining Lie*.

31 "Fact Sheet—Marijuana Suppression," John Paul Vann, Deputy for CORDS, May 1969, OPS, Vietnam Division, AIDNC, box 110, folder 7; Howard Groom to Michael McCann, "Assessment of Hoa-Hao Problem," July 17, 1969, Drug Abuse Council, 1973, EJE, box 12, folder 3.

32 "Fact Sheet for Brigadier General Timmenberg in Response to Some Sp.9 Heroin Detector Dogs," July, 1971, CIB, NA, box 3; "Dog Thwarts Drug Traffic," *Army Reporter*, June 1, 1970; "Adjutant General: Postal Operations," MACV, Vietnam folder, NA.

33 Public Safety Directorate, MACV, June 30, 1972, CIB, NA, box 1; Annual Narcotic Statistical Comparison, CIB, NA, box 2, folder 4.

34 E.g., USARV Report No. 6-87, Army CID, Serious Incident Report, 120125, June 1972, and USARV Report No. 6-84, Army CID, Serious Incident Report, CIB, NA, box 3, folder 2.

35 Aronson quoted in Alvin M. Shuster, "GI Heroin Addiction Is Epidemic in Vietnam," *New York Times*, May 16, 1971, A1.

36 "Memorandum for Secretaries of the Military Departments, Drug Abuse Prevention Week," May 11, 1970, CWP, box 44, folder 2; *Army Reporter*, February 11, 1971, 11.

37 "Amnesty Plan Saves Another," *Army Reporter*, March 15, 1971, 6; Daniel Southerland, "How Army Helps GI's Quit Drugs," *Christian Science Monitor*, June 18, 1971, 7; Terry Anderson, "GI Movement," 112.

38 Gard quoted in Anne Usher, "Many Soldiers Turning to Drugs to Deal," *Washington General News*, November 15, 2006; Simon, "GI Addicts"; Iver Peterson, "Army Discharges Many Addicts in Vietnam Despite Pledges," *New York Times*, December 19, 1971.

39 Spencer and Spencer, "Legal Problems," 14; Kunnes, *American Heroin Empire*, 169.

40 Michael McCann, attention Howard Groom, "Special Telephone Line," September 9, 1971, OPS, AIDNC, Vietnam, box 111, folder 3; Mike St. John, "Drug Booklet Distribution," Information Office, USAV, DP&P, box 4, folder 3; Department of Defense, *Drug Abuse: Game without Winners*; "Drug Abuse in the Military," USAV, May 1970, DP&P, box 44, 2; Thomas D. Drysdale, "DoD to Test Phoenix 'Dope Stop' Innovation," *Commander's Digest*, October 21, 1971, 3.

41 "Vung Tau Recreational Center for Troop Morale," General Jack J. Wagstaff to Lieutenant William J. McCaffrey, July 29, 1971, USAV, Military Personnel, Policy Division, M&W, box 13, folder 1; "Sammy Davis Visit as Part of Drug Education Field Team for MACV," John K. Singlaub to General William McCaffrey, Deputy Commanding General, April 12, 1972, DP&P, box 2, folder 11.

42 "Meeting with President and Top Civilian Leaders," Memorandum, Richard M. Nixon to Melvin R. Laird, June 3, 1971, EKP, box 32, folder Drug Abuse; Egil Krogh to John Ehrlichman, June 11, 1971, EKP, box 3, folder 2.

43 "Drug Abuse Program: A Future Model?" (1973), EJE, box 16, folder 2; Richard S. Wilbur, "Press Conference, A Follow-up of Vietnam Drug Users," Department of Defense, U.S. Army audiovisual center, NA.

44 Robins, *Vietnam Drug User Returns*, 67; Helmer, *Drugs and Minority Oppression*, 144.

45 Nicosia, *Home to War*, 179. Robert Reinhold, "Army's Drug Testing Program Stirs Sharp Dispute," *New York Times*, June 2, 1972, 1; "Drugs in the Military," *GI News & Discussion Bulletin*, January 1972, 41; Swarthmore Peace Collection, www.sirnosir.com/archives.

46 Paul Starr, "Drug (Mis)treatment for GIs," *Washington Post*, July 16, 1972, B1; Spencer and Spencer, "Legal Problems," 14.

47 "Correspondence Col. Bill Hart and Dr. Tom Robbins," Walter Reed Medical Museum archives, audiotape 102-5, July 14, 1971; Sanders, "Doper's Wonderland," 74.

48 Quoted in Starr, "Drug (Mis)treatment for GIs," B1.

49 Interview Egil "Bud" Krogh and interview Peter Bourne, *Frontline Drug Wars*, www.pbs.com.

50 Epstein, *Agency of Fear*. On Nixon as shrewd political tactician and pragmatist, see Hoff, *Nixon Reconsidered*.

51 See Kimball, *Nixon's War*; "National Police Anti-Corruption Action," September 18, 1972, USAID, OPS, East, Special Branch Forces in Southeast Asia, NA, box 278, folder 2. For an excellent analysis of the political function of the anti-corruption campaign, see Chomsky and Herman, "Saigon's Corruption Crisis," 23.

52 On Thieu's abysmal human rights record, see Luce and Brown, *Hostages of War*, 14; Chomsky, *At War with Asia*, 109–10. For corroboration of rampant GVN corruption, see "PSD Survey of Black Market Activities," April 16, 1964, USAID, OPS, East Asia Branch, box 285, folder Black Market; "Alleged National Police Misconduct (Shakedown) Office of the Assistant Chief of Staff," CORDS, March 18, 1972, USAID, OPS, East, Special Branch Forces in Southeast Asia, box 278, folder 2.

53 Edward M. Kennedy (D-Mass.) quoted in Keefer, *Foreign Relations*, 32.

54 House Committee on Foreign Affairs, *Foreign Assistance Act of 1971*, 296.

55 "Drugs and Smuggling," Department of State Telegram, Saigon, CIB, NA, box 11, folder 3.

56 "Summary of Vietnam Cables—Drugs," May 1971, Department of State Telegram, 070626, CIB, NA, box 11, folder 3; Memo for Egil "Bud" Krogh Jr., "Indo-Chinese Officials Removed or Shifted as a Result of Investigations in Drug Trafficking," August 3, 1971, EKP, box 30, folder 5; "GVN Reorganizes Attack on Drugs and Smuggling," American Embassy, Saigon, to Department of State, July 8, 1971, DP&P, box 286, folder 2.

57 "Drug Hunt Hits Saigon Customs," *Washington Post*, May 18, 1971, A14; "Anti-Smuggling Drive at Airport," *Pacific Stars and Stripes*, May 20, 1971, 6; "Smuggling Charges Answered," *Pacific Stars and Stripes*, May 13, 1971, 7; House Committee on Foreign Affairs, *The U.S. Heroin Problem in Southeast Asia* (1972), 46.

58 McCoy, *Politics of Heroin: CIA Complicity*, 1991 ed., 247–48; Father Tran Huu Thanh, "Indictment #1: The People's Front against Corruption for National Salvation and for Building Peace," Letter from Vietnam, Hue, September 1974, Douglas Pike Archive, Texas Tech University Vietnam Center, www.vietnam.ttu.edu; House Committee on Foreign Affairs, *Vietnam and Korea: Human Rights and U.S. Assistance* (1975), 7–8.

59 "Historical Narrative—PSD Support of Narcotic Control," Michael G. McCann, Director OPS, Bureau, to John Maopoli, Chief Vietnam Division, OPS, Office of the Assistant Chief of Staff, CORDS, DP&P, box 286, folder 2; Nelson Gross, "Bilateral and Multilateral Efforts to Intensify Drug Abuse Control Programs," *Department of State Bulletin*, April 3, 1972, DEAL; Peter Osnos, "U.S. Presses Saigon into War on Smuggling," *Los Angeles Times*, May 27, 1971, 2.

60 "Military Police: Drug Suppression Program," Headquarters, MACV Directive 190-4, January 14, 1972, OPS, Vietnam, Narcotics, box 12, folder 1; Roderic L.

O'Conner to John Hannah, "AID Representatives on Drug Matters," August 23, 1971, Personal File, Ogden Williams Papers, Texas Tech University Vietnam Center, www.vietnam.ttu.edu. On torture, see McCoy, *A Question of Torture*; Sydney H. Schanberg, "Saigon Torture in Jails Reported," *New York Times*, August 13, 1972, 1.

61 "JNID Confiscations, July 1, 1971 to May 31, 1972," USAV, DP&P, box 36, folder 7; "Antinarcotics Campaign in Viet-Nam," *Department of State Bulletin*, April 3, 1972, 508, DEAL; "Department of State Telegram," American Embassy, Saigon, to E.A Drug Coordinator, October 13, 1972, OPS, AIDNC, Vietnam, box 112, folder 8.

62 Peter Jay, "Saigon Launches Narcotics Drive," *Washington Post*, May 1, 1971, A10; "RVN Anti-Drug Suppression Campaign at Bien Hoa," May 6, 1971, DP&P, box 6, folder 2; "Narcotic Addict Treatment Survey," James L. Reinhart, Director CORDS, to Michael G. McCann, Saigon, July 3, 1972, OPS, box 29, folder 6; Brown and Luce, *Hostages of War*; "Visit to Bien Hoa Prison," memo, William C. Benson to Frank Walton, June 1, 1961, OPS, East Asia, box 287, Penology, folder 2.

63 "Decree Law No. 008/TT/SLU on the Eradication of Toxic Narcotic and Dangerous Substances, Promulgated by President Thieu," in House Committee on Foreign Affairs, *The U.S. Heroin Problem in Southeast Asia* (1972), 85; "Thieu Orders Death for Drug Pushers," *Washington Post*, August 14, 1972, A17; "Anti-Drug Advertisements," Army CID Files, DP&P, box 7, folder 1.

64 "Interview with Nguyen Cao Ky," *The Listener*, November 24, 1977. Ky admitted that the South Vietnamese government was "totally dependent" on the U.S. and that all major decisions were made in Washington. He also stressed the lack of political vision and frankly stated that what "South Vietnam needed, was a man like Ho [Chi Minh]!"

65 Fineman, *A Special Relationship*, 262; Bamrungsuk, *U.S. Foreign Policy*, 77.

66 "Proposals for Increased Anti-Narcotics Assistance to Thailand," Johnson F. Munroe, Deputy Director, OPS, to Nelson Gross, September 27, 1971, OPS, Thailand, AIDNC, box 212, folder 1; "Report of Illicit Traffic in Dangerous Drugs during the Year 1962," Byron Engle, Director Public Safety, to Philip Batson, Assistant Director Public Safety, March 17, 1972, BNDD, box 11, folder 1; Ralph White, "Observations on Hill-tribes and the Security of Thailand"; J. Marshall Thompson to Ambassador Ralph Ungar, January 30, 1962, RDS, Bureau of Far Eastern Affairs, Office of Southeast Asian Affairs, Thailand Files, 1960–1963, box 2.

67 Valentine, *Phoenix Program*, 358; Robbins, *Air America*, 244.

68 "AID Influence in Law Enforcement Community," Egil Krogh to Byron Engle, EKP, box 3, folder 2; Roger Ernst, Director U.S. Operations, Mission Bangkok, Thailand, to Joe W. Johnson, Audit Manager, Bangkok Office, Far-East Bureau, October 3, 1973, OPS, AIDNC, Thailand, box 212, folder 1; Fineman, *A Special Relationship*, 134–36; Lobe, *U.S. National Security Policy*, 23–24.

69 House Select Committee on Narcotics Abuse and Control, *Southeast Asian Narcotics* (1977), 2–3; McCoy, *Drug Traffic*, 346. On the human rights abuses of

Kittikachorn, see Chomsky and Herman, *Political Economy of Human Rights*, 1:222–25.

70 "Pramual case linked to Foreign Aid Bill," Department of State Telegram, American Embassy, Bangkok, to Secretary of State, November 15, 1972, and "Summaries of Recent Thai-language Press," American Embassy, Bangkok, to Secretary of State, October 5, 1972, both in USAID, OPS, box 212, folder 3; "Thanom: Why I Jailed Pramual," *Bangkok Post*, April 27, 1973; "Pramual: It Could Have Been 40 Years," *Bangkok Post*, April 25, 1973.

71 "The Task Forces of Thailand and Laos," 17; "Talking Points for Thailand Narcotics Action Control," to Interagency Working Group on Narcotics Control from Harriet Isom, Drug Control Coordinator, 1973, OPS, AIDNC, Thailand, box 212, folder 1; "Capture of Lo-Hsing Han," American Embassy, Rangoon, to Department of State, July 25, 1973, General RDS, 1970–1973, Thailand, box 3056, folder 1; "Top Drug Kingpin Captured," *Bangkok Post*, July 19, 1973; Delaney, "On Capturing an Opium King," 67.

72 See Packenham, *Liberal America and the Third World*; "Proposals for Increased Anti-Narcotics Assistance in Thailand," Johnson F. Munroe, Deputy Director, OPS to Nelson Gross, September 27, 1971, OPS, AIDNC, Thailand, box 212, folder 1; Renard, *Opium Reduction*, 75–82.

73 E.g., "Opium Production and Movement in Southeast Asia: Intelligence Report," Directorate of Intelligence, CIA Files, NA; Fineman, *Special Relationship*, 143; "Narcotics—Kriangsak Proposal," American Embassy, Bangkok, to Secretary of State, December 5, 1971, RDS, Thailand, box 3099; Senate Committee on Labor and Public Welfare, *The Narcotics Situation in Southeast Asia* (1973) 5; Jack Anderson, "Thai Opium Bonfire Mostly Fodder," *Washington Post*, July 31, 1972, B11; Flood, *United States and the Military Coup*.

74 "Narcotic Enforcement in Cambodia," Red Sutton to James Cretecos, June 14, 1971, OPS, Thailand, Narcotics, box 19, folder 4; McCoy, *Politics of Heroin: CIA Complicity*, 1991 ed., 251. On the destabilizing effect of the 1970 invasion and coup, see Kiernan, *How Pol Pot Came to Power*.

75 "Cambodian Drug Suppression Report #1," American Embassy, Phnom Penh, to Department of State, January 27, 1972, RDS, 1970–1973; and "Trafficking in Illicit Narcotics by Air in Southeast Asia," American Embassy, Phnom Penh, to Department of State, May 28, 1972, and "Narcotics Training Customs," American Embassy, Phnom Penh, to Secretary of State, June 1973, RDS, Cambodia, box 3057; Kiernan, *Pol Pot Regime*.

76 "Constabulary," Anti-Narcotics Unit, USAID, OPS, Philippines, NA, box 9, folder 1; "Testimony of Benedict J. Kerkvliet, Woodrow Wilson International Center for Scholars, Smithsonian Institute," in House Committee on Foreign Affairs, *Political Prisoners in South Vietnam and the Philippines* (1974), 74. On U.S.–Philippines relations, see Shalom, *United States and the Philippines*.

77 American Embassy, Vientiane, to Secretary of State, November 28, 1971, and Ambassador Godley to Assistant Secretary of State Marshall Greene, March 1971, RDS, Laos, box 3075, folder 6; "Public Safety Project, Laos—Termination

Phase-Out Study," May 1974, USAID, OPS Director, box 6, folder Laos; "Testimony of William Sullivan," in Senate Committee on Foreign Relations, *United States Security Agreements and Commitments Abroad—Part 2* (1969), 382.

78 Valentine, *Strength of the Wolf*, 188, 365; Ahearn Jr., *Undercover Armies*, 548. On U.S. policy toward Laos, see Charles A. Stevenson, *End of Nowhere*.

79 Sheldon B. Vance, "International Narcotics Control: A High Priority Program," *Department of State Bulletin*, January 27, 1975, DEAL; Ambassador Godley to Assistant Secretary of State Marshall Greene, March 1971, RDS, Laos, box 3075, folder 6; House Committee on Foreign Affairs, *The U.S. Heroin Problem in Southeast Asia* (1972), 33; "Narcotic Control Program Activities," American Embassy, Vientiane, to Secretary of State, July, 1972, USAID, East Asian Bureau, Program AIDNC, NA, Laos 1970–1976, box 1, folder 3; "Narcotic Law," American Embassy, Vientiane, to Secretary of State, August 27, 1971, RDS, Laos, box 3075; Fox Butterfield, "Laos' Opium Country Resisting Drug Law," *New York Times*, October 16, 1972, 12; Westermeyer, *Poppies, Pipes, and People*, 39, 65, 134.

80 "Laos Takes Steps to Implement Anti-Narcotics Law," American Embassy, Vientiane, to U.S. Information Service, Washington, D.C., November 1971, AMHI, MACV—Drug Abuse.

81 "Public Safety Project Laos, Phase-Out," May 1974, USAID, OPS, box 6, Laos; "Task Forces of Thailand and Laos," 17; Everingham, "Golden Triangle Trade," 28; U.S. A.I.D., U.S. Economic Assistance to the Royal Lao Government, *Mission to Laos, December 1972*, 8; House Committee on Foreign Affairs, *The U.S. Heroin Problem in Southeast Asia* (1972), 28.

82 "Narcotics Control," American Embassy, Vientiane, to Secretary of State, 1972, RDS, Laos, box 3075; "Report on Completion of Phase 2," AIDNC, Laos, box 1, folder 3; "U.S. Leads Global War on Drug Abuse," *Current Foreign Policy*, Department of State Medial Services, DEAL, International Control, 1961–1975 folder.

83 Westermeyer, "Pro-Heroin Effects," and *Poppies, Pipes, and People*, xv.

84 Joseph Westermeyer, "Methadone: An Orientation to Its Medical Uses," Public Health Division, USAID Laos, March 1972; "Meeting with Dr. Jaffe," White House SAODAP, and "Shipment of Methadone HCL for Laos Rehabilitation Program," American Embassy, Vientiane, to Secretary of State, June 1972, both in AIDNC, Laos, box 1, folder 3.

85 Arnold Abrams, "Lao Spies Help War on Opium," *Miami Herald*, April 18, 1972; Michael Parks, "CIA Reported Shifting Attention in Laos from Communists to Opium," *Baltimore Sun*, March 13, 1972.

86 "Opium Substitution Efforts in Laos—Phu Pha Dang Experimentation—Extension A Approach," American Embassy, Vientiane, to USAID, April 1, 1974; "Pha Dang agricultural station Vientiane A128—unclassified," AIDNC, Laos, box 1, folder 3; McCoy and Adams, *Laos*, 125. On the trauma of the war for the Hmong, see, e.g., John E. Woodruff, "A War-Exhausted People Seek a Way Out," *Baltimore Sun*, February 23, 1971.

87 "Politics and Narcotics Control in Laos," American Embassy, Vientiane, to Secretary of State, October 11, RDS, Laos, box 3076, folder 2; observer quoted in Haney, "Pentagon Papers," 276; Mullin, "Secret Bombing of Laos."

88 "Letter to Henry Kissinger," Walter F. Haney, Fa Ngun School, June 1972, NA, box 13, folder 4; Edward M. Kennedy, "Excerpts of Reports on U.S. Bombing in Laos by former American Personnel," June 28, 1970, Joel M. Halpern Papers, JFK, box 11; "U.S. Narcotics Suppression Program," Robert H. Nooter to Mr. Dworken, Political/Military Laotian Mission, June 11, 1973, and Edward Kennedy to John Hannah, July 13, 1973, both in AIDNC, Laos, box 1, folder 3.

89 See Cecil, Herbicidal Warfare; Neilands et al., Harvest of Death; Weisberg, Ecocide in Indo-China; McCoy, "America's Secret War," 301–5; Branfman, Voices from the Plain, 3; Stuart-Fox, History of Laos, 144.

90 Harold Levin to Charles Mann, Director USAID, Chief Lao Desk, June 24, 1971, AIDNC, Laos, box 1, folder 5; Discussion with Minister of Justice on Narcotics, American Embassy, Vientiane, to Secretary of State, May 1974, AIDNC, Laos, box 1, folder 4; Senate Committee on Armed Services, Staff Report on Drug Abuse in the Military (1971), 24; "Trip Report—Laos," February 7–10, 1973, AIDNC, Laos, box 1, folder 3; Everingham, "Golden Triangle Trade," 28; Robbins, Air America, 239; Senate Committee on Labor and Public Welfare, The Narcotics Situation in Southeast Asia (1973), 16–17; Westermeyer, Poppies, Pipes, and People, 52.

91 Fox Butterfield, "Laos' Opium Country Resisting Drug Law," New York Times, October 16, 1972, 12; "Anti-Narcotics Legislation/Permits for Cultivation," G. McMurtrie Godley to Honorable William Sullivan, Deputy Assistant Secretary, Department of State, June 9, 1971, RDS, Laos, box 3075.

92 Senate Committee on Foreign Relations, Post-War Southeast Asia (1976), 8; Stuart-Fox, History of Laos, 173–74; Westermeyer, Poppies, Pipes, and People, xv; McCoy, Politics of Heroin: CIA Complicity, 1991 ed., 261; Robert Solomon, "Rise and Fall," 169–70.

93 Senate Committee on Interstate and Foreign Commerce, Production and Abuse of Opiates in the Far East (1971); "Army Criminal Investigation Division Report, June 1972," CIB, NA, box 1, folder 3; Jack Anderson, "Saigon Dope Dealers Riding High," Washington Post, December 30, 1972, B11.

94 Quoted in Mitchell Satchell, "U.S. Drug Reports Differ," Washington Star-News, August 16, 1972, 3.

95 McCoy, Drug Traffic, 364; Richard Phalon, "Federal Drug Traffic Figures Contested," New York Times, June 10, 1972, 29.

96 On social dislocation and the black market economy, see Allison, "Black Market"; Fitzgerald, Fire in the Lake; Senate Committee on the Judiciary, Civilian Casualty and Refugee Problems in South Vietnam (1968); Luce and Brown, Hostages of War, 56.

97 McCoy, Politics of Heroin: CIA Complicity, 2003 ed., 253; Keefer, Foreign Relations, 32; "PSD Survey of Black Market Activities," April 16, 1964, USAID, OPS, East Asia Branch, NA, box 285, folder Black Market.

98 "Alleged Corrupt Practices of Nguyen Huy Thong, Chief, Narcotics Bureau," Frank Walton to Charles Vopat, March 31, 1971, OPS, Narcotic Control, Vietnam, box 112, folder 4; Henry Kamm, "Drive Fails to Halt Drug Sale in Vietnam," *New York Times*, August 30, 1971, 1; "Drug Abuse Program: A Future Model?" EJE, box 16, folder 2.

99 Snepp, *Decent Interval*, 14; Prados, *Hidden History*, 68; Chomsky and Herman, "Saigon's Corruption Crisis," 22; Senate Committee on Government Operations, *Fraud and Corruption in the Management of Military Club Systems* (1969), 275–79.

100 Memorandum for Egil Krogh, "Indo-Chinese Officials Removed or Shifted as a Result of Investigations in Drug Trafficking," August 3, 1971; "Meeting August 3, 1971, Request for Executive Session Appearance of the Attorney General Re Alleged Involvement of South Vietnamese Officials in Drug Traffic," August 3, 1971; "Senator McGovern and Drugs," July 31, 1972; all in EKP, box 32, folder 2.

101 See Shad Liang, *Burma's Foreign Relations*; Egil Krogh, White House, to Chairman Ne Win, November 23, 1971, BNDD, box 19, folder 1; Weimer, "Seeing Drugs," 233; Renard, *Burmese Connection*, 60.

102 George P. Schultz, Secretary of the Treasury, to Department of State, September 11, 1973, RDS, Burma, box 3056, folder 2; Lintner, "Heroin and Highland Insurgency," 274; House Select Committee on Narcotics Abuse and Control, *Southeast Asian Narcotics* (1977), 2–3.

103 "Human Rights in Burma," General Bo Mya to Congressman Wolff, April 28, 1977, and Thomas Schwab, "Legality and Human Rights: A View of Anti-Narcotics Policy in the Burmese-Shan-Thailand Triangle," both in House Select Committee on Narcotics Abuse and Control, *Southeast Asian Narcotics* (1977), 45, 188. On the civil war in Burma and savagery of Ne Win's army, see Lintner, *Land of Jade*.

104 "Narcotics Trafficking and Dissidents," American Consulate, Chiang Mai, to American Embassy, Bangkok, July 17, 1973, RDS, Burma, box 3056, folder 12; "Testimony Mathea Falco, State Department," in House Select Committee on Narcotics Abuse and Control, *Southeast Asian Narcotics* (1977), 45, 67. In response to the letter, Falco called Bo Mya a "terrorist" deserving of government repression and assault; American Embassy, Rangoon, to Department of State, October 10, 1973, Memo for John Hannah, Office of the Administration, September 1, 1973, RDS, Burma, box 3056, folder 2.

105 House Select Committee on Narcotics Abuse and Control, *Southeast Asian Narcotics* (1977), 120; House Committee on International Relations, *Proposal to Control Opium from the Golden Triangle* (1975).

106 House Select Committee on Narcotics Abuse and Control, *Southeast Asian Narcotics* (1977), 8.

107 Chomsky and Herman, *Political Economy of Human Rights*, vol. 1; McMahon, *Limits of Empire*; Lintner, *Burma in Revolt*; House Committee on Foreign Affairs, *Foreign Assistance Act of 1971*, 296.

7. "GET UP YOU DOPED UP BASTARD!"

Epigraphs

Edelman, "Viet Vets Talk About 'Nam' Films."

Ehrhart, *Madness of It All*, 24.

1 See the discussion in Lembcke, *Spitting Image*, 157.

2 See Berg, "Losing Vietnam," 136; Don Irwin, "U.S. Owes No Debt to Hanoi, Carter Says," *Los Angeles Times*, March 5, 1977, 1. Quote from professor in Ngo Vinh Long, "The War and the Vietnamese," 234; McMahon, "Contested Memory," 166, 171; Chomsky, "United States and Indo-China," 10.

3 See Franklin, *Vietnam and Other American Fantasies*; Sturken, *Tangled Memories*.

4 Biskind, *Easy Riders*.

5 Martini, *Invisible Enemies*; Chomsky and Herman, *After the Cataclysm*.

6 Julian Smith, *Looking Away*; Shapiro, "Vietnam War," 10; *Greetings*; Devine, *Vietnam at 24 Frames a Second*, 47.

7 See Katzman, "From Outcast to Cliché"; Dionisopoulos, "Images of the Warrior Returned."

8 Southern Illinois University Foundation, *Wasted Men*, 1; "Study Cites Bias against Vietnam GIs," *Washington Post*, April 6, 1972, A3.

9 E.g., "I Ain't Marchin' Anymore," October 10, 1974; "Poisoned Snow," September 11, 1975; and "Merchants of Death," November 20, 1975, all in *Streets of San Francisco*.

10 Swiers, "Demented Vets," 198.

11 Julian Smith, *Looking Away*, 164.

12 Doherty, *Projections of War*, 288; Turner, *Echoes of Combat*, 50; Englehardt, *End of Victory Culture*, 254–55.

13 Fuchs, "All the Animals Come Out at Night."On the broader political implications, see Flamm, "Politics and Pragmatism."

14 *Winter Soldier*. See also Vietnam Veterans Against the War, *Winter Soldier Investigation*; Kerry, *New Soldier*.

15 Footage from the documentary *Only the Beginning* of soldiers throwing their medals was also featured in *Sir! No Sir!* and mentioned in Berg, "Losing Vietnam," 136, and Franklin, *Vietnam and Other American Fantasies*, 61.

16 See Meyrowitz and Campbell, "Vietnam Veterans and War Crimes Hearings," 138. Tellingly, many supposedly objective academic historians have internalized the demonizing process, even though the revelations of systematic atrocities have been confirmed by archival evidence. Moyar, for example, bases part of his defense of the Phoenix Program, *Phoenix and the Birds of Prey*, on the argument that K. Barton Osborne, who testified before Congress that "no witness ever survived interrogation alive," suffered from psychiatric problems and hence was not a reliable source. Lewy in *America in Vietnam* and Jenkins in *Decade of Nightmares* write of the "tendentiousness" of the Winter Soldiers, dismissing their testimony on similar grounds. Other examples abound.

17 Lembcke, *Spitting Image*, 105. On the PTSD phenomenon, see Chaim Shatan, "The Post-Vietnam Syndrome," *New York Times*, May 6, 1973; Allen Young,

Harmony of Illusion. The absence of this consciousness was true even on the left, with many liberal intellectuals becoming advocates of a renewed use of military force on humanitarian grounds, particularly after the Cold War. See Chomsky, *New Generation.*

18 *Gordon's War,* 1973.

19 Chepesiuk and Gonzalez, *Superfly,* 96. The title of the film refers to the misguided idealism, tactical blunders, and suicidal heroism of the Spartan warriors at the Battle of Thermopylae, as recounted by Herodotus: "Go Tell the Spartans, thou that passeth by, that here, obedient to their laws, we lie."

20 Schulzinger, *Time for Peace,* 156; Janet Maislin, "Screen, Company C," *New York Times,* February 28, 1978, C15.

21 Scholars who promote this myth include Jenkins, *Decade of Nightmares,* 34–36; and Jonnes, *Hep Cats, Narcs, and Pipe Dreams,* 200.

22 For soldiers who viewed themselves as legions of empire see Ehrhart, *Passing Time;* Franklin, "Making Children Behave."

23 Torture and massacres of civilians were in fact more synonymous with the U.S.-ARVN side. See Franklin, *Vietnam and Other American Fantasies,* 27; Cumings, *War and Television;* Lehman, "Well, What's It Like Over There?," 136.

24 On the pervasiveness of these stereotypes in Western culture, see Said, *Culture and Imperialism;* Appy, *Cold War Constructions.* On the reinforcement of the frontier myth and patriotic themes, see Hellmann, *American Myth,* 171–88; Englehardt, *End of Victory Culture,* 306.

25 Roginski, "Who'll Stop the Rain," 57; Powers, "Review of *Dog Soldiers,*" 101.

26 McInerney, "Apocalypse Then," 27; Lasch, *Culture of Narcissism.*

27 Vincent Canby, "The Screen: *Apocalypse Now,*" *New York Times,* August 15, 1979, C15; McIrneny, "Apocalypse Then," 22; Levin, "Francis Coppola," 137–38.

28 Marsha Kinder, "Power of Adaptation," 20; Lembcke, *CNN's Tailwind Tale,* 73–74.

29 Chown, *Hollywood Auteur,* 138; Marcus, "Journey Up the River," 55; Nguyen Khac Vien, "*Apocalypse Now* Viewed."

30 See Desser, "Charlie Don't Surf," 77.

31 Lembcke, *CNN's Tailwind Tale,* 73–74. Lembcke interestingly argues that this admiration reinforces not only a stereotyped view of the "Vietcong" but also the film's underlying conservative message that the United States could have won the war had it been unhampered by civilian constraints and allowed to fight like the enemy.

32 See Kranz, "*Apocalypse Now* and *The Deer Hunter.*"

33 See Beattie, *Scar That Binds,* 21–22; Scruggs and Swerdlow, *To Heal a Nation;* Broyles, "Remembering a War"; Powell, "Healing Nation."

34 *Uncommon Valor; Missing in Action I* and *II;* Jeffords, *Remasculinization of America.* On the denigration of antiwar protestors as a general Hollywood theme, fitting with the Reagan ethos, see, e.g., *Hamburger Hill; Gardens of Stone;* Franklin, *Vietnam and Other American Fantasies,* 57. For critical analysis of Rambo

and its jingoistic message, see Studler and Desser, "Never Having to Say You're Sorry."

35 See Claude Smith, "Clean Boys"; Hagopian, "Social Memory of the Vietnam War," 201–2; *In-Country*; *Jacknife*; *Cutter's Way*.

36 Vincent Canby, "*The Big Chill*: Reunion of 1960s Activists," *New York Times*, September 23, 1983, C14. For the story of real-life vets engaged in solidarity work through the 1980s, see Clements, *Witness to War*; Christina Smith, *Resisting Reagan*, 39.

37 Taylor, "Colonialist Subtext"; Engelhardt, *End of Victory Culture*, 384. For Stone's rejoinder on this critique, see "Playboy Interview—Oliver Stone," 51. For a corrective, see Tang, *Vietcong Memoir*.

38 "Playboy Interview—Oliver Stone," 51. In a subsequent interview with historian Christian G. Appy, Stone stated that the Vietnam War lacked "moral purpose and was fought without any moral integrity; *Patriots*, 256.

39 Lembcke, *CNN's Tailwind Tale*, 77.

40 Anthony Lewis, "Another Senate Test," *New York Times*, July 9, 1973; McCoy, "America's Secret War"; Stuart-Fox, *History of Laos*, 144. The total tonnage of bombs may have reached or exceeded three million.

41 Branfman, *Voices from the Plain*; Browning and Forman, "Bombing in Laos"; "Letter to Henry Kissinger," Walter F. Haney, Fa Ngun School, June 1972, National Security Files, Nixon Presidential Materials, NA, box 13, folder 4; Edward M. Kennedy, "Excerpts of Reports on U.S. bombing in Laos by former American personnel stationed in Laos," June 28, 1970, Joel M. Halpern Papers, JFK, box 111. Estimates place the number of deaths during the secret war at 350,000 and villages destroyed at 3,500.

42 T. D. Allman, "Ruined Town a Vignette of War in Laos," *New York Times*, October 17, 1969, 2; Fred Branfman, "A Lake of Blood," *New York Times*, April 7, 1971, 43.

43 "Laos Air War Leans Heavily on Meo Tribe," *Los Angeles Times*, October 19, 1972; Shaplen, *Time Out of Hand*, 348; Corn, *Blond Ghost*, 161.

44 Stuart-Fox, *History of Laos*, 81–82, 93–94; Herring, *America's Longest War*, 264.

45 "Thicker than Blood," February 26, 1981, "By Its Cover," March 31, 1983, and "Please Don't Eat the Snow in Hawaii Parts 1 & 2," October 1980..

46 *Magnum P.I.*, "All for One, Parts 1 & 2," January 31 and February 7, 1985; Haines, "Pride Is Back," 117–18. On U.S. support for Cambodia in the war against Vietnam, see Martini, *Invisible Enemies*, 106–7.

47 "Golden Triangle, Parts 1 & 2," January 11 and 18, 1985; "Back In the World," December 6, 1985; and "Stone's War," October 3, 1986.

48 For comparative perspective, see Klein, *Cold War Orientalism*; Auster, "Reflections," 327; "Paradise Lost," March 28, 1988, and "Saigon 1 & 2," January 3, 10, 1988, *Tour of Duty*.

49 See, in particular, Zinberg, "Heroin Use in Vietnam," 488, "GI's and OJ's in Vietnam," *New York Times Magazine*, December 5, 1971; "Blood Brothers," *Tour of Duty*; Miller, "Primetime Television's Tour of Duty."

50 "Soldiers," February 16, 1988; "Nowhere to Run," December 17, 1988; "Bodyguard of Lies," October 28, 1989; "Necessary End," November 4, 1989; and "Cloud Nine," November 11, 1989.

51 "Pilot," April 26, 1988; "One Giant Leap," March 13, 1991; "Cherry," February 1, 1989.

52 On post-Vietnam foreign policies, see Mamdani, "Cold War after Indochina."

8. THE CRACKDOWN
Epigraph
Quoted in Davenport-Hines, *Pursuit of Oblivion*, 351.

1 Morley, "What Crack Is Really Like."

2 Morley, "Aftermath of a Crack Article"; "Testimony of William Bennett, Director Office of National Drug Control Policy," in House Committee on Government Operations, *National Drug Control Strategy* (1989). Bennett also called Morley "an irresponsible upper-class guy fooling around with crack and writing about the pleasures of it."

3 Jack Keller, "Our Worries: Crime, Drugs Top Economy," *USA Today*, August 15, 1984; Currie, *Confronting Crime*, 4.

4 Reagan quoted in Baggins, *Drug Hate*, 98.

5 House Committee on Government Operations, *Initiatives in Drug Interdiction—Part I* (1985), 141; Bourne, "President Carter's Commitment," 2–3.

6 House Select Committee on Narcotics Abuse and Control, *Drug Abuse among the U.S. Armed Forces* (1979), 56; Nield, "U.S. Police Assistance," 68. On the spread of cocaine, see House Select Committee on Narcotics Abuse and Control, *Cocaine: A Major Drug Issue of the Seventies* (October 1979); and Nicholas Von Hoffman "The Cocaine Culture: New Wave for the Rich and Hip," *Washington Post*, April 23, 1975, B1, B6.

7 House Select Committee on Narcotics Abuse and Control, *South America Study Mission* (1977), 104; Jack Anderson, "Mexico's War on Poppy Growers," *Washington Post*, January 10, 1978, B11; Senate Committee on the Judiciary, *The Mexican Connection* (1978). Carter and Bourne faced particular criticism from the pro-marijuana lobby for spraying Mexican marijuana fields with a herbicidal defoliant, paraquat.

8 Bourne, "President Carter's Commitment," 11; House Select Committee on Narcotics Abuse and Control, *Oversight Hearings on Federal Drug Strategy—1979*, 135; House Select Committee on Narcotics Abuse and Control, *United States Bureau of Prisons Staff Study* (1979), 2.

9 Trebach, *Heroin Solution*; Interview with Dr. Peter Bourne in *PBS Drug War Front Line*, 1999, www.pbs.com. For a similar view of cocaine, see Grinspoon and Bakalaar, *Cocaine*.

10 "Statement of Carleton Turner," November 19, 1981, CTF, box 10, folder Narcotics; Robert Reinhold, "Wide Marijuana and Cocaine Use Reported among Professionals," *New York Times*, July 22, 1978, 7; Johnston, *Illicit Drug Use*; Wright, *Great American Crime Myth*, 5.

11 "PRIDE National Newsletter," July 1985, CTF, box 7, folder 3; Massing, *The Fix*, 185; Mann, *Marijuana Alert*; Thomas Gleaton, "PRIDE's Man of the Decade: Gabriel Nahas, a Man of Our Time," CTF, Box 5; Nahas, *Cocaine*; Cohen, "Health Hazards," 12.

12 Wilson, *Thinking about Crime*, 1–2; Francis Allen, *Decline of the Rehabilitative Ideal*.

13 Hirschi and Gottfredson, "The True Value of Lambda"; Wilson, *Thinking about Crime*, 127–45; Austin and Irwin, *It's About Time*; Murray, *Losing Ground*. For an excellent analysis, see Garland, *Culture of Control*.

14 Interview with Dr. Peter Bourne, *PBS Drug War Front Line*, 1999, www.pbs.com.

15 Michael Getler, "Drug Abuse Casts Shadow on Army's Readiness," *Washington Post*, November 19, 1978, A20; Bernard Weintraub, "A Fog and a Furor over GI Drug Use," *New York Times*, July 30, 1978, 22.

16 House Select Committee on Narcotics Abuse and Control, *Drug Abuse in the Military* (1978), 2.

17 George C. Wilson, "Autopsies Reveal 6 on Nimitz Had Drugs in Their Systems," *Washington Post*, June 17, 1981, A1; House Select Committee on Narcotics Abuse and Control, *Drug Abuse in the Military—1981*, 4; Robert Reinhold, "Congressman Says Most Killed in Nimitz Crash Showed Traces of Drugs," *Washington Post*, June 17, 1981, A20.

18 "Drugs Nation's No. 1 Concern, but Politics Blurs Facts," *New York Times*, September 9, 1984, 12; Sobel, "The Polls."

19 Dornan quoted in "Liquor, Drugs—The GI's Biggest Foe," 7; House Select Committee on Narcotics Abuse and Control, *Drug Abuse in the Military* (1978), 149.

20 Thomas Walker, *Revolution and Counterrevolution*; Farber, *Iran Hostage Crisis*.

21 Carter, "Energy and National Goals," 1303.

22 E.g., Jenkins, *Decade of Nightmares*, 160; Schulman, *The Seventies*.

23 Dallek, *Ronald Reagan*.

24 On domestic policies, see esp. Phillips, *Politics of Rich and Poor*. On foreign policy, see Kornbluh and Klare, *Low-Intensity Warfare*; Fitzgerald, *Way Out There*; Chomsky, *Culture of Terrorism*.

25 Slotkin, *Gunfighter Nation*, 643; Troy, *Morning in America*.

26 Reagan, "Address to the Nation on the Campaign against Drug Abuse," 1181, and "Remarks on Signing," 629.

27 "1984 National Strategy for Prevention of Drug Abuse and Drug Trafficking," September 10, 1984, Counter-Terrorism and Narcotics, NSC, box 92258; Dale Russakoff, "U.S. to Use CIA Informers, Military to Expand Drug War," *Washington Post*, June 14, 1983, A1; House Select Committee on Narcotics Abuse and Control, *Narcotics Interdiction and Enforcement Efforts in South Florida* (1986); George H. W. Bush, "Speech before the Hartford County Bar Association," March 24, 1988, NSC, box 92258, folder 3.

28 Bagley, "Colombia and the War on Drugs," 78.

29 E.g.,"The Evil Empire," 14. On Escobar's rivalry with Cuban exiles, see Gugliotta and Leen, *Kings of Cocaine.*
30 "New Battle Plan Sought for War on Drugs," *Miami Herald,* October 18, 1981;
   Guy Guggliotta, "DEA Feebly Attempts to Slay Drug Dragon in Colombia," *Miami Herald,* October 14, 1981; House Select Committee on Narcotics Abuse and
   Control, *Federal Drug Law Enforcement and Interdiction* (1984), 2.
31 House Committee on Government Operations, *Military Assistance to Civilian
   Narcotics Law Enforcement* (May 1982); "Posse Comitatus," 17.
32 Reagan, "Radio Address to the Nation on Law Enforcement and Crime," 1017.
33 E.g., Carleton E. Turner, Memo to Mrs. Reagan, September 24, 1985, CTF,
   box 1, OA943213; Robert Ackerman, "Anti-Drug Movement Now Petitions World
   Leaders," *Atlanta Journal,* June 30, 1983.
34 "How Drugs Sap the Nation's Strength," 55; Jackson and Wright quoted in
   House Select Committee on Narcotics Abuse and Control, *Drug Education—
   Part II* (1986), 4, 5, 12.
35 "Nancy Reagan: Letter to 6th Graders," November 1983, CTF, box 8, folder 2.
36 Carleton Turner to John M. Keller, "Cocaine—One Man's Poison," October 18,
   1982, CTF, box 10, folder 1; "Going After Hollywood," 20.
37 Reagan, "Remarks on Substance Abuse in the Workplace," 1156; Winston Williams, "Navy Is Cracking Down at Biggest Training Base," *New York Times,*
   February 26, 1982, A14.
38 Timothy S. Robinson, "Court Upgrades Army Drug Discharges," *Washington
   Post,* November 29, 1979; Carleton Turner to Edwin Meese, "Urinalysis Program in the Military," December 1, 1982, CTF, box 8, folder 3; Philip Smith,
   "Crackdown on Drug Use in Marines Draws Fire," *Washington Post,* March 27,
   1982, B1.
39 Klare, *Beyond the Vietnam Syndrome.* At least one humdred civilians died as a
   result of errant bombing, including mental patients in a hospital destroyed in
   the attack. See Gordon K. Lewis, *Grenada,* 103.
40 Howell Raines, "Optimism in Nation Is Increasing, Poll Finds," *New York
   Times,* January 21, 1985, A1; Reagan quoted in Pease, "Hiroshima," 374.
41 Keith B. Richburg, "Reagan Order Defines Drug Trade as Security Threat, Wid-
   ens Military Role," *Washington Post,* June 8, 1986, A28; William Walker, *Drug
   Control in the Americas,* 203, 212, 221. On the Burmese and Thai programs, see
   Renard, *Burmese Connection,* 67; on Peru, see Cynthia McClintock, "War on
   Drugs."
42 After the OPS was disbanded for human rights abuses, its activities related to
   narcotics were undertaken by the State Department's International Narcotics
   Matters Bureau. See Marshall, *Drug Wars,* 76.
43 Lesley Gill, *School of the Americas;* Marshall and Scott, *Cocaine Politics,* 165–71;
   Freeman and Sierra "Mexico," 266. Regaldo was known by the nickname
   Dr. Death. He served as a top aide to Roberto D'Aubuisson, the head of the
   proto-fascist ARENA (Alianza Republicana Nacionalista) party, who was linked
   to the murder of Archbishop Oscar Romero and four U.S. nuns (along with a

large number of Salvadoran civilians in the dirty war waged by the government against the FMLN). Goff quoted in Stokes, *America's Other War*, 90.

44 E.g., "Counter-Insurgency and Anti-Narcotics Measures," 102; "Program for Enhanced Military to Military Relations with Peru" American Embassy, Lima, to Secretary of State, 070432, March 1988, and "The Military Response," American Embassy, Bogota, to Pete McNamara, both in NSC, box 58229, folder 3, www.gwu.org/~nsarchiv, document 5.

45 "Strategy for Narcotics Control in the Andean Region," Interagency Working Group Draft, June 18, 1989, section 19, NSA; "The Andean Strategy: Attacking Drugs by Hitting the Insurgency," electronic briefing book, NSA; Marshall, *Drug Wars*, 24–26; Huggins, "U.S.-Supported State Terror," 77.

46 Government Cable 1316297, American Embassy, Lima, to Washington, D.C., NSC, box 92270, folder 3; Waghelstein, "Latin-American Insurgency Status Report." These charges were echoed in the mainstream media and by anti-Communist lobbying groups and right-wingers. See Ehrenfeld, *Narco-Terrorism*; Cuban-American Foundation, *Castro's Narcotics Trade*.

47 Senate Committee on Labor and Human Resources, *Drugs and Terrorism* (1984), 5; U.S. Embassy cable, "Murtha and Marsh Visit Concentrates on Narco-Power and Insurgency," May 24, 1988, NSA, 4. On FARC, see Berquist, *Violence in Colombia*.

48 Thoumi, *Political Economy* and *Illegal Drugs*; Gugliotta and Leen, *Kings of Cocaine*.

49 Dunkerley, *Rebellion in the Veins*, 316. Most Contras consisted of former members of Anastasio Somoza's National Guard. The UN World Court condemned their invasion of Nicaragua as a violation of international law.

50 Kirk, *More Terrible Than Death*; Merrill Collett, "Colombia's Drug Lords Waging War on Leftists: Traffickers Seen Allied with Extreme Right," *Washington Post*, November 14, 1987, A1; Human Rights Watch Staff, *Colombia's Killer Network*.

51 Bagley, "Colombia and the War on Drugs," 78; and "New Hundred Years War," 46; Toro, *Mexico's War on Drugs*, 105; Cynthia McClintock, "War on Drugs," 131–32.

52 Kline, "How to Lose the Coke War"; Ledebur, "Bolivia," 149; "International Narcotics Control Programs in Peru and Bolivia," Memorandum 9CI-007, Ann Wroblenski (INM) to Sherman Funk (OIG), March 15, 1989; *48 Hours in the Cocaine War*, April 28, 1988, NA, Motion Pictures and Television Archive.

53 Frank White, Office of the (California) State Controller Department, "Operation Snowcap," March 9, 1988, NSA, 2; State Department Draft report, "Cocaine: A Supply Side Strategy" June 15, 1989, NSA, 10.

54 "International Narcotics Control," House of Representatives, March 17, 1988, NSC, box 92182, folder 1; Bullington, "Smuggler's Paradise."

55 Jamaica, NSC, box 92258, folder 1; Prashad, *Darker Nations*, 239; Letter, George Bush to Carleton Turner, January 1982, IMF, box 3, folder 2; "Continued Review of the Administration's Drug Interdiction Efforts, Southeast Asia," NSC, box 92258, folder 1.

56 Shalom, *Imperial Alibis*, 166–67; "Guatemala," NSC, box 92258, folder 1. In 1999, the Guatemalan Commission for Historical Clarification (ironically headed by Rios Montt's brother, a Catholic bishop) found the Reagan administration responsible for providing technical, financial, and military support for genocide. Gramajo was later awarded a scholarship at the Kennedy School of Government. The killings were not isolated but an intensification of previous counterinsurgent campaigns following the illegal 1954 overthrow of the democratically elected President Jacobo Arbenz by the CIA. See Grandin, "History, Motive, Law and Intent"; "Counterinsurgency Operation in El Quiche," CIA secret cable, February 1982, NSA, 14; Guatemala, "Over 100 Indians Reputedly Massacred in Quiche," State Department cable, June 16, 1982, 004310, Digital NSA, www.gwu.edu/~nsarchiv.

57 Grandin, *Empire's Workshop*, 216; Leslie Gill, *School of the Americas*, 168; Jelsma, *Vicious Circle*; Simmons, *Colombia*, 13; Goti, "Reinforcing Poverty"; Cynthia McClintock, "War on Drugs," 134.

58 "Operational Spraying," John Negroponte to Barry Kelley, and "Media Reaction Report—Proposed Tebuthiron Use in Peru," both in NSC, box 92181, folder 2; Eugene Robinson, "U.S. Pushes for Herbicide Use on Coca," *Washington Post*, June 16, 1988; José Gonzalez, "Guerrillas and Coca."

59 George H. W. Bush, "Speech before the Hartford County Bar Association," March 24, 1988, NSC, box 92258, folder 3. Lehder later cut a deal to testify at Manuel Noriega's trial and had his sentence reduced to 55 years. Some suspect that he was subsequently placed in the FBI's witness protection program.

60 Bagley, "Colombia and the War on Drugs," 77; Gugliotta and Leen, *Kings of Cocaine*, 351.

61 E.g., Marshall and Scott, *Cocaine Politics*, 23–50; Webb, *Dark Alliance*; Lifschultz, "Pakistan"; Rubin, *Fragmentation of Afghanistan*, 103; Mary Thornton, "Sales of Opium Reportedly Fund Afghan Rebels," *Washington Post*, December 17, 1983, A32; Nadelmann, *Cops Across Borders*, 251–312.

62 Dayle had also served as a DEA agent in the Middle East. He is quoted in Peter D. Scott, *Deep Politics*, 167.

63 Peter D. Scott, "Honduras"; Rosenberg, "Narcos and Politicos." A CIA asset, Martinez was also trained at the School of the Americas, and after he was forced into exile for his crimes was hired by the RAND Corporation as an expert on counterinsurgency.

64 See Senate Committee on Foreign Relations, *Drugs, Law Enforcement, and Foreign Policy* (1987), 83; Seymour Hersh, "Panama Strongman Said to Trade in Drugs, Arms and Illicit Money," *New York Times*, June 12, 1986; Dinges, *Our Man in Panama*.

65 Congressional Hearings on Narcotics Certification, Testimony Norman Bailey, Senate Foreign Relations Committee, Western Hemisphere, April 20, 1986, NSC, box 92182, folder 4.

66 D'Amato quoted in Congressional Hearings on Narcotics Certification, NSC, box 921956, folder 4; see also "Mondale Vows War on Drugs," *Washington Post*, October 4, 1984, A12.

67 William Walker, *War on Drugs*; Bagley, "Colombia and the War on Drugs," 78; Senate Committee on Foreign Relations, *Drugs, Law Enforcement, and Foreign Policy* (1987), 30.

68 Toro, *Mexico's War on Drugs*, 5.

69 See Menzell, *Fire in the Andes*, 21; Lee, "Cocaine Dilemma," 64.

70 National Security Council Memo, Ted McNamara from U.S. Mail, "Intelligent Use and Use of Intelligence," May 20, 1988, NSC, box 58229, folder 3; José Gonzales, "Guerrillas and Coca," 109; Rojas, "Peru," 213.

71 On the social acceptability of coca chewing see Catherine J. Allen, *The Hold That Life Has*; Spedding, "Coca Use in Bolivia."

72 E.g., Reinarman and Levine, *Crack in America*, 5, 35; Jones, *The Dispossessed*, 273–84; Chomsky, *Year 501*, 277. Chomsky writes of spiritual despondency resembling that of a "shattered peasant society" in American inner-city communities as one cause of the high rates of addiction.

73 Cole, *Never Too Young to Die*; Beckett, *Making Crime Pay*, 56.

74 Dan Rather, *CBS News* and Peter Jennings, *ABC News*, quoted in "The Crack Attack: Politics and Media in the Crack Scare," in Reinarman and Levine, *Crack in America*, 20.

75 Richard M. Smith, "The Plague Among Us."

76 Inciardi, "Beyond Cocaine"; National Institute on Drug Abuse, *National Household Survey on Drug Abuse, 1988*; Reinarman and Levine, "The Crack Attack," in *Crack in America*, 33.

77 Weissman, "I Was a Drug Hype Junkie: 48 Hours on Crock Street," 12; Richard Harwood, "Hyperbolic Epidemic," *Washington Post*, October 1, 1989, D6, and *New York Times*, October 4, 1988; Campbell and Reeves, *Cracked Coverage*.

78 Goode and Ben-Yehudah, "The American Drug Panic of the 1980s," in *Moral Panics*, 88. For similar polling data, see Blachman and Sharpe, "War on Drugs," 138; "Mrs. Lucille Dean to Charles Rangel," CTF, box 11, Rangel Files.

79 Ronald Reagan and Nancy Reagan, "Radio Address to the Nation on Drug Abuse and Aid to Nicaragua," 1265.

80 Kerry quoted in Marsahll and Scott, *Cocaine Politics*, 14.

81 Ravenal quoted in Mabry, "U.S. Military and the War on Drugs," 53; Jane Perlez, "Koch Asks Airport Strip-Searches for Drugs," *New York Times*, May 25, 1984, A17. Joseph Lieberman (D-Conn.) was also calling to eliminate the executive order making it illegal for the United States to assassinate such enemies as major drug kingpins like Escobar.

82 Hyde quoted in Joanne Omang, "Crackdown on Drugs Is Urged, Lawmakers Suggest," *Washington Post*, March 20, 1985, A3. Bennett quoted in "Off With Their Heads? Thoughts from the Drug Czar," *Washington Post*, June 20, 1989, 21.

83 "Gates Says Casual Users Ought to Be Shot," *Los Angeles Times*, September 6, 1990, A1.

84 Saletan, "Jar Wars"; R. W. Apple, "Drugs Dominate Florida Campaign," *New York Times*, October 5, 1986, 35.

85 "House Passes $6 Billion Anti-Drug Bill," *Congressional Quarterly*, September 13, 1986, 2125; House Select Committee on Narcotics Abuse and Control, *Implementation of the Anti-Drug Abuse Act of 1986*.

86 McCurdy quoted in *Time*, September 12, 1986, 36; Schroeder in "House Passes $6 Billion Anti-Drug Bill," *Congressional Quarterly*, September 13, 1986, 2125; Peter Kerr, "Anatomy of an Issue: Drugs, the Evidence, the Reaction," *New York Times*, November 7, 1986, A1.

87 Perl, "International Narco-policy," 89.

88 House Select Committee on Narcotics Abuse and Control, *Oversight of the Anti-Drug Abuse Act of 1986 and the Federal Drug Strategy*; Senate Committee on Foreign Relations, *Drugs in Massachusetts* (1990), 16.

89 E.g., Duster, "Pattern, Purpose and Race"; Lusane, *Pipe Dream Blues*; Rosenblatt, *Criminal Injustice*.

90 Nadelmann, "Drug Prohibition in the United States," 293; Belenko, *Crack and the Evolution of Anti-Drug Policy*, 119.

91 Beckett, *Making Crime Pay*, 33–36; Michael Issikoff, "Drug Buy Set Up for Bush Speech: DEA Lured Seller to Lafayette Park," *Washington Post*, September 22, 1989, A1.

92 On the Panama invasion and its humanitarian toll, which was largely neglected in mainstream media accounts, see Johns, *State Crime*. Ironically, narcotics rates increased under Noriega's corrupt successor, Guillermo Endara. On Bush's broader militarization of the War on Drugs, see Mabry, "The U.S. Military and the War on Drugs," 43–61.

93 E.g., Trebach, *The Great Drug War*; Nadelmann, "U.S. Drug Policy—A Bad Export."

94 Milton Friedman, "An Open Letter to Bill Bennett," *Wall Street Journal*, September 7, 1989; also in Boaz, *Crisis in Drug Prohibition*, 115–16.

CONCLUSION

1 See Shrecker, *Cold War Triumphalism*; Chalmers Johnson, *Blowback*. One important revisionist work on Vietnam is Lind's *Vietnam*.

2 In my own teaching experience, usually not one student in a survey course is aware of these events. See Chomsky, "United States and Indo-China," 10.

3 Steven Macko, "General McCaffrey Leads the Battle against Drugs," *Emergency News New Service*, April 21, 1996, www.emergency.com.

4 For a critical view of Plan Colombia, see Petras and Morley, "Geo-Politics of Plan Colombia."

5 McCaffrey quoted in Kitfield, *Prodigal Soldiers*, 34; Trebach and Zeeze, *Drug Prohibition*.

6 For a deconstruction of the administrative perspective, see Chalmers Johnson, *Nemesis*; Chomsky, *Failed States*.

7 See Brigham, *Is Iraq Another Vietnam?*

8 See Lesley Gill, "Disordering the Andes," in *School of the Americas*, 163–97; Isaacson, "U.S. Military in the War on Drugs," 56; Grandin, *Empire's Workshop*, 220.

9 Balko, *Overkill.*

10 See Dreyfuss, "Bush's War on Pot"; Mirken, "Marijuana and the Media," 145.

11 Anne Usher, "Many Soldiers Turning to Drugs to Deal," *Washington General News,* November 15, 2006; Department of Defense, *Survey of Health Related Behaviors,* 11; Department of the Army, *Regulation 600-85.*

12 Doug Saunders, "Corruption Eats Away at Afghan Government," *Toronto Globe and Mail,* April 10, 2008, 1, 12; Kolhatkar and Ingalls, *Bleeding Afghanistan;* Peter D. Scott, *Road to 9/11;* Patrick Cockburn, "Opium Fields Spread across Iraq as Farmers Try to Make Ends Meet," *The Independent,* January 24, 2008, www.zmag.org.

13 E.g., Amy Schlesing, "Drugs, Booze Easy for GIs to Get in Iraq," *Arkansas Democrat-Gazette,* January 3, 2005; Thomas Harding, "Stressed US Troops in Iraq 'Turning to Drugs,'" *London Telegraph,* July 23, 2005; Anne Usher, "Many Soldiers Turning to Drugs to Deal," *Washington General News,* November 15, 2006; Susan Milligan, "Drug Use Seen on Rise in Iraq: Porous Borders, Lack of Security Are Cited as Cause," *Boston Globe,* August 23, 2003, A33. On the climate of corruption in Iraq bred by the illegal U.S. occupation, see Chandrasekaran, *Imperial Life.*

14 E.g., *American Gangster.* See McCoy, *Politics of Heroin: CIA Complicity,* 2003 ed.; Peter D. Scott, *Drugs, Oil and War.*

15 E.g., "Veterans and Drugs," *20/20,* ABC, November 30, 2007; William M. Welch, "Trauma of Iraq War Haunting Thousands Returning Home," *USA Today,* February 28, 2005.

16 Dave Goldner, "Druggie Marines? 'More than Possible' at Haditha, Says Wife," *New York Daily News,* June 5, 2006, 12.

17 Herr, *Dispatches,* 260.

BIBLIOGRAPHY

Abramsky, Sasha. *American Furies: Crime, Punishment and Vengeance in the Age of Mass Imprisonment.* Boston: Beacon Press, 2007.

Acker, Caroline Jean. *Creating the American Junkie: Addiction Research in the Classic Era of Narcotic Control.* Baltimore: Johns Hopkins University Press, 2002.

Ackerman, Henry F. *He Was Always There: The U.S. Army Chaplain Ministry in the Vietnam Conflict.* Washington, D.C.: Department of the Army, 1989.

Adas, Michael. *Dominance by Design: Technological Imperatives and America's Civilizing Mission.* Cambridge, Mass.: Belknap Press of Harvard University Press, 2006.

"The Agency's Brief." *Harper's Magazine,* October 1972, 116–19.

Ahern Jr., Thomas L. *Undercover Armies: CIA and Surrogate Warfare in Laos, 1961–1973.* Washington, D.C.: Center for Studies in Intelligence, 2006.

Air America. Directed by Roger Spottswood. Tri-Star, 1990.

Allen, Catherine J. *The Hold That Life Has: Coca and Cultural Identity in an Andean Community.* Washington, D.C.: Smithsonian Institute, 2002.

Allen, Douglas. "Scholars of Asia and the War." In Allen and Ngo, *Coming to Terms,* 211–49.

Allen, Douglas, and Ngo Vinh Long, eds. *Coming to Terms: Indochina, the United States and the War.* Boulder, Colo.: Westview Press, 1991.

Allen, Francis. *The Decline of the Rehabilitative Ideal.* New Haven: Yale University Press, 1981.

Allison, William. "The Black Market, Currency Manipulation and Corruption." In *Military Justice in Vietnam,* 140–67.

———. *Military Justice in Vietnam: The Rule of Law in an American War.* Lawrence: University of Kansas Press, 2007.

Alsop, Stewart. "The City Killer." *Newsweek,* February 8, 1971, 104.

———. "The GI's Other Enemy: Heroin." *Newsweek,* May 24, 1971, 26.

———. "The Smell of Death." *Newsweek,* February 1, 1971, 76.

———. "Worse than My Lai." *Newsweek,* May 24, 1971, 108.

American Gangster. Directed by Ridley Scott. Universal, 2007.

Anderegg, Michael, ed. *Inventing Vietnam: The War in Film and Television.* Philadelphia: Temple University Press, 1991.

Anderson, Jack. *Peace, War and Politics: An Eyewitness Account.* New York: Tom Doherty, 1999.

Anderson, Jack, and Drew Pearson. *The Case Against Congress: A Compelling Indictment of Corruption on Capitol Hill.* New York: Simon & Schuster, 1968.

Anderson, Terry. "The GI Movement and the Response from the Brass." In *Give Peace a Chance: Exploring the Vietnam Anti-War Movement,* edited by Melvin Small and William D. Hoover, 93–116. Syracuse: Syracuse University Press, 1992.

———. *The Movement and The Sixties.* New York: Oxford University Press, 1995.

"Another Check-Up on Drug Use by GIs," *U.S. News and World Report*, August 31, 1970, 33.

Anslinger, Harry J., and Courtney R. Cooper, "Marihuana: Assassin of Youth," *American Magazine*, July, 1937: 18.

Anslinger, Harry J., and Will Oursler. *The Murderers: The Story of Narcotics Gangs.* New York: Farrar, Straus & Cudahy, 1961.

Anslinger, Harry J., and William F. Tompkins. *The Traffic in Narcotics: Addiction in America.* New York: Funk & Wagnalls, 1953.

Appy, Christian G., ed. *Cold War Constructions: The Political Culture of United States Imperialism, 1945–1966.* Amherst: University of Massachusetts Press, 2000.

———. *Patriots: The Vietnam War Remembered from All Sides.* New York: Viking, 2004.

———. *Working-Class War: American Combat Soldiers in Vietnam.* Chapel Hill: University of North Carolina Press, 1993.

Apocalypse Now. Directed by Francis Ford Coppola. United Artists-Zoetrope, 1979.

Aptheker, Herbert. *Mission to Hanoi.* New York: International Publishers, 1966.

Aronson, James. "The Media and the Message." In *Critical Essays,* edited by Noam Chomsky and Howard Zinn, vol. 5 of Gravel, *The Pentagon Papers,* 41–59. Boston: Beacon Press, 1972.

Ashley, Richard. *Heroin: The Myths and Facts.* New York: St. Martin's Press, 1972.

Astorga, Luis. "Mexico: Drugs and Politics." In *The Political Economy of the Drug Industry: Latin America and the International System,* edited by Menno Villenga, 85–103. Gainesville: University Press of Florida, 2004.

Auster, Albert. "Reflections of the Way Life Used to Be: *Tour of Duty, China Beach,* and the Memory of the Sixties." In *Historical Memory and Representations of the Vietnam War,* edited by Walter Hixson, 327–37. New York: Garland, 2000.

Auster, Albert, and Leonard Quartz. *How the War Was Remembered: Hollywood and Vietnam.* New York: Praeger, 1988.

Austin, James, and John Irwin. *It's About Time: America's Imprisonment Binge.* Rev. ed. Belmont, Calif.: Wadsworth, 2001.

Ausubel, David P. *Drug Addiction: Physiological, Psychological, and Sociological Aspects.* New York: Random House, 1958.

Baggins, David. *Drug Hate and the Corruption of American Justice.* New York: Praeger, 1998.

Bagley, Bruce M. "Columbia and the War on Drugs." *Foreign Affairs* 61, no. 1 (Fall 1988): 70–92.

———. "The New Hundred Years War? U.S. National Security and the War on Drugs in Latin America." In Mabry, *The Latin American Narcotics Trade,* 43–59.

Bagley, Bruce, and William O. Walker III. *Drug Trafficking in the Americas.* New Brunswick, N.J.: Transaction, 1994.

Baker, S. L., Jr. "U.S. Army Heroin Abuse Identification Program in Vietnam, Implications for a Methadone Program." *American Journal of Public Health* 62, no. 6 (June 1972): 857–60.

Balko, Radley. *Overkill: The Rise of Paramilitary Police Raids in America.* Washington, D.C.: Cato Institute, 2006.

Bamrungsuk, Surachert. *United States Foreign Policy and Thai Military Rule, 1947–1977.* Bangkok: Editions Duang Kamol, 1988.

Barkan, Stephen A. *Criminology: A Sociological Perspective.* Englewood Cliffs, N.J.: Prentice Hall, 2001.

Bartels, John R., Jr. "The Mission Before Us." *Drug Enforcement Administration Magazine,* Fall 1973, 1.

———. "The Nation's War on Drugs Is Now Under Way," *Drug Enforcement Administration Magazine,* Fall 1973, 1.

Baskir, Lawrence M., and William A. Strauss. *Chance and Circumstance: The Draft, the War and the Vietnam Generation.* New York: Alfred A. Knopf, 1978.

Baum, Dan. *Smoke and Mirrors: The War on Drugs and the Politics of Failure.* Boston: Little Brown, 1996.

Beattie, Keith. *The Scar That Binds: American Culture and the Vietnam War.* New York: New York University Press, 1998.

Becker, Howard S., ed. *Campus Power Struggle.* New York: Transaction Books, 1970.

———. "History, Culture and Subjective Experience: An Exploration of the Social Bases of Drug-induced Experiences." *Journal of Health and Social Behavior* 8, no. 3 (September 1967): 163–76.

———. *Outsiders: Studies in the Sociology of Deviance.* New York: Free Press, 1963.

Beckett, Katherine. *Making Crime Pay: Law and Order in Contemporary American Politics.* New York: Oxford University Press, 1997.

Belenko, Steven. *Crack and the Evolution of Anti-Drug Policy.* Westport, Conn: Greenwood Press, 1993.

Bender, Thomas. *A Nation among Nations: America's Place in World History.* New York: Hill & Wang, 2006.

Bennett, William J. *The Devaluing of America: The Fight for Our Culture and Our Children.* New York: Simon & Schuster, 1992.

Bentel, David, and David Smith. "Drug Abuse in Combat: The Crisis of Drugs and Addiction among American Troops in Vietnam." *Journal of Psychedelic Drugs* 4 (Fall 1971): 23–30.

Berg, Rick. "Losing Vietnam: Covering the War in an Age of Technology." In *The Vietnam War and American Culture,* edited by John C. Rowe and Rick Berg, 115–48. New York: Columbia University Press, 1991.

Berman, Larry. *No Peace, No Honor: Nixon, Kissinger and Betrayal in Vietnam.* New York: Free Press, 1999.

Berquist, Charles, Ricardo Penranda, and Gonzalo Sanchez. *Violence in Colombia: The Contemporary Crisis in Historical Perspective.* Wilmington, Del: Scholarly Resources, 1992.

Berry, John Stevens. *Those Gallant Men: On Trial in Vietnam.* Novato, Ca: Presidio, 1984.

Bertram, Eva, Morris Blachman, Kenneth Sharpe, and Peter Andreas. *Drug War Politics: The Price of Denial.* Berkeley: University of California Press, 1996.

Beschner, George M., and A. S. Friedman. *Youth Drug Abuse: Problems, Issues, Treatment.* Washington, D.C.: Lexington Books, 1979.

Bey, Douglas R., and Vincent A. Zecchinelli. "GI's against Themselves: Factors Resulting in Explosive Violence in Vietnam." *Psychiatry* 37, no. 3 (August 1974): 221–28.

The Big Chill. Directed by Lawrence Kasdan. Columbia Pictures, 1983.

"Big Gains in Drive to Cut Off Narcotics, Jailed Kingpins and Record Seizures Attest to Progress Against Drug Menace." *U.S. News & World Report,* December 25, 1972, 32–34.

Biskind, Peter. *Easy Riders, Raging Bulls: How the Sex-Drugs-and-Rock 'n' Roll Generation Saved Hollywood.* New York: Simon & Schuster, 1998.

Blachman, Morris, and Kenneth Sharpe. "The War on Drugs: American Democracy Under Assault." *World Policy Journal* 7, no. 1 (Winter 1989/1990): 135–63.

Black, Samuel, Kenneth L. Owens, and Ronald P. Wolff. "Patterns of Drug Use: A Study of 5,482 Subjects." *American Journal of Psychiatry* 127 (October 1970): 420–23.

Black Sunday. Directed by John Frankenheimer. Paramount Pictures, 1977.

Blaufarb, Douglas S. *The Counter-Insurgency Era: U.S. Doctrine and Performance.* New York: Free Press, 1977.

Block, Alan A. "Anti-Communism and the War on Drugs." In *Perspectives on Organizing Crime,* 209–26. London: Kluwar Academic Publishers, 1991.

Bloomquist, Edward R. *Marijuana.* Beverly Hills, Calif.: Glencoe Press, 1968.

Blum, Richard H. *Utopiates.* London: Travistock, 1965.

Blumer, Herbert, Alan Sutter, Samir Ahmed, and Roger Smith. *The World of Youthful Drug Use.* Berkeley: School of Criminology, University of California, 1967.

Boaz, David, ed. *Crisis in Drug Prohibition.* Washington, D.C.: Cato Institute, 1990.

Bonnie, Richard, and Charles H. Whitehead II. *The Marihuana Conviction: A History of Marijuana Prohibition in the United States.* Charlottesville: University Press of Virginia, 1974.

Born on the Fourth of July. Directed by Oliver Stone. Mexico, Universal Pictures, 1989.

Bourgeois, Philippe. *In Search of Respect: Selling Crack in El Barrio.* New York: Cambridge University Press, 1995.

Bourne, Peter G. *Men, Stress, and Vietnam.* Boston: Little Brown, 1970.

———. *Methadone: Benefits and Shortcomings.* Washington, D.C.: Drug Abuse Council, 1975.

———. "President Carter's Commitment to a Combined State, Local and Federal Effort." *Drug Enforcement Administration Magazine,* August 1977, 2–3.

———. *The Psychology and Physiology of Stress.* New York: Academic Press, 1969.

———. "The Vietnam Veteran." In *The Vietnam Veteran in Contemporary Society,* IV-83–86. Washington, D.C.: Department of Medicine and Surgery, Veterans Administration, 1972.

Boyle, Richard. *Flower of the Dragon: The Breakdown of the U.S. Army in Vietnam.* San Francisco: Ramparts Press, 1972.

The Boys in Company C. Directed by Sidney Furie. Columbia Pictures, 1978.

Branfman, Fred. *Voices from the Plain of Jars: Life Under an Air War.* New York: Harper & Row, 1972.

Brecher, Edward M. *Licit and Illicit Drugs.* Boston: Little Brown, 1977.

Brigham, Robert. *ARVN: Life and Death in the South Vietnamese Army.* Lawrence: University Press of Kansas, 2006.

———. *Guerilla Diplomacy: The NLF's Foreign Relations and the Vietnam War.* Ithaca: Cornell University Press, 1998.

———. *Is Iraq Another Vietnam?* New York: Public Affairs, 2006.

Brown, Bertram S. "The Treatment and Rehabilitation of Narcotics Addicts in the United States." In National Commission on Marihuana and Drug Abuse, *Drug Use in America,* 4:127–43.

Browning, Frank. "An American Gestapo." *Playboy Magazine,* February 1976, 80–82.

Browning, Frank, and Dorothy Forman, eds. *The Wasted Nations: Report of the International Commission of Enquiry into United States Crimes in Indochina.* New York: Harper & Row, 1972.

———. "Bombing in Laos—A Crime Against Humanity." In *The Wasted Nations,* 63–80.

Browning, Frank, and Banning Garrett. "The New Opium War." *Ramparts,* May 1971, 32–39.

Broyles, William, Jr. "Remembering a War We Want to Forget: A Veteran Reflects on Healing the Wounds of War," *Newsweek,* November 22, 1982, 82–83.

Brush, Peter. "Higher and Higher: Drug Use among U.S. Forces in Vietnam." *Vietnam* 15, no. 4 (December 2002) 46–53, 70. Also available online at www.library.vanderbilt.edu/central/brush/American-drug-use-vietnam.htm.

Bullington, Bruce. "A Smuggler's Paradise: Cocaine Trafficking through the Bahamas." In McCoy and Block, *War on Drugs,* 209–31.

Bundy, William P. *A Tangled Web: The Making of Foreign Policy in the Nixon Presidency.* New York: Hill and Wang, 1998.

Burchett, Wilfred. *Vietnam Will Win: Why the People of South Vietnam Have Already Defeated U.S. Imperialism and How They Have Done It.* New York: Monthly Review Press, 1969.

Burkett, B. G., and Glenna Whitley. *Stolen Valor: How the Vietnam Generation Was Robbed of Its Heroes and Its History.* Dallas: Verity Press, 1998.

Caldwell, Malcolm, and Lek Tan. *Cambodia in the Southeast Asian War..* New York: Monthly Review Press, 1973.

Camp, Norman, William C. Marshall, and Robert H. Stretch. *Stress, Strain, and Vietnam.* New York: Greenwood Press, 1988.

Campbell, Richard, and Jimmie L. Reeves. *Cracked Coverage: Television News, the Anti-Cocaine Crusade, and the Reagan Legacy.* Durham, N.C.: Duke University Press, 1994.

Caputo, Philip. *A Rumor of War.* New York: Ballantine Books, 1977.

Carmichael, Stokely. "Speech at the University of California at Berkeley, October 1966." In *Stokely Speaks: Black Power Back to Pan-Africanism*, 45–61. New York: Random House, 1971.

Carpenter, Ted G. *Bad Neighbor Policy: Washington's Futile War on Drugs in Latin America*. New York: Palgrave Macmillan, 2003.

Carter, Jimmy. "Energy and National Goals: Address to the Nation." July 15, 1979. *Public Papers of the Presidents of the United States: Jimmy Carter, 1977–1981*. Vol. 2. Washington, D.C.: GPO, 1979.

Cecil, Paul. *Herbicidal Warfare: The Ranch Hand Project in Vietnam*. New York: Praeger, 1986.

Chambliss, William J. *Power, Politics, and Crime*. Boulder, Colo.: Westview Press, 1999.

Chandrasekaran, Rajiv. *Imperial Life in the Emerald City: Inside Baghdad's Green Zone*. New York: Alfred A. Knopf, 2006.

Chavez, Ernesto. *'Mi Raza Primero!' (My People First): Nationalism, Identity, and Insurgency in the Chicano Movement in Los Angeles, 1966–1978*. Berkeley: University of California Press, 2002.

Chepesiuk, Ron. *Hard Target: The U.S. War against International Drug Trafficking, 1982–1997*. Jefferson, N.C.: McFarland, 1989.

Chepesiuk, Ron, and Anthony Gonzalez. *Superfly: The True Untold Story of Frank Lucas, American Gangster*. New York: Street Certified Entertainment, 2007.

China Beach. "Pilot." April 26, 1988; "Cherry." February 1, 1989; "One Giant Leap." March 13, 1991. "The Always Goodbye." May 8, 1991; "Juice." March 13, 1991. NBC Television.

Chomsky, Noam. "An Editorial Statement on Vietnam." *Ramparts*, December 2, 1967, 2.

———. *American Power and the New Mandarins*. New York: Vintage Books, 1969.

———. *At War with Asia: Essays on Indo-China*. New York: Vintage Books, 1970.

———. *The Culture of Terrorism*. Boston: South End Press 1987.

———. *Failed States: The Abuse of Power and the Assault on Democracy*. New York: Metroplitan Books, 2006.

———. *For Reasons of State*. (1973.) London: New Press, 2003.

———. *A New Generation Draws the Line: Kosovo, East Timor, and the Standards of the West*. London: Verso, 1999.

———. The Responsibility of Intellectuals." In *American Power and the New Mandarins*, 323–66.

———. "The United States and Indo-China: Far From an Aberration." In Allen and Ngo, *Coming to Terms*, 161–89.

———. "Visions of Righteousness." In *The Vietnam War and American Culture*, edited by John C. Rowe and Rick Berg, 21–52. New York: Columbia University Press, 1991.

———. *Year 501: The Conquest Continues*. Boston: South End Press, 1993.

Chomsky, Noam, and Edward S. Herman. *After the Cataclysm: Postwar Indo-China and the Reconstruction of Imperial Ideology*. Boston: South End Press, 1979.

———. *Manufacturing Consent: The Political Economy of the Mass Media.* New York: Pantheon Books, 1989.

———. *The Political Economy of Human Rights.* Vol. 1, *The Washington Connection and Third World Fascism;* vol 2, *Postwar Indochina and the Reconstruction of Imperial Ideology.* Boston: South End Press, 1979.

———. "Saigon's Corruption Crisis: The Search for an Honest Quisling." *Ramparts,* December 1975, 21–26.

Chown, Jeffrey. *Hollywood Auteur: Francis Coppola.* New York: Praeger, 1988.

"The CIA's Flourishing Opium Trade." *Ramparts,* June 13, 1968, 8.

Cincinnatus. *Self-Destruction: The Disintegration and Decay of the U.S. Armed Forces in the Vietnam Era.* New York: Norton, 1981.

Citizens Commission of Inquiry, ed. *The Dellums Committee Hearings on War Crimes in Vietnam.* New York: Vintage, 1972.

Clark, Janet [pseud.]. *The Autobiography of a Girl Drug Addict as told to Howard S. Becker.* Edited by Helen MacGill Hughes. Boston: Houghton Mifflin, 1961.

Clements, Charles. *Witness to War: An American Doctor in El Salvador.* New York: Bantam, 1984.

Cobrun, Judith. "Asian Scholars and Government: The Chrysanthemum on the Sword." In *America's Asia: Dissenting Essays,* edited by Edward Friedman and Mark Selden, 67–108. New York: Vintage, 1971.

Cohen, Sidney. *The Beyond Within: The LSD Story.* New York: Atheneum, 1964.

———. *The Drug Dilemma.* New York: McGraw-Hill, 1969.

———. "Health Hazards of Cocaine." *Drug Enforcement Administration Magazine,* Fall 1982, 12.

Colbach, Edward. "Marijuana Use by GIs in Vietnam." *American Journal of Psychiatry* 128, no. 2 (August 1971): 198–204.

Colbach, Edward M., and S. M. Willson. "The Binoctal Craze." *U.S. Army Medical Bulletin* 14 (May–June 1969): 40–44.

Colby, William, and Peter Forbath. *Honorable Men: My Life in the CIA.* New York: Simon & Schuster, 1978.

Cole, Lewis. *Never Too Young to Die: The Death of Len Bias.* New York: Alfred A. Knopf, 1989.

Collins, Jack P. "Traffic in Traffickers." In National Commission on Marihuana and Drug Abuse, *Drug Use in America,* 3:481–90.

Columbo. NBC Television, 1968–2008.

Coming Home. Directed by Hal Ashby. United Artists, 1978.

Corn, David. *Blond Ghost: Ted Shackley and the CIA's Crusades.* New York: Simon & Schuster, 1994.

Corson, William R. *The Betrayal.* New York: W. W. Norton, 1968.

Cortright, David. *Soldiers in Revolt: The American Military Today.* New York: Anchor, 1975.

"Counter-Insurgency and Anti-Narcotics Measures Become Intertwined in Upper-Huallaga Valley." *The Andean Report,* June 1987, 102.

Courtwright, David T. *Dark Paradise: A History of Opiate Abuse in America.* Cambridge, Mass.: Harvard University Press, 1982.

Craig, Richard B. "La Campaa Permanente: Mexico's Anti-Drug Campaign in the 1970s." *Journal of Inter-American Studies and World Affairs* 20, no. 1 (May 1978): 107–31.

Cuban American National Foundation. *Castro's Narcotics Trade.* Miami: Cuban-American National Foundation, 1983.

Cumings, Bruce. *War and Television.* London: Verso, 1992.

Currey, Cecil B. *Edward Lansdale: The Unquiet American.* Boston: Houghton Mifflin, 1988.

———. *Long Binh Jail: An Oral History of Vietnam's Notorious Military Prison.* Washington, D.C.: Brassey's, 1999.

Currie, Elliot. *Confronting Crime: An American Challenge.* New York: Pantheon, 1985.

———. *The Reckoning: Drugs, the Cities, and the American Future.* New York: Hill & Wang, 1992.

Cutter's Way. Directed by Ivan Passer. United Artists, 1981.

Dallek, Robert. *Partners in Power: Nixon and Kissinger.* New York: HarperCollins, 2007.

———. *Ronald Reagan and the Politics of Symbolism.* New York: Cambridge University Press, 1984.

Davenport-Hines, Richard. *The Pursuit of Oblivion: A Global History of Narcotics, 1500–2000.* London: Weidenfeld & Nicolson, 2001.

de Alarcón, R. "The Spread of Heroin Abuse in a Community." *Bulletin on Narcotics* 3 (July–September 1969): 17–22.

"DEA International Training Program." *Drug Enforcement Administration Magazine,* Winter 1976, 18.

Dean, Eric T. *Shook Over Hell: Post-Traumatic Stress, Vietnam, and the Civil War.* Cambridge, Mass.: Harvard University Press, 1997.

The Deer Hunter. Directed by Michael Cimino. Universal Studios, 1978.

Deforest, Orin, and David Chanoff. *The Rise and Bitter Fall of American Intelligence in Vietnam.* New York: Pocket Books, 1991.

Delaney, William P. "On Capturing an Opium King: The Politics of Lo Hsing Han's Arrest," In *Drugs and Politics,* edited by Paul E. Rock, 67–89. Brunswick, N.J.: Transaction Books, 1977.

Denson-Gerber, Judianne. *We Mainline Dreams: The Odyssey House Story.* New York: Doubleday, 1973.

DeRienzo, Paul. "Interview with Alfred McCoy." November 9, 1991. www.pdr. autono.net/mccoy.htm.

Desser, David. "Charlie Don't Surf: Race and Culture in Vietnam War Films." In Anderegg, *Inventing Vietnam,* 81–103.

Devine, Jeremy L. *Vietnam at 24 Frames a Second.* Jefferson: N.C: McFarland, 1995.

Different Strokes. "The Reporter," March 19, 1983, NBC.

Dikötter, Frank, Lars Laaman, and Zhou Xun. *Narcotic Culture: A History of Drugs in China.* Chicago: University of Chicago Press, 2004.

Dinges, John. *Our Man in Panama: How General Noriega Used the United States and Made Millions in Drugs and Arms.* New York: Harper & Row, 1989.

Dionisopoulos, George N. "Images of the Warrior Returned: Vietnam Veterans in Popular American Film." In *Cultural Legacies of Vietnam: Uses of the Past in the Present*, edited by Richard Morris and Peter Ehrenhaus, 80–99. Norwood, N.J.: Ablex, 1990.

Dirty Harry. Directed by Don Siegel. Warner Brothers, 1971.

Dirty Harry—The Enforcer. Directed by James Fargo. Warner Brothers, 1976.

Dodd, Thomas J. *Freedom and Foreign Policy.* New York: Bookmailer, 1962.

Doherty, Thomas. *Projections of War: Hollywood Film, American Culture, and World War II.* New York: Columbia University Press, 1993.

Dole, Vincent P. "Detoxification of Sick Addicts in Prison." *Journal of the American Medical Association* 220 (April 17, 1972): 366–69.

Dorland, Gil. *Legacy of Discord: Voices of the Vietnam War Era.* Washington, D.C.: Brassey's, 2001.

Dreyfuss, Robert. "Bush's War on Pot." *Rolling Stone*, July 28, 2005, www.rollingstone.com/politics/story/7504250/bushs_war_on_pot/.

Dudziak, Mary L. *Cold War Civil Rights: Race and the Image of American Democracy.*Princeton: Princeton University Press, 2000.

Duffet, John, ed. *Against the Crime of Silence: Proceedings of the Russell International War Crimes Tribunal.* New York: O'Hare Books, 1968.

Duncan, Donald. "I Quit." *Ramparts*, February 1966, 41–46.

Dunkerley, James. *Rebellion in the Veins: Political Struggle in Bolivia, 1952–1982.* London: Verso, 1984.

DuPont, Robert L. "The Drug Abuse Decade." *Journal of Drug Issues* 8 (Spring 1978): 173–87.

———. *Getting Tough on Gateway Drugs: A Guide for the Family.* Washington, D.C.: American Psychiatric Press, 1984.

———. "Heroin Addiction Treatment and Crime Reduction." *American Journal of Psychiatry* 128 (March 1972): 856–60.

Duster, Troy. "Pattern, Purpose and Race in the Drug War." In Reinarman and Levine, *Crack in America*, 260–88.

Earlywine, Mitch, ed. *Understanding Marijuana: A New Look at the Scientific Evidence.* New York: Oxford University Press, 2002.

Ebert, James R. *A Life in a Year: The American Infantryman in Vietnam, 1965–1972.* Novato, Calif: Presidio, 1993.

Edelman, Rob. "Viet Vets Talk About 'Nam' Films." *Films in Review* 30, no. 9 (November 1979): 539–42.

Editors of *Ramparts* and Frank Browning. *Smack!* New York: Harrow, 1971.

Ehrenfeld, Rachel. *Narco-Terrorism.* New York: Basic Books, 1990.

Ehrenreich, Barbara. *Fear of Falling: The Inner Life of the Middle-Class.* New York: Pantheon Books, 1989.

Ehrhart, William D. *Busted: A Vietnam Veteran in Nixon's America.* Amherst: University of Massachusetts Press, 1995.

———. *The Madness of It All—Essays on War, Literature, and American Life.* Jefferson, N.C.: McFarland, 2002.

————. *Passing Time: Memoir of a Vietnam Veteran Against the War*. Amherst: University of Massachusetts Press, 1995.

Elliot, David W. P. *The Vietnamese War*. 2 vols. New York: M. E. Sharpe, 2003.

Englehardt, Tom. *The End of Victory Culture: Post-War America and the Disillusioning of a Generation*. New York: Basic Books, 1995.

Epstein, Edward J. *Agency of Fear: Opiates and Political Power in America*. New York: Putnam, 1977.

————. "The Incredible War against the Poppies." *Esquire*, December 1974, 148–50.

Ernst, John. *Forging a Faithful Alliance: Michigan State University and the Vietnam War*. East Lansing: Michigan State University Press, 1998.

Everingham, John. "The Golden Triangle Trade." *Asia Magazine*, March 23, 1975, 28.

"The Evil Empire." *Newsweek*, February 25, 1985, 14, 65.

Fall, Bernard. "Vietnam Blitz: A Report on the Impersonal War." *New Republic*, October 9, 1965, 19.

Fanon, Frantz. *The Wretched of the Earth*. New York: Grove, 1962.

Farber, David. *The Iran Hostage Crisis and America's First Encounter with Radical Islam*. Princeton: Princeton University Press, 2005.

Feingold, David A. "Opium and Politics in Laos." In McCoy and Adams, *Laos: War and Revolution*, 322–39.

Feldman, Harvey W. "Ideological Supports for Becoming and Remaining a Heroin Addict." *Journal of Health and Social Behavior* 9 (September 1968): 131–39.

————. "The Origins and Spread of Working-Class Use of Illicit Drugs: A Neighborhood Field Study." PhD diss., Florence Heller School for Advanced Studies in Social Welfare, Brandeis University, 1970.

Fineman, Daniel. *A Special Relationship: The United States and Military Government in Thailand, 1947–1958*. Honolulu: University of Hawai'i Press, 1997.

Finestone, Harold. "Cats, Kicks, and Color." *Social Problems* 5, no. 1 (July 1957): 3–13.

Finlator, John. *The Drugged Nation: A "Narc's" Story*. New York: Simon & Schuster, 1973.

Fisher, Allen H., Jr. *Preliminary Findings from the 1971 DOD Survey of Drug Use*. Technical Report 72-8. Alexandria, Virginia: Human Resources Research Organization, 1972.

Fitzgerald, Frances. *Fire in the Lake: The Vietnamese and the Americans in Vietnam*. Boston: Beacon Press, 1972.

————. *Way Out There in the Blue: Reagan, Star Wars, and the End of the Cold War*. New York: Simon & Schuster, 2000.

Flamm, Michael W. *Law and Order: Street Crime, Civil Unrest, and the Crisis of Liberalism in the 1960s*. New York: Columbia University Press, 2005.

————. "Politics and Pragmatism: The Nixon Administration." *White House Studies* 6, no. 2 (Spring 2007): 151–62.

Flanders, Joe. "The Heroin Labs of Marseille." *Drug Enforcement Administration Magazine*, Fall 1973, 10–15.

Flood, E. Thadeus. *The United States and the Military Coup in Thailand: A Background Study.* Washington, D.C.: Indochina Resource Center, 1976.

Ford, Gerald. "A Message to the Congress of the United States." *Drug Enforcement Administration Magazine,* Spring 1976, 17.

———. *A Time to Heal.* New York: Harper & Row, 1979.

Fort, Joel. *Alcohol: Our Biggest Drug Industry and Drug Problem.* New York: McGraw-Hill, 1972.

———. *The Pleasure Seekers: The Drug Crisis, Youth and Society.* Berkeley: University of California Press, 1969.

———. "Social Problems of Drug Use and Drug Policies." *California Law Review* 56, no. 1 (January 1968): 17–28.

Franklin, H. Bruce. "Making Children Behave." In *The Vietnam War in American Stories, Songs, and Poems,* edited by H. Bruce Franklin, 251. Boston: Bedford Books, 1996.

———. *M.I.A. or Mythmaking in America: How and Why Belief in Live POWs Has Possessed a Nation.* New York: Lawrence Hill Books, 1992.

———. *Vietnam and Other American Fantasies.* Amherst: University of Massachusetts Press, 2000.

Freeman, Laurie, and Jorge Luis Sierra. "Mexico: The Militarization Trap." In Youngers and Rosin, *Drugs and Democracy in Latin America,* 263–303.

"Fresh Disclosures on Drugs and GIs." *U.S. News & World Report,* April 6, 1970, 32–33.

Fromm, Erich. *The Sane Society.* New York: Rhinehart, 1955.

Fuchs, Cynthia J. "All the Animals Come Out at Night: Vietnam Meets Noir in *Taxi Driver.*" In Anderegg, *Inventing Vietnam,* 33–56.

Fussell, Paul. *Wartime: Understanding and Behavior in the Second World War.* New York: Oxford University Press, 1989.

Gabriel, Richard A., and Paul L. Savage. *Crisis in Command.* New York: Hill & Wang, 1978.

"Gains in the War on Drug Smugglers: Interview with Myles J. Ambrose." *U.S. News & World Report,* June 21, 1971, 60.

Gallup, George H. *The Gallup Poll: Public Opinion, 1972–1977.* Wilmington, Del.: Scholarly Resources, 1978.

Galvin, Katherine, and Richard Taylor. "Drug Education in Massachusetts." In National Commission on Marihuana and Drug Abuse, *Drug Use in America,* 2:411–55.

Gardens of Stone. Francis Ford Coppola. Delphi Premier Productions, 1986.

Gareau, Frederick H. "Washington's Support for State Terrorism in Argentina." In *State Terrorism and the United States: From Counterinsurgency to the War on Terrorism,* 102–6. London: Zed Books, 2004.

Garland, David. *The Culture of Control: Crime and Social Order in Contemporary Society.* Chicago: University of Chicago Press, 2001.

Gibson, James W. *The Perfect War: The War We Couldn't Lose and How We Did.* New York: Vintage, 1986.

Gill, Gerald. "Black Soldiers' Perspectives on the Vietnam War." In *The Vietnam Reader*, edited by Walter Capps, 173–86. New York: Routledge, 1991.

Gill, Lesley. *The School of the Americas: Military Training and Political Violence in the Americas*. Durham, N.C.: Duke University Press, 2004.

Ginsberg, Allen, "The First Manifesto to End the Bringdown." In *The Marihuana Papers*, edited by David Solomon, 183–200. New York: Signet, 1966.

Gioglio, Gerald. *Days of Decision: An Oral History of Conscientious Objectors in the Military during the Vietnam War*. Lavalette, N.J.: Broken Rifles Press, 1989.

Gitlin, Todd. *The Whole World Is Watching: Mass Media in the Making and Unmaking of the New Left*. Berkeley: University of California Press, 1980.

Glass, William J., and Leigh Henderson. *LSD: Still with Us after All These Years*. San Francisco: Jossey-Bass, 1994.

Glassner, Barry. *The Culture of Fear: Why Americans Are Afraid of the Wrong Things*. New York: Basic Books, 1999.

Go Tell the Spartans. Directed by Ted Post. Mar Vista Films, 1978.

"Going After Hollywood: Critics Call for Deglamorization of Drugs." *Newsweek*, August 11, 1986, 20.

Goldberg, Peter. "The Federal Government's Response to Illicit Drugs, 1969–1978." In *e*, Drug Abuse Council, *The Facts about Drug Abuse*, 20–63.

Goldman, Peter L., Tony Fuller, and Richard Manning. *Charlie Company: What Vietnam Did to Us*. New York: Ballantine, 1983.

Goldstein, Joseph, Burke Marshall, and Jack Schwartz. *The My Lai Massacre and Its Cover-up: Beyond the Reach of Law? The Peers Report with a Supplement and Introductory Essay on the Limits of Law*. New York: The Free Press, 1976.

Gonzalez, Arturo, Jr. "The Vietcong's Secret Weapon: Marijuana." *Science Digest*, April 1969, 17–18.

Gonzales, José. "Guerrillas and Coca in the Upper-Huallaga Valley." In *Shining Path of Peru*, edited by David S. Palmer. 105–22. New York: St. Martin's Press, 1992.

Goode, Erich, and Nachman Ben-Yehuda. *Moral Panics: The Social Construction of Deviance*. Malden, Mass.: Blackwell, 1994.

Goodman, Amy. "Interview with Alfred McCoy." February 18, 2006. www.zmag.org.

Goodman, Paul. *Growing Up Absurd: Problems of Youth in the Organized Society*. New York: Random House, 1960.

Gordon's War. Directed by Ossie Davis. Palomar Pictures, 1973.

Goscha, Christopher E. *Thailand and the Southeast Asian Networks of the Vietnamese Revolution, 1885–1954*. London: Curzon, 1999.

Goti, Jaime Malamud. "Reinforcing Poverty: The Bolivian War on Cocaine." In McCoy and Block, *War on Drugs*, 67–84.

Gottschalk, Marie. *The Prison and the Gallows: The Politics of Mass Incarceration in America*. New York: Cambridge University Press, 2006.

Graham, Herman, III. *The Brothers' Vietnam War: Black Power, Manhood, and the Military Experience*. Gainesville: University Press of Florida, 2003.

Grandin, Greg. *Empire's Workshop: Latin America, the United States, and the Rise of the New Imperialism.* New York: Metropolitan Books, 2006.

———. "History, Motive, Law and Intent: Methods in Understanding Guatemala's 1981–83 Genocide." In *The Specter of Genocide: Mass Murder in Historical Perspective*, edited by Robert Kiernan and Ben Kiernan, 339–53. New York: Cambridge University Press, 2003.

Gravel, Mike, ed. *The Pentagon Papers: The Defense Department History of the United States Decision-Making in Vietnam.* 5 vols. Boston: Beacon Press, 1971.

Gray, Mike. *Drug Crazy: How We Got Into This Mess and How We Can Get Out.* New York: Routledge, 1998.

Greenberg, David. *Nixon's Shadow: The History of an Image.* New York: W. W. Norton, 2003.

Greenway, H. D. S. "The Book the CIA Couldn't Put Down: A Review of *The Politics of Heroin* by Alfred W. McCoy." *Life Magazine*, October 20, 1972.

Greetings. Directed by Brian DePalma. West End Films, 1968.

Grinspoon, Lester. "Marijuana in a Time of Psychopharmacological McCarthyism." In *Searching for Alternatives: Drug Control Policy in the United States*, edited by Melvin B. Krauss and Edward P. Lazear, 379–89. Palo Alto: Hoover Institution Press, 1991.

———. *Marijuana Reconsidered.* Cambridge, Mass: Harvard University Press, 1971.

Grinspoon, Lester, and James Bakalaar. *Cocaine: A Drug and Its Social Evolution.* New York: Basic Books, 1976.

Gritz, James "Bo." *A Nation Betrayed.* Las Vegas: Lazarus Publishers, 1989.

Gugliotta, Guy, and Jeff Leen. *Kings of Cocaine: Inside the Medellin Cartel.* New York: Harper, 1990.

Hagopian, Patrick. "The Social Memory of the Vietnam War." PhD diss., Johns Hopkins University, 1993.

Haines, Harry W. "The Pride Is Back: *Rambo, Magnum PI* and the Return Trip to Vietnam." In *Cultural Legacies of Vietnam: Uses of the Past in the Present*, edited by Richard Morris and Peter Ehrenhaus, 99–124. Norwood, N.J.: Ablex, 1990.

Halberstam, David. *The Making of a Quagmire.* New York: Random House, 1965.

Hallin, Daniel C. *The "Uncensored War": The Media and Vietnam.* New York: Oxford University Press, 1986.

Halstead, Fred. "The New Anti-War Army." *International Socialist Review*, January 1972, 24–31.

Hamburger Hill. Directed by John Irvin. Artisan, 1987.

Hamilton-Paterson, James. *The Greedy War.* New York: David McKay, 1971.

Haney, Walt. "The Pentagon Papers and U.S. Involvement in Laos." In *Critical Essays*, edited by Noam Chomsky and Howard Zinn, vol. 5 of Gravel, *The Pentagon Papers*, 248-93. Boston: Beacon Press, 1972.

Harris, Louis, and Associates, Inc. *Myths and Realities: A Study of Attitudes toward Vietnam-era Veterans.* Washington D.C.: Veterans Administration, 1980.

Harris, T. George, and Jerome H. Jaffe. "As Far as Heroin Is Concerned, the Worst Is Over." *Psychology Today*, August 1973, 68–79, 85.

Haseltine, Pat, Jerry Meldon, Charles Knight, Mark Selden et al. *The Trail of the Poppy: Heroin and Imperialism. Bulletin of the Committee of Concerned Asian Scholars.* Somerville, Mass.: New England Free Press, 1972.

Hauser, William L. *America's Army in Crisis: A Study in Civil-Military Relations.* Baltimore: Johns Hopkins University Press, 1973.

Hawaii Five-O. CBS Television, 1968–1980.

Heinl, Col. Robert D., Jr. "The Collapse of the Armed Forces." *Armed Forces Journal* 7 (June 1971): 30–37.

Hellmann, John. *American Myth and the Legacy of Vietnam.* New York: Columbia University Press, 1986.

Helmer, John. *Bringing the War Home: The American Soldier in Vietnam and After.* New York: Free Press, 1974.

———. *Drugs and Minority Oppression.* New York: Seabury Press, 1975.

Herbert, Anthony, with James T. Wooten. *Soldier.* New York: Holt, Rinehart & Winston, 1972.

"The Heroin Plague: What Can Be Done?" *Newsweek,* July 5, 1971, 27–32.

Herman, Edward S. *Atrocities in Vietnam.* Boston: Pilgrim Press, 1970.

"Heroin: A New and Growing Threat." *Reader's Digest,* June 1972.

Herr, Michael. *Dispatches.* New York: Alfred A. Knopf, 1977.

Herring, George. *America's Longest War.* New York: McGraw-Hill, 1996.

Hersh, Seymour. *My La 4: A Report on the Massacre and Its Cover-up.* New York: Random House, 1970.

———. *Price of Power: Kissinger in the Nixon White House.* New York: Bantam, 1987.

Hinckle, Warren, and Robert Scheer. "The University on the Make (or How MSU Helped Arm Madame Nhu)." *Ramparts,* May 1965, 11–20.

Hirschi, Travis, and Michael R. Gottfredson. "The True Value of Lambda Would Appear to Be Zero: An Essay on Career Criminals, Criminal Careers, Selective Incapacitation, Cohort Studies, and Related Topics." *Criminology* 245 (February 1986): 213–33.

Hodgson, Godfrey. *The World Turned Right-Side Up: A History of the Conservative Ascendancy in America.* Boston: Houghton Mifflin, 1996.

Hoff, Joan. *Nixon Reconsidered.* New York: Basic Books, 1994.

Hogan, Michael A. *Cross of Iron: Harry S. Truman and the Origins of the National Security State, 1945–1954.* New York: Cambridge University Press, 1998.

Holloway, Harry C., et al. "Drug Abuse in Military Personnel." *Annual Progress Report.* Washington, D.C.: Walter Reed Army Institute of Research, 1972.

———. "Epidemiology of Heroin Dependency among Soldiers in Vietnam." *Military Medicine* 139, no. 2 (February 1974): 108–13.

Hougan, Jim. *Spooks: The Haunting of America—The Private Use of Secret Agents.* New York: Bantam, 1979.

"How Drugs Sap the Nation's Strength." *U.S. News & World Report,* May 16, 1983, 55–60.

Huffman, Edward. "Which Soldiers Break Down: Survey of 610 Psychiatric Patients in Vietnam." *Bulletin of Menninger Clinic* 34 (March 1970): 343–51.

Huggins, Martha K., *Political Policing: The United States and Latin America.* Durham, N.C.: Duke University Press, 1998.

———. "U.S.-Supported State Terror: A History of Police Training in Latin America." In *Vigilantism and the State in Modern Latin America,* edited by Martha K. Huggins, 219–42. New York: Praeger, 1991.

Human Rights Watch Staff. *Colombia's Killer Networks: The Military-Paramilitary Partnership and the United States.* New York: Human Rights Watch, 1986.

Hunt, Andrew E. *The Turning: A History of Vietnam Veterans Against War.* New York: New York University Press, 1999.

Hunt, Leon, and Carl D. Chambers. *The Heroin Epidemics: A Study of Heroin Use in the United States.* New York: Spectrum, 1976.

In Country. Directed by Norman Jewison. Warner Brothers, 1989.

Inciardi, James A. "Beyond Cocaine: Basuco, Crack, and Other Coca Products." *Contemporary Drug Problems* 14 (Fall1987): 461–92.

———. *The War on Drugs: Heroin, Cocaine, Crime, and Public Policy.* Palo Alto: Mayfield Publishing, 1984.

Ingraham, Larry H. "The Myth of Illicit Drug Use and Military Incompetence." *Medical Bulletin of the US Army, Europe,* New York: HQ, 7th Medical Command, 36, no. 4 (July/August 1979): 18–21.

———. "'The Nam' and 'The World': Heroin Use by U.S. Army Enlisted Men Serving in Vietnam." *Psychiatry* 37 (May 1974): 114–28.

———. "Sense and Nonsense in the Army's Drug Abuse Prevention Effort." *Parameters, Journal of the U.S. Army War College* 9 (March 1981): 60–70.

"Interview with Timothy Leary." *Playboy Magazine* September 1966, 93–112, 250–56.

Isaacson, Adam. "The U.S. Military in the War on Drugs." In Youngers and Rosin, *Drugs and Democracy in Latin America,* 15–61.

Ives, John O. "Profiles in Disaster." *New York Times Magazine,* April 6, 1973.

Jacknife. Directed by David Jones. Cineplex Odeon, 1988.

Jacob's Ladder. Directed by Adrian Lyne. Tri-Star, 1990.

Janecek, E., J. Casper, and H. Martinelli. "Marijuana in Vietnam." *USARV Medical Bulletin* 11 (Pamphlet 40, 1968): 60–72.

Jeffords, Susan. *The Remasculinization of America: Gender and the Vietnam War.* Bloomington: Indiana University Press, 1989.

Jelsma, Martin. *Vicious Circle: The Chemical and Biological "War on Drugs."* Amsterdam: Transnational Institute Press, 2001.

Jenkins, Philip. *Decade of Nightmares: The End of the Sixties and the Making of Eighties America.* New York: Oxford University Press, 2006.

Johns, Christina J. *Power, Ideology, and the War on Drugs: Nothing Succeeds Like Failure.* New York: Praeger, 1992.

———. *State Crime, the Media, and the Invasion of Panama.* Westport, Conn: Greenwood Press, 1993.

Johnson, Bruce D. "Once an Addict, Seldom an Addict." *Contemporary Drug Problems* 7 (Spring 1978): 48–49.

Johnson, Chalmers. *Blowback: The Costs and Consequences of the American Empire.* New York: Owl Books, 2000.

———. *Nemesis: The Last Days of the American Republic*. New York: Metropolitan Books, 2006.

Johnson, Haynes, and George C. Wilson. *Army in Anguish: The Washington Post National Report*. New York: Pocket Books, 1972.

Johnston, Lloyd D. *Illicit Drug Use: Smoking and Drinking by America's High-School Students, College Students, and Young Adults*. Washington, D.C.: GPO, 1988.

Johnson, Lloyd D., Patrick M. O'Malley, and Jerald G. Bachman. *Drug Use among American High School Students, College Student, and Other Young Adults: National Trends through 1985*. Washington, D.C.: National Institute on Drug Abuse, 1986.

Jones, Jacqueline. *The Dispossessed: America's Underclass from the Civil War to the Present*. New York: Basic Books, 1992.

Jonnes, Jill. *Hep-Cats, Narcs, and Pipe-Dreams: A History of America's Romance with Illegal Drugs*. Baltimore: Johns Hopkins University Press, 1996.

Kahin, George McT. *Intervention: How America Became Involved in Vietnam*. New York: Alfred A. Knopf, 1986.

Kaplan, Joel H. "Marijuana and Drug Abuse in Vietnam." *Annals of the New York Academy of Science* 1 (February 1971): 261–69.

Kaplan, John. *The Hardest Drug: Heroin and Public Policy*. Chicago: University of Chicago Press, 1983.

———. *Marijuana: The New Prohibition*. New York: World Publishing, 1970.

Karnow, Stanley. *Vietnam: A History*. New York: Viking, 1983.

Kashimba, David. "Uncle Sam, Pusher." *The Nation*, September 20, 1971, 226–45.

Katzman, Jason. "From Outcast to Cliché: How Film Shaped, Warped and Developed the Image of the Vietnam Veteran, 1967–1990." *Journal of American Culture* 16, no. 1 (Spring 1993): 7–24.

Kazin, Michael. *The Populist Persuasion: An American History*. New York: Basic Books, 1995.

Keating, Edward. *Free Huey*. San Francisco: Ramparts Press, 1971.

Keefer, Edward, ed. *Foreign Relations of the United States, 1969–1976*. Vol. 6, *Vietnam, January 1969 to July 1970*. Washington, D.C.: GPO, 2006.

Kendrick, Alexander. *The Wound Within*. Boston: Little Brown, 1974.

Kerry, John, and Vietnam Veterans Against the War. *The New Soldier*. Edited by David Thorne. New York: Macmillan, 1971.

Kiernan, Ben. *How Pol Pot Came to Power*. New York: Columbia University Press, 1985.

———. *The Pol Pot Regime: Race, Power, and Genocide Under the Khmer Rouge, 1975–1979*. New Haven: Yale University Press, 1996.

Kiljunen, Kimmo, ed. *Kampuchea: Decade of the Genocide*. London: Zed Press, 1984.

Kimball, Jeffrey. *Nixon's War*. Lawrence: University of Kansas Press, 1999.

———. "The Stab-in-the-Back Legend and the Vietnam War." *Armed Forces and Society* 14, no. 3 (Spring 1988): 433–58.

Kinder, Douglas Clark. "Bureaucratic Cold Warrior: Harry J. Anslinger and Illicit Narcotics Traffic." *Pacific Historical Review* 50, no. 2 (May 1981): 169–91.

Kinder, Douglas Clark, and William O. Walker III. "Stable Force in a Storm: Harry J. Anslinger and United States Foreign Narcotics Policy, 1930–1962." *Journal of American History* 72, no. 4 (March 1986): 908–27.

Kinder, Marsha. "The Power of Adaptation in *Apocalypse Now*." *Film Quarterly* 33, no. 2 (Winter 1979–1980): 12–20.

Kirk, Robin. *More Terrible than Death: Massacres, Drugs, and America's War in Colombia.* New York: Public Affairs, 2003.

Kitfield, James. *Prodigal Soldiers: How the Generation of Officers Born in Vietnam Revolutionized the American Style of War.* New York: Simon & Schuster, 1995.

Klare, Michael T. *Beyond the Vietnam Syndrome: U.S. Interventionism in the 1980s.* Washington, D.C.: International Policy Institute, 1981.

Klare, Michael T., and Cynthia Aronson. *Supplying Repression: U.S. Support for Authoritarian Regimes Abroad.* Washington, D.C.: Institute for Policy Studies, 1981.

Klein, Christina. *Cold War Orientalism: Asia in the Middlebrow Imagination, 1945–1961.* Berkeley: University of California Press, 2003.

Kline, David. "How to Lose the Coke War." *Atlantic Monthly*, May 1987, 22–27.

Knock, Thomas J. "Come Home America: The Story of George S. McGovern." In *Vietnam and the American Political Tradition: The Politics of Dissent*, edited by Randall B. Woods, 81–121. New York: Cambridge University Press, 2003.

Kolb, Lawrence. *Drug Addiction: A Medical Problem.* Springfield, Ill.: C. C. Thomas, 1962.

Kolhatkar, Sonail, and James Ingalls. *Bleeding Afghanistan: Washington, Warlords, and the Propaganda of Silence.* New York: Seven Stories Press, 2006.

Kolko, Gabriel. *Anatomy of a War: Vietnam, the United States, and the Modern Historical Experience.* New York: Pantheon, 1985.

Kolko, Gabriel, Richard A. Falk, and Robert J. Lifton, eds. *Crimes of War: A Legal, Political-Documentary, and Psychological Inquiry into the Responsibility of Leaders, Citizens, and Soldiers for Criminal Acts in Wars.* New York: Harper & Row, 1971.

Kornbluh, Peter, and Michael T. Klare, eds. *Low-Intensity Warfare: Counterinsurgency, Pro-Insurgency, and Antiterrorism in the Eighties.* New York: Pantheon, 1988.

Kranz, Rachel. "*Apocalypse Now* and *The Deer Hunter*: The Lies Aren't Over." *Jump Cut* 23 (October 1980): 18–20.

Krogh, Egil, Jr. "Heroin Politics and Policy under President Nixon." In Musto, *One Hundred Years of Heroin*, 39–43.

Kruger, Henrik. *The Great Heroin Coup: Drugs, Intelligence, and International Fascism.* Boston: South End Press, 1980.

Kunnes, Richard. *The American Heroin Empire: Power, Profits, Politics.* New York: Dodd & Mead, 1972.

Kwitny, Jonathan. *The Crimes of Patriots: A True Tale of Dope, Dirty Money, and the CIA.* New York: W. W. Norton, 1987.

Laing, Ronald D. *The Politics of Experience and the Birds of Paradise.* London: Penguin, 1967.

Laing, Ronald D., and Aaron Esterson. *Sanity, Madness and the Family*. London: Penguin, 1967.

Lansdale, Edward G. *In the Midst of Wars: An American's Mission to Southeast Asia*. New York: Harper & Row, 1972.

Lasch, Christopher. *The Culture of Narcissism: American Life in an Age of Diminishing Expectations*. New York: Warner Books, 1979.

Latham, Michael E. *Modernization as Ideology: American Social Science and "Nation Building" in the Kennedy Era*. Chapel Hill: University of North Carolina Press, 2000.

Leary, Timothy F. *Flashbacks: A Personal and Cultural History of an Era: An Autobiography*. New York: Putnam, 1990.

———. "The Politics, Ethics, and Meaning of Marijuana." In *The Marihuana Papers*, edited by David Solomon. New York: New American Library, 1966.

———. *The Politics of Ecstasy*. Berkeley, Calif.: Ronin Publishing, 1968.

———. *Tune In, Turn On, and Drop Out*. Berkeley, Calif.: Ronin Publishing, 1965.

Leary, Timothy, George H. Litwin, and Ralph Metzner. "Reactions to Psilocybin Administered in a Supportive Environment." *Journal of Nervous and Mental Diseases* 137, no. 6 (December 1963): 561–73.

Leary, William M. *Perilous Missions: Civil Air Transport and CIA Covert Operations in Asia*. Birmingham: University of Alabama Press, 1984.

Lebedur, Kathryn. "Bolivia: Clear Consequences." In Youngers and Rosin, *Drugs and Democracy in Latin America*, 143–85.

Lederer, William J. *The Anguished American*. London: Victor Gallanz, 1968.

Lee, Martin A., and Bruce Shlain. *Acid Dreams: The CIA, LSD, and the Sixties Rebellion*. New York: Grove Press, 1985.

Lee, Rensselaer W., III. "The Cocaine Dilemma in South America." In Mabry, *The Latin American Narcotics Trade*, 59–75.

———. "Perversely Harmful Effects of Counter-Narcotics Policy in the Andes." Chapter 10 of *The Political Economy of the Drug Industry: Latin America and the International System*, edited by Menno Villenga. Gainesville: University Press of Florida, 2004.

———. *The White Labyrinth: Cocaine and Political Power*. Bruinswick, N.J.: Transaction, 1989.

Lehman, Peter. "Well, What's It Like Over There? Looking for Vietnam in *The Deer Hunter*." *North Dakota Quarterly* 51, no. 3 (Summer 1983): 137.

Lembcke, Jerry. *CNN's Tailwind Tale: Inside Vietnam's Last Great Myth*. Lanham, Md.: Rowman & Littlefield, 2003.

———. *The Spitting Image: Myth, Memory, and the Legacy of Vietnam*. New York: New York University Press, 1998.

Lernoux, Penny. *Cry of the People*. New York: Doubleday, 1980.

Lethal Weapon. Directed by Richard Donner. Warner Brothers, 1987.

Levin, G. Roy. "Francis Coppola Discusses *Apocalypse Now*." *Millimeter* 7 (October 1979): 136–39.

Levine, Stanley, and Edward T. Grimes. "Pulmonary Edema and Heroin Overdose in Vietnam." *Archives of Pathology* 95, no. 5 (May 1973): 330–32.

Lewis, Flora. "Heroin and the CIA." Review of The Politics of Heroin in Southeast Asia, by Alfred W. McCoy. *Atlantic Monthly*, November 1972.

Lewis, Gordon K. *Grenada: The Jewel Despoiled*. Baltimore: Johns Hopkins University Press, 1994.

Lewis, Paul H. *Paraguay Under Stroessner*. Chapel Hill: University of North Carolina Press, 1980.

Lewy, Guenter. *America in Vietnam*. New York: Oxford University Press, 1979.

Lieven, Anatol. *America Right or Wrong: An Anatomy of American Nationalism*. New York: Oxford University Press, 2004.

Lifschultz, Lawrence. "Pakistan: The Empire of Heroin." In McCoy and Block, *War on Drugs*, 309–52.

Lifton, Robert Jay. *Death in Life: Survivors of Hiroshima*. New York: Random House, 1968.

———. "The 'Gook Syndrome' and Numbed Warfare." *Saturday Review*, November 18, 1972, 66–72.

———. *Home From the War: Vietnam Veterans: Neither Victims nor Executioners*. Boston: Beacon Press, 1973.

Lind, Michael. *Vietnam: The Necessary War*. New York: Free Press, 1999.

Linden, Eugene. "The Demoralization of an Army: Fragging and Other Withdrawal Symptoms." *Saturday Review*, January 8, 1972, 12–17, 55.

Lindesmith, Alfred R. *The Addict and the Law*. New York: Vintage Books, 1965.

———. "'Dope Fiend' Mythology." *Journal of Criminal Law & Criminology* 31, no. 2 (July–August 1940): 199–208.

———. *Opiate Addiction*. Bloomington, Ind.: Principia Press, 1947.

Lintner, Bertil. *Burma in Revolt: Opium and Insurgency since 1948*. Bangkok: White Lotus, 1994.

———. "The Golden Triangle Opium Trade: An Overview." *Asia-Pacific Media Services*, www.asiapacficms.com.

———. "Heroin and Highland Insurgency in the Golden Triangle." In McCoy and Block, *War on Drugs*, 281–319.

———. *Land of Jade: A Journey Through Insurgent Burma*. Edinburgh: Kincade Publishing, 1990.

"Liquor, Drugs—The GI's Biggest Foe." *U.S. News & World Report*, September 28, 1981, 7.

Lobe, Thomas. J. *U.S. National Security and Aid to the Thailand Police*. Denver: University of Denver Graduate School of International Studies 1977.

Louria, Donald B. *The Drug Scene*. New York: McGraw-Hill, 1968.

———. *Nightmare Drugs*. New York: Pocket Books, 1966.

Luce, Don, and Holmes Brown. *Hostages of War: Saigon's Political Prisoners*. Washington, D.C.: Indochina Mobile Education Project, 1973.

Lusane, Clarence. *Pipe Dream Blues: Racism and the War on Drugs*. Boston: South End Press, 1991.

Lyfoung, Touby. *An Authentic Account of the Life of a Hmong Man in the Troubled Land of Laos*. Minneapolis: Burgess Publishing, 1966.

Mabry, Donald, ed. *The Latin American Narcotics Trade and U.S. National Security*. New York: Greenwood Press, 1989.

Mabry, Donald. "The U.S. Military and the War on Drugs in Latin America." *Journal of Inter-American Studies and World Affairs* 30, no. 2 (Summer–Fall 1988): 53–76.

Maclear, Michael. *The Ten Thousand Day War: Vietnam, 1945–1975*. New York: Avon Books, 1981.

Magnum P. I. "All for One 1 & 2." January 31, 1985; February 7, 1985. NBC Television.

Malloy, Michael. "Harvest Home." *Far Eastern Economic Review*, July 24, 1971, 38–39.

Mamdani, Mahmood. "The Cold War after Indochina." In *Good Muslim, Bad Muslim: America, the Cold War, and the Roots of Terror*, 63–118. New York: Random House, 2004.

Mann, Peggy. *Marijuana Alert*. New York: McGraw-Hill, 1985.

Mannatt, Marsha. *Parents, Peers, and Pot*. Rev. ed. Rockland, Md: U.S. Department of Health Services, 1987.

Marcovitz, Eli, and Henry J. Myers. "The Marihuana Addict in the Army." *War Medicine* 6 (December 1944): 382–91.

Marcus, Greil. "Journey Up the River." *Rolling Stone*, November 1979, 51–57.

Marcuse, Herbert. *Eros and Civilization: A Philosophical Inquiry into Freud*. Rev. ed. Boston: Beacon Press, 1966.

"Marijuana—The Other Enemy in Vietnam." *U.S. News & World Report*, January 26, 1970, 68–69.

Marshall, Jonathan. "CIA Assets and the Rise of the Guadalajara Connection." In McCoy and Block, *War on Drugs*, 201–5.

——. *Drug Wars: Corruption, Counter-Insurgency, and Covert Operations in the Third World*. San Francisco: Cohan & Cohan, 1991.

——. "Opium and the Politics of Gangsterism in Nationalist China." *Bulletin of Concerned Asian Scholars* 8 (July–September 1976): 19–48.

——. "The White House Death Squad." *Inquiry*, March 5, 1979, 15–21.

Marshall, Jonathan, and Peter Dale Scott. *Cocaine Politics: Drugs, Armies, and the CIA in Central America*. Berkeley: University of California Press, 1991.

Martin, Brian G. *The Shanghai Green Gang: Politics and Organized Crime, 1919–1937*. Berkeley: University of California Press, 1996.

Martini, Edwin A. *Invisible Enemies: The American War on Vietnam, 1975–2000*. Amherst: University of Massachusetts Press, 2007.

Marx, Karl. "The Opium Trade." In *On Colonialism*, by Karl Marx and Frederich Engels, 219–20. New York: International Publishers, 1972.

"Mary Jane in Action." *Newsweek*, November 6, 1967, 40.

M*A*S*H. Directed by Robert Altman. 20th Century Fox, 1970.

Mason, Robert. *Richard Nixon and the Quest for a New Majority*. Chapel Hill: University of North Carolina Press, 2004.

Massing, Michael. *The Fix*. Berkeley: University of California Press, 1998.

Matusow, Allen J. *The Unraveling of America: A History of Liberalism in the 1960s*. New York: Harper & Row, 1984.

McClintock, Cynthia. "The War on Drugs: The Peruvian Case." *Journal of Inter-American Studies and World Affairs* 30, no. 2/3 (Summer–Fall 1988): 127–42.

McClintock, Michael. *Instruments of Statecraft: U.S. Guerrilla Warfare, Counter-Insurgency, and Counter-Terrorism, 1940–1990.* New York: Pantheon, 1992.

McCombs, Maxwell, and Donald Shaw. "The Agenda-Setting Function of the Mass Media." *Public Opinion Quarterly* 36, no. 2 (January 1972): 176–87.

McCoy, Alfred W. "Subcontracting Counter-Insurgency: Academics in Thailand, 1954–1970." *Bulletin of Concerned Asian Scholars,* February 1971, 56–70.

McCoy, Alfred W. "America's Secret War in Laos, 1955–1975." In Young and Buzzanco, *Companion to the Vietnam War,* 283–315.

———. "The Author Responds." *Harper's Magazine,* October 1972, 118–20.

———. *Drug Traffic: Narcotics and Organized Crime in Australia.* Sydney: Harper & Row, 1980.

———. "Flowers of Evil: The CIA and the Heroin Trade." *Harper's Magazine,* July 1972, 47–53.

———. "Heroin as a Global Commodity: A History of South East Asia's Opium Trade." In McCoy and Block, *War on Drugs,* 237–81.

———. *The Politics of Heroin in Southeast Asia.* With Cathleen B. Read and Leonard Adams. New York: Harper & Row, 1972.

———. *A Question of Torture: CIA Interrogation from the Cold War to the War on Terror.* New York: Metropolitan Books, 2006.

McCoy, Alfred W., and Nina S. Adams. *Laos: War and Revolution.* New York: Harper & Row, 1970.

McCoy, Alfred W., and Alan A. Block, eds. *War on Drugs: Studies in the Failure of U.S. Narcotics Policy.* Boulder, Colo.: Westview Press, 1992.

McGovern, George. "Toward an End to Drug Abuse." *Journal of Drug Issues* 2, no. 2 (Spring 1972): 1–4.

McInerney, Peter "Apocalypse Then: Hollywood Looks at Vietnam." *Film Quarterly* 33, no. 2 (Winter 1979–1980): 21–32.

McMahon, Robert J. "Contested Memory: The Vietnam War and American Society, 1975–2001." SHAFR Presidential Address. *Diplomatic History* 26, no. 2 (Fall 2002): 159–84.

———. *The Limits of Empire: The U.S. and Southeast Asia Since World War II.* New York: Columbia University Press, 1999.

McPherson, Myra. *Long Time Passing: Vietnam and the Haunted Generation.* New York: Doubleday, 1984.

McSherry, J. Patrice. *Predatory States: Operation Condor and Covert War in Latin America.* New York: Rowman & Littlefield, 2004.

McWilliams, John C. *The Protectors: Harry J. Anslinger and the Federal Bureau of Narcotics.* Newark: University of Delaware Press, 1990.

———. "Through the Past Darkly: The Politics and Policies of America's Drug Wars." In *Drug Control Policy: Essays in Historical and Comparative Perspective,* edited by William O. Walker III, 5–42. University Park: Pennsylvania State University Press, 1992.

Menzell, Sewall. *Fire in the Andes: U.S. Foreign Policy and Cocaine Politics in Bolivia and Peru.* New York: University Press of America, 1996.

Merry, Robert W. "Stewart and Vietnam: Like a Tethered Goat at a Tiger Shoot." *Taking on the World: Joseph and Stewart Alsop—Guardians of the American Century,* 437–45. New York: Viking, 1996.

Mirken, Bruce. "Marijuana and the Media: Science, Propaganda, and Sloppy Reporting in the U.S. Media." In *Pot Politics: Marijuana and the Costs of Prohibition,* edited by Mitch Earlywine, 141–59. New York: Oxford University Press.

Meyer, Roger E. *Guide to Drug Rehabilitation: A Public Health Approach.* Boston: Beacon Press, 1972.

Meyrowitz, Elliott L., and Kenneth J. Campbell. "Vietnam Veterans and War Crimes Hearings." In *Give Peace a Chance: Exploring the Vietnam Antiwar Movement,* edited by Melvin Small and William D. Hoover, 129–40. New York: Syracuse University Press, 1992.

Michael, Laurie Beth. "An Investigation of the Substance Abuse Behavior of Men of the Vietnam Generation." PhD diss., Columbia University, 1980.

Miller, Daniel. "Primetime Television's Tour of Duty." In Anderegg, *Inventing Vietnam,* 166–90.

Mills, James. *Underground Empire: Where Crime and Governments Embrace.* New York: Dell, 1986.

Mirin, S. M., and G. J. McKenna. "Combat Zone Adjustment: The Role of Marihuana Use." *Military Medicine* 140 (January 1975): 482–85.

Missing in Action I, II. Directed by Joseph Zito. Cannon, 1984, 1985.

Morley, Jefferson. "Aftermath of a Crack Article." *Nation,* November 20, 1989, 592.

———. "What Crack Is Really Like." *New Republic,* October 2, 1989, 12–13.

Morris, Roger. *Uncertain Greatness: Henry Kissinger and Foreign Policy.* New York: Harper & Row, 1977.

Moser, Richard. *The New Winter Soldiers: GI and Veteran Dissent during the Vietnam Era.*New Brunswick, N.J.: Rutgers University Press, 1996.

Moskos, Charles. *The American Enlisted Man: The Rank and File in Today's Military.* New York: Russell Sage, 1970.

Moyar, Mark. *Triumph Forsaken: The Vietnam War, 1954–1963.* New York: Cambridge University Press, 2006.

———. *Phoenix and the Birds of Prey.* Annapolis: Naval Institute Press, 1997.

Mullin, Christopher. "The Secret Bombing of Laos: The Story Behind Nine Years of U.S. Attacks." *Asia Magazine,* May 12, 1974, 3–8.

Murray, Charles. *Losing Ground: American Social Policy, 1950–1980.* New York: Basic Books, 1984.

Musto, David F. *The American Disease: The Origins of Narcotics Control.* New Haven: Yale University Press, 1973.

———, ed. *One Hundred Years of Heroin.* Westport, Conn.: Greenwood, 2002.

Musto, David F., and Pamela Korsmeyer. *The Quest for Drug Control: Politics and Federal Policy in a Period of Increasing Substance Abuse.* New Haven: Yale University Press, 2002.

Nadelmann, Ethan A. *Cops Across Borders: The Internationalization of U.S. Criminal Law Enforcement.* University Park: Pennsylvania State University Press, 1993.

———. "Drug Prohibition in the United States: Costs, Consequences and Alternatives." In Reinarman and Levine, *Crack in America.*

———. "U.S. Drug Policy—A Bad Export." *Foreign Policy* 70 (Spring 1988): 83–108.

Nahas, Gabriel. *Cocaine: The Great White Plague.* Middlebury, Vt: Paul S. Eriksson, 1975.

———. *Marihuana—Deceptive Weed.* 2nd ed. New York: Raven Press, 1975.

Nashel, Jonathan. *Edward Lansdale's Cold War.* Amherst: University of Massachusetts Press, 2005.

National Commission on Marihuana and Drug Abuse. *Drug Use in America: Problem in Perspective. 4 vols. Washington, D.C.: GPO, 1973.*

———. *Marihuana: A Signal of Misunderstanding.* Report Commissioned by President Richard M. Nixon, March 1972. Washington, D.C.: GPO, 1972.

National Institute on Drug Abuse. *National Household Survey on Drug Abuse, 1988.* Washington, D.C.: GPO, 1988.

Neilands, J. B., et al. *Harvest of Death: Chemical Warfare in Vietnam and Cambodia.* New York: Macmillan, 1972.

"A New GI for Pot." *Newsweek,* February 2, 1970, 24.

"The New Public Enemy No. 1." *Time,* June 28, 1971, 20.

Newsday, by the staff and editors. *The Heroin Trail: The Ugly Odyssey From Blossom To Bloodstream.* New York: Holt, Rinehart & Winston, 1973.

"NFL Stars Line Up Against Drug Abuse." *Drug Enforcement Administration Magazine,* September 1973, 8.

Ngo Vinh Long. "The War and the Vietnamese." In *Vietnam Reconsidered: Lessons From a War,* edited by Harrison Salisbury. New York: Harper & Row, 1984.

Ngu Khac Vien. "Apocalypse Now Viewed by a Vietnamese." In *The Vietnam Era: Media and Popular Culture in the United States and Vietnam,* edited by Michael Klein. London: Pluto Press, 1990.

Nicosia, Gerald. *Home to War: A History of the Vietnam Veterans Movement.* New York: Avalon, 2001.

Nield, Rachel. "U.S. Police Assistance and Drug Control Policy." In Youngers and Rosin, *Drugs and Democracy in Latin America,* 61–99.

Nixon, Richard M. "Message before Congress." July 14, 1969. *Public Papers of the Presidents of the United States: Richard Nixon, 1969–1974.* Vol. 1. Washington, D.C.: GPO, 1969.

———. "Message to the Congress Transmitting Reorganization Plan 2 of 1973 establishing the Drug Enforcement Administration." March 28, 1973. *Public Papers of the Presidents of the United States: Richard Nixon, 1969–1974,* vol. 1, 228–33. Washington, D.C.: GPO, 1973.

———. *No More Vietnams.* New York: Arbor House, 1985.

———. *The Real War.* New York: Warner Books, 1980.

———. "Remarks to Athletes Attending White House Sponsored Conference on Drug Abuse." February 3, 1973. *Public Papers of the Presidents of the United States: Richard Nixon, 1969–1974. Vol.1.* Washington, D.C.: GPO, 1973.

———. "Special Message to the Congress on Drug Abuse Prevention and Control." June 17 1971. *Public Papers of the Presidents of the United States: Richard Nixon, 1969–1974.* Vol.1. Washington, D.C.: GPO, 1972.

———. "What Has Happened to America?" *Reader's Digest*, October 1967, 50.

Nurco, David N., Thomas E. Hanlon, and Timothy Kinlock. "Heroin Use in the United States: History and Present Developments." In *Heroin in the Age of Crack Cocaine*, edited by James A. Inciardi and Lana D. Harrison, 1–31. London: Sage, 1998.

Nyswander, Marie. *The Drug Addict as a Patient.* New York: Grune & Stratton, 1956.

O'Donnell, John A. *Narcotic Addicts in Kentucky.* Washington, D.C.: Department of Health, Education and Welfare, 1969.

O'Donnell, J. A., H. L. Voss, R. R. Clayton, G. L. Slatin, and R. G. W. Room. *Young Men and Drugs—A Nationwide Survey.* Washington, D.C: National Institute on Drug Abuse, 1976.

Olson, James S., and Randy Roberts. *Where the Domino Fell: America and Vietnam, 1945–1990.* New York: St. Martin's, 1990.

Only the Beginning, documentary. Director unknown. Washington, D.C., Vietnam: Newsreel (April 1971).

Owen, Taylor, and Ben Kiernan. "Bombs Over Cambodia: New Light on US Air War." *Japan Focus*, May 12, 2007. Also available online at www.japanfocus.org/products/details/2420.

Packenham, Robert A. *Liberal America and the Third World: Political Development Ideas in Foreign Aid.* Princeton: Princeton University Press, 1973.

Pach, Chester, Jr. "The War on Television: TV News, the Johnson Administration, and Vietnam." In Young and Buzzanco, *Companion to the Vietnam War*, 470–91.

Parenti, Christian. *Lockdown America: Police and Prisons in an Age of Crisis.* London: Verso, 1999.

Pease, Donald. "Hiroshima, the Vietnam Veterans War Memorial and the Gulf War: Post-National Spectacles." In *Cultures of United States Imperialism*, edited by Amy Kaplan and Donald Pease, 557–81. Durham, N.C.: Duke University Press, 1994.

Peele, Stanton. *Diseasing of America: Addiction Treatment Out of Control.* Lanham, Md.: Lexington Books, 1989.

Peers, William R., and Dean Brelis. *Behind the Burma Road.* London: Robert Hale, 1964.

Perl, Raphael. "International Narco-policy and the Role of the U.S. Congress." In Mabry, *The Latin American Narcotics Trade*, 89–105.

Perlstein, Rick. *Nixonland: The Rise of a President and the Fracturing of America.* New York: Scribner, 2008.

Petras, James, and Morris Morley. "The Geo-Politics of Plan Colombia." In *Masters of War: U.S. Militarism and Blowback in the Age of Empire*, edited by Carl Boggs, 83–111. New York: Public Affairs, 2004.

Phillips, Kevin P. *The Politics of Rich and Poor: Wealth and the American Electorate in the Reagan Aftermath*. New York: HarperCollins, 1991.

Pike, Andrew, and Eric Goldstein. "History of Drug Use in the Military." In National Commission on Marihuana and Drug Abuse, *Drug Use in America*, 1: 1115–35.

"Playboy Panel—The Drug Revolution." *Playboy Magazine*, February 1970, 53.

"Playboy Interview—Oliver Stone." *Playboy Magazine*, February 1988, 51.

Platoon. Directed by Oliver Stone. Hemdale, 1986.

Podhoretz, Norman. *Why We Were in Vietnam*. New York: Simon & Schuster, 1982.

Polner, Murray. *No Victory Parades: The Return of the Vietnam Veteran*. New York: Holt, 1971.

"Posse Comitatus." *Drug Enforcement Administration Magazine*, Summer 1982, 17.

Postel, Wilfred B. "Marijuana Use in Vietnam: A Preliminary Report." *USARV Medical Bulletin*, September–October 1968, 56–59.

Powell, Stewart. "The Healing Nation." *U.S. News & World Report*, April 15, 1985, 35–37.

Powers, Thomas. "Review of *Dog Soldiers*." *Commonwealth*, January 1974, 101, 241.

Prados, John. *The Hidden History of the Vietnam War*. Chicago: Ivan R. Dee, 1995.

———. *Lost Crusader: The Secret Wars of CIA Director William Colby*. New York: Oxford University Press, 2003.

———. *Safe for Democracy: The Secret Wars of the CIA*. Chicago: Ivan R. Dee, 2006.

Prashad, Vijay. *The Darker Nations: A People's History of the Third World*. New York: New Press, 2007.

Preble, Edward J., and John J. Casey, Jr. "Taking Care of Business: The Heroin Users' Life on the Streets." *International Journal of the Addictions* 4, no. 1 (March 1969): 1–24.

Race, Jeffrey. *War Comes to Long An: Revolutionary Conflict in a Vietnamese Province*. Berkeley: University of California Press, 1972.

Rae, William R., Stephen B. Forman, and Howard G. Olson. *Future Impact of Dissident Elements within the Army on the Enforcement of Discipline, Law, and Order*. McLean, Va.: Research Analysis Corporation, 1972.

Rambo: First Blood, Part II. Directed by George Cosmatos. Tri-Star, 1985.

Ratner, Richard A. "Drugs and Despair in Vietnam." *University of Chicago Magazine*, January 1972, 15–23.

Reagan, Ronald. "Address to the Nation on the Campaign against Drug Abuse." September 14, 1986. *Public Papers of the President of the United States: Ronald Reagan, 1981–1989*. Vol. 2. Washington, D.C.: GPO, 1986.

———. "Radio Address to the Nation on Law Enforcement and Crime." July 7, 1984. *Public Papers of the President of the United States: Ronald Reagan, 1981–1989*. Vol. 2. Washington, D.C.: GPO, 1984.

———. "Remarks on Signing the Just Say No to Drugs Week Proclamation." May 20, 1986. *Public Papers of the President of the United States: Ronald Reagan, 1981–1989*. Vol. 1. Washington, D.C.: GPO, 1986.

———. "Remarks on Substance Abuse in the Workplace." Durham, North Carolina, February 8, 1988. *Public Papers of the President of the United States: Ronald Reagan, 1981–1989*. Vol. 1. Washington D.C.: GPO, 1988.

Reagan, Ronald, and Nancy Reagan. "Radio Address to the Nation on Drug Abuse and Aid to Nicaragua." February 6, 1988. *Public Papers of the President of the United States: Ronald Reagan, 1981–1989*. Vol. 2. Washington, D.C.: GPO, 1988.

Regus, Nicholas. *The Drug Addiction Business: A Denunciation of the Dehumanizing Politics and Practices of the So-Called Experts*. New York: Dial Press, 1971.

Reinarman, Craig, and Harry G. Levine, eds. *Crack in America: Demon Drugs and Social Justice*. Berkeley: University of California Press, 1997.

Renard, Ronald. *The Burmese Connection: Illegal Drugs and the Making of the Golden Triangle*. Boulder, Colo.: Lynne Riener, 1996.

———. *Opium Reduction in Thailand, 1970–2000: A 30-Year Journey*. Bangkok: Silkworm Books, 2001.

Rinaldi, Matthew. "Olive Drab Rebels: Military Organizing during the Vietnam Era." *Radical America* 8, no. 3 (May–June 1974): 17–52.

Robbins, Tom. *Air America: The Story of the CIA's Airlines*. New York: Putnam, 1979.

Robin, Ron. *The Making of the Cold War Enemy: Culture and Politics in the Military-Intellectual Complex*. Princeton: Princeton University Press, 2001.

Robins, Lee N. "The Interaction of Setting and Predisposition in Explanatory Novel Behavior: Drug Initiations Before, In, and After Vietnam." In *Longitudinal Research on Drug Use*, edited by Denise Kandel, 179–96. Washington, D.C.: Hemisphere, 1978.

———. *The Vietnam Drug User Returns*. Special Action Office Monograph, series A, no 2. Washington, D.C.: GPO, 1974.

Robins, Lee N., John Helzer, and Darlene H. Davis. "Narcotic Use in Southeast Asia and Afterward: An Interview of 898 Vietnam Returnees." *Archives of General Psychiatry* 32, no. 8 (August 1975): 955–61.

Robins, Lee N., John Helzer, Michi Hesselbrock and Eric Wish. "Vietnam Veterans Three Years after Vietnam: How Our Study Changed Our Views of Heroin." In *The Yearbook of Substance Use and Abuse*, edited by Leon Brill and Charles Winick, 213–30. New York: Human Science Press, 1980.

Roffman, Roger A. "Survey of Marijuana Use: Prisoners Confined in the USARV Installation Stockade as of July 1, 1967." In Pike and Goldstein, "History of Drug Use in the Military," 1118.

Roffman, Roger A., and Ely Sapol. "Marijuana in Vietnam: A Survey of Use among Army Enlisted Men in the Two Southern Corps." *International Journal of the Addictions* 5, no. 1 (March 1970): 1–42.

———. "Marijuana in Vietnam: A Survey of Use among Army Enlisted Men in the Two Southern Corps." *Journal of the American Pharmaceutical Association* 9, no. 12 (December 1969): 615–30.

Roginski, Ed. "Who'll Stop the Rain." Film Quarterly 32, no. 2 (Winter 1978–79): 57–61.

Rojas, Isaías. "Peru: Drug Control Policy, Human Rights and Democracy" In Youngers and Rosin, Drugs and Democracy in Latin America, 185–231.

Rose, Kenneth D. Myths and the Greatest Generation: A Social History of Americans in World War II. New York: Routledge, 2008.

Rosenberg, Mark. "Narcos and Politicos: The Politics of Drug Trafficking in Honduras." Journal of Inter-American Studies and World Affairs 30, nos. 2–3 (Summer–Fall 1988): 143–65.

Rosenblatt, Elihu, ed. Criminal Injustice: Confronting the Prison Crisis. Boston: South End Press, 1996.

Roszak, Theodore. The Dissenting Academy. New York: Pantheon, 1967.

———. The Making of a Counter Culture: Reflections on the Technocratic Society and Its Youthful Opposition. New York: Doubleday, 1969.

Roth, Jeffrey A. "Psychoactive Substances and Violence." U.S. Department of Justice, 1994. Available online at www.druglibrary.org.

Rubin, Barnett. The Fragmentation of Afghanistan: State Formation and Collapse in the International System. 2nd ed. New Haven: Yale University Press, 2002.

Rublowsky, John. The Stoned Age: A History of Drugs in America. New York: Putnam 1974.

Russo, Anthony J. A Statistical Analysis of the U.S. Crop Spraying Program in South Vietnam. Santa Monica, Calif.: RAND Corporation, 1967.

Ruybal, Jay Dee. Culture and Imperialism. New York: Pantheon, 1993.

———. The Drug Hazed War in Southeast Asia. Albuquerque, N.M.: Creative Designs, 1998.

Said, Edward W. Orientalism. New York: Vintage, 1979.

———. Culture and Imperialism. New York: Pantheon, 1993.

Saletan, William. "Jar Wars: From Kissing Babies to Pissing in Bottles." New Republic, October 2, 1989, 13–14.

Sanders, Clinton R. "Doper's Wonderland: Functional Drug Use by Military Personnel in Vietnam." Journal of Drug Issues 3, no. 1 (Winter 1973): 65–78.

Schaller, Michael. The U.S. Crusade in China, 1938–1945. New York: Columbia University Press, 1979.

Schanche, Don A. Mister Pop. New York: McKay, 1970.

Schell, Jonathan. The Village of Ben Suc. New York: Harper, 1967.

Schoultz, Lars. Beneath the United States: A History of U.S. Policy toward Latin America. Cambridge Mass.: Harvard University Press, 1998.

———. Human Rights and United States Foreign Policy in Latin America. Princeton: Princeton University Press, 1981.

Schulman, Bruce J. The Seventies: The Great Shift in American Culture, Society and Politics. New York: Free Press, 2001.

Schulzinger, Robert D. A Time for Peace: The Legacy of the Vietnam War. New York: Oxford University Press, 2006.

———. A Time for War: The United States in Vietnam, 1941–1975. New York: Oxford University Press, 1997.

Scott, Peter D. "Air America: Flying the U.S. into Laos." *Ramparts*, February 1970, 39–42, 52–54.

———. *Coming to Jakarta: A Poem about Terror* New York: New Directions, 1989.

———. *Deep Politics and the Death of JFK.* Berkeley: University of California Press, 1993.

———. *Drugs, Oil, and War: The United States in Afghanistan, Colombia, and Indochina.* New York: Rowman & Littlefield, 2004.

———. "Honduras: The Contra Support Networks and Cocaine: How the U.S. Government Has Augmented America's Drug Crisis." In McCoy and Block, *War on Drugs*, 125–77.

———. *The Road to 9/11: Wealth, Empire, and the Future of America.* Berkeley: University of California Press, 2007.

———. *The War Conspiracy.* New York: Bobbs Merrill, 1972.

Scott, Wilbur J. *The Politics of Readjustment: Vietnam Veterans since the War.* New York: Aldine Press, 1993.

Scruggs, Jan, and Joel Swerdlow. *To Heal a Nation: The Vietnam Veterans Memorial.* New York: HarperCollins, 1986.

Selden, Mark. *The Yenan Way in Revolutionary China.* Cambridge, Mass.: Harvard University Press, 1971.

Shad Liang, Chi. *Burma's Foreign Relations: Neutralism in Theory and Practice.* New York: Praeger, 1990.

Shalom, Stephen R. *Imperial Alibis: Rationalizing U.S. Intervention after the Cold War.* Boston: South End Press, 1993.

———. *The United States and the Philippines: A Study of Neo-Colonialism.* Philadelphia: Institute for the Study of Human Issues, 1981.

Shapiro, Herbert. "The Vietnam War and the American Historical Professor." In *Vietnam and the Antiwar Movement: An International Perspective*, edited by John Dumbrell, 7–34 Brookfiled, Vt.: Avebury, 1989.

Shaplen, Robert. *Time Out of Hand.* New York: Harper & Row, 1970.

Shawcross, William. *Sideshow: Kissinger, Nixon, and the Destruction of Cambodia.* New York: Pocket Books, 1979.

Sheehan, Neil. *A Bright Shining Lie: John Paul Vann and America in Vietnam.* New York: Harper, 1986.

Sherrill, Robert. "Justice, Military Style." *Playboy Magazine*, February, 1970, 217–18.

Sherry, Michael. *In the Shadow of War: The United States Since the 1930s.* New Haven: Yale University Press, 1995.

Shrecker, Ellen, ed. *Cold War Triumphalism: The Misuse of History at the End of the Cold War.* New York: Oxford University Press, 2000.

"Shrinking the Drug Specter." *Time*, August 9, 1971, 21.

Siegel, A. J. "The Heroin Crisis among U.S. Forces in Southeast Asia: An Overview." *Journal of the American Medical Association* 223, no. 11 (March 12, 1973): 1258–61.

Silberman, Charles E. *Criminal Violence, Criminal Justice.* New York: Random House, 1978.

Siler, J. F. "Marijuana Smoking in Panama." *Military Surgeon* 73 (November 1933): 269–80.

Simmons, Geoff. *Colombia: A Brutal History.* London: Saqi, 2004.

Simon, Samuel A. "GI Addicts: The Catch in Amnesty. *The Nation,* October 4, 1971.

Sir! No Sir! The Suppressed Story of the GI Movement to End the War in Vietnam. Directed by David Geiger. Displaced Films, 2006.

Slack, Edward R. *Opium, State, and Society: China's Narco-Economy and the Guomindang, 1924–1937.* Honolulu: University of Hawai'i Press, 2001.

Slotkin, Richard. *Gunfighter Nation: The Myth of the Frontier in Twentieth-Century America.* New York: Atheneum, 1992.

Small, Melvin. *Johnson, Nixon, and the Doves.* New Brunswick, N.J.: Rutgers University Press, 1988.

Smith, Christian. *Resisting Reagan: The U.S. Central American Peace Movement.* Chicago: University of Chicago Press, 1999.

Smith, Claude J., Jr. "Clean Boys in Bright Uniforms: The Rehabilitation of the U.S. Military in Films Since 1978." *Journal of Popular Film and Television* 11, no. 4 (Winter 1984): 144–51.

Smith, David E. "Lysergic Acid Diethylamide: An Historical Perspective." *Journal of Psychedelic Drugs* 1 (January 1967): 1–7.

Smith, Julian. *Looking Away: Hollywood and Vietnam.* New York, Scribner & Sons, 1975.

Smith, Richard M. "The Plague Among Us." *Newsweek,* June 16, 1986, 16.

Smuckler, Ralph H., and Members of the Police Team. *Report on the Police of Vietnam.* East Lansing: Michigan State University, Vietnam Technical Assistance Project, 1955.

Snepp, Frank. *Decent Interval.* New York: Random House, 1977.

Sobel, Richard. "The Polls—A Report: Public Opinion about U.S. Intervention in El Salvador and Nicaragua." *Public Opinion Quarterly* 53, no. 1 (Spring 1989): 114–28.

Solis, Gary. *Marines and Military Law in Vietnam: Trial by Fire.* Washington, D.C.: Marine Corps, 1989.

Solomon, Robert. "The Rise and Fall of the Laotian and Vietnamese Opiate Trades." *Journal of Psychedelic Drugs* 11, no. 9 (July–September 1979): 159–71.

Solomon, David, ed. *LSD: The Consciousness-Expanding Drug.* New York: Putnam, 1967.

Some Kind of Hero. Directed by Richard Pryor. Paramount, 1982.

Southern Illinois University Foundation. *Wasted Men: The Reality of the Vietnam Veteran.* Edwardsville: Southern Illinois University, 1972.

"Sparks or Sputters." *Newsweek,* August 21, 1972, 60.

Spedding, Allison. "Coca Use in Bolivia: A Tradition of Thousands of Years." In *Drug Use and Cultural Contexts: Beyond the West,* edited by Ross Coomber and Nigel South, 46–64. London: Free Association Books, 2003.

Spencer, Bob, and Carol Spencer. "Legal Problems: Addiction in the Army." *Civil Liberties,* November 1971, 1–14.

Stanton, Morris D. "Drug Use in Vietnam: A Survey among Army Personnel in Two Northern Corps." *Archives of General Psychiatry* 26, no. 3 (March 1972): 279–86.

———. "Drugs, Vietnam and the Vietnam Veteran: An Overview." *American Journal of Drug and Alcohol Abuse* 3, no. 4 (March 1976): 557–70.

Stanton-Candlin, A. H. *Psycho-Chemical Warfare: The Chinese Drug Offensive against the West*. New Rochelle, N.Y.: Arlington House, 1973.

Stapp, Andy. *Up against the Brass*. New York: Simon & Schuster, 1971.

Starr, Paul. *The Discarded Army: Veterans after Vietnam—The Nader Report on Vietnam Veterans and the Veterans Administration*. New York: Charterhouse, 1975.

Stearn, Jess. *The Seekers: Drugs and the New Generation*. New York: Harper & Row, 1969.

Steinbeck, John, IV. "The Importance of Being Stoned in Vietnam." *Washingtonian Magazine*, January 1968, 33–38.

———. *In Touch*. New York: Alfred A. Knopf, 1969.

Stevens, Jay. *Storming Heaven: LSD and the American Dream*. New York: Atlantic Monthly Press, 1987.

Stevenson, Charles A. *The End of Nowhere: U.S. Policy toward Laos Since 1954*. Boston: Beacon Press, 1972.

Stevenson, Jack. *Highway to Hell: The Myth and Menace of Drugs in American Cinema*. New York: Creation Books, 1999.

Stokes, Douglas. *America's Other War: Terrorizing Colombia*. London: Zed Books, 2005.

Stone, Robert. *Dog Soldiers*. Boston: Houghton Mifflin, 1974.

The Stone Killer. Directed by Michael Winner. Columbia Pictures, 1973.

Strock, Carl. "No News from Laos." *Far Eastern Economic Review*, January 30, 1971, 18.

Stuart-Fox, Martin. *A History of Laos*. New York: Cambridge University Press, 1997.

Studler, Gaylan, and David Desser. "Never Having to Say You're Sorry: *Rambo's* Rewriting of the Vietnam War." *Film Quarterly* 42 (Fall 1988): 9–16.

Sturken, Marita. *Tangled Memories, The Vietnam War, the AIDS Epidemic and the Politics of Remembering*. Berkeley: University of California Press, 1997.

Sutherland, Edwin H. *The Professional Thief*. Chicago: University of Chicago Press, 1937.

———. *White Collar Crime*. New York: Dryden Press, 1949.

Sutter, Alan G. "The World of the Righteous Dope Fiend." *Issues in Criminology* 2 (February 1966): 177–222.

Swiers, George. "Demented Vets and Other Myths: The Moral Obligation of Veterans." In *Vietnam Reconsidered: Lessons From a War*, edited by Harrison Salisbury, 196–202. New York: Harper & Row, 1984.

Szasz, Thomas. *Ceremonial Chemistry: The Ritual Persecution of Drugs, Addicts and Pushers*. New York: Anchor, 1975.

———. "The Ethics of Addiction: An Argument in Favor of Letting Americans Take Any Drug They Want to Take." *Harpers.*, April 1972, 74–79.

————. *The Myth of Mental Illness: Foundations of a Theory of Personal Conduct.* New York: Hoeber and Harper, 1961.

————. "Scapegoating Military Addicts: The Helping Hand Strikes Again." *Transaction* 9 (January 1972): 4–6.

Talbott, John A., and James W. Teague. "Marihuana Psychosis: Acute Toxic Psychosis Associated with the Use of Cannabis Derivatives." *Journal of the American Medical Association* 210, no. 2 (October 1969): 299–302.

Tang, Truong Nhu, David Chanoff, and Doan Van Toi. *A Vietcong Memoir.* New York: Vintage, 1986.

"The Task Forces of Thailand and Laos." *Drug Enforcement Administration Magazine,* September 1973, 17.

Taxi Driver. Directed by Martin Scorsese. Columbia, 1976.

Taylor, Clyde. "The Colonialist Subtext in *Platoon.*" In *From Hanoi to Hollywood: The Vietnam War in American Film,* edited by Linda Dittmar and Gene Michaud. 171–85. Brunswick, N.J.: Rutgers University Press, 1990.

Terry, Wallace. *Bloods.* New York: Harper & Row, 1984.

Thompson, Hunter S. *Fear and Loathing in Las Vegas: A Savage Journey to the Heart of the American Dream.* New York: Warner, 1971.

Thoumi, Francisco E. *Illegal Drugs, Economy, and Society in the Andes.* Washington, D.C.: Woodrow Wilson Center Press, 2003.

————. *Political Economy and Illegal Drugs in Colombia.* Boulder, Colo: Lynne Riener, 1995.

Torgoff, Martin. "Next Stop Is Vietnam." In *Can't Find My Way Home: America in the Great Stoned Age, 1945–2000,* 174–96. New York: Simon & Schuster, 2004.

Toro, Maria Celia. *Mexico's "War" on Drugs: Causes and Consequences.* Boulder, Colo: Lynne Riener, 1995.

Tour of Duty. "Pilot Episode." August 31, 1987; "Saigon 1 & 2." January 3, 10, 1988; "Paradise Lost." March 28, 1988; "Soldiers." February 16, 1988; "Blood Brothers." March 12, 1988; "Nowhere to Run." December 17, 1988. CBS Television.

Tour of Duty. "Bodyguard of Lies." October 28, 1989; "Necessary End." November 4, 1989; "Cloud Nine." November 11, 1989. CBS Television, special edition DVD.

Tracks. Directed by Henry Jaglon. Rainbow, 1976.

Treanor, John J., and James N. Skirpol. "Marijuana in a Tactical Unit in Vietnam." *USARV Medical Bulletin* 24 (Pamphlet 40, 1970): 29–37.

Trebach, Arnold. *The Great Drug War—And Radical Proposals That Could Make America Safe Again.* New York: Macmillan, 1987.

————. *The Heroin Solution: The Story of the World's Most Feared Drug—With a Persuasive Plan for How We Can Live with It Sensibly.* New Haven: Yale University Press, 1982.

Trebach, Arnold, and Kevin B. Zeese, eds. *Drug Prohibition and the Conscience of a Nation.* Washington, D.C.: Drug Policy Foundation, 1990.

Trocki, Carl A. *Opium, Empire and the Global Political Economy: A Study of the Asian Opium Trade, 1750–1950.* London: Routledge, 1999.

"The Troubled U.S. Army in Vietnam." *Newsweek*, January 11, 1971, 29.

Troy, Gil. *Morning in America: Ronald Reagan and the Invention of the 1980s.* Princeton: Princeton University Press, 2005.

Turnbull, James. *Chinese Opium Narcotics—A Threat to the Survival of the West.* Washington, D.C.: The Committee for a Free China, 1972.

Turner, Fred. *Echoes of Combat: The Vietnam War in American Memory.* New York: Anchor, 1996.

Uncommon Valor. Directed by Ted Kotcheff. Paramount, 1983.

U.S. A.I.D., U.S. Economic Assistance to the Royal Lao Government, 1962–1972. *Mission to Laos, December 1972.* Washington, D.C.: GPO, 1972.

U.S. Attorney General. *1972 Annual Report of the Attorney General of the United States.* Washington, D.C.: GPO, 1973.

U.S. Cabinet. Committee on International Narcotics Control. *The World Opium Survey, 1972.* Washington, D.C.: GPO, 1972.

U.S. Congress. House. Committee on Armed Services. *Alleged Drug Abuse in the Armed Services.* Hearings before the Special Subcommittee to Investigate Alleged Drug Abuse in the Armed Services. 91st Cong., 2nd sess., September 22 to December 15, 1970.

———. Committee on Armed Services. *Inquiry into Alleged Drug Abuse in the Armed Services.* Report of the Special Subcommittee to Investigate Alleged Drug Abuse in the Armed Services. 92nd Cong., 1st sess., September through December, 1971.

———. Committee on Foreign Affairs. *Foreign Assistance Act of 1971.* Hearings. 92nd Cong., 1st sess., May 5, 1971.

———. Committee on Foreign Affairs. *The International Narcotics Trade and Its Relation to the United States.* Report of a Special Study Mission. 92nd Cong., 2nd sess., February 1972. H. Doc. Report No. 92-836.

———. Committee on Foreign Affairs. *Political Prisoners in South Vietnam and the Philippines.* Hearings before the Subcommittee on Asian and Pacific Affairs. 93rd Cong., 2nd sess., June 5, 1974.

———. Committee on Foreign Affairs. *The U.S. Heroin Problem in Southeast Asia.* Report of a Staff Survey Team. 92nd Congress, 2nd sess., December 1972.

———. Committee on Foreign Affairs. *U.S. Narcotics Control Programs Overseas: An Assessment.* Report on a Staff Study Mission. 99th Cong., 1st sess., February 22, 1985.

———. Committee on Foreign Affairs. *Vietnam and Korea: Human Rights and U.S. Assistance.* Study Mission Report. Washington, D.C.: GPO, 1975.

———. Committee on Government Operations. *Continued Review of the Administration's Drug Interdiction Efforts.* Hearings before the Subcommittee on Government Information, Justice, and Agriculture. 98th Cong., 2nd sess. March 21–23, June 14, August 1, and September 6, 1984.

———. Committee on Government Operations. *Evaluating the Federal Effort to Control Drug Abuse.* Hearings before a Special Studies Subcommittee. 93rd Cong., 1st sess., 1993.

————. Committee on Government Operations. *Initiatives in Drug Interdiction—Part 1.* Hearings before the Subcommittee on Government Information, Justice, and Agriculture. 99th Cong., 1st sess., March 1985.

————. Committee on Government Operations. *Military Assistance to Civilian Narcotics Law Enforcement.* Hearings. 97th Cong., 2nd sess., February 22, May 19 and 20, and August 18, 1982.

————. Committee on Government Operations. *National Drug Control Strategy.* Hearing before the Legislation and National Security Subcommittee and Joint Hearings. 101st Cong., 1st sess., October, 1989.

————. Committee on International Relations. *Proposal to Control Opium from the Golden Triangle and Terminate the Shan Opium Trade.* Hearings before the Subcommittee on Future Foreign Policy, Research, and Development. 94th Cong., 1st sess., 1975.

————. Committee on Labor and Public Welfare. *Federal Drug Abuse and Drug Dependency Prevention, Treatment and Rehabilitation Act of 1970.* Hearings before the Special Subcommittee on Alcohol and Narcotics. 91st Cong., 2nd sess., April 1970.

————. Select Committee on Crime. *Crime in America—Illicit and Dangerous Drugs.* Hearings. 91st Cong., 1st sess., October 1969.

————. Select Committee on Crime. *Drugs in Our Schools.* Hearings. 92nd Cong., 2nd sess., September–December, 1972.

————. Select Committee on Crime. *Narcotics Research, Rehabilitation and Treatment.* Hearings. 92nd Cong., 1st sess., June 1971.

————. Select Committee on Narcotics Abuse and Control. *Cocaine: A Major Drug Issue of the Seventies.* Hearings. 96th Cong., 1st sess., July 24 and 26, 1979; October 10, 1979.

————. Select Committee on Narcotics Abuse and Control. *Drug Abuse among the U.S. Armed Forces.* Report. 95th Cong., 2nd sess., February 1979.

————. Select Committee on Narcotics Abuse and Control. *Drug Abuse in the Military.* Hearings. 95th Cong., 2nd sess., April 1978.

————. Select Committee on Narcotics Abuse and Control. *Drug Abuse in the Military—1981.* Hearings. 97th Cong., 1st sess., September 17, 1981.

————. Select Committee on Narcotics Abuse and Control. *Drug Education—Part II.* Hearings. 97th Cong., 2nd sess., May 21, 1986.

————. Select Committee on Narcotics Abuse and Control. *Federal Drug Law Enforcement and Interdiction.* Hearings. 98th Cong., 2nd sess., May 22, 1984.

————. Select Committee on Narcotics Abuse and Control. *Implementation of the Anti-Drug Abuse Act of 1986.* Report, together with additional views. 100th Cong., 1st sess., 1986.

————. Select Committee on Narcotics Abuse and Control. *Narcotics Interdiction and Enforcement Efforts in South Florida.* Hearings. 99th Cong., 2nd sess., May 16, 1986.

————. Select Committee on Narcotics Abuse and Control. *Oversight Hearings on Federal Drug Strategy—1979.* Hearings. 96th Cong., 1st sess., May 31, 1979.

———. Select Committee on Narcotics Abuse and Control. *Oversight of the Anti-Drug Abuse Act of 1986 and the Federal Drug Strategy.* Hearing, 100th Cong., 1st sess., December 8, 1987.

———. Select Committee on Narcotics Abuse and Control. *South America Study Mission.* Hearings. 95th Cong., 1st sess., August 9–23, 1977.

———. Select Committee on Narcotics Abuse and Control. *Southeast Asian Narcotics.* Hearings. 95th Cong., 1st sess., July 12–13, 1977.

———. Select Committee on Narcotics Abuse and Control. *United States Bureau of Prisons Staff Study—Institutional Drug Abuse Treatment Programs and Utilization of Prescription Drugs at Five Institutions.* Report. 96th Cong., 2nd sess., October 1979.

U.S. Congress. Senate. Committee on Armed Services. *Drug Abuse in the Military.* Hearings before the Subcommittee on Drug Abuse in the Military. 92nd Cong., 2nd sess., February 29 to April 6, 1972.

———. Committee on Armed Services. *Review of Military Drug and Alcohol Programs.* Hearings before the Subcommittee on Drug Abuse in the Military. 93rd Cong., 1st sess., September 1973.

———. Committee on Armed Services. *Staff Report on Drug Abuse in the Military.* Report of the Subcommittee on Drug Abuse. 92nd Cong., 1st sess., July 1971.

———. Committee on Foreign Relations. *Drugs in Massachusetts: The Domestic Impact of a Foreign Invasion.* Report by Senator John Kerry. 101st Cong., 1st sess. Washington. D.C.: GPO, 1990.

———. Committee on Foreign Relations. *Drugs, Law Enforcement, and Foreign Policy.* Report by the Senate Subcommittee on Terrorism, Narcotics, and International Operations. 100th Cong., 2nd sess., December 1988.

———. Committee on Foreign Relations. *Hearings before the Senate Committee on Foreign Relations.* 92nd Cong. 1st sess., July–August 1971.

———. Committee on Foreign Relations. *Heroin: Can the Supply Be Stopped?* Report by Senator William Spong. 92nd Cong., 2nd sess., September 18, 1972.

———. Committee on Foreign Relations. *Post-War Southeast Asia—A Search for Neutrality and Independence.* Report by Senator Mike Mansfield. 94th Cong., 2nd sess., 1976.

———. Committee on Foreign Relations. *United States Security Agreements and Commitments Abroad, Part 2: Kingdom of Laos.* Hearings before the Senate Subcommittee on United States Security. 91st Cong., 1st sess., October, 1969.

———. Committee on Government Operations. *Drug Abuse Prevention and Control.* Hearings before the Joint Subcommittee on Executive Reorganization and Government Research and the Subcommittee on Intergovernmental Relations. 92nd Cong., 1st sess., July 1971.

———. Committee on Government Operations. *Federal Drug Enforcement.* Hearings before the Permanent Subcommittee on Investigations. 94th Cong., 1st sess., June–July 1975.

———. Committee on Government Operations. *Federal Drug Enforcement.* Hearings before the Permanent Subcommittee on Investigations. 94th Cong., 2nd sess., July 1976.

———. Committee on Government Operations. *Fraud and Corruption in the Management of Military Club Systems.* 91st Cong., 1st sess., October 8, 1969.

———. Committee on Government Operations. *Hearings before the Joint Subcommittee on Executive Reorganization and Government Research and the Subcommittee on Intergovernmental Relations.* 93rd Cong., 1st sess., September 1973.

———. Committee on Interstate and Foreign Commerce. *Production and Abuse of Opiates in the Far East.* Report of the Subcommittee on Public Health and Environment. 92nd Cong., 1st sess., September 1971.

———. Committee on the Judiciary. *Civilian Casualty and Refugee Problems in South Vietnam.* Findings and recommendations of the Subcommittee to Investigate Problems Connected with Refugees and Escapees. 90th Cong., 2nd sess., May 9, 1968.

———. Committee on the Judiciary. *Drug Abuse in the Armed Forces.* Hearings before the Subcommittee to Investigate Juvenile Delinquency. 90th Cong., 2nd sess., March 4, 5, 6, 1968.

———. Committee on the Judiciary. *Drug Abuse in the Armed Forces.* Hearings before the Subcommittee to Investigate Juvenile Delinquency. 91st Cong., 2nd sess., March 24 to October 30, 1970.

———. Committee on the Judiciary. *Drug Abuse in the Military.* Report of the Subcommittee to Investigate Juvenile Delinquency, based on Hearings and Investigations, 1966–1970. Washington, D.C.: GPO, 1971.

———. Committee on the Judiciary. *Methadone Use and Abuse.* Hearings before the Subcommittee to Investigate Juvenile Delinquency. 92nd Cong., 2nd sess., November 1972.

———. Committee on the Judiciary. *The Mexican Connection.*: Hearings before the Subcommittee to Investigate Juvenile Delinquency. 95th Cong., 1st sess., February 1978.

———. Committee on the Judiciary. *Narcotics Legislation.* Hearings held before the Subcommittee to Investigate Juvenile Delinquency., pursuant to S. Res. 48, investigation of juvenile delinquency in the United States. 91st Cong., 1st sess., 1969.

———. Committee on the Judiciary. *Poppy Politics: Cultivation, Use, Abuse and Control of Opium.* Hearings before the Senate Subcommittee to Investigate Juvenile Delinquency. 94th Cong., 1st sess., March 1975.

———. Committee on the Judiciary. *War-Related Civilian Problems in Indochina.* Hearings before the Subcommittee to Investigate Problems Connected with Refugees and Escapees. 92nd Cong., 1st sess., April 21, 1971.

———. Committee on the Judiciary. *World Drug Traffic and Its Impact on U.S. Security.* Hearings before the Subcommittee to Investigate the Administration of the Internal Security Act and Other Internal Security Laws. 92nd Cong., 2nd sess., September 1972.

———. Committee on Labor and Human Resources. *Drugs and Terrorism.* Hearing before the Subcommittee on Alcoholism and Drug Abuse of the Committee on Labor and Human Resources. 98th Cong., 2nd sess., August 2, 1984.

———. Committee on Labor and Public Welfare. *Drug and Alcohol Abuse in the Military*. Hearings before the Special Subcommittee on Alcoholism and Narcotics. 91st Cong., 2nd sess. November 17 to December 3, 1970.

———. Committee on Labor and Public Welfare. *Federal Drug Abuse and Drug Dependence Prevention, Treatment, and Rehabilitation Act of 1970*. Hearings before the Special Subcommittee on Alcohol and Narcotics. 91st Cong., 2nd sess., Summer 1970.

———. Committee on Labor and Public Welfare. *Hearings before the Special Subcommittee on Alcoholism and Narcotics*. 91st Cong., 2nd sess., 1970.

———. Committee on Labor and Public Welfare. *Hearings before the Special Subcommittee on Alcohol and Narcotics*. 93rd Cong., 1st sess., April 22–23, 1973, Philadelphia, Pa.

———. Committee on Labor and Public Welfare. *Military Drug Abuse, 1971*. Hearings before the Subcommittee on Alcoholism and Narcotics. 92nd Cong., 1st sess., June 9 and 22, 1971.

———. Committee on Labor and Public Welfare. *The Narcotics Situation in Southeast Asia*. Report of the Special Study Mission of the Subcommittee on Alcoholism and Narcotics. 93rd Cong., 1st sess., January–February 1973 and March 1974.

———. Committee on Labor and Public Welfare. *The World Heroin Problem*. Report of the Special Study Mission of the Subcommittee on Alcoholism and Narcotics. 92nd Cong., 1st sess., May 27, 1971.

———. Select Committee to Study Governmental Operations with respect to Intelligence Activities. *Final Report of the Select Senate Committee to Study Governmental Operations with respect to Intelligence Activities*, book 1. 94th Cong., 2nd sess., 1974.

U.S. Department of the Army. *Regulation 600-85. Army Substance Abuse Program*. Washington, D.C.: Army Headquarters, 2006. www.army.mil/usapa/epubs/edf/r600-85.pdf.

U.S. Department of Defense. *Survey of Health Related Behaviors among Active Duty Military Personnel: A Component of the Lifestyle Assessment Program*. Washington, D.C.: RTA International, 2006.

———. *Drug Abuse: Game without Winners: A Basic Handbook for Commanders*. Washington, D.C.: GPO, 1968.

U.S. Department of State. Bureau of International Narcotics Matters. *Narcotics Control in Mexico: Environmental Analysis of Effects, April 1979*. Washington, D.C.: GPO, 1979.

U.S. Treasury, Advisory Committee to the Federal Bureau of Narcotics. *Interim Report of the Joint Committee of the American Bar Association and American Medical Association, 1958*. Washington, D.C.: Bureau of Narcotics, 1959.

U.S. Veterans Administration. *Drug and Alcohol Dependency Program, FY 1973*. Washington, DC: GPO, 1973.

Valentine, Douglas. *The Phoenix Program*. New York: William Morrow, 1991.

———. *The Strength of the Wolf: The Secret History of America's War on Drugs*. London: Verso, 2004.

Vargas Meza, Ricardo. *Democracy, Human Rights, and Militarism in the War on Drugs in Latin America.* Amsterdam: Transnational Institute Press, 1997.

Verrone, Richard Burks, and Laura M. Calkins. *Voices from Vietnam: Eye-Witness Accounts of the War, 1954–1975.* Devon, U.K.: David & Charles, 2005.

Vietnam Veterans Against the War. *The Winter Soldier Investigation: An Inquiry into U.S. War Crimes.* Boston: Beacon Press, 1972.

The Visitors. Directed by Elia Kazan. United Artists, 1972.

Waghelstein, John. "A Latin American Insurgency Status Report." *Military Review* 58, no. 2 (February 1987): 46–47.

Wakefield, Dan, ed. *The Addict.* New York: Premier Books, 1963.

———. "The Hallucinogens: A Reporter's Objective View." In Solomon, *LSD: The Consciousness-Expanding Drug,* 60–61.

Wald, Patricia, et al. *Dealing with Drug Abuse—A Report to the Ford Foundation.* New York: Praeger, 1972.

Walker, Thomas. *Revolution and Counterrevolution in Nicaragua.* Boulder, Colo: Westview, 1991.

Walker, William O., III. *Drug Control in the Americas.* Rev. ed. Albuquerque: University of New Mexico Press, 1989.

———. *Opium and Foreign Policy: The Anglo-American Search for Order in Asia, 1912–1954.* Chapel Hill: University of North Carolina Press, 1991.

———, ed. *The War on Drugs: An Odyssey of Cultures in Conflict.* Wilmington, Del.: Scholarly Resources, 1996.

Walt, Lewis W. *Strange War, Strange Strategy: A General's Report on Vietnam.* New York: Funk & Wagnalls, 1970.

Walton, Frank, Paul Skuse, and Wendell Motter. *A Survey of the Laos National Police.* U.S. State Department Report, May 15, 1965.

Warner, Roger. *Backfire: The CIA's Secret War in Laos and Its Link to the Vietnam War.* New York: Simon & Schuster, 1995.

Waterhouse, Larry, and Mariann G. Wizard. *Turning the Guns Around: Notes on the GI Movement.* New York: Praeger, 1971.

Webb, Gary. *Dark Alliance: The CIA, the Contras, and the Crack Cocaine Explosion.* New York: Seven Stories Press, 1998.

Weil, Andrew T. *The Natural Mind: A New Way of Looking at Drugs and the Higher Consciousness.* Boston: Houghton Mifflin, 1972.

Weimer, Daniel. "Drugs as Disease: Heroin, Metaphors, and Identity in Nixon's Drug War." *Janus Head* 6, no. 2 (June 2003): 260–81.

———. "Seeing Drugs: The American Drug War in Thailand and Burma, 1970–1975." PhD diss., Kent State University, 2003.

Weir, William. *In the Shadow of the Dope Fiend: America's War on Drugs.* New York: Archon Books, 1995.

Weisberg, Barry, ed. *Ecocide in Indo-China: The Ecology of War.* San Francisco: Canfield, 1970.

Weissman, Adam Paul. "I Was a Drug Hype Junkie: 48 Hours on Crock Street." *New Republic,* October 6, 1986, 12–13.

Welcome Home, Soldier Boys. Directed by Richard Compton. 20th Century Fox, 1972.

Weldon, Charles. *Tragedy in Paradise: A Country Doctor at War in Laos.* Bangkok: Asia Books, 1999.

Wells, Tom. *The War Within: America's Battle over Vietnam.* Berkeley: University of California Press, 1994.

Westermeyer, Joseph. *Poppies, Pipes, and People: Opium and Its Uses in Laos.* Berkeley: University of California Press, 1982.

———. "The Pro-Heroin Effects of Anti-Opium Laws in Asia." *Archives of General Psychiatry* 33, no. 9 (September 1976): 1135–39.

Westheider, James E. *Fighting on Two Fronts: African Americans and the Vietnam War.* New York: New York University Press, 1997.

Westin, Av, and Stephanie Schaffer. *Heroes and Heroin: The Shocking Story of Drug Addiction in the Military.* New York: Pocket Books, 1972.

Westmoreland, William C. *A Soldier Reports.* New York: Doubleday, 1976.

"When 30,000 GIs Are Using Heroin, How Can You Fight a War? An Interview with Representative Morgan Murphy," *Drug Forum,* October 1971, 94.

"When Johnny Comes Marching Home." *MAD Magazine,* March 1972.

White, William L. "Trick or Treat: A Century of American Responses to Heroin Addiction." In Musto, *One Hundred Years of Heroin,* 131–49.

Who'll Stop the Rain. Directed by Karel Reisz. United Artists, 1979.

Wilbur, Richard S. "The Battle against Drug Dependency within the Military—A View from the Front." *Journal of Drug Issues* 4 (Winter 1974): 11–31.

Williams, William A. *The Tragedy of American Diplomacy.* Cleveland: World Publishing, 1959.

Wilson, James Q. *Thinking About Crime.* New York: Vintage Books, 1977.

Winter Soldier. Winterfilm Collective Cast. Winterfilm Collective, 1972.

"White, Suburban, Middle Class." *Newsweek,* July 5, 1971, 28.

"The Wonderland of Opium." *Far Eastern Economic Review,* July 17, 1971, 37–41.

Wright, Kevin N. *The Great American Crime Myth.* Westport, Conn: Greenwood Press, 1985.

Wyant, William, Jr. "Addiction in Vietnam: Coming Home with a Habit." *The Nation,* July 5, 1971, 7–10.

Yablonsky, Lewis. *The Tunnel Back: Synanon.* New York: Macmillan, 1965.

Ybarra, Lea. *Vietnam Veteranos: Chicanos Recall the War.* Austin: University of Texas Press, 2004.

Yongming, Zhou. *Anti-Drug Crusades in Twentieth-Century China: Nationalism, History, and State-Building.* New York: Rowman & Littlefield, 1999.

Young, Allen. *Harmony of Illusion: Inventing Post-Traumatic Stress Disorder.* Princeton: Princeton University Press, 1995.

Young, Jock. *The Drug Takers: The Social Meaning of Drug Use.* London: Paladin, 1970.

Young, Marilyn B. *The Vietnam Wars: 1945–1991.* New York: Harper Perennial, 1991.

Young, Marilyn B., and Robert Buzzanco, eds. *A Companion to the Vietnam War.* Malden, Mass.: Blackwell, 2003.

Youngers, Colletta, and Eileen Rosin, eds. "Drugs and Democracy in Latin America: The Impact of U.S. Policy." Special Report of the Washington Office on Latin America, November 2004. Also available online at www.wola.org/media/ddhr_exec_sum_brief.pdf.

———, eds. *Drugs and Democracy in Latin America: The Impact of U.S. Policy.* Boulder, Colo: Lynne Rienner, 2005.

Zimmer, Lynn, and John P. Morgan. *Marijuana Myths, Marijuana Facts.* New York: Lindesmith Center, 1997.

Zinberg, Norman. *Drug, Set, and Setting: The Basis for Controlled Intoxication Use.* New Haven: Yale University Press, 1987.

———. "GI's and OJ's in Vietnam," *New York Times Magazine,* December 5, 1971, 120.

———. "Heroin Use in Vietnam and the United States: A Contrast and Critique." *Archives of General Psychiatry* 26, no. 5 (May 1972): 955–61.

———. "Rehabilitation of Heroin Users in Vietnam." *Contemporary Drug Problems,* March 1972, 263–294.

———. "The Search for a Rational Approach to Heroin Use." In *Addiction,* edited by Peter Bourne, 149–74. New York: Academic Press, 1974.

Zinberg, Norman, and Leon Hunt. *Heroin Use: A New Look.* Washington, D.C.: The Drug Abuse Council, 1976.

Zinberg, Norman, and John A. Robertson. *Drugs and the Public.* New York: Simon & Schuster, 1972.

Zinberg, Norman, and Andrew T. Weil. "A Comparison of Marijuana Users and Non-Users." *Nature* 226 (April 11, 1970): 119–23.

AUTHOR INTERVIEWS

Hannon, Tom. Boston Mass., May 17, 2004.

Jaffe, Jerome H. Telephone interview, February 24, 2005.

Leary, William. Revere, Mass., January, 24, 2004.

Lembcke, Jerry. Worcester, Mass., January 17, 2004.

Levy, Marc. Gloucester, Mass., February, 2004.

Olson, Neil. Lubbock, Tex., March 25, 2007.

Pham, Chet. Lubbock, Tex., March 24, 2007.

Pierson, Jay. Lubbock, Tex., March 24, 2007.

Peterson, Joel. Boston Mass., April 27, 2004.

Randle, Eddie. Lubbock, Tex., March 24, 2007.

Rodriguez, Jaime. Boston Mass., April 20, 2004.

Roffman, Roger A. Telephone interview, November 1, 2004.

Sanders, Clinton R. Telephone interview, November 6, 2004.

Scott, Peter Dale. Telephone, April 05, 2005.

Thornton, F. Wayne. Lubbock, Tex., March 24, 2007.

Civil Air Transport (CAT), 78, 213n12

civil commitment program, 49, 105, 110, 219n21

Clinton, William J. ("Bill"), 191

coca, 118, 178–80; farmers, 176–77, 183; and Tebithurion, 180. *See also* crops, cocaine

cocaine, 11; crack, 116, 183–84, 186; community effect of, 173; decriminalization of, 168–69; and drug traffic, 118, 167, 172–81; and heroin, 18–19; legislation, 57, 119, 186; media portrayal of, 161, 174, 184; research, 119. See also coca; drug traffic

Cohen, Sidney, 57, 59, 169

Colbach, Edward, 29

Cold War, 41, 89, 118, 171; end of, 190; role of, in drug traffic, 78, 85; and Vietnam, 131, 189

Columbia, 116, 167, 172, 176–82, 190–91. *See also* cartels; Latin America

Columbo, (NBC, television series), 150

Coming Home (Ashby, film), 151

Committee of Concerned Asian Scholars (CCAS), 79, 89

Committee on Foreign Affairs, 51, 53

Committee on Juvenile Delinquency, 115

Committee on Narcotics Abuse and Control, 176

communism, 89, 116; fight against, 9, 78, 83, 86; and foreign policy, 88, 97

communist(s), 42, 49, 79, 104, 146; aggression, 81; anti-, 43, 75, 80, 132, 144; antidrug, 141, 167; drug police, 67; and drug traffic, 38–41, 45, 59, 122, 143; during 1960s, 3; media portrayal of, 161–62, 241n46; propaganda, 20, 126; Southeast Asian parties, 134, 144–45, 216n56; threat of, 171, 189, 207n31, 214n26; and U.S. operations, 84, 92, 214n26. *See also* Chinese Communist Party; drug

traffic; Guomindang; Indonesian Communist Party

Comprehensive Crime Control Act. *See under* drug traffic: legislative acts

Conein, Lucien ("Lou") (pseud. Black Luigi), 82, 115, 124

conservatives, 7–10, 14, 100, 189; antidrug agenda of, 9, 11–12, 59, 154, 159, 186–87; neo-, 7; New Right, 76, 100, 102; and social context, 58, 151, 218n86

Constitution (U.S.), 110, 175; and Watergate, 112, 119

Coppola, Francis Ford, 155–57

corruption, 4, 9, 120, 143; anti-, 86, 132; in Latin America, 177; in Middle East, 181; police, 113, 117, 119, 125, 133; in South Vietnam, 44, 77–78, 86–91, 32, 123, 142; spiritual, 81, 153; and U.S. allies, 51, 85–88, 108, 122, 134, 190; and U.S. government, 4, 9, 40, 76–77, 84, 141

Corson, William, 76. *See also* Green Berets

counterinsurgency, 84, 138, 176; and American doctrine, 33, 181; and U.S. training, 116–20, 140, 176, 242n63; in Southeast Asia, 121, 134. *See also* narco-insurgency

counternarcotics, 4, 87, 141; funding, 118, 135; training, 124, 132, 176–78. *See also* military: U.S. Operations

court-martial, 30, 128, 159, 170

crack. *See* cocaine

Cranston, Alan, 222

C-rations, 102, 199

Criminal Investigation Division (CID), 26–27, 32, 34, 87–88, 142; antinarcotics brigade, 126, 128. *See also* military: U.S. Army

crop(s): defoliation, 4, 12, 117–18, 127, 180, 187; drug suppliers, 80, 84,

115–18, 138–45, 179, 191; substitution, 4, 116–23, 127, 136, 139,
144–46, 167, 176, 180. *See also*
farmers; marijuana; opium
crystal methamphetamines, 11
Cuba, 172; Bay of Pigs, 86, 113
culture, 7, 63, 164, 174–75; of 1950s, 3;
of 1960s, 30, 175, 191; of 1980s,
157; class based, 62, 64; counter-,
3, 12, 30, 38, 95, 103–10; disease,
155; drug, 6, 8, 14, 130, 152, 162; of
fear, 35; media portrayal of, 14, 44;
mythologies, 189; and nationalism,
104; of permissiveness, 1, 166; of
resistance, 31, 130; in Southeast
Asia, 28, 89, 143
Cushman, John H., 126

Da Nang. *See* Danang
Dai, Bao (emperor), 122, 225n4
Danang, 59, 123–24, 164
Dang Vang Quang, *See* Quang, Dang
Vang
Daniels Act. *See* drug traffic: legislative
acts
DARE. *See* Project DARE
Date of Expected Return from Overseas
(DEROS), 69
Davis, Ossie, 152
Davis, Raymond, 21
DEA. *See* Drug Enforcement
Administration
death squad(s), 118, 176, 181
decriminalization, 110, 168
The Deer Hunter (Cimino, film), 154
defoliants, 116–17, 140, 160, 179–80.
See also crop(s)
DeForest, Orin, 86
De Mau Mau, 31. *See also* Black Power
demilitarized zone (DMZ), 17, 107
democracy, 3, 8; and drug control, 12,
136; doves, 6, 95; liberal, 6; in
South Vietnam, 49, 96; Western-
style, 156. *See also* liberals;
conservatives

DePalma, Brian, 149
Department of Agriculture, 115, 118, 136
Department of Defense (DOD), 17, 27,
97, 108; antidrug initiatives of,
126–29, 163, 173; and drug traffic,
18; and funding, 46; military
testing by, 19, 21, 129, 175; and
research, 25–26, 68; role of, in
myth, 50. *See also* drug traffic;
military
deviance, 61, 103; criminal, 68; model,
57, 63
Dienbienphu, 82, 122, 126
Diem, Ngo Dinh, 78–79, 82, 86, 96,
122; repression, 123, 198n22
differential association theory, 61
Dirty Harry (Siegel, film), 151
disease model of addiction, 58–59, 68,
74, 105, 130, 221n41. *See also* Jaffe,
Jerome H.
DMZ. *See* demilitarized zone
DOD. *See* Department of Defense
Dodd, Thomas J., 32, 48–51; and
antidrug hearings, 50, 59–60; on
military drug use, 49; as myth
proponent, 8; and My Lai, 32–33;
and no-knock regulation, 107
Don, Tran Van, 123
Donfeld, Jeffrey, 52, 106, 108
Dong Ap Bia Hill, 30
Dornan, Robert R., 171
Drug Abuse Education Act, 107
Drug Abuse Research and Education.
See Project DARE
drug control: legislative acts, 105–7, 131,
173, 185; and Old Guard, 56, 62,
66–69, 73–74, 192; programs, 29,
136–37, 141–43, 167; public support
of, 108, 165; U.S. policies, 12–13,
53, 118, 137, 179, 185–87; War on
Drugs, 76, 114–18, 166. *See also*
Drug Enforcement Administration; drug traffic; Federal Bureau
of Narcotics; military: U.S.
operations

JNID. *See* Joint Narcotics Investigation Division

Johnson, Dwight, 45

Johnson, Lyndon B., 3, 7, 97, 105, 110, 115, 218n10. *See also* drug traffic: legislative acts

Johnston, Lloyd, 34

Joint Narcotics Investigation Division (JNID), 132, 142

junkie(s), 10, 14, 44–50, 109, 148, 150, 173; and antiwar movement, 75, 78; and myth of Nam, 33–37

Just Say No campaign, 174. *See also* Reagan, First Lady Nancy

Kachin Rangers, 89

Kaplan, Joel H., 59–60

Karabaic, Bill, 22

Karen National Liberation Army, 144

Karnow, Stanley, 86, 199n53

Kashimba, David, 23

Kellenbenz, Daniel, 46–47

Kennedy, Edward M., 140

Kennedy, John F., 81, 110, 114–15

Kerry, John, 2, 181, 184

Khan Sa, 16

Khe Sanh, 21, 173

Khmer Rouge revolution, 137, 162, 207n31

Khun Sa (pseud. Chiang Chi Foo), 136

Kissinger, Henry, 8, 107, 118–19, 160, 218n10, 224n95

Kolb, Lawrence, 58

Kolko, Gabriel, 23

Korea, 38, 55, 68, 78, 129, 150

Krogh, Egil, 34, 47, 115; and antidrug campaign, 109, 129–30, 135, 143; and corruption, 108; and drug war policy, 102, 106–8; and Latin America, 116; and ODALE, 113; and Watergate, 112

Kulak, Victor ("Brute"), 40

Kunnes, Richard, 93

Ky, Nguyen Cao, 77–80, 84, 93, 125, 213n10, 230n64

Lacata, Victor, 38

Laird, Melvin, 98, 107, 129

Lansdale, Edward G., 40, 82, 84, 124, 134

Laos, 4, 8, 63, 92; and corruption, 40, 87; covert operations in, 4, 46, 77, 79–80, 88, 134; crop defoliation in, 140–44; and drug control programs, 137–42, 146; drug laboratories in, 52, 141; and drug traffic, 78, 93, 97, 122, 141–42, 216n56; media portrayal of, 151, 160; "secret war" in, 82–85, 191; and war expansion, 37, 189. *See also* Air America; crops; heroin; opium

Lasch, Christopher, 155

Latin American, 11–12; agreements with, 116; covert operations in, 113, 176, 181, 183; crops, 12, 119, 140, 179, 190, 193; human rights, 182, 193; narco-guerrillas, 11, 167, 177, 180; resistance to U.S. policies, 182; and War on Drugs, 11–12, 184, 191. *See also* Argentina; Bolivia; Brazil; Columbia; Paraguay; Peru; Venezuela

LaVerne, Albert A., 60

Lawyers Military Defense Committee, 128

Leary, Timothy, 56–68; and antipsychiatry, 62–64, 73; and countercultural movement, 56, 64, 104; imprisonment of, 105, 219n17; and psychedelic research, 57, 64–65, 211n27. *See also* psychedelic drugs

Leary, William, 24

Lembcke, Jerry, 18, 31, 45, 198n22, 236n31

Lemon, Peter, 53

Lethal Weapon (Donner, film), 158

Levy, Marc, 22, 26, 28

Lewis, Flora, 42, 96

liberals/liberalism, 103–4, 108, 110, 190; Great Society, 3, 169; New Left, 3. *See also* conservatives

Lifton, Robert Jay, 9, 70–72, 81
Lindsey, Douglas, 24
Livingstone, Gordon, 71
Li Wen-Huan, 136
Lo Hsing-Han, 135
Long Binh jail. *See* prison
Longo, Michael, 47
Long Tien, 86, 137, 151
Lon Nol government, 44
Los Tres activists, 95
Louria, Donald B., 56–58, 128
Lysergic Acid Diamelythide (LSD), 3,
    56, 65, 81, 104–5, 107. *See also*
    psychedelic drugs

M-13, 179
MACV. *See* Military Assistance
    Command Vietnam
Magnum PI (CBS, television series),
    161
mandatory minimum sentencing, 103,
    185, 199n54, 219n28
Mann, Peggy, 168
Mansfield, Mike, 96
Marcos, Ferdinand, 137
Marcuse, Herbert, 64
marijuana. *See also* cannabis; crops;
    drug control; drug traffic
  —and alcohol use, 28
  —and antidrug legislation, 13, 57,
    105, 169, 185, 119n54
  —and antidrug programs, 3, 57, 127,
    137
  —as symbol of antiwar stance, 31
  —crops: demand for, 16; destruction
    of, 4, 116, 127; in Mexico, 115–16,
    157, 179, 238n7; replacement pro-
    grams, 123–24
  —domestic hearings on, 50, 59
  —media portrayal of, 7, 37–44, 150,
    157–65
  —military use of, 4–5; usage rates, 5,
    123; related to war crimes, 8, 32–33,
    60, 72–74, 205n5
  —pro-use action, 5, 65, 81, 104–5, 168

  —research on: 17, 58, 66, 196; de-
    sensitization to war, 23; effects on
    military performance, 20–21, 25,
    60; Long Binh, 17, 72; medicinal
    use, 66, 192; prior to enlistment,
    17–18; social origins, 61; use after
    military discharge, 34, 119
  —related arrests, 5, 13, 57, 105, 113,
    168
  —tetra-hydrocanibinol (THC), 59
  —as threat to national security, 170
  —use with opium, 16, 26, 41, 44
Marines (U.S.). *See under* military
Marx, Karl, 90
Marxism, 50, 64, 175, 180
"Mary Jane," 125–27. *See also* marijuana
*M*A*S*H* (Altman, film), 150
Massachusetts Institute of Technology
    (MIT), 79
Matthiak, Marvin, 21
McCaffrey, Barry R., 191, 193
McCoy, Alfred W., 75, 88, 214n26; and
    antiwar movement, 92–95, 192;
    and corruption, 75–79, 84–85, 160,
    216n56; and drug traffic, 83–84,
    90, 142, 214n30; and heroin, 75,
    83–84, 88–92; role of, in myth, 82.
    See also antiwar movement; drug
    traffic; heroin
McGee, Gale, 91
McGovern, George S., 95–96, 99, 143
McLellan, John, 98
McMurtry, Mrs. William, 48
McNamara, Robert S., 81, 123
media, the
  —and addiction reports, 19–21, 189
  —atrocity coverage of, 32, 43, 192,
    207n31
  —and alcohol use, 29
  —on drug use: by the military, 1, 10,
    14, 31–39, 170; in the U.S., 13, 43,
    54–55, 105, 114, 166
  —and political manipulation, 9, 53,
    174, 208n46
  —racial coverage of, 52

Ribicoff, Abraham, 98
Ridenhour, Ronald, 32–33
RLG. *See* Royal Lao Government
Robins, Lee N., 33–34, 71, 129
Robinson v. California, 105
Rockefeller, Nelson, 102, 114
Roffman, Roger A., 17, 27, 38, 49, 68, 73
Royal Lao Air Force, 51, 83
Royal Lao Government (RLG), 92,
    137–38
Royal Thai police, 135
RPI. *See* Renesselear Polytechnic
    Institute
Rubin, Jerry, 64
Rudin, Stanley A., 67
Rumsfeld, Donald, 53, 115
Rural Mobile Police Patrol Units
    (UMOPAR), 178, 183
Rush, Kenneth, 145
Rusk, Dean, 49, 137
Russian roulette, 58, 154
Ruybal, Jay Dee Sgt., 22

Saigon, 24, 44, 83, 124, 189, 193; and
    drug treatment, 27–28; and drug
    traffic, 45, 53–54, 77–78, 80, 86,
    133; and policy training, 124–25,
    132; and U.S. corruption, 96. *See
    also* drug control; drug traffic
Sanders, Clinton R., 69–70, 211n27
SAODAP. *See* Special Action Office on
    Drug Abuse Prevention
Sapol, Ely, 17
Sarit, Thanarat, 84, 87, 91
schizophrenia, 60
Schultz, Augie, 81
Schultz, George P., 183
Scorsese, Martin, 151
Scott, Peter Dale, 77–78, 80, 82, 152,
    192, 213n12
Sea Supply, 88. *See also* Central
    Intelligence Agency: police
    training
Sendero Luminoso (Shining Path), 180
Shining Path. *See* Sendero Luminoso

sicarios, 182
Siegel, A. Carl, 129
Sirik Matak, 136–37
Slotkin, Richard, 6
Smith, Charles, 170
Smith, David, 70–71
Smith, Julian, 149–50
Smith, Prentice B., 29
Smith, Roger, 111
social condition, 10, 35, 112; chaos, 53;
    public perception of, 9; oppression,
    93
social context, 5, 14, 22, 55, 64; of
    alcohol abuse, 28–29; of drug use;
    69, 71; of the right, 57
social control, 10, 95, 111
social deviance, 61–62, 103, 169
social environmentalists, 57, 67, 73,
    90, 168
social movements, 3, 10, 31, 103, 177,
    186
Socialist ideology, 101, 144. *See also*
    communism; communists
solitary confinement, 130
Soul Alley, 52
Southeast Asia: and corruption, 75–79,
    94, 189–90; crops in, 4, 8, 88–89,
    176; drug abuse by military in, 22,
    29, 97–98, 113; drug traffic in, 9,
    34, 52, 75–91, 94–98, 115, 140–43,
    155, 185; and funding, 97; media
    portrayal of, 10, 34, 44, 149; people
    of, 97, 143, 165; U.S. destruction of,
    14; U.S. operations in, 78, 83–86,
    146, 189; U.S. policies toward, 78,
    83–86, 146, 189. *See also* counter-
    insurgency; drug traffic, military:
    U.S. operations; narco-insurgency
South Vietnamese Army. *See* Army of
    the Republic of South Vietnam
Special Action Office on Drug Abuse
    Prevention (SAODAP), 109–10
Special Forces, 4, 18, 77, 156, 176, 179.
    See also Green Berets, military:
    specific U.S. branches

drug policy speeches in, 96–98, 106; and funding, 3, 109, 118, 132; and legislation, 176; and Medal of Honor, 25, 45; role of, in myth, 170, 174; testimony before, 2, 17, 23, 29, 32, 73, 129, 142, 170, 235n16. *See also* United States Congress: House; United States Congress: Senate

United States Congress: House, 115, 176, 179, 185

United States Congress: Senate, 77; Ethics Committee, 50; Foreign Relations Committee, 2, 8, 49, 75; investigation by, 170; reports, 21; subcommittee hearings of, 98, 205n78

Upper Huallaga Valley (UHV), 167, 176, 178. *See also* Peru

urinalysis test, 4, 19, 109, 121, 129–30, 146, 175, 189

USAID. *See* United States Agency of International Development

USO. *See* United Service Organizations

U Thant, 9

Vang Pao, 80, 84–86, 92, 137

Vann, John Paul, 52, 127

Venezuela, 116. *See also* Latin America

Vientiane, 52, 83, 136, 138, 140; Air Vientiane, 87. *See also* drug traffic

Vietnam era, 11, 160, 170, 184, 190; antiwar, 7; pre–, 10

Vietnam Era Research Project, 34

Vietnam Veterans Against the War (VVAW), 2, 45, 68

Vietnamization strategy, 42, 109, 131, 134, 190

Vinh, Tap, 113

The Visitors (Kazan, film), 151

Vogel, Victor H., 58

Vung Tau, 39, 129

VVAW. *See* Vietnam Veterans Against the War

Walt, Lewis W., 20, 123

Walter Reed Army Medical Center, 19, 70, 121, 135

Walter Reed Army Medical Institute, 70

Walters, John, 12

war crimes, 2, 32, 151, 224n95, 235n16; tribunal, 27

War on Drugs. *See* drug control; Nixon, Richard M.; Reagan, Ronald W.

wasted nations, 189

Watergate. *See* Constitution (U.S.)

Weil, Andrew, 66

Welcome Home Soldier Boys (Compton, film), 150

West, Charles, 32

Westmoreland, William C., 20, 26–27

White House Drug Abuse Council, 174

WHO. *See* World Health Organization

Who'll Stop the Rain (Reisz, film), 154

Wilbur, Richard, 18, 27–28, 129

Wilkinson, Charles ("Bud"), 107, 175

Winter Soldier (Winterfilm Collective), 151, 235n16

Withers, Paul, 79

Wolff, Lester, 97–98, 142–45, 170

World Bank, 131

World Health Organization (WHO), 76–77

World War I, 6, 71, 89

World War II, 48, 89, 104, 160; and drug abuse, 27; media portrayal of, 149; post–, 11, 54; and psychiatric rate, 68

Xuyen, Binh, 78, 122–23

Zinberg, Norman, 66–69, 90, 130